The 1967 Arab-Israeli War

Origins and Consequences

The June 1967 War was a watershed moment in the history of the modern Middle East. In six days, the Israelis defeated the Arab armies of Egypt, Syria, and Jordan and seized large portions of territory including the West Bank, East Jerusalem, the Gaza Strip, the Sinai Peninsula, and the Golan Heights. With the hindsight of four decades and access to recently declassified documents, two veteran scholars of the Middle East bring together some of the most knowledgeable experts in their fields to reassess the origins of the war and its regional reverberations. Each chapter takes a different perspective from the vantage point of a different participant, those that actually took part in the war, and the world powers – the United States, Soviet Union, Britain, and France – that played important roles behind the scenes. Their conclusions make for sober reading. At the heart of the story was the incompetence of the Egyptian high command under the leadership of Gamal Abdel Nasser and the rivalry between various Arab players who were deeply suspicious of each other's motives. Israel, on the other side, gained a resounding victory for which, despite previous assessments to the contrary, there was no master plan.

Wm. Roger Louis is the Kerr Professor of English History and Culture at the University of Texas at Austin and Honorary Fellow of St. Antony's College, Oxford. A past President of the American Historical Association, he is the editor-in-chief of *The Oxford History of the British Empire*. His books include *The British Empire in the Middle East, 1945–1951* (1984) and *Ends of British Imperialism: The Scramble for Empire, Suez, and Decolonization* (2006).

Avi Shlaim is a Fellow at St. Antony's College and Professor of International Relations at the University of Oxford. He is the author of many books, including *The Iron Wall: Israel and the Arab World* (2000); *Lion of Jordan: King Hussein's Life in War and Peace* (2007); and *Israel and Palestine: Reappraisals, Revisions, Refutations* (2009). He edited with Eugene Rogan *The War for Palestine: Rewriting the History of 1948, Second Edition* (2007).

Cambridge Middle East Studies

Editorial Board

Charles Tripp (general editor)
Julia Clancy-Smith, F. Gregory Gause, Yezid Sayigh, Avi Shlaim,
Judith E. Tucker

The 1967 Arab-Israeli War

Origins and Consequences

Edited by

Wm. ROGER LOUIS
University of Texas at Austin

AVI SHLAIM
University of Oxford

CAMBRIDGE
UNIVERSITY PRESS

CAMBRIDGE UNIVERSITY PRESS
Cambridge, New York, Melbourne, Madrid, Cape Town,
Singapore, São Paulo, Delhi, Tokyo, Mexico City

Cambridge University Press
32 Avenue of the Americas, New York, NY 10013-2473, USA
www.cambridge.org
Information on this title: www.cambridge.org/9780521174794

First published 2012

Printed in the United States of America

A catalog record for this publication is available from the British Library.

Library of Congress Cataloging in Publication Data
The 1967 Arab-Israeli war: origins and consequences / edited by
Wm. Roger Louis and Avi Shlaim.
   p.   cm. – (Cambridge Middle East studies; 36)
Includes bibliographical references and index.
ISBN 978-1-107-00236-4 (hardback) – ISBN 978-0-521-17479-4 (paperback)
1. Israel-Arab War, 1967.   I. Shlaim, Avi.   II. Louis, William Roger, 1936–
DS127.A55   2012
956.04'6–dc23   2011021659

ISBN 978-1-107-00236-4 Hardback
ISBN 978-0-521-17479-4 Paperback

Contents

Notes on Contributors

Tewfik Aclimandos is based in a research centre in Cairo. He was an associate professor at Cairo University (2000) and the American University of Cairo (2007), and a visiting professor at the Sorbonne (2008). His doctoral thesis is on the rise of political activism in the Egyptian army during the early 1950s. He has written several articles on the Muslim Brotherhood. He is currently writing a biography of Gamal Abdel Nasser.

Jean-Pierre Filiu is an associate professor at Sciences Po in Paris. He was a visiting professor at Columbia and Georgetown universities. An Arabist and historian, he has published several books in French with Librairie Arthème Fayard, including *Mitterrand and Palestine* (2005), *The Boundaries of Jihad* (2006), and *The Nine Lives of Al-Qaida* (2009). His *Apocalypse in Islam* (University of California Press, 2011) was awarded the Augustin-Thierry Prize by the French History Convention.

Fawaz A. Gerges is Professor of the International Relations of the Middle East and director of the Middle East Centre at the London School of Economics. He is author of two recent books: *Journey of the Jihadist: Inside Muslim Militancy* (2007) and *The Far Enemy: Why Jihad Went Global* (2005, second edition 2009). His other books include *The Superpowers and the Middle East: Regional and International Politics* (1994) and *America and Political Islam: Clash of Cultures or Clash of Interests?* (2000).

Rami Ginat is Professor of Middle Eastern Studies in the Department of Political Studies, Bar-Ilan University, Israel. His books include *The Soviet*

Union and Egypt (1993) and *Syria and the Doctrine of Arab Neutralism* (2005). His most recent books are *A History of Egyptian Communism: Jews and Their Compatriots in Quest of Revolution* (2011) and *Egypt and the Second Palestinian Intifada: Policy Making with Multifaceted Commitments* (2011).

Laura M. James is a Middle East analyst specialising in Egypt and Sudan. She received a doctorate in International Relations from the University of Oxford, and her book *Nasser at War: Arab Images of the Enemy* was published in 2006. After working for the Economist Intelligence Unit and for DFID, she is now the Economic Adviser to the Assessment and Evaluation Commission supporting the North-South peace agreement in Sudan.

Rashid Khalidi is the Edward Said Professor of Arab Studies at Columbia University and past President of the Middle East Studies Association. His books include *Sowing Crisis: American Dominance and the Cold War in the Middle East* (2009), *The Iron Cage: The Story of the Palestinian Struggle for Statehood* (2006), *Resurrecting Empire: Western Footprints and America's Perilous Path in the Middle East* (2004), and *Palestinian Identity: The Construction of Modern National Consciousness* (1997).

David W. Lesch is Professor of Middle East History and Chair of the Department of History at Trinity University, San Antonio, Texas. He has published nine books, including *The Middle East and the United States: History, Politics, and Ideologies* (fifth edition 2011); *The Arab-Israeli Conflict: A History* (2008); *The New Lion of Damascus: Bashar al-Asad and Modern Syria* (2005); and *1979: The Year That Shaped the Modern Middle East* (2001).

Wm. Roger Louis is Kerr Professor of English History and Culture at the University of Texas at Austin and Honorary Fellow of St. Antony's College Oxford. A past President of the American Historical Association, he is editor-in-chief of *The Oxford History of the British Empire*. His books include *The British Empire in the Middle East, 1945–1951* (1984) and *Ends of British Imperialism: The Scramble for Empire, Suez, and Decolonization* (2006).

Wendy Pearlman is Assistant Professor of Political Science and the Crown Junior Chair in Middle East Studies at Northwestern University. She is the author of *Violence, Nonviolence, and the Palestinian National Movement* (2011) and *Occupied Voices: Stories of Everyday Life from* *the Second Intifada* (2003), as well as articles in *Journal of Palestine Studies, International Security,* and *Journal of Conflict Resolution.* She holds a PhD in Government from Harvard University.

Eugene Rogan teaches Modern History of the Middle East at the University of Oxford. He authored *The Arabs: A History* (2009), which has been translated into several European and Middle Eastern languages, and *Frontiers of the State in the Late Ottoman Empire* (1999), which was awarded the Albert Hourani Book Award of the Middle East Studies Association and the Fuad Köprülü Prize of the Turkish Studies Association. He edited with Avi Shlaim *The War for Palestine: Rewriting the History of 1948* (second edition 2007).

Avi Shlaim is Professor of International Relations and a Fellow of St. Antony's College, University of Oxford. He is a Fellow of the British Academy. His books include *War and Peace in the Middle East: A Concise History* (1995); *The Iron Wall: Israel and the Arab World* (2000); *Lion of Jordan: The Life of King Hussein in War and Peace* (2007); and *Israel and Palestine: Reappraisals, Revisions, Refutations* (2009).

Charles D. Smith is Professor of Middle East history at the University of Arizona. He authored *Islam and the Search for Social Order in Modern Egypt* (1983) and *Palestine and the Arab-Israeli Conflict* (1988, now in its seventh edition). He is published widely on U.S. Middle East policy and the Arab-Israeli conflict and was an invited commentator on a panel on the 1967 War sponsored by the U.S. State Department in 2004.

Chronology of the June 1967 War

28 May 1967	First meeting between Israeli government and Israel Defence Force (IDF) high command; Eshkol delivers hesitant speech to the nation
30 May 1967	Egypt and Jordan sign mutual defence pact in Cairo
31 May 1967	Mossad chief Meir Amit meets with U.S. Secretary of Defence Robert McNamara and Central Intelligence Agency (CIA) officials
1 June 1967	Government of National Unity formed in Jerusalem, with Moshe Dayan taking over as Minister of Defence; Egyptian General Riad assumes command of the Jordanian armed forces
2 June 1967	Second meeting between the Israeli government and high-ranking military officials; Nasser warns senior officers of imminent Israeli strike
4 June 1967	Israeli Cabinet decides to go to war; CIA alerts King Hussein of impending Israeli attack on Egypt
5 June 1967	Israel launches surprise attack on Egypt's air force, destroying most of it on the ground; Israel urges King Hussein to stay out of the war; Jordanians open hostilities against Israel; Israeli air force destroys most of Syrian air force
6 June 1967	IDF conquers Gaza; Egypt orders a general retreat; Jordan retreats from the West Bank
7 June 1967	IDF captures East Jerusalem; Nasser turns down UN ceasefire initiative
8 June 1967	IDF occupies Hebron and destroys Jordanian bridges; Israeli forces attack USS *Liberty*; Egypt accepts ceasefire
9 June 1967	United Nations passes Resolution 235 calling for immediate end to hostilities between Syria and Israel; IDF captures the Golan Heights; Israeli forces reach the Suez Canal; Nasser accuses United States and Britain of aiding Israel
10 June 1967	The Soviet Union breaks off diplomatic relations with Israel
27 June 1967	Israel annexes East Jerusalem
1 September 1967	Arab League summit at Khartoum rejects negotiations and reconciliation with Israel
22 November 1967	UN Security Council Resolution 242 calls on the Arabs to make peace with Israel and calls on Israel to withdraw from the territories it occupied during the war

The 1949 Armistice Lines

LEBANON
Damascus
N

SYRIA

Acre
Safed
DMZ
Sea of Galilee

Haifa
Nazareth
DMZ

Mediterranean Sea

Nablus

Tel Aviv
Jaffa

JORDAN

Amman

Latrun
Jerusalem
R. Jordan

ISRAEL
Bethlehem

Gaza
Hebron
Dead Sea

Rafah
Beersheba

Dimona
DMZ

EGYPT

1949 Armistice Lines
Israel
Area of Palestine under Jordanian Control
Area of Palestine under Egyptian Control
Demilitarized Zone (DMZ)

Eilat
Aqaba

25 miles
50 kilometres

MAP 1. 1949 Armistice Lines

MAP 2. The Middle East after the June 1967 War

Acknowledgements

We received a great deal of advice, encouragement, and support along the road that led to the publication of this book. Our greatest debt is to the British Academy for a generous grant for a conference at which preliminary drafts of the chapters in this book were presented. We would also like to thank the Department of Politics and International Relations at the University of Oxford for helping to prepare the application to the British Academy and for administering the grant.

The conference was held under the auspices of the Middle East Centre at St. Antony's College, Oxford, in October 2009. Our thanks go to Dr. Eugene Rogan, the director of the centre who is also a contributor to this volume; Julia Cook, the ever-helpful administrator; the graduate students of the centre for their critical contribution to our discussions; and Professor Margaret MacMillan, the Warden of St. Antony's, for her participation in the conference and for putting up four Antonians in the Warden's Lodgings.

We would also like to record our very special thanks to two of our graduate students, Noa Schonmann and Maximillian Thompson, for the invaluable part they played in organizing the conference, editing the conference papers, and preparing the manuscript for publication.

Last but not least, we wish to express our gratitude to the editorial team at Cambridge University Press, and especially to Marigold Acland and Joy Mizan, for their help in the editing and production of this book.

March 2011

Introduction

The June 1967 War was a turning point in the evolution of the Arab-Israeli conflict and a watershed moment in the history of the modern Middle East. A vast literature on this war, popularly known as the Six-Day War, covers the subject from all angles. But the time has come for reassessment. Many previous accounts deal with the military operations on the Egyptian, Jordanian, and Syrian fronts during the period of 5–10 June 1967. In this volume, the focus is not on the military operations but on the political aspects of the conflict, especially during the prolonged period of crisis that eventually erupted in all-out war. The aim is to reconstruct in some detail and in some depth the history of this fateful war from the perspective of its principal protagonists. These include the great powers and the regional powers. A major theme of the volume is the relationship between the great powers and their local allies on the road to war.

The contributors to this volume are area specialists. One of its strengths is that the authors have examined recently declassified material not only in English, French, and Russian but also in Hebrew and Arabic. The volume, however, is not merely a collection of articles with up-to-date material regarding different aspects of the war by different scholars. All the contributors were guided by the same overarching plan. Our collective aim has been to reinterpret the history of the June 1967 War by drawing as much as possible from the official documents and primary sources now available in all the relevant languages.

One objective of this volume is to reassess the outbreak of the war, the origins of which were as complex as its consequences have been far-reaching. Of the manifold causes that contributed to the outbreak of this war, three are of paramount importance: the long-standing hostility between the Arab states and Israel; inter-Arab politics; and the involvement of external powers in the affairs of the region. The secondary literature about the origins of the war is extensive, but there is no consensus on the relative weight of these three contributing causes. The authors have shed new light on all three dimensions and on the complex interplay among them.

A pronounced asymmetry between the primary sources available on the Arab and Israeli sides exists. Israel follows the practice prevalent in liberal democracies of reviewing and declassifying its official documents. Arab countries do not. Official Israeli and British documents for 1967 were recently declassified under the thirty-year rule. American documents for this period are readily accessible in the National Archives in Washington, D.C., and in the Lyndon Baines Johnson Library in Austin, Texas. A large selection of documents is also published in the relevant volumes of the Foreign Relations of the United States series. A substantial collection of documents for 1967 was published by the French Ministry of Foreign Affairs in Paris in 2008 under the title *Documents Diplomatiques Français*. One needs privileged access to see official documents from the Russian Foreign Ministry, the General Staff, and the KGB (*Komitet gosudarstvennoy bezopasnosti*, or Committee for State Security) in Moscow, but photocopies of at least some of the documents regarding the June 1967 War are also available at the Cummings Centre for Russian Studies at Tel Aviv University. Arab governments do not normally open their records for research by independent scholars, but a substantial body of memoirs by Egyptian, Jordanian, and Syrian politicians and soldiers deal with the war.

The other major objective of this volume is to reassess the consequences of the war. Some of the results are obvious: the military balance shifted dramatically in Israel's favour. Pan-Arabism suffered a shattering defeat. Israel expanded its territory considerably by capturing the Golan Heights, the West Bank, and the Sinai Peninsula. Israel's neighbours went from simply supporting the Palestinians to having a direct stake in the conflict. The Palestine Liberation Organization (PLO) emerged as a major player in the struggle for Palestine. A longer perspective suggests that Israel gradually began to lose international legitimacy in the aftermath of the war as a result of its intransigence, while the PLO began to gain international recognition as a national liberation movement. Over and beyond that, this volume establishes the war as marking not only a political and military transformation of the Middle East but also a shift in the emotional and intellectual climate of the region. The two concluding chapters of the volume are an overview and an examination of the scope and nature of this transformation.

A substantial part of the existing literature views the war from a Western perspective; we have tried to redress the balance by paying more attention to the local powers. Western scholars have often written about the international politics of the Middle East as if the local powers hardly mattered. We do not deny the importance of the great powers in shaping the history and politics of the region. We do, however, believe in devoting equal attention to the role played by the local powers. In short, we examine this major event in the history of the region not only from the outside looking in but also from the inside looking out.

In this introduction, we try to place the June 1967 War in its historical context. The Middle East has been one of the most volatile and violent subsystems in the international political system since the end of the World War II. Postwar history in the Middle East has been punctuated by an unusually high number of armed conflicts: full-scale, interstate, and civil wars. A major source of this instability has been the conflict between Israel and the Arabs. This was one of the bitterest, most profound, and most protracted conflicts of the twentieth century and the principal precipitant of wars in the Middle East.

The Israeli-Palestinian dimension and the Israeli-Arab dimension are the two major dimensions of this conflict. The origins of the conflict go back to the end of the nineteenth century, when the Zionist movement promoted the idea of building an independent state for the Jewish people in Palestine. Zionism met with strong opposition on the part of the Arab population of the country. The upshot was a clash between two national movements for the possession of Palestine. There were two peoples and one land – hence the conflict.

The neighbouring Arab states became involved in the conflict on the side of the Palestinian Arabs during the late 1930s. In 1947, the struggle for Palestine entered its most critical phase. In February of that year, Britain announced its decision to relinquish its mandate over Palestine, which it had received from the League of Nations in the aftermath of World War I. On 29 November 1947, the United Nations, the successor to the League of Nations, passed a resolution calling for the partition of mandatory Palestine into two states: one Jewish, one Arab. The Jews accepted the partition resolution; the Palestinians, the Arab states, and the Arab League rejected it and went to war to prevent it. This long war was divided into two main phases. The first phase lasted from 1 December 1947 until 14 May 1948, when Britain's mandate over

Palestine expired and the state of Israel was proclaimed. During this phase, the Palestinians suffered a military defeat, Palestinian society was decimated, and the first large wave of refugees was set in motion. The second phase began on 15 May 1948 with the invasion of Palestine by the regular armies of the neighbouring Arab states, and it ended with a cease-fire on 7 January 1949. This phase also ended with a Jewish victory and a comprehensive Arab defeat. After the guns fell silent, Israel concluded armistice agreements with all its neighbours: Lebanon, Syria, Jordan, and Egypt. These agreements gave Israel the only internationally recognized borders it has ever had. The main losers in the first Arab-Israeli war were the Palestinian Arabs. About 730,000 Palestinians, more than half the total, became refugees, and the name "Palestine" was wiped off the map.[1]

Regarding the basic cause of the conflict there are widely divergent views. Most Arabs maintain that the root cause is the dispossession and dispersal of the Palestinian Arabs, an original sin that was compounded by Israel's subsequent territorial acquisitions. In their view, Israel is an inherently aggressive and expansionist state and the real source of violence in the region.[2] Most Israelis maintain that the fundamental cause of the conflict is not territory but is the Arab rejection of Israel's very right to exist as a sovereign state in the Middle East. According to this view, the basic Arab objective is the liquidation of the state of Israel, whereas Israel acts only in self-defence and in response to the Arab challenges.[3] But whatever one's view are of the origins and nature of the Arab-Israeli dispute, there can be no doubt that the dispute has been a major cause of wars in the Middle East.

A second source of tension and instability, which at least on one occasion, in June 1967, helped tip the balance in favour of war, is to be found in the relations among the Arab states. In theory, all Arab states subscribe to the ideal of Arab unity, but in practice, inter-Arab relations are characterized more by conflict than by cooperation. Israel is widely held to be one of the few solid pillars propping up Arab unity, the one issue on which all Arabs, whatever their other differences, usually agree. Opposition to Israel follows naturally from the belief that the inhabitants

---

[1] Eugene L. Rogan and Avi Shlaim, eds., *The War for Palestine: Rewriting the History of 1948* (Cambridge: Cambridge University Press, 2001; 2nd ed., 2007).

[2] See, e.g., David Hirst, *The Gun and the Olive Branch: The Roots of Violence in the Middle East* (London: Faber and Faber, 1977).

[3] See, e.g., Yehoshafat Harkabi, *Arab Strategies and Israel's Response* (New York: Free Press, 1977).

of the various Arab states, including the Palestinians, form a single nation and that Israel has grossly violated the sacred rights of this nation.

A distinction needs to be made, however, between the rhetorical and operational levels of Arab foreign policy at the time. Whereas, at the rhetorical level, the Arab states were largely united in their commitment to oppose Israel, at the operational level they remained deeply divided. The conservative states tended to advocate containment of the Jewish state, while the radical states tended to advocate confrontation. As a number of scholars have pointed out, the conflict with Israel has imposed enormous strain on the inter-Arab system.[4] Far from serving as a unifying force, the question of how to deal with Israel has been a serious source of dissension and discord in inter-Arab politics.

A third source of instability and violence in the Middle East has been the involvement of the great powers in the affairs of the region. Two features of the Middle East help account for the interest and rivalry it has evoked among them: its geostrategic importance and its oil reserves. Great power involvement is not a unique feature of the Middle East, but instead affects, in varying degrees, all regions of the world. What distinguishes the Middle East is the intensity, pervasiveness, and profound impact of this involvement. No other part of the world has been so thoroughly and ceaselessly caught up in great power rivalries. No other subsystem of the international political system has been as penetrated as in the Middle East.[5]

The dominant great powers in the Middle East throughout the course of the twentieth century were the Ottoman Empire until its dissolution in 1918; Britain and France until, roughly, the Suez Crisis of 1956; the United States and the Soviet Union from Suez until the dissolution of the Soviet Union in 1991; and the United States alone since 1991. So much stress has been laid on the role of these external powers that the history of the modern Middle East, in the words of Malcolm Yapp, has often been written as though the local states were "driftwood in the sea of international affairs, their destinies shaped by the decisions of others."[6]

---

[4] Malcolm Kerr, *The Arab Cold War: Gamal Abd al-Nasir and his Rivals, 1958–1970* (London: Oxford University Press, 1971); Michael C. Hudson, *Arab Politics: The Search for Legitimacy* (New Haven, CT: Yale University Press, 1977); Fouad Ajami, *The Arab Predicament: Arab Political Thought and Practice since 1967* (Cambridge: Cambridge University Press, 1981); Stephen M. Walt, *The Origins of Alliances* (Ithaca, NY: Cornell University Press, 1987).

[5] L. Carl Brown, *International Politics and the Middle East: Old Rules, Dangerous Game* (Princeton, NJ: Princeton University Press, 1984), 4.

[6] M. E. Yapp, *The Near East since the First World War* (London: Longman, 1991), 3.

Yet this is a false picture, popular as it is with Middle Easterners and outsiders alike.

The dominant feature in the relations between international and regional powers is the manipulation of the former by the latter. A survey of the period from 1955 to 1967 by Fawaz Gerges reaches the conclusion that the superpowers were rarely able to impose their will on the smaller states of the Middle East.[7] Although the local states depended on their superpower patrons for diplomatic support, economic aid, and the supply of arms, they managed to retain considerable freedom of action. Yet, obviously, no account of the origins of Arab-Israeli wars would be complete if it ignored the role played by outside powers.

When the role of the great powers is considered alongside the Arab-Israeli disputes and inter-Arab relations, we begin to get some idea of why the international politics of the Middle East are so complex, endemically unstable, and prone to violence and war. Against this background, what is surprising is not that eight full-scale Arab-Israeli wars have erupted during the postwar period, but that some of the other crises in this volatile region stopped short of war. Our next task is to review briefly the specific events that catapulted the Middle East into a third Arab-Israeli war.

Our main conclusion is that the June 1967 War was not the result of deliberate planning, and was still less a grand design on the part of any of the participants, but was rather the result of a crisis slide, of a process that no one was able to control. Accounts that attribute the outbreak of war to a deliberate decision fall into two categories: those that claim Israel instigated the war in order to expand its territory, and those that claim President Gamal Abdel Nasser of Egypt wilfully chose to embark on the path to war in order to defeat Israel. We maintain that both Israel and Egypt on the whole simply reacted to events. The claim that Israel planned the war from the beginning simply does not stand up to serious critical scrutiny in the light of the evidence. From Israel's perspective, this was a war of self-defence, not a war of conquest. Nasser's motives are much more difficult to pin down. Chapters 2 and 6 of this volume are devoted to Nasser's motives, and several of the other chapters deal with how these motives were interpreted by the other participants. The consensus we reach is that Nasser neither wanted war nor expected a war to take place. What he did do was to embark on an exercise in brinkmanship that went over the brink.

---

[7] Fawaz A. Gerges, *The Superpowers and the Middle East: Regional and International Politics, 1955–1967* (Boulder, CO: Westview Press, 1994).

It is undeniable that Nasser appeared to challenge Israel to a duel. On 13 May 1967, he received a Soviet intelligence report claiming that Israel was massing troops on Syria's border. Nasser responded by taking three successive steps that made war virtually inevitable: he deployed his troops in the Sinai close to Israel's border, he expelled the UN Emergency Force (UNEF) from the Sinai, and, on 22 May, he closed the Straits of Tiran to Israeli shipping. In Israeli eyes, this was a *casus belli*, a cause for war. On 5 June, Israel seized the initiative and launched the short, sharp war that ended in a resounding military defeat for Egypt, Syria, and Jordan.

In triggering the crisis that led to the June 1967 War, inter-Arab rivalry was decisive. It may sound ironic to suggest that the war owed more to the rivalries between the Arab states than to the dispute between these states and Israel, but such a view is supported by the facts. The Arab world was in a state of turmoil arising from the conflicts and suspicions between the radical and conservative regimes. A militant Ba'th regime rose to power in Syria in February 1966 and started the push for a war to liberate Palestine. President Nasser came under growing pressure to stop hiding behind the United Nations and to come to the rescue of the embattled regime in Damascus. Nasser suspected his Syrian allies of wanting to drag him into a war with Israel, while they suspected that if push came to shove, he would leave them to face Israel on their own. Nasser's first move, the deployment of the Egyptian army in the Sinai, was not intended as a prelude to an attack on Israel but as a political manoeuvre designed to deter the Israelis and to shore up his prestige at home and in the Arab world. This move, however, started a chain reaction that Nasser was unable to control.

In early May 1967, the old quarrel between Israel and the Arabs seemed almost irrelevant. As Malcolm Kerr observed in *The Arab Cold War*, the Arabs were more preoccupied with one another than they were with Israel. A football analogy seems appropriate because the World Cup was on everyone's mind during the spring of that year. Even when the Israelis first appeared on the scene, they were merely there as a football for the Arabs, kicked onto the field first by the Syrian hotheads and then again by Nasser. The Israelis, however, took a different view of themselves. It became a case of the football kicking the players.[8]

The superpowers did little to prevent the slide towards war. The Soviets gave Nasser a misleading report about Israeli troop concentrations and supported his deployment of Egyptian troops in the Sinai in the interest

[8] Kerr, *The Arab Cold War*, 126.

of bolstering the left-wing regime in Damascus and in the hope of deterring Israel from moving against it. Their subsequent attempts to restrain Nasser had little effect. They probably hoped to make some political gains by underlining their own commitment to the Arabs and the pro-Israeli orientation of American foreign policy. But they seriously miscalculated the danger of war and were swept up in a fast-moving crisis that they had helped unleash.

America features prominently in Arab conspiracy theories purporting to explain the causes and outcome of the June 1967 War. Mohamed Heikal, Nasser's confidant, for example, claims that President Lyndon Johnson was obsessed with Nasser and that Johnson conspired with Israel to bring him down.[9] Such explanations, however, are transparently self-serving in that they assign all the blame for the war to America and Israel and overlook the part played by Arab provocations and Arab miscalculations.

The war provides a striking illustration of the perennial predicament of the Arab states: they cannot act separately and they cannot act collectively; they keep getting in one another's way. On this occasion, the level of incompetence displayed by the Arab leaders was staggering. After ten years of preparation for what was often referred to as the battle of destiny, and after raising popular passions to a fever pitch with their blood-curdling rhetoric, the leaders of the confrontational states were caught by complete surprise when Israel took their threats at face value and landed the first blow.

The United States did not plan the war. The American position during the upswing phase of the crisis was hesitant, weak, and ambiguous. President Johnson initially tried to prevent war by restraining Israel and issuing warnings to the Egyptians and the Soviets. Because these warnings had no visible effect and because American forces were tied down in Vietnam, some of Johnson's advisers toyed with the idea of unleashing Israel against Egypt. American policy was neither clear-cut nor constant: it evolved gradually and eventually underwent a significant shift. As a result of these domestic constraints, President Johnson sent Israel mixed messages. His last signal to the Israelis amounted to what William Quandt termed "a yellow light," but like most motorists, Israel treated the yellow

---

[9] Mohamed Heikal, *1967: Al-Infijar* [1967: The Explosion] (Cairo: Al-Ahram, 1990), 371–2.

light as a green one.[10] America thus played a critical role in the outbreak of war by leaving Israel a free hand to respond as it saw fit to the perceived Egyptian challenge. Thus, although the crisis of May 1967 sprang out of inter-Arab rivalries, Israel's decision to go to war could be reached only after it had secured the tacit support of its superpower ally.

The 1967 war has often been described as a premeditated war on the part of Israel. But Chapter 1 shows that the archival records and other contemporary evidence reveal almost the opposite. Military officers in the Israel Defence Force (IDF) had occasionally made reckless and belligerent public statements, but the government of Levi Eshkol had no intention of provoking a war with the Arabs and still less of expanding the dominion of Israel. Territorial aims developed during the war. The Israelis responded to Nasser's actions: the deployment of troops in the Sinai, the demand for the withdrawal of the UNEF, and on 22 May, the closing of the Straits of Tiran, which virtually everyone in the Israeli Cabinet regarded as an act of war. During the previous weeks, Eshkol had kept his eye on the most vital part of the problem – to make sure that the U.S. government and the president would not respond negatively to the IDF's engagement with the Egyptian army. Moshe Dayan, who became defence minister in early June, summed up the Israeli mood when he said that it would be "lunacy" to wait any longer. Dayan guided the course of the war, often giving orders that should have been issued by the Chief of Staff. Dayan's actions were erratic, contradictory, and irresponsible, but he got away with it because of the resounding military victory. Once wound up and released, the Israeli war machine sprang into action with devastating speed, first in the destruction of the Egyptian air force and army, then in the occupation of East Jerusalem and the West Bank, and finally in the hard-fought battle over the Golan Heights.

No master plan existed. Israeli tanks rolled to a halt mainly along natural frontiers such as the River Jordan and the Suez Canal. As a result, the war rekindled irredentist aims, especially on the eastern front. What began as a war to destroy the Egyptian army led to the occupation of territory inhabited by more than a million Arabs and, in the north, the conquest of a region that embittered Syrians at the time and has continued

---

[10] William B. Quandt, *Peace Process: American Diplomacy and the Arab-Israeli Conflict since 1967* (Berkeley: University of California Press, 2001), 48.

to do so. The Old City of Jerusalem was the unintended prize, the result of a Jordanian decision to follow Nasser's lead and to attack Israel. Within the Israeli government, Eshkol proved to be an effective leader, despite near rebellion of the younger corps of officers in the IDF and the virtual insubordination of Dayan. None of the military or civilian members of the government would have predicted the outcome. The territorial aims were confused, convoluted, and complex, but the result was a "Greater Israel" that largely endures to the present.

For Nasser, the destruction of the Egyptian air force and a substantial part of the army was an unprecedented disaster. Chapter 2 uses contemporary evidence and postwar testimony of Egyptian generals and others within the authoritarian elite to explain Nasser's own misconceptions and mistakes. The Egyptians as well as the Arabs generally believed their own extravagant rhetoric and underestimated Israel's military capacity. Nasser thought that the United States was the archenemy and that Israel would follow American orders. He needed to be careful not to make Egypt appear to be the aggressor and thus to sustain an Israeli attack. He believed the Egyptian army could engage the IDF without provoking American intervention while bringing about an international crisis that would work to Egypt's advantage. Such assumptions can be detected in his response to one of the air force generals, Sidqi Mahmoud, who told him realistically that the Egyptian air force could not survive a first strike by Israel: "Sidqi," replied Nasser, "do you accept the first attack or do you want go fight the United States?" Nasser calculated that Egypt could endure a prolonged defensive battle that would bring about "global confrontation" – which in turn would result in a cease-fire favourable to Egypt. The other part of the gamble was that war might be averted. If there were no war, Nasser would achieve a pan-Arab victory. In either case, Egypt would emerge victorious.

Nasser actually thought that the Israelis might attack on 5 June. But such was the mistrust within the Egyptian government that his generals refused to believe him. Nasser accepted assurances that the Egyptian armed forces were capable of holding the IDF at bay, which seemed to be the only plausible strategy because the Egyptian army was trained for defensive and not offensive warfare. Throughout the crisis, Nasser remained confident. His three moves of deploying troops in the Sinai on 14 May, demanding the withdrawal of the UNEF on 16 May, and closing the Gulf of Aqaba on 22 May were taken to shore up his prestige in Egypt and to sustain his credibility as the leader of the Arabs. His decisions were not made as part of a plan, but neither were they accidental. Nasser knew he was playing for high stakes. But he had no idea of the extent of the impending catastrophe. He apparently knew that American and British aircraft had not assisted the Israelis, but he agreed to broadcast what became known as the "Big Lie," thus poisoning American and British public sentiment. He correctly believed that the Soviet Union would not come to his rescue, but after the defeat, he became increasingly dependent on Soviet military and economic assistance. Nasser lost the leadership of Arab nationalism. But together with King Hussein, a chastened Nasser pursued a much more moderate policy towards Israel in an attempt to regain the West Bank and Old Jerusalem.

The origins of the 1967 war and its outbreak can be traced in part to the highly charged tension between Syria and Israel. Chapter 3 describes the Ba'th government in Damascus as militant and aggressively committed. Riven with political jealousies and conflicts between the younger and older members, the Ba'th Party also reflected differing aims of urban politicians, intellectuals, rural minorities, and tribes. But there was unity on one point. General sentiment in Syria held that Egypt, and Nasser in particular, had failed to promote Arab unity and that the creation of the state of Israel was the cause of an ongoing regional crisis. The Syrians did not, however, anticipate an actual war. They were unprepared. The Syrians were astonished by Nasser's closing of the Straits. But the Ba'thist regime assumed that the Soviet Union would either prevent the outbreak of war or protect the radical Arab states, Syria no less than Egypt. A few months before, during the spring of 1967, an incident between Israel and Syria had brought about mobilization of troops on both sides. Many observers at the time believed that Israel might attack on the Syrian frontier. Thus public attention throughout the world focused on the Syrian border. When war broke out instead in the Sinai, the Syrians not only were caught by surprise but also initially did very little.

When the war expanded, the Syrians aimed at any cost to prevent the Israelis from capturing the Golan Heights, the juncture of Lebanon, Syria, Jordan, and Israel. Though less than 1 percent of Syria's landmass – only 690 square miles – the Golan Heights nevertheless possessed agricultural and water resources. The Syrians fought ferociously to prevent an Israeli takeover. Compared with the destruction of the Egyptian army and the loss of the Sinai, the Syrian defeat was small. But the Golan Heights became a symbol of Israeli aggressiveness and a source of Syrian irredentism. The mistake during the war was to assume that the Soviet Union would protect Syria – but the Russians calculated that the loss of the Golan Heights was not worth the risk of a third world war.

The combination of Syrian miscalculation and Russian ambivalence helps explain the complicated reasons why the war broke out when it did.

Chapter 4 explains that when King Hussein made his fateful visit to conclude a defence pact with Egypt in late May 1967, he believed it to be virtually inevitable that Jordan would participate along with the other Arab states in a war against Israel. The argument later became useful in covering up disastrous mistakes. Foremost among Hussein's errors of judgement was his capitulation to Nasser's demand that the Jordan army be placed under Egyptian command. Within three days of the Israeli attack on 5 June, Hussein lost half his kingdom. Old Jerusalem and the West Bank were now under Israeli occupation. The defeated Jordanian army was close to disintegration, and a new wave of refugees strained the resources of the Jordanian state to its breaking point. How can this series of catastrophes be explained? A few months before the outbreak of the war, the IDF attacked the Jordanian village of Samuʿ on the West Bank. It was a ferocious raid, but Hussein misinterpreted its significance. He believed the Israelis had revealed their intention to occupy the West Bank and to regard Jordan as an enemy rather than as a partner in trying to maintain a precarious coexistence.

Hussein became obsessed with what he believed to be an Israeli betrayal. Israeli Prime Minister Eshkol was furious with the IDF because of the raid. In May 1967 the Israeli government wanted Jordan to keep out of any war with Egypt, and it had no plans for the conquest of the West Bank or East Jerusalem. The Israelis sent Hussein no fewer than three messages saying they had no hostile intent towards Jordan. But it was now too late. Hussein had thrown in his hand with Nasser. He regarded Nasser as "behaving like a mad man" in closing the Straits of Tiran and thus precipitating the war, but he followed Nasser. Hussein proved that he was loyal to the Arab cause. Despite the catastrophe, he could later look back on a redeeming outcome. Nasser became an ally. Jordan was now accepted by other Arab states as having fought gallantly against Israel. Jordan could now stand up to Syria and the PLO without being maligned as a collaborator with Israel. Jordan's part in the war lent legitimacy to the Hashemite regime in Jordan.

Chapter 5 places Palestinian nationalism in the context of the antecedents and consequences of the war. The Palestinian movement was significant before and after the war – but not during the war. As a result of the 1967 transformation of the region, Israel occupied virtually all of what had been known as British Palestine. The demography of the Palestinians in the wake of the earlier upheaval in 1948 is revealing for both the response of the Arab states and the Palestinians two decades later. More than seven hundred thousand Palestinians became refugees after the Zionist victories and the creation of the state of Israel: 37 percent ended up on the West Bank, while 10 percent ended up in Jordan (thus, nearly half were under the jurisdiction of the state of Jordan); 26 percent went to the Gaza Strip, which was administered by Egypt; 14 percent to Lebanon; 10 percent to Syria; and 1 percent to Egypt. Each of the Arab states attempted to control or influence the Palestinian movement. Nasser hoped to integrate the Palestinians into the larger pan-Arab movement under his control, and most Palestinians looked to Nasser to liberate their homeland. A smaller contingent believed in direct guerrilla attacks against Israel by commandos, the *fedayeen*. In the latter grouping, the faction named Fatah became predominant, not least because of the support it received from the regime in Damascus. Fatah upheld the view that the mass of the Palestinian population had to be organized ideologically as well as militarily. A unified organization taking its own initiative would force action on the part of the Arab states.

Nasser believed that Fatah was attempting to drag him into war. Syria supported the guerrillas in part to challenge Nasser. In Jordan, the Palestinians became increasingly a state within a state and a danger to the Hashemite dynasty. King Hussein feared that mobilization of the Palestinians in the West Bank would precipitate an Israeli invasion. He thus concluded the pact with Nasser in May 1967. Growing militancy on the West Bank and the danger of an Israeli occupation set the Palestinian context of the 1967 war. Hussein finally cracked down on the Palestinians in 1970, expelling the leadership and most of its cadres. But in 1969, Arafat emerged as the leader of the PLO, thus marking a long-term revival of the movement and sustaining the belief, in Palestinian eyes, of honour and eventual redemption.

The Egyptian involvement in the civil war in Yemen, as Chapter 6 demonstrates, had a direct bearing on Egyptian preparedness for war in 1967. Since the beginning of the Yemeni revolution in 1962, Nasser had deployed Egyptian forces against the Yemeni monarchy in the hope of creating a revolutionary state that would be pro-Egypt and anti–Saudi Arabia. With his relations already strained with Syria, Nasser had to deal with Saudi Arabia's and, to a lesser extent, Jordan's support for the royalist side. Though Egypt's relations with Saudi Arabia and Jordan had improved by 1967, the war in Yemen made it difficult to forge a united coalition against Israel. Nasser had a further aim beyond Yemen. He intended to drive the British out of the Arabian Peninsula. But in the years leading up to the end of the British Empire, Aden became increasingly important as a base for military headquarters in the Middle East and for the protection of oil in the Gulf. The British were determined not to allow Nasser to extend influence or control over Yemen or southwards towards Aden. By 1967, one-third of Egyptian forces had been committed to the Yemeni war, and fifteen thousand soldiers had been killed. But Radio Cairo proclaimed victories. Most Egyptians, including perhaps Nasser, believed their own propaganda.

Even though his military commanders advised Nasser to withdraw, he refused. To Nasser, the war in Yemen was a political operation. His political aims claimed priority over military setbacks. When he launched subversive guerrilla actions against the British in Aden, the conflict broadened internationally. The British not only conducted covert operations but also, in a manner reminiscent of the Suez operation in 1956, approached the French and the Israelis to support the royalist movement in Yemen. British covert involvement was managed by the "Aden group," a small but influential number of patriots within the government, including Julian Amery and former intelligence officers dedicated to sustaining the British Empire and defeating Nasser. The French secretly sent mercenaries with previous experience in Algeria and the Congo. They were small in number, only about fifteen, but highly effective. The Israelis also lent support by dropping arms and ammunition to the royalist troops. The Israelis thus gained invaluable information about the deployment of Egyptian forces. The Aden group, together with French volunteers and Israeli assistance, prevented the royalist movement from collapsing for the time being. But in 1966, British Prime Minister Harold Wilson announced that the British would withdraw from Aden. By then there were sixty thousand Egyptian soldiers and airmen in Yemen. The military commitment strained the Egyptian economy and prevented the upkeep of military maintenance, including the building of hangars for the Egyptian air force. Egyptian airplanes were thus left exposed in 1967. The war in Yemen distracted Nasser from the Sinai front. He again refused to listen to his military advisers, who urged him that Egypt must strike first in a war against Israel. Egyptian forces would not survive an Israeli offensive. Their judgement was vindicated when the Israelis virtually destroyed the Egyptian air force. But there was one positive development for the Egyptians. The sixty thousand troops in Yemen survived intact to fight another day.

Chapter 7 addresses one of the most controversial questions of the war: did President Johnson signal to the Israelis his approval of their intent to attack Egypt? Johnson made up his own mind. He chose certain advisers to whom he would listen closely, including not only staff members of the National Security Council (NSC) but also certain American Jews, such as Abraham Feinberg (a New York banker) and Arthur Krim (head of the Democrat Party Campaign), whose wife Mathilde was a guest in the White House when Johnson made some of his key decisions. His confidants also included Abe Fortas, an Associate Justice of the Supreme Court, and Eppie Evron, a counsellor at the Israeli embassy. By contrast, Secretary of State Dean Rusk was cut out of some of the critical discussions. Relations between the United States and Egypt had deteriorated, and Johnson had little sympathy for the Arab or Palestinian cause. His methods and disposition were markedly different from those of the president a decade earlier. During the Suez Crisis, President Dwight Eisenhower not only consulted heads of departments and agencies but also warned Israel in advance not to assume that the upcoming presidential elections would cause him to accept an attack on Egypt. Eisenhower's subsequent insistence that Israel withdraw from the Sinai Peninsula angered Johnson, who was in the Senate at the time. Always sensitive to public sentiment, Johnson instructed his staff during the 1967 war to answer individually some 160,000 letters, mainly pro-Israel. But Johnson was not uncritical or unaware of Israeli motives. He resented Jewish pressure and at one point reprimanded members of his staff for being "Zionist dupes." For Johnson and some of his principal advisers, including Walt Rostow, the 1967 war was a diversion from Vietnam. Johnson acquiesced in State Department guidance in mid-May when he declared that the United States would respect the territorial integrity of all states in the Middle East. But once war began, he disregarded the State Department and listened mainly to those within his White House circle of advisers.

The major historical question has been: when did Johnson flash an amber light at the Israelis, signifying danger but not opposition to an Israeli preemptive strike? Johnson had many lights flashing at him during late May and early June 1967, and none of them were red. His contacts accurately though nervously detected his mood. For Johnson, it came as no surprise when the Israelis attacked (though it did to Rusk, who was "shocked and angry"). Johnson had concluded that war was inevitable, but unlike Eisenhower, he would not try to curb it. Like most others, Johnson subsequently believed that the Israelis would return most of the conquered territory. Whether they would actually do so depended on, in the words of one NSC staff member, "how hard LBJ is willing to lean on Israel." Johnson received no assurance about Israeli willingness to negotiate over the occupied territories. But with Ambassador Arthur Goldberg working as the president's right-hand man at the United Nations, the United States did help provide the basis for UN Resolution 242, which set the principle that peace in the Middle East should be established by adjusting the frontiers of territories lost in the war (but not the territories themselves, which made the formula acceptable to the Israelis). From beginning to end, Johnson was astutely pro-Israel and reoriented the American position in the Middle East. Subsequently, the United States replaced France as the principal supplier to Israel of military equipment, including tanks and jet aircraft.

On the basis of Russian and Eastern European archives, Chapter 8 assesses Soviet involvement in the origins of the crisis. The chapter begins with a comprehensive review of the historical literature, much of which has attributed a high degree of calculation and manipulation to the Russians. For example, Soviet influence in the Middle East depended on total support for the Arab cause. Even if Israel were to emerge victorious in the 1967 conflict, the Soviet Union would champion Egypt and Syria in the United Nations and the United States would emerge as the enemy of the Arabs. In this interpretation as well as many others based on supposition rather than evidence, historians have overrated the accuracy of Soviet intelligence and the effectiveness of their decisions. Soviet Military Intelligence was mixed, with no coherent or systematic method of making decisions. Far from concocting the crisis, the Soviets sent the famous warning of 13 May as a realistic probability of Israeli troop concentration on the Syrian frontier. Nasser did not know of plans for Israeli troop deployment, and he responded by evicting the UNEF on the frontier with Israel and then blockading the Gulf of Aqaba. He did not consult his Russian allies.

The Soviets believed that Nasser's move was, in the words of Leonid Brezhnev, "ill-advised." But the Soviets continued to support Nasser. They perhaps could have imposed more restraint, but paradoxically they wound up following Nasser's lead. Soviet intelligence in any event tended to overestimate Egypt's military capacity while picking up at face value reports that Israeli military officers planned to attack Syria and occupy Damascus. The Soviet regime regarded the Israelis as they did Russian Jews, "downtrodden, intellectuals, artists." By late May there was apathy rather than active planning in Moscow. A certain irony exists that at high levels within the Soviet government there was as much lack of communication as there was between the White House and the State Department. Soviet intelligence reports were contradictory and poorly digested. At the outbreak of the war, the Russians had no choice but to support the Arab cause. They certainly did not orchestrate the crisis. The origins of the 1967 war are not to be found in Moscow or for that matter Washington, but rather in the Middle East.

Chapter 9 challenges the conventional interpretation of the part played by the British government during the 1967 war. Conventional wisdom holds that the British asserted strict neutrality, issuing strenuous denials of involvement in Parliament and the United Nations. Foreign Secretary George Brown, according to this view, managed only superficially to rebuild damaged relations with the Arab states. The deteriorating economic circumstances in the aftermath played into the decision to recall all British troops east of Suez. It must be said that this negative set of lamentable events, lamentable at least to the British, is entirely true, but there are other levels of interpretation. An examination of the archival records reveals that the Wilson government played a vigorous role in the crisis from beginning to end, at first participating in the debate about the withdrawal of the UN contingent from the Sinai and finally making a signal contribution with Lord Caradon's drafting of UN Resolution 242. The Wilson government is often depicted as feeble and indecisive, but those within the Cabinet saw themselves as the equal of previous proconsuls dealing with the Middle East, lineal descendants of Curzon, Milner, and Balfour. The statecraft of 1967 dealt with the war as part of the larger crisis of civil war in Aden and the end of the British Empire in the Middle East, but the Wilson government aimed to sustain British influence rather than liquidate it.

The British response to the war can also be interpreted as a study in irony. Fifty years after the Balfour Declaration, and a decade after the Suez Crisis of 1956 and 1957, the British reaped the whirlwind of previous commitments. To the Arabs, the sheer scope of their defeat led to the conclusion that Israel alone could not have inflicted it. The British now paid the ultimate price for Suez in what the British and Americans called the Big Lie. To the Arabs, the logic of collusion seemed as compelling as it had been in 1956. How else could the cataclysm be explained? Anti-British demonstrations and rioting erupted throughout the Middle East. Even as it became clear that neither the British nor the Americans had intervened to support Israel, state-controlled radios in the Arab countries continued to broadcast news of an imperialist plot in which the Western countries had used Israel for their own purposes. The long-range consequences were severe, above all because Israel now occupied virtually all of Arab Palestine. Britain's Middle East hands believed that the war damaged the British position in the Middle East more seriously than any episode since the creation of the state of Israel in 1948.

Charles de Gaulle was consistent before, during, and after the crisis. As Chapter 10 makes clear, de Gaulle believed that the Israeli-Arab conflict must be seen as a dimension of the Cold War, in which France occupied an equal place along with the United States, the Soviet Union, and Britain. Though originally pro-Zionist, in 1967 de Gaulle demonstrated that France respected Arab independence and had moved beyond colonial episodes such as Indo-China, Suez, and Algeria. France was still Israel's main source of military strength and had provided critical assistance in the development of the nuclear plant opened at Dimona during 1966. But in 1967, de Gaulle warned Israel as well as the Arab states that the French would remain neutral (even though he authorized the sending of critical spare parts to the IDF on the second day after the outbreak of war, 7 June). In the early days of the conflict, some thirty thousand French demonstrated in favour of Israel, a figure that bore comparison with the average of one thousand who would turn up at protests against the American presence in Vietnam.

De Gaulle remained silent on the question of who fired the first shot on 5 June, but he believed the Soviets had been caught off guard and that the Americans could not make up their minds. De Gaulle rebuffed Israel's plea for assistance and made his views exceedingly clear to Egypt and Syria. "Who is your enemy?" he asked the Syrian deputy prime minister, "the United States or Israel?" "Do not make a bet," he continued, "on the Russians coming to the rescue." As if giving advice to a friend, he pointed out that the state of Israel had been created mainly by the United States, not France, but that Israel must now be seen as a reality. During the months following the end of the war, de Gaulle persistently stated that Israel had to return the occupied territories and that the Arab states had to recognize Israel. Despite overwhelming public and political pressure, he managed to reverse a consistently pro-Israeli outlook on the part of France. It came to be known in France as "the divorce." But de Gaulle believed he was taking a long view of history and that the Israelis would remain enemies of the Arabs until the restoration of East Jerusalem, the West Bank, and Gaza. When the UN Security Council voted in favour of Resolution 242, the French translation called on Israel to withdraw from "the territories" and not "territories occupied in the recent conflict." The definitine article implied total withdrawal. There could be no mistake about French intent.

Chapter 11 makes a critical distinction between Arab nationalism, which includes the identity of a people with a common culture, and the ideal of Arab unity. Nasser was the apostle of Arab nationalism. Though his flowery rhetoric often expressed the aim of a unified Arab state, his motive was to further the cause of Egypt. He was wary and even sarcastic about a union with Syria before and after the failed experiment of merging the two states in 1958. He always made clear that he should never be blamed for the disappointment – or for that matter, for any other breakdown of Arab unity. At least to his followers, his charisma usually allowed him to rise above mistakes and contradictions. Nasser was certainly capable of precipitous action and errors of judgement, as he proved during the crisis of 1967, but on the whole he was consistently pragmatic and shrewd. In short, he was nonideological.

Arab nationalism was also nonideological. But there are three exceptions in which ideology seemed to drive commitment. One of them was the war in Yemen. Perhaps Nasser allowed himself to be drawn in because the "Free Officers" of Yemen compared their revolt with his own revolt in 1952 (but so did the Iraqi revolutionaries in 1958 and he had held them at a distance). In any event, there was an idealistic or ideological dimension to Yemen that made it virtually unique even after independence. The second exception to the general rule of nonideological Arab nationalism was the case of Syria. The Ba'th regime in Damascus between 1966 and 1970 was one of the most ideologically committed of any in the region at any time. The ideological resolve of the Damascus regime thus helps explain the drive for confrontation with Israel that played a large part in the origins of the 1967 war. The third exception to nonideological Arab nationalism was the Palestinian movement, in which the Fatah faction eventually prevailed. Fatah in 1967, and later the PLO under Arafat's leadership, believed in "Palestine first" – Palestinian autonomy and militancy against Israel. Fatah was supported by the regime in Damascus, but Nasser and many other Arabs of the time believed that it was not only dangerous but also irresponsible for Fatah and the Syrians to provoke a war with Israel. The cases of Yemen, Syria, and Palestine are thus three examples in which ideology was a driving force. Nasser was influenced by simple realpolitik. The defeat of 1967 was profoundly demoralizing to the Arabs. But Arab nationalism remained the same. What faded was hope for Arab unity and, at least in the short run, victory over Israel.

Within a period of days, the 1967 war led to an Arab defeat that at the time seemed to be as disastrous and far-reaching as that of the prolonged conflict of 1948. The long-term consequences of 1967 led to the revival of the pan-Islamist movement. But Chapter 12 shows that few at the time made the connection between religion and the political setback for Arab nationalism. Such was the rapidity and shock of events that it took time to reflect on causes and consequences. Yet even in the immediate aftermath it seemed that the foundations of Arab civilization had been shaken. It became immediately clear that Nasser would never again have the same charismatic appeal that he had previously possessed as the leader of Arab nationalism. Since the early 1950s, his popularity and moral standing had rested on championing the Palestinian cause against Israel and on combating the continued influence of Western powers in the Arab world, including Saudi Arabia and the Gulf states. Nasser emerged from the 1967 trauma as a wiser and diminished figure. He now had to restructure the Egyptian government and economy as well as to rebuild the army. He became increasingly dependent on Soviet and Saudi assistance.

Nasser demanded that Egyptians take a more realistic view of their resources and strength at the same time that Arab intellectuals and writers throughout the Middle East assessed the underlying causes of the 1967 military defeat. They asked far-reaching questions that became known as the searching of the Arab soul. For example, what were the Arab assumptions of power and prestige that in retrospect appeared as grandiose and exaggerated, even delusional? What were the reasons for the lead of the West in technology and science? Had there been a moral and perhaps religious decline that helped to explain the catastrophe of 1967? Perhaps the defeat was divine punishment? Eventually no one could establish a direct link between the war and the Islamic revival of the 1970s, but Arab introspective thoughts and the darkened mood of despair, as well as subsequent political events, help to explain it. After Nasser's death in 1970, Anwar Sadat succeeded him. He pursued a different course, not only concluding peace with Israel but also purging Egypt of pan-Arabism and espousing the Islamic movement. The temper of the times changed. Just as the Egyptian state in the period before 1967 sponsored the ideology of pan-Arabism, so it now embraced the cause of religion and, to a lesser extent, political Islam. The oil revolution of the 1970s fuelled the pan-Islamic movement and marginalized Arab nationalism. The reasons for the transformation of Arab politics during the 1970s were thus complex, and the cultural and political context should be viewed against the role of the state as well as the oil revolution. The phrase "Nasser and his thugs" sums up the de-Nasserization campaign as it became known under Sadat.

Throughout the Middle East, however, Sadat's enemies viewed him as no less than a traitor to the cause of Arab nationalism.

We wish to acknowledge the work of historians of an earlier generation who have provided the foundations on which this book is based. In this introduction we have cited Malcolm Kerr, whose *Arab Cold War* remains fundamentally significant. Many other books and articles can be traced in the footnotes. We especially want to mention *The Six-Day War*, edited by Richard B. Parker, a symposium that brought participants of the war together with historians on the war's twenty-fifth anniversary. It stimulated a vigorous and invaluable inquiry into motives as well as evidence and remains a point of departure in the historical literature. As we now approach the fiftieth anniversary, we hope the same might be said of this volume sometime in the future when the war and its consequences are bound to be reassessed.

Wm. Roger Louis and Avi Shlaim

I

Israel

Poor Little Samson

Avi Shlaim

In early June 1967, Israel won the swiftest and the most spectacular military victory of its entire war-filled history. Defence Minister Moshe Dayan quickly branded it the "Six-Day War" in a conscious allusion to the six days of the Creation in the book of Genesis. With a few exceptions, Israelis regard this war as a defensive war, a morally justified war, and a war of no-choice, a war imposed on them by their predatory Arab foes. In the Arab world, this war is viewed as a wilful act of aggression with a secret agenda of territorial expansion. The widely held view is that during the summer of 1967 Israel was ready for war, well prepared, and only waiting for an opportunity to launch it. Many Egyptians go further and claim that Israel laid a trap for Gamal Abdel Nasser and that Nasser fell into it.[1] Jordanians believe that there was a trap and consider it part of an Israeli strategy to draw the neighbouring Arab states into a war for which they were not prepared. The notion that Israel was constantly planning and plotting to capture the West Bank is central to the Jordanian understanding of the origins of the war. In a speech on 25 January 1967, King Hussein declared that "the enemy's present objective is the West Bank; after that it will be the East Bank and after that they will expand throughout the Arab homeland to achieve their aims and ambitions."[2] This view of Israel's conduct in 1967 is entirely consistent with the predominant Arab perception of themselves as the innocent victims and of Israel as

---

[1] Richard B. Parker, ed., *The Six-Day War: A Retrospective* (Gainesville: University of Florida, 1996), 61–2.
[2] Samir A. Mutawi, *Jordan in the 1967 War* (Cambridge: Cambridge University Press, 1987), 69.

an inherently aggressive and expansionist state, an outpost of Western imperialism.[3] The reality is more complex on both sides of the equation.

The purpose of this chapter is to reexamine the Arab claims of a premeditated war plot in the light of the evidence that is now available. Why did Israel launch a surprise attack on 5 June 1967? What were its war aims? Did they include territorial expansion at the expense of its neighbours? Was this a defensive or an offensive war? Was it a war of choice or a war of no-choice? These are some of the main questions to be explored here. Fortunately, the primary sources available regarding Israel's conduct in 1967 are extraordinarily rich. Israel emulated Britain's thirty-year rule for the review and declassification of official documents and applied it in an admirably liberal fashion. The primary sources regarding the June War that have been declassified include the verbatim records of Cabinet meetings; the papers of the Ministry of Foreign Affairs, the verbatim records of the meetings of the Israel Defence Force (IDF) General Staff, the papers of the Chief of Staff, and the minutes of countless consultative meetings involving military and civilian officials. Whatever one might think of Israel's policy towards the Arabs, it is very much to its credit that it allows researchers such remarkably free access to its internal records.

Close study of these records has led me to the conclusion that the theory of a premeditated plan is simply wrong. The picture that emerges from the records is not one of central planning and direction from the top, but is one of conflict and confusion in the heart of the government, an almost chronic inability to decide, and leaders who constantly trailed behind events. No overall strategic plan for the conduct of this war existed. War aims were not formulated by the government in advance; they emerged gradually in response to changing circumstances. Decision making during the crisis and war was complex, cumbersome, contradictory, gravely affected by the panic that gripped the country, and in some instances almost haphazard.[4] Israel's resounding victory in the war inaugurated a new era of arrogance. It is important to recall, however, that before the war Israel was nowhere as confident or self-assured as it was to become in its aftermath. The victory bred triumphalism, and triumphalism affected all aspects of Israeli policy after the war.

---

[3] See, e.g., Y. Harkabi, *Arab Attitudes to Israel* (Jerusalem: Israel Universities Press, 1974).

[4] For a rigorous analysis of Israeli decision making see Michael Brecher, *Decisions in Israel's Foreign Policy* (London: Oxford University Press, 1974), ch. 7; and Michael Brecher with Benjamin Geist, *Decisions in Crisis: Israel, 1967 and 1973* (Berkeley: University of California Press, 1980).

The Two Faces of Israel

When he became Israel's third prime minister in 1963, Levi Eshkol confronted a state with a conflicted identity, which combined military superiority with an acute sense of vulnerability, in the Yiddish words *Shimshon der nebechdikker* – poor little Samson.[5] While appearing hesitant, Israel was capable of acting decisively and of using force in a crushing manner when its security was challenged. This duality is the hallmark of Israeli politics in the Eshkol era and a key to understanding Israel's behaviour during May and June 1967.[6]

The government and the army represented two different faces of Israel, two distinct schools of thought on how to deal with the Arabs – the diplomatic school and the military school. With some notable exceptions, the civilian leadership consisted of middle-aged or elderly politicians who held moderate views and were intent, desperate to find a peaceful solution to the crisis. The IDF General Staff consisted largely of young, dynamic, battle-hardened officers who were contemptuous of diplomacy and confident of their ability to smash the Arab war machine without any external help. The average age of the generals was twenty-one years less than that of the ministers. Throughout the crisis, most of the army leaders were chomping at the bit; they had the scent of battle in their nostrils and were not about to turn back. They felt that their political masters were too hesitant, overly cautious, and utterly incompetent, and they bitterly resented the constraints that these men placed on their freedom of action. Like soldiers throughout history, they protested at being made to fight the enemy with one hand tied behind their backs. These young men in a hurry looked down on their elders as frightened Diaspora Jews who wasted precious time in endless discussions instead of taking the bull by the horns. It is a revealing fact that in General Staff meetings the ministers were sometimes referred to collectively as "the Jews."[7]

The military bore a large share of the responsibility for the escalation of the conflict with Syria, and this conflict was the trigger for a general Middle East war that nobody planned or wanted. Syria was seen as the main threat to Israel's security for four principal reasons: it had

---

[5] Avi Shlaim, *The Iron Wall: Israel and the Arab World* (New York: W. W. Norton, 2000), 219.

[6] For a perceptive portrait of Israeli society during this period, see Tom Segev, *1967: Israel, the War and the Year that Transformed the Middle East* (London: Little, Brown, 2007).

[7] Ami Gluska, *Eshkol, Give an Order! The IDF and the Political Leadership on the Road to the Six-Day War, 1963–1967* [in Hebrew] (Tel Aviv: Ma'arachot, 2004), 36.

been the spearhead of the United Arab Command's attempt to divert the headwaters of the River Jordan; it harassed Israeli farmers in the three demilitarized zones (DMZs) on the border between the two countries; its radical Ba'th regime preached a popular war for the liberation of Palestine; and it actively supported the Palestinian guerrilla forces of Fatah in launching cross-border raids into Israel.[8] The IDF constantly raised the level of violence in the border skirmishes in order to prepare the ground for a full-scale showdown with Syria. It also had a rigid intelligence conception; believing that Egypt would not intervene in the event of an Israeli war with Syria as long as it remained bogged down in the war in Yemen. This conception was soon to be disproved by events. IDF leaders added to the tension by issuing a series of threats to act against the Syrian regime unless it stopped its support for Palestinian guerrillas who were operating against Israel. On 12 May 1967, in a newspaper interview, Chief of Staff Yitzhak Rabin threatened to occupy Damascus and overthrow the Syrian regime. His words caused a storm. They contradicted the official line that Israel did not interfere in the internal politics of the Arab states but only acted in self-defence against Arab aggression. Several ministers criticised the Chief of Staff at the next Cabinet meeting and the prime minister reprimanded him.

Rabin's strong language was widely interpreted in the Arab world as a signal of Israel's intent to overthrow the Syrian regime by force. But there was no agreed policy and no coherent strategy regarding how to deal with Syria. Here the defensive ethos of the government clashed with the offensive ethos of the IDF. The misplaced confidence that Egypt would not intervene, combined with weak civilian control, allowed the army to continue to escalate the conflict with Syria in sharp contradiction of the overarching goal of the government, which was to prevent war. Thus, as Ami Gluska has argued in his illuminating study of civil-military relations during this period, the military leadership embroiled the state of Israel in an escalation that provoked a crisis that ended in a war which Israel did not intend, a war that from the beginning was undesirable and unnecessary.[9] Eshkol made his government's commitment to the status quo clear before the Knesset Committee on Defence and Foreign Affairs on 17 May: "We are not heading for war, we do not want war . . . we do

---

[8] Interview with Lieutenant General Yitzhak Rabin, 22 August 1982, Tel Aviv. Published version: "An Interview with Yitzhak Rabin, 22 August 1982," [in Hebrew] *Iyunim Bitkumat Israel* 8 (1998), 665–86.

[9] Gluska, *Eshkol, Give an Order!* 200, 405.

not want from any of our neighbours anything, except the status quo."[10]
The government, however, was unable to control the course of events
that would lead to the abrogation of its armistice agreements with Egypt,
Jordan, and Syria.

The Egyptian Challenge

Extraregional actors contributed inadvertently to the drift towards war.
Concern for their Syrian client prompted the Soviet leaders to intervene
in the crisis. On 13 May, they sent a report to Nasser that Israel was
concentrating forces on its northern front and planning to attack Syria.
The report was untrue, and Nasser knew that it was untrue but he was in a
quandary. A third of his best troops were pinned down in an inconclusive
war in Yemen, and he knew that Israel was militarily stronger than all
the Arab confrontation states taken together. Yet politically he could not
afford to remain inactive because his leadership of the Arab world was
being challenged. Since the end of 1966, the Jordanians had been accusing
him of cowardice and of hiding from the Israelis behind the skirts of the
UN Emergency Force (UNEF) in Sinai.[11] Egypt had a defence pact with
Syria that compelled it to go to Syria's aid in the event of an Israeli attack.
Clearly, Nasser had to do something to preserve his own credibility as an
ally and to restrain the hotheads in Damascus. He chose to embark on
an exercise in brinkmanship, which was to carry him over the brink with
disastrous consequences for Egypt and its Arab allies.

Nasser took three steps, all of which were intended to impress Arab
public opinion and to deter Israel from attacking Syria; they were not a
conscious prelude to war with Israel. The first step, on 14 May 1967,
was to send two divisions to reinforce his army in Sinai. The second
step, on 16 May, was to request the removal of the UNEF from Sinai.
The third and most fateful step, taken on 22 May, was to close the
Straits of Tiran, at the southern end of the Gulf of Aqaba, to Israeli
shipping. The removal of the UN peacekeepers from Sharm al-Sheikh
exposed Nasser to powerful pressure from his Arab neighbours to close
the straits to Israeli shipping. He succumbed to the pressure, although he
fully realized the risks involved. To the Supreme Executive Committee he

---

[10] Yemima Rosenthal, ed., *Yitzhak Rabin: Prime Minister of Israel, 1974–1977, 1992–
      1995: Selected Documents, Volume 1, Early Years and Military Career, 1922–1967* [in
      Hebrew] (Jerusalem: Israel State Archives, 2005), 445.

[11] Avi Shlaim, *Lion of Jordan: King Hussein's Life in War and Peace* (London: Allen Lane,
      2007), 235–6.

gave the following assessment: "Now with our concentrations in Sinai, the chances of war are fifty-fifty. But if we close the Strait, war will be one hundred per cent certainty."[12]

The Egyptian president announced this decision in a speech in front of pilots at the Egyptian air base in Bir Gafgafa in Sinai. To add insult to injury, he went on to say, "The Jews threaten war – and we say *ahlan wa-sahlan* [welcome]. We are ready!" For Israel this deliberately provocative act constituted a *casus belli*. The narrow passage led from the Red Sea to the Israeli port city of Eilat. Oil tankers from Iran could only reach Eilat by this route. The blockade was illegal and cancelled the main achievement of the Suez War of 1956. The Israeli economy could possibly survive the closure of the straits but the deterrent image of the IDF most certainly could not. Nasser understood the psychological significance of this step. He knew that Israel's entire defence philosophy was based on imposing its will on its enemies, not on submitting to unilateral diktats by them. In a remarkably perceptive newspaper article, Mohamed Hasanein Heikal, Nasser's friend and confidant, explained:

The closure of the Gulf of Aqaba...means first and last that the Arab nation represented by the UAR [United Arab Republic] has succeeded for the first time, *vis à vis* Israel, in changing by force a *fait accompli* imposed on it by force.... To Israel this is the most dangerous aspect of the current situation – who can impose the accomplished fact and who possesses the power to safeguard it. Therefore it is not a matter of the Gulf of Aqaba but of something bigger. It is the whole philosophy of Israeli security. Hence I say that Israel must attack.[13]

This was precisely how Israel's military leaders viewed the closure of the Straits of Tiran: they saw it as a declaration of war. They had been watching Nasser's moves with mounting concern. The introduction of large forces into Sinai made them realize the mistake in their estimation that Egypt would not dare provoke a crisis with Israel as long as it was involved in the war in Yemen. At a meeting with the Chief of Staff, in the morning of 19 May, Ezer Weizman, the Chief of the General Staff Branch and former commander of the air force, reported that Egyptian warplanes had penetrated Israel's airspace and taken photographs of the nuclear reactor in Dimona. Weizman also mentioned that Mohamed

[12] Anwar el-Sadat, *In Search of Identity: An Autobiography* (New York: Harper and Row, 1978), 172.
[13] *Al Ahram*, 26 May 1967. Quoted in Michael Howard and Robert Hunter, *Israel and the Arab World: The Crisis of 1967*, Adelphi Paper no. 41 (London: International Institute for Strategic Studies, October 1967), 24.

Hasanein Heikal referred in his articles in *Al Ahram* to the possibility of attacking the nuclear reactor. The conclusion of the meeting was that the situation was tense, Nasser had thrown down the gauntlet, and the United Nations was bankrupt.[14]

Rabin was depressed, downcast, and burdened by a sense of personal responsibility for the crisis. He could not be blamed for thinking that too much was expected of him. Rabin was Eshkol's principal military adviser, and during the crisis he carried a heavy burden of responsibility that was made even heavier by being constantly called to attend meetings of the Cabinet, the Ministerial Committee for Defence, and the Knesset Committee on Defence and Foreign Affairs. On 22 May Rabin felt the need to talk to David Ben-Gurion, the founder of the state and the great guru of its defence establishment, but instead of fortifying his spirits, the "Old Man" gave him a dressing down. "I very much doubt whether Nasser wanted to go to war, and now we are in serious trouble," said Ben-Gurion. He claimed that the mobilization of the reserves had been a mistake. Rabin replied that he had recommended mobilization in order to make sure they were ready. "In that case you, or whoever gave your permission to mobilize so many reservists, made a mistake," repeated Ben-Gurion. "You have led the state into a grave situation. We must not go to war. We are isolated. You bear the responsibility."[15] The words struck Rabin like hammer blows and contributed to the breakdown he was to suffer on the evening of the following day.

News of the blockade of the Straits of Tiran reached Rabin in the early hours of 23 May. His instinctive feeling was that when closing the straits, Nasser probably understood that he was going to war.[16] Rabin was in a state of complete mental and physical exhaustion, but he convened a meeting with Eshkol and senior officers for eight o'clock in the morning in the General Headquarters underground command post, known as "the Pit." It was obvious to the military experts that war was now unavoidable. Aharon Yariv, the director of Military Intelligence, spoke first. He was in favour of immediate military action. Weizman agreed with him. All eyes turned to the Chief of Staff. Rabin was in a pensive mood and far from raring to go. He said, "My opinion too is that we have to respond immediately. But the war is not a matter of a day or two. The behaviour

[14] Minute of a consultative meeting in the office of the Chief of Staff, 19 May 1967, Israel Defence Force Archive [hereinafter referred to as IDF].
[15] Yitzhak Rabin, *The Rabin Memoirs* (London: Weidenfeld and Nicolson, 1979), 58–9.
[16] Interview with Lieutenant General Yitzhak Rabin, 22 August 1982, Tel Aviv.

of Jordan and Syria will depend on the extent of our success in the Egyptian theatre," he added in a slow, soft voice, "For us it is a question of survival."

"The Waiting Period"

Eshkol was not ready to rule in favour of military action. He was anxious to prevent an inadvertent war and preferred to defer action until all the avenues for a diplomatic solution had been exhausted. For him, the announcement of the blockade was not the same as the actual stopping of an Israeli ship. He pointed out that an oil tanker was due to pass through the straits a week later and suggested that they use the intervening period for diplomatic activity.[17] The general atmosphere, however, was one of gloom. Abba Eban called the closure of the straits the "Day of Wrath." "For the whole of that day in Tel Aviv," he wrote, "and far into the night in Jerusalem, our minds revolved round the question of survival."[18]

The central political problem for Israel was to secure American backing in the event that war became inevitable. Everyone remembered that in the aftermath of the Suez War, President Dwight Eisenhower had compelled Israel to pull out its troops from Sinai and few politicians were willing to risk another crisis in U.S.-Israel relations. Following the closure of the straits, Eshkol received a message from the Johnson administration urging Israel to refrain from any military action in order to allow this matter to be handled by diplomatic means.[19] A meeting of the Ministerial Committee for Defence was convened on 23 May to decide what to do. At this meeting Rabin reviewed recent developments and recommended an air strike against the Egyptian air force followed by a ground offensive against the Egyptian forces in Sinai. He explained that failure to respond immediately to the blockade would undermine Israel's credibility and could have grave long-term consequences. Although he favoured immediate action, he did not rule out a delay of forty-eight hours to gain American backing. Most of the ministers supported such a delay but were divided on what to do next if a diplomatic solution could not be found.

---

[17] Eitan Haber, *Today War Will Break Out: The Reminiscences of Brigadier-General Israel Lior, Aide-de-Camp to Prime Ministers Levi Eshkol and Golda Meir* [in Hebrew] (Tel Aviv: Edanim, 1987), 163–5.

[18] Abba Eban, *Live or Perish* (unpublished manuscript, 1969), 4.

[19] Department of State, *Foreign Relations of the United States, 1964–1968, vol. XIX, Arab-Israeli Crisis and War, 1967* (Washington, DC: U.S. Government Printing House, 2004), 62–3 [hereinafter referred to as *FRUS*].

Eshkol was in a quandary. He was slowly moving to the conclusion that war might be inescapable, but he was afraid to go to war without the backing of America and other Western powers. He therefore supported the forty-eight-hour delay, but he continued to worry about the risk of a surprise attack by the enemy. The committee resolved to wait.[20]

Meanwhile the Egyptian army continued the buildup of forces in Sinai, the Jordanian army went on high alert and began to reinforce its presence on the West Bank, and intelligence was received that other Arab countries, like Iraq and Kuwait, were ready to send forces and take part in the battle. At an emergency meeting with the army chiefs on 25 May, Eshkol was told that they feared that a coordinated Egyptian-Syrian attack may be staged two days later. Eshkol's military advisers stressed that the key issue was no longer freedom of navigation but the concentration of Egyptian forces in Sinai that threatened Israel's very existence. They reckoned that, with the passage of time, military cooperation among the Arab states would grow and the danger of a surprise attack on Israel would increase.

Later on in the evening, another consultation took place. Yariv, the director of Military Intelligence, reported the possibility of an Egyptian air strike that night or the following evening. Israel informed the United States, which promptly warned Cairo against any act of aggression against Israel.[21] After the war it emerged that there was a plan for a surprise attack, code-named Fajr – "Operation Dawn." Its objective was to sever the southern Negev and the port of Eilat from Israel. It was due to be launched at dawn on 27 May. International pressure, however, persuaded Nasser to cancel this plan at the last minute and to replace it with a defensive strategy of absorbing a first Israeli strike and then delivering what he thought would be a devastating counterattack.[22]

In the days after the closure of the Straits of Tiran to Israeli shipping, Nasser kept raising the stakes. He seemed to be goading Israel into a military showdown. In a speech to Arab trade unionists on 26 May, he declared, "Taking such action also meant that we were ready for a general

---

[20] Yemima Rosenthal, ed., *Levi Eshkol – The Third Prime Minister: Selected Documents, 1895–1969* [in Hebrew] (Jerusalem: Israel State Archives, 2002), 532.

[21] Ibid., 534–5.

[22] Mohamed Heikal, *1967: The Explosion* [in Arabic] (Cairo: Al-Ahram, 1990), 371–4; Michael Oren, *Six Days of War: June 1967 and the Making of the Modern Middle East* (Oxford: Oxford University Press, 2002), 120–1; Moshe Shemesh, *Arab Politics, Palestinian Nationalism and the Six Day War: The Crystallization of Arab Strategy and Nasir's Descent to War 1957–1967* (Brighton, UK: Sussex Academic Press, 2008), 197–201.

war with Israel. It is not a separate operation. . . . If Israel embarks on an aggression against Syria or Egypt, the battle against Israel will be a general one . . . and our basic objective will be to destroy Israel."[23] Other Arab leaders indulged in blood-curdling rhetoric and the Arab media reported the rapidly growing popular enthusiasm for war. The IDF General Staff took Nasser's threats at face value. It placed the regular army units on high alert, continued to mobilize the reserves, and stepped up its preparations for an all-out war with Egypt. The army was now like a coiled spring. The air force, which for a number of years had been rehearsing a plan code-named Moked, was ready to mount a lightning strike against the Egyptian air force.[24]

The operational plans for the southern front changed countless times in the lead up to the war. But all of them included a surprise air strike and the capture of the Gaza Strip. The difference lay in the scope of the ground operations in Sinai: some had El Arish as the outer limit whereas others extended farther east to Jabl Libni. In all of these plans, the capture of territory was intended not for retention but for bargaining purposes after the guns fell silent. The Egyptian challenge, however, rekindled an expansionist streak that had been largely dormant for the best part of two decades. Some of the generals, and former generals such as Yigal Allon, wanted to seize the opportunity to finish the unfinished business of the first Arab-Israeli war. In particular, they longed to capture the West Bank – a plan that Ben-Gurion had vetoed in 1948.[25] At a meeting of the General Staff, on 26 May, Major General Rehavam Ze'evi, a chisel-jawed, ultra-right-wing nationalist officer, opined that after the victory they would have a large kingdom. He suggested that the IDF should start preparing practical plans for keeping all the land it was about to occupy during the course of the fighting. The Chief of Staff cut him short to discourage this expansionist streak. He stated that the point of departure of the government was to insist on a peace settlement after the war and that it intended to hold on to the territories until it achieved a settlement.[26] The message was clear: the purpose of the war – if and when

[23] Quoted in Robert Stephens, *Nasser: A Political Biography* (London: Penguin Books, 1971), 479.

[24] Major General Motti Hod, "Operation 'Moked' – Why It Is Not a Gamble?" in *The Six-Day War*, ed. Benny Michalson [in Hebrew] (Tel Aviv: the Israeli Society for Military History, 1996), 91–7.

[25] Avi Shlaim, *Collusion across the Jordan: King Abdullah, the Zionist Movement, and the Partition of Palestine* (Oxford: Clarendon Press, 1988), 303–11, 406–7.

[26] Verbatim Record of the IDF General Staff, 26 May 1967, IDF Archive.

it came about – was to defend Israel's security, not to extend it borders. To paraphrase Karl Von Clausewitz's famous words, war was to be the extension of policy by the admixture of other means.

The top brass stepped up the pressure on the government to launch a preemptive strike against Egypt. They were afraid that while the diplomats were dilly-dallying, Egypt might seize the opportunity to land the first blow. By his deeds and his defiant speeches, Nasser succeeded in eroding the deterrent power of the IDF. Much talk circulated among the generals about the need to rebuild the IDF's deterrent image. They wanted to deal a knockout blow to the Egyptian army and sear deep in its consciousness the lesson that it could never defeat the Israeli army on the battlefield. They saw a chance to destroy the Egyptian war machine once and for all and were anxious to seize the moment. While the ministers were preoccupied with asserting Israel's legal right of passage through the Straits of Tiran, the generals were more troubled by the ground forces and the warplanes that Nasser kept pouring into Sinai and by the change in their posture from a defensive to a potentially offensive one. The issue of the straits had become almost irrelevant for them. If the government was wedded to the diplomatic track, at the very least the generals hoped to shift the focus from the issue of the straits to that of the troop concentration on Israel's southern border.[27] At one meeting convened by the Chief of Staff, all those present expressed strong reservations about the government's policy of postponing military action. Once again, they drew attention to the danger of a surprise attack on the nuclear reactor in Dimona.[28]

The government hesitated on the brink: it was paralyzed by a sense of international isolation, the fear of war and its destructiveness, concern over casualties, and conflicting currents of opinion within its ranks. It took the government the best part of two weeks to decide on military action. These two weeks were not wasted, however. They were used to prepare the ground for the action that followed. Nevertheless, it was a traumatic experience for the Israeli public and went down in history as the infamous "waiting period." During this time, tensions were heightened to a fever pitch and the entire nation succumbed to a collective psychosis. The memory of the Holocaust was a powerful psychological force that deepened the feeling of being abandoned and accentuated the perception

[27] Interview with Colonel (Ret.) Mordechai Bar-On, 12 May 2009, Jerusalem.
[28] Minute of a consultative meeting in the office of the Chief of Staff, 26 May 1967, IDF Archive.

of threat. Israel was only nineteen years old at the time. Some of its citizens could remember Adolf Hitler's threats from the 1930s. Although, objectively speaking, Israel was much stronger than its enemies, many Israelis genuinely believed that their country faced a threat of imminent destruction. Their image of themselves was that of a little David facing a modern-day Goliath. The big question for them was not the Straits of Tiran but a question of survival. Weak leadership was partly responsible for permitting this panic to spread from the politicians to the people at large. Paradoxically, Eshkol and Rabin, who had done so much to equip the IDF for war, now seemed unequal to the task of leading the nation in a crisis that involved a high risk of war. Faced with a crisis of the supreme magnitude, they faltered, and Rabin suffered a temporary breakdown. Acute anxiety, lack of sleep, and excessive smoking incapacitated him for thirty-six hours, after which he returned to his desk.

Eshkol's performance also was impaired by crisis-induced stress, his own relative lack of experience in foreign affairs, and domestic political pressures. His former colleagues in the Labour Party, who had split off to form the Rafi faction in 1965, became his most outspoken critics, conducting a merciless campaign to undermine his authority. Ben-Gurion, Shimon Peres, and Dayan, who had been languishing in opposition, tried to make political capital out of the crisis by persistently drawing attention to Eshkol's shortcomings. Of the three, Dayan was the most cynical, devious, manipulative, and power-hungry. "I don't care about prestige," he used to say, "especially other people's prestige." He was also unusually opinionated and arrogant, even by Israeli standards. Eshkol refused to step down as prime minister in favour of Ben-Gurion, but was eventually forced to hand over the defence portfolio to Dayan. Eshkol was never much of an orator but the fluffing of his lines in a live radio broadcast, on 28 May, fatally undermined his standing as a national leader.

The domestic political crisis was resolved on 1 June by the formation of a national unity government that included the two main opposition parties: Gahal and Rafi. Dayan, the popular war hero with the black eye patch, entered the government as minister of defence while two Gahal leaders, Menachem Begin and Yosef Sapir entered it as ministers without portfolio. Dayan was brought in despite strong opposition from Golda Meir, the Labour Alignment's Secretary-General. She proposed to give the defence portfolio to Allon, the minister of labour, and most of her party colleagues supported her. But the National Religious Party threatened to quit the coalition unless a national unity government was set up with Dayan as minister of defence. Dayan's appointment was a painful personal blow to Eshkol, but it helped to restore the confidence of the public and the army in the government. Change in the composition of the government also brought with it the possibility of a change in its policy.

The Generals' "Revolt"

The pressure exerted by the military on the Cabinet to sanction immediate military action against Egypt was unrelenting. Before agreeing to military action, Eshkol and the majority of his ministers wanted to ascertain the current American view of the pledge made to Israel in 1957 after inducing it to hand back the Sinai Peninsula to Egypt. On 23 May, the Cabinet had decided to send Eban on a mission to Paris, London, and Washington in order to secure international action to reopen the Straits of Tiran. Eban was a brilliant orator, eloquent in seven languages, but with the backbone of a noodle. Although he greatly valued Eban's diplomatic skills, Eshkol sometimes referred to him as "the clever fool." Eban returned three days later empty-handed. His most important meeting was with President Lyndon Johnson. Johnson told Eban that it was the unanimous view of his military experts that there was no sign that the Egyptians were planning to attack Israel and that if they did attack, the Israelis would "whip the hell out of them." Johnson promised to act with other maritime powers to open the Straits of Tiran to Israeli shipping. He warned against the initiation of hostilities by Israel. He repeated several times, "Israel will not be alone unless it decides to go alone."[29] Johnson reiterated the warning against preemptive action in a letter to Eshkol who had just received a threatening letter from Moscow.

The Cabinet convened at three o'clock in the afternoon on 28 May. Eban reported on the disappointing results of his trip and on the messages from the Western powers. The Chief of Staff argued that waiting would not solve the basic problem. But by a majority that included Eshkol, the Cabinet decided to wait two weeks.[30] Of the eighteen ministers, only Moshe Carmel, the minister of transport and a former general, was prepared to vote for immediate military action. His argument was that with every passing day, the possibility of an Egyptian surprise attack would grow. Eban was sceptical of the vehemence with which some advisers were telling the Cabinet that every hour was likely to bring

---

[29] Abba Eban, *Personal Witness: Israel through My Eyes* (New York: Putnam, 1992), 386–91.
[30] Rosenthal, *Levi Eshkol*, 540–1; Rosenthal, *Yitzhak Rabin*, 469–74.

"the destruction of the Third Jewish Commonwealth." Eshkol asked him to read the messages they received that day from President Johnson and Secretary of State Dean Rusk. The president said that "Israel must not take any preemptive military action and thereby make itself responsible for the initiation of hostilities." Rusk warned that "unilateral action by Israel would be irresponsible and catastrophic." Eshkol said that he had intended to ask for a drastic decision, but the representations from Washington put a new aspect on the matter. He was especially impressed by Rusk's report of the progress being made with the international naval-escort plan. He was therefore prepared to advise the Cabinet to give the United States a chance over the next two weeks to bring the project to fulfilment. One minister after another followed Eshkol in this course. The final vote was 17:1. The decision to postpone military action was subjected to fierce criticism after the victory. Eban defended it as the "courageous and mature decision taken almost unanimously on May 28."[31]

That evening Eshkol went to a meeting with the General Staff to explain the decision of the Cabinet. The meeting was stormy. The generals used blunt language, charging the civilian leadership with weakness, muddle, and confusion. They stressed again and again that the central problem was not the right of passage through the Straits of Tiran but the threat to the survival of the state of Israel. From the beginning, they had scoffed at the idea that the maritime powers would pull their chestnuts out of the fire for them. Some argued that the maritime powers should not even be allowed to break the Egyptian blockade, the IDF had to do it on its own, and this was the only way to restore its deterrent capability. All the speakers stressed that time was of the essence, because the longer they waited, the price of victory would be heavier in terms of casualties. Eshkol replied firmly that if bloodshed could possibly be avoided, it should be. He stressed the importance of working in concert with Israel's friends. He disputed that the only way to preserve Israeli deterrence was by launching an immediate attack and elaborated on his reasons against preventive war. "Would we live forever by the sword?" he asked, his voice rising in anger. The atmosphere became so intolerable that the meeting had to be adjourned. Eshkol left in a huff. What was said on "the night of the generals" was so blunt and harsh that it could be seen as verging on an open rebellion. The prime minister, according to his aide-de-camp,

---

[31] Eban, *Live or Perish*, 157–65. For the full text of the messages from Johnson and Rusk, see *FRUS*, 162–4.

regarded what he heard as a vote of no confidence in himself and in his government.[32]

Eshkol never underestimated what was at stake. In a speech on 29 May he said, "In the balance lies not only the fate of the State of Israel but the fate of the Jewish people."[33] Despite all the pressures, Eshkol kept his nerve. For some of the military leaders, however, the tension became unbearable. In the early afternoon of 1 June, Eshkol had with him Yaacov Shimshon Shapira, the minister of justice, when Ezer Weizman, the mercurial general, burst into his office without making a prior appointment and in gross violation of protocol. Weizman cried in front of the ministers. "The state is being destroyed," he yelled, "everything is being destroyed." Eshkol was stunned. "Eshkol," screamed Weizman, "give an order and Tsahal [the IDF] will go to war. Why do you need Moshe Dayan? Who needs Yigal Allon? You have a strong army and it is only waiting for your order. Give us an order to go to war and we'll win. We'll win and you'll be the head of the government of the victory." At this point Shapira started to weep while Weizman tried to remove the general's insignia from his shirt as he stormed out of the room. It was a scene of hysteria and utter confusion that was symptomatic of the mood of the entire country.[34]

On 2 June, there was a joint meeting of the Ministerial Committee for Defence and the General Staff in the Pit at General Headquarters in Tel Aviv. The generals presented their unanimous view that war was inescapable and the sooner they could launch it, the better. The Chief of Staff emphasized that time was not on their side. None of them wanted war for its own sake, he observed. However, they were liable to lose the military advantage and face a serious threat to the existence of the state. With every day that passed, the Egyptian army improved its position in Sinai and its self-confidence increased. Rabin felt that the noose was being tightened round their neck, and he doubted that anyone but they could break it. He had no doubt that their primary aim should be to deal a crushing blow to Nasser and thereby transform the entire landscape of the Middle East. Motti Hod, the commander of the air force, stated that his pilots were completely ready to go into action; there was no need to wait, not even twenty-four hours. The best defence against an attack, added Rabin, was to hit the Egyptian air force and cripple it.

---

[32] Haber, *Today War Will Break Out*, 194–9.
[33] Michalson, *The Six-Day War*, 18.
[34] Haber, *Today War Will Break Out*, 203.

Major General Ariel Sharon, who had recently assumed command of a division in the south, reported that the army was ready for action as it had never been before. He warned that the deterrent power of the IDF was being constantly eroded and, consequently, that the primary aim of the attack should be to hit the Egyptian army so hard that they would not want to fight Israel again for ten or twenty years, or even for a generation. The IDF must do it alone, Sharon insisted. Collaboration with outside powers would be seen as a sign of weakness as it had been in 1956. Above all, if they wanted to live in the region, they had to stand up for their rights with no compromises, "kowtowing" to foreign powers, or appeasement. Other officers also joined in the chorus addressed to the ministers: why are we waiting? Mattityahu Peled, the Quartermaster General, addressed the ministers in an angry and menacing tone, "The General Staff has not received an explanation – what are we waiting for? I can understand that we are waiting for something. If so, bring out the secret and let us know what we are waiting for!" Eshkol replied that they were waiting in order to keep their few friends in the world, notably the American president, whose help might be needed to rebuild Israel's power after the war is over. He concluded what was undoubtedly the most bad-tempered encounter between the government and the high command in Israel's entire history by pointing out that "a military victory will not end the matter. The Arabs are staying here."[35]

The Amber Light

The military became progressively disenchanted with their political masters. They certainly had no confidence in Eban or in his report of the American position. Eban epitomized the polished, but pusillanimous, diplomat that they despised. They even suspected him of misrepresenting the message of the American president in order to stay their hand. Yariv suggested to Eshkol that Meir Amit, the director of the Mossad, be sent to the United States on a secret mission. Amit, like his colleagues in the army, thought that Israel was making a grave mistake by simply sitting like a "dead duck."[36] Amit's task was to clarify how the Americans saw the situation, whether they planned to take action to break the blockade, and how they would react if Israel seized the initiative.

---

[35] Verbatim Record of a Meeting of the General Staff and the Ministerial Committee for Defence, 2 June 1967, IDF Archive.
[36] Parker, *The Six-Day War*, 124.

Amit's arrival coincided with a change in American policy. The centre of gravity had shifted from the State Department to the Pentagon. The Pentagon chiefs had a more permissive attitude towards the resort to force by Israel. President Johnson had told Eban that America planned to organize an international armada to open the straits, and he had therefore asked Israel to wait. By the time Amit arrived, American policy had moved in favour of unleashing Israel against Nasser. Amit shifted the emphasis from the legal issue of the straits to the strategic issue of the Egyptian forces in Sinai. He informed Secretary of Defense Robert McNamara that, on his return, he was personally going to recommend to his government that they go on the offensive. Amit specifically told McNamara that he did not need to respond. He did this in order to avoid charges of collusion between America and Israel in the aftermath of the attack on Egypt. As Dayan's deputy during the Suez War, Amit remembered only too well the damage to Israel's reputation that resulted from collusion with the colonial powers. McNamara told Amit that it was alright, the president knew about the visit, and he had a direct line to the president. Amit then asked McNamara for three things: American diplomatic support at the United Nations, American backing in the event of Soviet intervention, and, if the need arose, American replenishment of Israel's military arsenal. McNamara recognized that America had a moral responsibility to open the straits, but he preferred Israel to do it because America was tied down in Vietnam and because the Central Intelligence Agency (CIA) estimated that Israel could defeat the Egyptian army without any outside help. In effect he gave Israel a green light to launch a preemptive strike against Egypt.[37]

In his next message to Eshkol, Johnson mentioned that they had a full and frank exchange of views with General Amit.[38] Significantly, he did not mention any reservations or objections to the course of action he knew that Amit was going to recommend to his government on his return home. Some scholars maintain that President Johnson gave Israel the green light to attack Egypt while others claim that he only flashed an amber light.[39] For political reasons the president could not possibly give the Israelis a *carte blanche* as is implied by a green light. His message to

---

[37] Ibid., 140; Meir Amit, "The Road to the Six Days: The Six Day War in Retrospect," *Ma'arachot* 325 (June–July 1992).

[38] Johnson to Eshkol, 3 June 1967, *FRUS*, 262–4.

[39] William B. Quandt, *Peace Process: American Diplomacy and the Arab-Israeli Conflict since 1967* (Berkeley: University of California Press, 1993), ch. 2.

them was to proceed with caution, and this is best indicated by an amber light. Amit insisted that he neither requested nor received a green light to attack Egypt. But in a conference on the Six-Day War in 1996, he listed three phases in America's attitude towards Israel during the crisis: "a. Wait! b. Consult! c. Do what you like!"[40]

Amit reported on the result of his mission to a small group of advisers that met in the prime minister's house at six o'clock in the evening of Saturday, 3 June. The new defence minister was impatient with the discussion of Foreign Ministry cables and wanted to go straight to what for him was the only issue – waging war. Amit said that the American intelligence estimates of Arab military capabilities did not differ materially from the Israeli ones. "I have the impression," he said, "that the Americans would welcome an operation if we succeed in smashing Nasser." He used the colloquial Hebrew word *lefatspets*, which means to shatter or to dash to pieces. Nor could Amit detect signs of any serious American preparation of a maritime task force for opening the straits. With characteristic decisiveness he declared, "The armada for opening the straits will not happen!" American caution, coupled with its tacit approval of an Israeli strike, seemed to clinch the case for going to war. But at this point Amit surprised his listeners by suggesting that they could wait a week in order to establish a firm *casus belli* by sending an Israeli ship through the straits.

Dayan, Amit's former commanding officer and friend, pressed for immediate action and adamantly refused to contemplate any further procrastination. The only alternative, he said angrily, was to wait for the Egyptians to attack first and that meant the loss of the Land of Israel. Waiting a week, added Dayan, would entail thousands of casualties: "It is illogical to wait. I prefer that we move first. Let us deal the first blow and then proceed to diplomatic activity. It is imperative to do that despite the political disadvantages.... It is lunacy to wait," he repeated with some vehemence. This was the moment when it became clear that Israel was going to war. All those present realized this. Although they were bitter political rivals, Allon agreed with Dayan. They became the most fervent advocates of immediate military action against Egypt in the enlarged Cabinet. From this point on, the two of them led the inexorable march

---

[40] Major General Meir Amit, "The Considerations of the Supreme Command of Tsahal and of the General Staff in their Contacts with the Political Echelon in the Preparations for the Six-Day War and during the War," in Michalson, *The Six-Day War*, 34.

towards war. By this time it was past midnight. Everybody was exhausted but the point of no return had been reached.[41]

Decision Point

The next day, Sunday, 4 June, the Cabinet met at quarter after eight in the morning and made the decision to go to war. The foreign minister gave an exhaustive and exhausting survey of the diplomatic scene. Three days earlier he had reached the conclusion that there was no diplomatic solution to the crisis and that military action was now unavoidable. The military experts set the tone in the discussion that followed. Yariv reviewed the reinforcement of the eastern front by Jordan and Iraq and the deployment, by Egypt, of two hundred tanks in a preattack position facing Eilat. Dayan said that they must not lose the initiative, the situation was deteriorating from the military point of view, and the question of who fired the first shot was completely unimportant. "We have to act as quickly and as early as possible," he insisted. Some of the ministers remained unconvinced. Others continued to ask questions about sending a ship through the straits, but they were clutching at straws. Allon cut them short. The diplomatic avenue had been exhausted, he said in an authoritative tone, and it was time to act. He was ready for Israel to be condemned for its actions as long as it continued to live. Allon then turned to his nervous colleagues with the eminently sensible suggestion: leave to future historians the task of dealing with the question of who fired the first shot.

For Eshkol, the controlling consideration in the decision to go to war was the amber light from the White House. Despite the hysteria in the country at large, political intrigues behind his back, and revolt of the generals, he firmly stood his ground until he received a nod and a wink from the most powerful man in the world. To his Cabinet colleagues Eshkol explained that President Johnson's position had relaxed. He would have dearly wanted, he said, to grant the president's wish for another week had he not seen "the danger of life and death confronting the State of Israel." Accordingly, he proposed "to give an order to the army to choose the time, place and method that suited it." Eshkol remained true to his democratic and collegial style of chairing Cabinet meetings to the end. He put to the vote a proposal for continuing with political activity and avoiding war, but the proposal was supported by only two ministers.

---

[41] Amit, "The Road to the Six Days"; Haber, *Today War Will Break Out*, 216–18.

Dayan then suggested the text of the historic decision to embark on what was soon to be called "the Six-Day War."[42] The text of the decision follows:

a. After hearing reports on the military and political situation from the Prime Minister, the Foreign Minister, the Defence Minister, the Chief of Staff, and the Director of Military Intelligence, the Cabinet states that the armies of Egypt, Syria, and Jordan are deployed for a multi-front and immediate attack which threatens the existence of the State of Israel.

b. The Cabinet decides to undertake military action to free Israel from the noose of aggression which is tightening around it.

c. The Cabinet authorizes the Prime Minister and the Minister of Defence to sanction to the General Staff the time of the operation.[43]

War Aims

The IDF opened hostilities with a stupendous air strike on the Egyptian air fields at 7:45 A.M. on Monday, 5 June. When the fighting started, Levi Eshkol went on Israeli radio and said that Israel had no territorial ambitions. Dayan issued an Order of the Day to the armed forces. One of the first things he said was that Israel had no objectives of conquest.[44] These statements accurately reflected the view of the government and the army that this was a defensive war. Clearly, the main enemy was Egypt. But even after issuing the long-awaited order to strike, the government did not give the army any specific guidelines about its territorial aims. The immediate aims were to open the Straits of Tiran, destroy the Egyptian army in Sinai, and restore the deterrent power of the IDF. Territorial war aims only emerged during the course of the fighting. They did so in a piecemeal, confused, and contradictory fashion.

All along, Eshkol's conception of the war was defensive and limited: to remove the Egyptian threat to Israel's security by military means once all the diplomatic efforts had been exhausted. The Operations Department of the General Staff Branch prepared two major war plans. One plan, Atzmon, called for the capture of the Gaza Strip and the southern flank

[42] Haber, *Today War Will Break Out*, 218–21; Rosenthal, *Levi Eshkol*, 551.

[43] Cabinet Secretariat, Decision No. 51/b of the Cabinet Committee for Defence, 4 June 1967, Israel State Archives, Jerusalem.

[44] Moshe Dayan, *Milestones: An Autobiography* [in Hebrew] (Jerusalem: Yediot Aharonot, 1976), 436.

of al-Arish. The second plan, Kardom, a hatchet in Hebrew, called for
the capture of the Gaza Strip and eastern part of the Sinai Peninsula up to
Jabl Libni. Both plans envisaged holding the territory until Egypt agreed
to open the Straits of Tiran. The allocation of forces for the northern and
eastern fronts was only for defensive purposes – to contain an attack by
Syria or Jordan if such an attack took place.

On 24 May, when Rabin was incapacitated, Major-General Chaim
Bar-Lev, who was soon to be appointed deputy Chief of Staff, presented
the two plans at a meeting with Eshkol and his senior advisers. Eshkol
readily accepted Bar-Lev's advice and approved the second plan. The
eastern front was not discussed at this meeting. There was a 1964 operational plan for the capture of the West Bank but only in response to a
Jordanian attack, not as an Israeli initiative. The allocation of forces that
Eshkol approved for the Jordanian and Syrian fronts catered purely to
the purpose of blocking an enemy advance.[45]

On becoming minister of defence, Dayan made two changes in the
second and larger plan. One change was to order the IDF to steer clear
of the Gaza Strip, which he described as a hornet's nest. The other was
to expand the area to be captured and add to it Sharm al-Sheikh, the
strategically vital point at the southern tip of the Sinai Peninsula. Control of Sharm al-Sheikh meant, in effect, control of the Straits of Tiran.
Dayan thus modified the underlying conception of the war without prior
discussion or decision by the Cabinet regarding the strategic objectives.[46]
As one of his aides has argued, Dayan changed the war aims in the south
from a limited war with Egypt and a "Gaza first" approach to war along
the entire length of Sinai. His hope was to inflict a crushing and comprehensive defeat on the Egyptian army along the entire front and leave no
room for doubt about Israel's invincibility. In short, he wanted not only
to restore Israel's deterrent image but also to reinforce it.[47] Dayan did
hope that after this war, unlike the Suez War, Israel would be able to keep
some Egyptian territory once the dust had settled. More specifically, he
hoped to keep a two hundred kilometre-long strip of land from just east
of Rafah down to Sharm al-Sheikh. But his primary aim was to destroy
the Egyptian army.[48]

---

[45] Interview with Lieutenant-General Chaim Bar-Lev, 8 August 1982, Tel Aviv.
[46] Zvi Lanir, "Political Aims and Military Objectives in Israel's Wars," in *War by Choice: A Collection of Articles* [in Hebrew] (Tel Aviv: Hakibbutz Hameuchad Publishing House, 1985), 129–31.
[47] Arie Brown, *Personal Imprint: Moshe Dayan in the Six-Day War and After* [in Hebrew] (Tel Aviv: Ma'arachot, 1997), 35–9.
[48] Interview with Colonel (Ret.) Mordechai Bar-On, 12 May 2009, Jerusalem.

Once Dayan had modified the Kardom operational plan, Rabin suggested that, from the military view, the most logical place for their forces to stop would be the Suez Canal. He argued that if the aim was to destroy the Egyptian army, then the most convenient stopping point was the waterway. Dayan thought it would be political madness to advance all the way up to the canal. He therefore gave a firm order to stop some distance from it. His reasoning was that the canal was an international, not an Egyptian, waterway and that Israel should leave it alone. He predicted that neither Nasser nor his Soviet backers would tolerate Israeli presence along the canal and that if the IDF tried to hold it, the war would go on for years. In the end, it was agreed that the stopping line would be the Mitla and the Giddi passes. When Dayan was informed, on the morning of 7 June, that an IDF patrol had reached the canal, he ordered that it be immediately recalled. That evening, however, Dayan cancelled his own order because he heard that the Security Council was about to call for a cease-fire, and he wanted to improve Israel's bargaining position.

In a postmortem on the war, Dayan summed up, "I was absolutely against reaching the canal. I issued an order to stop at a certain distance from it. But the army presented me with an accomplished fact."[49] It was not the views of the government or the orders of the minister of defence but the sheer momentum of the advance that propelled the Israeli army all the way to the eastern edge of the Suez Canal. The logic of war overwhelmed the minimalist conception of the politicians and the restrictions imposed by the minister of defence.

The Jordanian Front

Decision making in relation to the eastern front was even more haphazard. Prior to the outbreak of war the policy makers considered only minor modifications in the 1949 armistice line with Jordan. They wanted to establish territorial contiguity between West Jerusalem and the Israeli enclave on Mount Scopus on the Jordanian side of the line. Another wish was to capture the Latrun salient, overlooking the road from Tel Aviv to Jerusalem, which is something the IDF tried but failed to achieve during the 1948 war. Generally speaking, Eshkol and his party colleagues had a positive image of the Hashemite dynasty and continued to nourish hope of a settlement with Jordan. "There was nothing here," noted Eban later, "of the inhuman virulence which marked the attitude of other Arab

---

[49] Dayan, *Milestones*, 422; Moshe A. Gilboa, *Six Years – Six Days: Origins and History of the Six Day War*, 2nd ed. [in Hebrew] (Tel Aviv: Am Oved, 1969), 207.

nationalists towards Israel's existence. Even in wars, an unspoken assumption of ultimate accord hovered over the relations between Israel and Jordan."[50] In May and June 1967 Eshkol's government did everything in its power to confine the confrontation to the Egyptian front. Eshkol and his colleagues had to take into account the possibility of some fighting on the Syrian front because that was where the trouble had started. However, they wanted to avoid a clash with Jordan and the inevitable complications of having to deal with the predominantly Palestinian population of the West Bank.[51]

The fighting on the eastern front was initiated by Jordan, not by Israel. King Hussein was swept along by the powerful current of Arab nationalism, and he threw caution to the wind. On 30 May, he flew to Cairo and signed a defence pact with Nasser, placing his army under the command of an Egyptian general. In Israeli eyes this raised the spectre of a war on three fronts. Dayan described it in his diary as "the last straw that broke the camel's back."[52]

King Hussein received sensitive intelligence about the imminent Israeli air strike against Egypt. He was given a chance to pull back from the brink, but he missed it. On the evening of Sunday, 4 June, Jack O'Connell, the CIA station chief in Amman, went to see Hussein with some alarming news that the Israelis were going to attack Egypt's air force and airfields the following morning at 8:00 A.M. Hussein sent an urgent message to Cairo, through the Egyptian general who had in the meantime assumed command of the Jordanian army, to warn Nasser of the plan and urge him to take precautions. Nothing was done. The Egyptian armed forces were a sitting duck. After the war, Nasser confessed to Hussein that he did not act on his warning because he did not believe him.[53] This story is highly revealing of the deep mistrust and the staggering level of incompetence on the part of the Arab rulers who led their countries to war in June 1967, a war that the Arab media repeatedly referred to as "the battle of destiny." But the relevant point here is that it was King Hussein who made the decision to attack Israel, not the other way round.

On 5 June at 9:30 A.M., Jordanian artillery started shelling Israeli neighbourhoods in West Jerusalem and other Israeli settlements along the border. This could have been interpreted either as a salvo to uphold

---

[50] Abba Eban, *An Autobiography* (London: Weidenfeld and Nicolson, 1977), 408.
[51] Uzi Narkis, *Soldier of Jerusalem* [in Hebrew] (Tel Aviv: Ministry of Defence, 1991), 327.
[52] Dayan, *Milestones*, 420.
[53] Interview with Jack O'Connell, 4 October 2008, Connaught Hotel, London.

Jordanian honour or as a declaration of war. Eshkol decided to give King Hussein the benefit of the doubt. Through General Odd Bull, the Norwegian commander of the UN Truce Supervision Organization (UNTSO), he sent the following message on the morning of 5 June: "We shall not initiate any action whatsoever against Jordan. However, should Jordan open hostilities, we shall react with all our might, and the King will have to bear the full responsibility for the consequences." King Hussein told General Bull that it was too late, the die was cast. Hussein had already handed over command of his forces to an Egyptian general. Under Egyptian command, the Jordanian forces intensified the shelling, captured the Government House in Jerusalem, where UNTSO had its headquarters, bombed the airfield in Ramat David, and started moving their American-made tanks from the East Bank to the West Bank, in violation of an earlier understanding not to deploy American-made tanks on the West Bank.

At noon Jordanian Hunter planes attacked Netanya and the airfield in Kfar Syrkin. For the majority of Israel's civilian and military leaders it was not the 30 May pact with Nasser but the combined infantry, artillery, and air attack along the entire front that made this a defensive war.[54] Had King Hussein heeded Eshkol's warning, he would have kept the Old City of Jerusalem and the West Bank. No one in the Cabinet or the General Staff had proposed the capture of the Old City before the Jordanian bombardment began. By throwing in his lot with Nasser so ostentatiously and by his defiant response to Eshkol's suggestion, Hussein contributed to the rekindling of irredentist aspirations on the Israeli side.

During the evening of 5 June the Cabinet convened in the air-raid shelter of the Knesset in Jerusalem, because at that time the city was being bombarded by Jordanian artillery. Allon and Begin argued that Jordanian shelling gave Israel a historic opportunity to liberate the Old City of Jerusalem. Eban remonstrated that earlier that day the minister of defence had announced that Israel's purpose was not conquest. He was also concerned about the risk of damage to the Holy Places. Eshkol deferred a decision until Dayan and Rabin could be consulted.[55]

On 6 June Dayan allowed the IDF General Staff to encircle the Old City, but he ordered them not to enter it. He too worried about damage to the Holy Places and wanted to avoid fighting in a built-up area. He

---

[54] Dayan, *Milestones*, 434; interview with Lieutenant-General Chaim Bar-Lev, 8 August 1982, Tel Aviv.
[55] Verbatim record of Cabinet Meeting, 5 June 1967, Israel State Archives, Jerusalem.

also thought that international pressure would force Israel to withdraw from the Old City after the war, and he did not want to pay a heavy price in casualties. News that the United Nations was about to call for a cease-fire caused Dayan to change his mind. Without clearing it with the Cabinet, he gave the IDF the order to move into the Old City. By 10:00 A.M. the next day, 7 June, it was in Israeli hands. Three hours later, Dayan, Rabin and Uzi Narkis, head of Central Command, entered the city through the Lion's Gate. Standing by the Wailing Wall, Dayan declared, "The IDF liberated Jerusalem this morning. We reunited divided Jerusalem, the bisected capital of Israel. We have returned to our holiest places, we have returned in order not to part from them ever again."[56] This statement flatly contradicted the assurance that Dayan had given on the previous day, but in the heady atmosphere of victory nobody called him to account.

Decisions on the rest of the West Bank were also taken in stages. They were dictated by military developments, not by a political master plan. The Israeli reaction to the Jordanian shelling was initially restrained, in the hope that King Hussein would desist after satisfying Jordan's honour. After the Old City was captured, Dayan ordered his troops to dig in on the slopes east of Jerusalem. When an armoured brigade commander, on his own initiative, penetrated further east and reported having Jericho in his sights, Dayan angrily ordered him to turn his force around. It was only after Military Intelligence reported hours later that King Hussein had ordered his forces to retreat across the river that Dayan agreed to the capture of the entire West Bank. That evening Dayan met with senior officers to consider these unexpected developments. "How do we control a million Arabs?" asked Rabin, referring to the inhabitants of the West Bank. "One million, two hundred and fifty thousand," corrected a staff officer. It was a question to which no one had an answer.[57]

Narkis stressed the resistance of the government to military action in the sector for which he was responsible throughout the precrisis period. The Labour Party leadership, according to him, was intent on preserving the status quo with Jordan. Military Intelligence had estimated that Jordan would not join the battle. The Hussein-Nasser pact hit them like a bolt from the blue. Despite the pact, Rabin refused to allow Narkis to

---

[56] Quoted in Meron Benvenisti, *Jerusalem: The Torn City* (Jerusalem: Isratypeset, 1976), 84.

[57] Abraham Rabinovich, "Into the West Bank: The Jordanians Were Laughing," *International Herald Tribune*, 6–7 June 1992.

retain an armoured division in reserve because he persisted in thinking that there would be no fighting in that sector. Even after the Jordanians opened fire, all the proposals made by Narkis, to capture Latrun, for example, were turned down. Only when the Government House was captured did the Israeli military machine start to roll. There was a serious threat to Jerusalem's security, so he was allowed to send troops to Mount Scopus. Narkis summed up:

First, the Israeli government had no intention of capturing the West Bank. On the contrary, they were opposed to it. Second, there was not any provocation on the part of the IDF. Third, the rein was only loosened when a real threat to Jerusalem's security emerged. This is truly how things happened on 5 June although it is difficult to believe. The end result was something that no one had planned.[58]

Narkis made another important point: the speed of developments on the battlefield meant that the government could not exercise effective control over the actions of the army even if it had wanted to.

We are a disciplined army.... But we operated so quickly that the Israeli government did not have the time to determine national goals for that war.... The government could have ordered us not to capture Ramallah. The government could have ordered us not to capture Jericho, or to stop before Bethlehem, or before Hebron, or before Nablus. They didn't do it because I think they were overwhelmed by the situation and they did not have time to say stop.[59]

Rabin was also of the opinion that the final outcome of the conflict was determined not by political war aims but by military contingencies: "The war developed as a result of its own inner logic, and this development enclosed all the forces of the Jordanian army in Judea and Samaria and willy-nilly led to the capture of the natural border of the Land of Israel – the River Jordan."[60]

Another revealing account of how Israel came to occupy the entire West Bank was given by the principal policy maker, Eshkol, to his party colleagues. On the third day of the war, Eshkol said the following, in his characteristically lighthearted and convoluted style, to the secretariat of the Labour Party:

[58] Interview with Major-General Uzi Narkis, 20 July 1982, Jerusalem.
[59] Tad Szulc's interview with Major General Uzi Narkis, date not recorded, Record Group 19.005, the Gaynor I. Jacobson Collection, U.S. Holocaust Memorial Museum, Washington, DC. I am grateful to Dr. Avi Raz of Wolfson College, Oxford, for giving me a copy of this interview.
[60] Gilboa, *Six Years – Six Days*, 229.

God wanted to confuse the heads of the nations, and at the last minute Hussein too made an agreement with Nasser. He too tried to jump on the Nasserist bandwagon.... From that moment it was clear that there was no way but to be ready to stand simultaneously on three fronts.... I confess that for some reason there was a soft spot in my heart towards the Hashemite family although I had not met Hussein or his father or his grandfather. When the Jordanian attack on Jerusalem began, it was clear that there was no escape – a new mission was born: the liberation of the Old City.... It was clear that we were going to the Old City. It is easy to say but surrounding the Old City was not simple.... In the meantime the possibility arose of encircling and taking Sheikh Jarah, Mount Scopus, and Ramallah. A new mission opened by itself – to liberate the West Bank. This was not born in one minute. To this very day I hesitated to get this word out of my mouth: "the complete liberation of the West Bank."[61]

The Syrian Front

Nowhere was Dayan more erratic and unpredictable than in the decision-making process concerning the Syrian front. Here too the government had no clearly defined war aims. The IDF was deployed in a defensive mode on the Syrian front, as it was on the Jordanian front, when the lightning strike against Egypt was launched. Syria, for its part, wanted to stay out of this war. Although Syria had a defence pact with Egypt, it was remarkably passive during the critical first two days of fighting. Its air force made one feeble sortie that caused very little damage and its artillery bombarded Israeli settlements along the front line. But these were limited hostilities, and they practically ended with Israel's devastating counterattack on Syria's air force. After the magnitude of the Egyptian and Jordanian setbacks became apparent, Syria's motivation to do battle with the IDF evaporated altogether.[62] There was, therefore, no strategic need for Israel to open a third front. David Elazar ("Dado"), the combative head of Northern Command, exerted all the pressure of which he was capable for all-out war against Syria, but Dayan kept him under a very tight leash.[63]

During the nights of 5 and 6 June, Dayan and Rabin discussed the possibility of military action on the Syrian front. Dayan ruled that the

---

[61] A Speech by Levi Eshkol before the Labour Party Secretariat, 8 June 1967, Labour Party Archive, Beit Berl.

[62] Patrick Seale, *Asad: The Struggle for the Middle East* (London: I. B. Tauris, 1988), 137–9; Benny Michalson, "The War on the Syrian Front," in Michalson, *The Six-Day War*, 212–13.

[63] Hanoch Bartov, *Dado – 48 Years and 20 More Days*, vol. 1 [in Hebrew] (Tel Aviv: Ma'ariv, 1978), 125.

IDF must not cross the international border, but that it should take over all the DMZs on its side of the border. During the 1948 war, the Syrian army succeeded in capturing territory beyond the international border, and the IDF was unable to dislodge it. Under the terms of the 1949 Armistice Agreement, the area was demilitarized: Israel and Syria were allowed to have farmers but not soldiers on their side of the DMZ. Dayan now permitted the IDF to remilitarize – in effect unilaterally eradicating the DMZ – but not to invade Syria. This ruling was confirmed by a decision of the ministerial committee for defence on 6 June. The following day Eshkol held a consultation with Allon, Rabin, and Elazar. Eshkol had bitter memories of the water war with Syria during the mid-1960s. He proposed a much larger operation whose aim would be the capture of the sources of the Banias and Tel Azaziat, a fortified Syrian position on the Golan Heights. All the other participants supported this proposal. Rabin and Elazar wanted to go further than Tel Azaziat. Allon was insistent that they be given permission to do so. Dayan persisted in his opposition.

Eshkol repeated his proposal in different forums. At a meeting of the Knesset Committee on Foreign Affairs and Defence on 7 June, Dayan said that he personally was opposed to the capture of the Golan Heights "but if the cabinet decided on this conquest, it will be carried out." This was typical of Dayan's talent for giving himself the opportunity to claim credit for successes whilst shirking responsibility for failures. He nailed his colours firmly to the fence. He distinguished between capturing the Golan Heights and dealing a blow to the Syria army. He was against crossing the international border, not least on account of the special relationship between Syria and the Soviet Union. On 8 June, there was yet another consultation regarding Syria in Eshkol's office. Eshkol repeated his proposal; Allon, Rabin, and Elazar reiterated their support. They expected the war with Syria to be tough and involve heavy casualties. They did not consider it a price worth paying for the sake of the limited objective that Dayan had in mind. There was much criticism of Dayan behind his back.[64]

The farmers from the collective settlements and the *kibbutzim* from northern Galilee added their voice to the call to capture the Golan Heights. A whole settlement lobby sprang into action. They found in Eshkol a sympathetic listener. He even invited three representatives of the settlers from the Galilee panhandle to put their case directly to the Ministerial Committee for Defence, which met in the evening of 8 June. By this time,

---

[64] Haber, *Today War Will Break Out*, 246–7.

the Egyptian and Jordanian armies had disintegrated and Israel could turn its undivided attention to the Syrian front. The representatives of the settlements pleaded not to be left at the mercy of the Syrian guns. Their words made a strong impression on all those present, except Dayan.

Dayan was determined not to run the risk of Soviet military intervention on the side of Syria. He was also worried that their forces would become overextended. "We started the war in order to destroy the Egyptian force and open the Straits of Tiran," he said. "On the way we took the West Bank. I do not think that it is possible to open another campaign against Syria. If the idea is to go into Syria and change the border in order to make life easier for the settlements, I am against." Dayan pointed out that the Syrians would never accept the loss of their territory and the result would be never-ending conflict. Rather than trying to move the international border, he proposed moving ten settlements to a distance of several kilometres west of the border. Allon and Eshkol were outraged by this suggestion. It went against the whole spirit and ethos of the Zionist movement. Eshkol retorted that the Syrians could hardly hope for a greater victory. Allon, a member of Kibbutz Ginossar in the north, said that the entire Galilee panhandle did not amount to fifteen kilometres and that they could not possibly give up part of the country. Speaking as a former farmer, the prime minister stressed that the idea of uprooting settlements and moving them elsewhere was absolutely out of the question. The committee decided to defer making a decision regarding Syria for two or three days and, in the meantime, to ask the Chief of Staff to prepare an operational plan.[65] No other person except Dayan could have single-handedly blocked a proposal that enjoyed such strong political and military support.

Dayan's next move completely astounded his colleagues. Early in the morning of 9 June, a few hours after Syria requested a cease-fire, Dayan called Major General Elazar directly, bypassing the Chief of Staff, and ordered him to attack Syria and capture the Golan Heights.[66] It was the exclusive prerogative of the Chief of Staff to give operational orders, but on this occasion Rabin had "no desire to quibble when the Syrians were about to get their just deserts [*sic*] for malicious aggressiveness and arrogance."[67] Eshkol did not receive the news with the same equanimity.

---

[65] Shlomo Nakdimon, "The Secret Battle for the Golan Heights," *Yediot Aharonot*, 30 May 1997.

[66] Bartov, *Dado*, 134–6.

[67] Rabin, *The Rabin Memoirs*, 90.

He suspected that Dayan was trying to steal all the glory for himself and even considered cancelling his order. "What a vile man," he muttered in the presence of his aide-de-camp.[68]

What prompted Dayan to change his mind so suddenly was a message from Nasser to the Syrian president, Nur al-Din al-Atasi, which was intercepted on the night of 8 and 9 June by Israeli intelligence:

I believe that Israel is about to concentrate all her forces against Syria in order to destroy the Syrian army and regard for the common cause obliges me to advise you to agree to the ending of hostilities and to inform U Thant [the UN secretary-general] immediately, in order to preserve Syria's great army. We have lost this battle. May God help us in the future. Your brother, Gamal Abdel Nasser.

Dayan claimed that this message completely changed the situation and led him to give the order to storm the Golan Heights and capture even more territory than had been proposed the previous day. His order was to "Do whatever can be done." In the margin of the text of Nasser's message, Dayan scribbled, "Eshkol, 1. In my opinion this cable obliges us to capture the maximal military lines. 2. Yesterday I did not think that Egypt and Syria (the political leadership) would collapse in this way and give up the continuation of the campaign. But since this is the situation, it must be exploited to the full. A great day. Moshe Dayan."[69]

Having changed his mind, Dayan prosecuted the war on the Syrian front with great vigour. But he greatly underestimated the strength and determination of the enemy. He told Elazar that the Syrian units were crumbling and their soldiers had begun fleeing even before the IDF assault. The Syrian units fought obstinately and with all their strength. But by the evening of 10 June, when the cease-fire that Israel had persistently disregarded went into effect, the Golan Heights were in Israeli hands.

Dayan's Confession

Although Dayan got most of the glory for the victory over Syria, he later regarded the decision to go to war as a mistake. In his 1976 off-the-record conversations with the journalist Rami Tal, Dayan confessed that on the fourth day of the June War he had failed in his duty as minister of defence by agreeing to the war with Syria. There was really no pressing reason, he admitted, to go to war with Syria. The kibbutz residents who

[68] Haber, *Today War Will Break Out*, 246–51.
[69] Ibid., 252–3.

pressed the government to take the Golan Heights did so less for security than for the farmland. Dayan conceded that these civilians had suffered a great deal at the hands of the Syrian soldiers: "But I can tell you with absolute confidence, the delegation that came to persuade Eshkol to take the heights was not thinking of these things. They were thinking about the land." This confidence was unjustified. The verbatim record of the meeting of the Ministerial Committee for Defence on 8 June shows that the kibbutz leaders spoke only about the nightmarish security situation and not of the opportunity to acquire more land.

The allegation that Israel went to war against Syria because the kibbutz residents coveted Syrian land provoked strong indignation in Israel. There was even greater anger at Dayan's allegations from the grave, through an interview published after his death, that Israel's security was not threatened by the Syrians. For it became an article of faith among Israelis that the Golan Heights were seized in 1967 in order to stop the Syrians from shelling the settlements down below. Rami Tal tried to make this argument but Dayan cut him short: "Look, it's possible to talk in terms of the Syrians are bastards, you have to get them and this is the right time, and other such talk, but that is not policy. You don't strike at every enemy because he is a bastard but because he threatens you. And the Syrians, on the fourth day of the war, were not a threat to us."[70]

Dayan's various accounts of the reasons for the war against Syria are so glaringly inconsistent as to raise questions not only about his integrity but also about his sanity. Three days after the victory, Dayan launched a scathing attack on the conduct of the war at a meeting of the Knesset Committee for Foreign Affairs and Defence. This was the most poorly planned war in Israel's history, he charged. During the Sinai War, the military moves were dictated by the goals and the guidelines that had been agreed on in advance. During the recent war, by contrast, no clear instructions were given to the army on where and how far to go. "Here," said Dayan, "we had no intention whatsoever to take the West Bank, or Jerusalem, or to get into a war with Syria and anyone who presents this campaign as planned in advance is simply wrong."[71] What Dayan omitted to say was that he gave the army most of the orders during the war and that he did not always consult the Cabinet or the

---

[70] Rami Tal, "Moshe Dayan: Soul Searching," *Yediot Aharonot*, 27 April 1997; Serge Schmemann, "General Dayan Speaks from the Grave," *International Herald Tribune*, 12 May 1997.

[71] Verbatim Record of the Knesset Foreign Affairs and Defence Committee, 13 June 1967, Israel State Archives, Jerusalem.

prime minister. Hard as he tried, Israel Lior, Eshkol's aide-de-camp, was unable to fathom Dayan's intentions. Lior thought that Dayan's decisions needed to be examined by a psychologist no less than by a historian: "The fickleness of the decisions was extraordinary – but maybe ordinary for Moshe Dayan."[72]

Fickleness is not a word that comes immediately to mind in relation to the government that led Israel during May and June 1967. But it was not a model of coherence or consistency either. What emerges most clearly from its verbatim records is that this government did not have a political plan for the conduct of the war. The government was divided internally, debated options endlessly, improvised, and seized opportunities as and when they presented themselves. It hoped for a war on one front, was drawn to war on a second front, and ended up by initiating war on a third front. The one thing it did not have was a master plan for territorial aggrandizement. Its territorial aims were not defined in advance but in response to developments on the battlefield. Appetite comes with the eating, as the French saying goes.

Conclusion

On the first day of the war, the prime minister and the minister of defence proclaimed that their country had no territorial ambitions. Later that summer, Secretary of State Rusk reminded his opposite number of this. Eban simply shrugged his shoulders and said: "We've changed our minds."[73] This answer was surprising but truthful. The alternative explanation of a premeditated conspiracy to draw the Arab states into a war in order to expand Israel's borders is simply not supported by the evidence. It is utterly baseless. Individual ministers harboured some expansionist designs in different directions: Eshkol's priority was in the north; Dayan's preoccupation was with the south, while Allon coveted the territory to the east, the biblical land of Israel. But none of them advocated going to war in order to acquire more territory. The government as a whole most certainly did not have an agreed-upon, collective agenda of territorial aggrandizement.

The decision-making process of the Eshkol government during the crisis slide and the six days of fighting were complex, confused, and

---

[72] Haber, *Today War Will Break Out*, 246.
[73] Dean Rusk, *As I Saw It: A Secretary of State's Memoirs* (London: I. B. Tauris, 1991), 332.

convoluted. It did not bear much resemblance to what political scientists like to call the "the rational actor model." Precisely because the government was so divided, it experienced great difficulty when it came to reigning in the military. The government and the army were at one in recognizing the seriousness of the Egyptian threat to the country's security. Some of them even defined it as a question of survival. The difference lay in how to deal with this threat: the government preferred multilateral diplomacy whereas the army preferred the unilateral use of force. The General Staff was more united than the government but it was not entirely monolithic when it came to the question of borders. Individual members, like Weizman and Rechvam Ze'evi, clearly wanted to change the borders. But the General Staff as a whole was collectively committed to the territorial status quo.

This chapter began with a question: Why did Israel go to war on 5 June 1967? The evidence reviewed here suggests a straightforward answer: Israel went to war because the leaders believed its security and possibly even its very survival were threatened. Its government did everything in its power between 15 May and 4 June to prevent war, and it sanctioned the use of force reluctantly, as a last resort, and only after all other avenues had been exhausted. It can therefore be stated quite categorically: the June 1967 War was a defensive war, not an offensive war, let alone an expansionist war. At the height of the crisis, Allon begged his colleagues to leave it to future historians to determine who fired the first shot. My own view is that it was Nasser who, for all intents and purposes, fired the first shot on 22 May 1967 by illegally closing the Straits of Tiran to Israeli shipping. In doing so, he put the match to the barrel of gunpowder.

The question of whether this was a "war of choice" or "war of no-choice" is more difficult to answer. On 8 August 1982, during the first Lebanon war, Prime Minister Begin gave a talk at the Staff College about this theme. He admitted that the Lebanon War was a war of choice, but he argued that the Suez War, waged by his Labour predecessors, had also been a war of choice. Regarding the Six-Day War he had this to say: "In June 1967 we again had a choice. The Egyptian army concentrations in the Sinai approaches do not prove that Nasser was really about to attack us. We must be honest with ourselves. We decided to attack him."[74] That Israel initiated hostilities is not in question. The question is: did it have any reasonable alternative? Opinion on this question is likely to remain

---

[74] Meron Medzini, ed., *Israel's Foreign Relations: Selected Documents, 1982–1984*, vol. 8 (Jerusalem: Ministry of Foreign Affairs, 1990), 134.

divided. My own conclusion is that the June War was neither a classic war of choice nor an unambiguous war of no-choice but something in between – an inescapable war of choice. Israel could have allowed Nasser to get away with violating its maritime rights in the hope that there would be no further provocations. But that would have been an act of faith, not an act of statesmanship.

The long-term consequences of the Six-Day War lie outside the scope of this study. But even regarding the immediate outcome, there were sharply contrasting views. The myopic view of the military was typified by Sharon whereas the civilian view was best represented by Eshkol. After the guns fell silent, a group of newspaper editors visited Sharon in his command post in Sinai. Sharon gave them a briefing on the war and concluded by saying: "The Egyptian army is destroyed. My generation will not fight again."[75] In the immediate aftermath of victory, Eshkol began to sport a Churchillian V sign. His wife Miriam said to him, "Eshkol, what are you doing? Have you gone mad?" With characteristic humour Eshkol replied, "No. This is not a V sign in English. It is a V sign in Yiddish! *Vi krikht men aroys?*" Roughly translated, this means, "How do we get out of this?" It is a question to which Eshkol's compatriots have not yet found an answer.

[75] Quoted in Michalson, *The Six-Day War*, 241.

2

Egypt

Dangerous Illusions

Laura M. James

In the June 1967 War Egypt lost not only ten thousand men in five days and the Sinai desert but also more intangible assets, such as regional and international credibility and national self-confidence. The scale of this disaster, combined with Egypt's own role in its initiation, provokes many questions. One of the most enduring mysteries concerns the intentions of Egyptian President Gamal Abdel Nasser. Did he plan a war? Did he expect one? Or did he simply blunder into it through a process of uncontrolled escalation? This chapter argues that Nasser made war neither by accident nor by design. He took a set of actions primarily aimed at reaping political gains, but he was well aware that they carried a high risk of precipitating military hostilities.

This chapter endorses the vital importance of the international system to the development of the crisis in May, including the Cold War context and Arab regional competition. It focuses, however, on the Egyptian regime – its authoritarian structure, internal divisions, and deeply rooted preconceptions. Within this framework, it argues that particular and deeply ingrained elite images of Egypt's enemies guided policy in the crisis. For the Egyptian regime, the enemy in late 1966 and early 1967 was threefold. Imperialism, represented by the United States and Britain, was linked to the "Arab reactionaries" as well as to Zionist Israel, typically described as an "imperialist base in the heart of the Arab homeland." Imperialism, especially that of the United States, was seen as by far the most powerful and rhetorically salient enemy up to and during the early stages of the 1967 crisis, while the other hostile states were "only satellites spinning in the United States orbit and following its steps."[1]

---

[1] Cairo Radio, 15 May 1967, *BBC Summary of World Broadcasts*, ME2467. For a much
more detailed delineation of the development and nature of these hostile images, see Laura

One of the root causes of war was Nasser's own perception that the United States was his primary enemy. Nasser's idea of America as an all-powerful adversary encouraged his fundamental underestimation of Israel's capacity for independent and effective military action – although the most that regime members expected was to hold their own rather than to win a military victory. These two concepts constantly led to the misinterpretation of incoming information to fit preconceived patterns during the prewar crisis, as well as during the conflict and its aftermath.

In the early 1960s, Egypt had essentially agreed with the U.S. administration to keep its difference with Israel "in the ice-box" – a stock phrase in diplomatic correspondence of the time. This was helped by the presence of UN peacekeeping forces on the Sinai border. As a result, Cairo initially managed to stay removed some distance from the Arab-Israeli dispute over the division of water from the River Jordan. The series of Arab summits that had begun in response to this dispute not only failed to contain it but also contributed to the formation of Palestinian guerrilla organizations that had carried out a series of attacks on Israel across the Syrian and Jordanian borders. Although Egypt was not directly involved, given the UN peacekeeping forces on the Sinai border, incidents such as the Israeli raid on the Jordanian village of Samuʿ in November 1966 demanded a response from any country claiming to lead the Arab world. Added to this, the Soviet Union was pressing Egypt to ally with a new radical regime in Syria, culminating in the Egypt-Syria Defence Agreement, also in November 1966. This made it harder for Nasser to remain uninvolved – for example, in an incident in April 1967, when Israeli planes shot down six MiGs over Syrian territory and overflew Damascus. Border incidents continued into late April and early May, allowing the conservative Arab states to increase their public criticism of Nasser. But few observers expected an imminent war.

The June 1967 crisis blew up quickly, and many of the key escalatory steps were initiated by the Egyptian government. Some U.S. and other foreign representatives believed at the time that the Egyptians had a plan, due to small indications of forethought and organization, the speed of the movement into Sinai, and the atmosphere of overwhelming confidence.[2] However, subsequent Egyptian accounts emphasize that there was a high

M. James, *Nasser at War: Arab Images of the Enemy* (London: Palgrave Macmillan, 2006).

[2] Richard B. Parker, *The Politics of Miscalculation in the Middle East* (Bloomington: Indiana University Press, 1993), 90.

degree of confusion and improvisation. The evidence in Nasser's own speeches is mixed. On 22 May he asserted that "we had no plan prior to 13th May."[3] Four days later, he implied the opposite – but was perhaps merely trying to appear in control of events. Although the Egyptian military certainly had contingency plans for this sort of situation, the specific occasion seems to have come as a surprise.

Step 1: The Mobilization in Sinai

On 13 May the Egyptian regime received reports from Moscow that Israeli troops were massing in force on the Syrian border. These were discussed that evening by Nasser, his military chief, Marshal Abdel-Hakim Amer, and Anwar Sadat, who had just returned from Moscow.[4] The following day, the Egyptian armed forces mobilized on full alert, concentrating troops in the Sinai desert. The Chief of Staff, General Mohamed Fawzi, was sent to Syria and assured the Damascus regime of Egyptian support.[5] The aim at this stage appears to have been to deter Israel from aggression against Syria, rather than to start a war.[6] This is partially confirmed by the fact that Egyptian troops passed through Cairo in ostentatious procession, rather than secretly.[7] Nasser later claimed that he estimated the likelihood of war at only 20 percent at this time.[8] General Fawzi was ordered by Marshal Amer to implement the "Conqueror" (*qāhir*) plan, which was defensive rather than offensive in nature. He was also told that the aim was "to make this mobilization and deployment of troops like we did in 1960."[9]

There remains the question of why the Egyptian regime reacted so strongly and rapidly to an unconfirmed report of an Israeli threat to Syria. Although such reports had been received before, this one was more

---

[3] *BBC Summary*, ME2473; *Wathā'iq 'abd al-nā sir*, vol. 1 [Nasser's Documents] (Cairo: Al-Ahram Centre for Political and Social Studies, n.d.), 173.

[4] Parker, *The Politics of Miscalculation*, 42–3, 62.

[5] Brian Lapping Associates, interview transcripts, *The Fifty Years War: Israel and the Arabs*, Middle East Centre Archive, St. Antony's College, University of Oxford: Fawzi interview.

[6] Anwar Sadat, *In Search of Identity* (London: Collins, 1978), 172; author interview with Mohamed Fayek, Cairo, 25 March 2004; Brian Lapping Associates, *Fifty Years War*: Fawzi and Badran interviews.

[7] Michael B. Oren, *Six Days of War: June 1967 and the Making of the Modern Middle East* (Oxford University Press, 2002), 58–9.

[8] 23 June 1967, *BBC Summary*, ME2525.

[9] Brian Lapping Associates, *Fifty Years War*: Fawzi interview.

convincing. First, circumstantial detail was provided regarding the nature and location of the alleged thirteen brigades massing on the border. Second, there were fewer troops than usual in the Israeli Independence Day parade in Jerusalem on 15 May, which was intended as a gesture to reduce provocation, but interpreted, due to the preconception of an aggressive Israel, as evidence that they were busy elsewhere.[10] Third, the information was received through several channels, including Syria, Lebanon, and the Soviet Union, which gave it particular emphasis.[11] Even so, this report alone seems insufficient to explain the Egyptian decision, especially because it was soon contradicted. General Fawzi was sent to Syria to investigate on 14 May, but he found no evidence of abnormal troop concentrations. He was told by the Syrian air force chief that the report was merely based on threats and past raids. Fawzi reported fully to Amer on his return to Cairo on 15 May.[12] In addition, the Israelis repeatedly denied, through the United States, the Soviet Union, and a secret channel previously used by Mossad, that unusual numbers of troops were present on the border.[13] The United States confirmed this. However, due to the fixed Egyptian belief in Israeli and American hostility, neither was believed. The military build-up therefore continued into late May.

The real reason for the mobilization was less the presence of troop concentrations and more the fixed image of Israel as having aggressive intentions, which caused contrary evidence to be discounted or ignored. Egyptian General Intelligence assessed, according to Salah Bassiouny of the Foreign Ministry, that stable U.S.-Israel relations and increasing U.S.-Egypt tension "could push Israel to undertake a military action against Syria to embarrass the Egyptian leadership in the Arab world." One might argue that the Soviet report was never taken literally, as it was seen to represent a political rather than a military reality.[14] It is certainly true that, because Israel could mobilize within hours, the lack of troop concentrations was not in itself significant. The perception that Israel intended to attack Syria may therefore have been more closely related to

---

[10] Department of State, *Foreign Relations of the United States, 1964–1968*, vol. XIX (Washington, DC: U.S. Government Printing Office, 2004), 5 [hereinafter referred to as *FRUS*].

[11] Parker, *The Politics of Miscalculation*, 5–6; Christopher Andrew and Oleg Gordievsky, *KGB* (London: Sceptre, 1990), 501.

[12] Mohamed Fawzi, *Harb al thalāth sanawāt, 1967–1970* [The Three Year War, 1967–1970] (Cairo: Dar al-Mustaqbal al-Arabiyy, 1983), 71–2; Brian Lapping Associates, *Fifty Years War*: Fawzi interview.

[13] Oren, *Six Days of War*, 62–3.

[14] Winston Burdett, *Encounter with the Middle East* (New York: Atheneum, 1969), 213.

recent statements uttered by Israeli decision makers that were interpreted as belligerent.

However, even an Israeli threat to Syria was not necessarily a sufficient reason for action. Syria was no longer part of the United Arab Republic, as it had been when Nasser mobilized in 1960, and the Egyptian-Syrian Defence Agreement, concluded in late 1966, did not mandate a response to minor border raids. The statements of Israeli leaders and reported troop movements attacked Nasser's prestige by showing that he was unable to protect Syria and laid him open to deeper criticism from America's "reactionary" Arab allies.[15] But they seemed all the more threatening because they were perceived in the context of a U.S. conspiracy against Egypt. Bassiouny claims that the Foreign Ministry saw the reports as credible because Israel had reached the level at which it could find strategic alliance with the United States.[16] The U.S. chargé believed that the Egyptian government "had talked itself" into believing in a "U.S.-Israeli plot" in order to create an incident resulting in the stationing of UN Emergency Force (UNEF) along the border between Israel and Syria.[17] On 12 May, Heikal had written the final article in a series about the clash between Egypt and America, in which he depicted the United States as finally prepared to deal the *coup de grâce*. In this atmosphere of danger, the heavy emphasis laid by the Soviet Union on the warning of troop movements seemed an opportunity not to be missed, implying an invitation for Egypt to confront its enemies with Soviet support.[18]

Step 2: Expelling the United Nations Emergency Force

On 16 May, General Fawzi wrote to Major General Indar Jit Rikhye, the commander of the UNEF in Sinai, asking him to withdraw "all UN troops which install Observation Posts along our borders" immediately.[19] Rikhye had no authority to agree and referred the matter to UN Secretary-General U Thant, who made it clear that the UNEF could be expelled but would not in the meantime stand aside to allow the resumption of

---

[15] Author interview with Mohamed Fayek, Cairo, 25 March 2004.
[16] Brian Lapping Associates, *Fifty Years War*: Bassiouny interview.
[17] 21 May 1967, *FRUS*, 28.
[18] Nadav Safran, *From War to War* (New York: Pegasus, 1969), 277–8; Mohammed Hassanein Heikal, *Sphinx and Commissar: The Rise and Fall of Soviet Influence in the Arab World* (London: Collins, 1978), 170, 181.
[19] Indar Jit Rikhye, *The Sinai Blunder: Withdrawal of the United Nations Emergency Force Leading to the Six-Day War of June 1967* (London: Frank Cass, 1980), 16.

hostilities. Therefore, Foreign Minister Mahmoud Riad sent him a second letter, containing a formal request "to terminate the existence of UNEF on the soil of the United Arab Republic and in the Gaza Strip."[20] Again, although Nasser does not seem to have intended war, he acknowledged that this action raised its probability – to anything from 20 percent to 80 percent, depending on the source.[21] General Fawzi apparently failed to realize the significance at the time, but Riad claims to have become aware of the possibility of a military confrontation immediately upon reading the first letter.[22] Rikhye thought it would make war inevitable, especially when he was cheerfully told by his Egyptian liaison, Brigadier General Sharkawy: "We have arrived at this decision after much deliberation and are prepared for anything. If there is war, we shall next meet at Tel Aviv."[23]

Some ambiguity exists regarding precisely who took these decisions and what they intended. Nasser certainly ordered both letters. He planned the first on the morning of 14 May in consultation with his Advisor for Foreign Affairs, Mahmoud Fawzi, delegating the task to Marshal Amer, who then gave instructions to Mohamed Fawzi. However, when Nasser saw the English version, he displayed concern about the wording because he wanted to make it quite clear that the UNEF could remain in Gaza and Sharm al-Sheikh. He apparently asked Amer to change "withdraw" to "redeploy" and cross out "all" before "these troops." Amer reported that this was not possible, as the letter was already being delivered.[24] Therefore it seems likely that, two days later, Nasser ordered Riad to request the full withdrawal reluctantly, with no alternative that would not lead to loss of face.[25] In the long term, he had been seeking an opportunity to get rid of the UNEF, which the leadership saw as infringing on Egyptian national sovereignty.[26] At this juncture it led to confused changes of plan and raised new political issues for which the regime was not prepared.[27] However, once the lines had been drawn, in accordance

---

[20] Quoted in Safran, *From War to War*, 268.

[21] Parker, *The Politics of Miscalculation*, 47.

[22] Brian Lapping Associates, *Fifty Years War*: Fawzi interview; Mahmoud Riad, *The Struggle for Peace in the Middle East* (London: Quartet Books, 1981), 18.

[23] Rikhye, *The Sinai Blunder*, 21.

[24] Oren, *Six Days of War*, 67; Brian Lapping Associates, *Fifty Years War*: Fawzi interview.

[25] Mohammed Hassanein Heikal, *Li-misr ila li-'abd al-nā sir* [For Egypt or for Abdel Nasser] (Cairo: Al-Ahram, 1987), 117; author interview with Mohamed Fayek, Cairo, 25 March 2004.

[26] Fawzi, *Harb al thalāth sanawāt*, 69.

[27] Safran, *From War to War*, 287.

with his customary practice he had no intention of seeking a graceful way to back down. He advised U Thant not to send an appeal that would certainly be refused.[28]

It seems possible that Amer intended the complete termination of the UNEF from the beginning. He had suggested it twice previously, telegraphing Nasser from Pakistan with a recommendation to that effect as early as December 1966, in response to Jordanian and Saudi propaganda. Afterwards, watching an infantry brigade setting out from Suez to Yemen, he suggested sending it to Sharm al-Sheikh instead, but the president once again refused.[29] Moreover, the Egyptian army, which Amer controlled, preempted the UNEF withdrawal, demanding access not only to the border posts but also to Sharm al-Sheikh.[30] The occupation of Sharm al-Sheikh was the crucial difference between the withdrawal and the redeployment of the UNEF because the military certainly never considered the option of leaving it empty.[31]

Amer apparently decided to occupy Sharm al-Sheikh on 16 May, the very day that the UNEF was asked to withdraw from the border. General Noufal, then assistant to the Chief of Operations, claims that he called Amer that afternoon to ask if troops should be sent to replace the UNEF there as well. After a delay of two hours, Amer called back to say that they should. However, when the link to the Straits of Tiran and the potential for war was pointed out to him, Amer met with his top military officers and decided not to send troops to Sharm al-Sheikh. Later that evening, Amer changed his mind again and told him to send troops after all, as soon as possible. They had to arrive by 18 May. Paratroops were to be sent instead of the Fourth Brigade, as previously planned.[32] Rikhye reports that he was asked to include Sharm al-Sheikh in the initial withdrawal, evacuating it on the evening of 16 May, despite the fact that it was not mentioned in Fawzi's letter, and that at around 2 P.M. on 18 May a group of Egyptian officers arrived by helicopter, saying that they had come to take over the camp and demanding a reply within fifteen minutes.[33]

---

[28] Rikhye, *The Sinai Blunder*, 51; author interview with Ambassador Mohammed Abdel Wahab, Cairo, 30 March 2004.

[29] Fawzi, *Harb al thalāth sanawāt*, 73; Brian Lapping Associates, *Fifty Years War*: Fawzi interview. See also Oren, *Six Days of War*, 39.

[30] Rikhye, *The Sinai Blunder*, 19.

[31] Mohamed Gamasy, *The October War* (Cairo: AUC Press, 1993), 26.

[32] Brian Lapping Associates, *Fifty Years War*: Noufal interview.

[33] Rikhye, *The Sinai Blunder*, 19, 37. See also U Thant's 26 June 1967 "Report on the Withdrawal of UNEF," in *International Documents on Palestine, 1967* (Beirut: Institute for Palestine Studies, 1970), 211–15.

Because Amer seems to have been aware that the occupation of Sharm al-Sheikh would force the closure of the Tiran Straits, thus provoking Israel, this suggests that he – although not perhaps all of his fellow officers – may already have planned war in mid-May.[34]

Nasser, by contrast, was looking primarily to increase the political gains from his previous move. Amer and his military supporters saw Israel as the primary enemy, and their delusion that it was militarily inferior to Egypt was the key factor determining action. Nasser's calculations were more complex because his emphasis on the hostility of the United States caused him to pay greater attention to the global situation. Unlike Amer, who apparently never seriously considered the option of a partial UNEF withdrawal, Nasser was probably not committed to the occupation of Sharm al-Sheikh until at least 17 May, when U Thant refused to merely evacuate the border posts.[35] However, after that date, he must have approved it. Rikhye, in his discussions of the handover, communicated largely with General Fawzi, who was avowedly Nasser's man. At 2 P.M. on 17 May, Fawzi definitely confirmed that the UNEF had to withdraw from Sharm al-Sheikh within forty-eight hours. When Rikhye, hoping to delay the removal until U Thant arrived in Cairo, asked for three extra days, it was Fawzi who refused, but granted him until 22 May as an act of cooperation.[36] This particular date was almost certainly chosen because it was the day on which Nasser intended to announce the closure of the Gulf of Aqaba, which depended on an Egyptian military presence in Sharm al-Sheikh. It was therefore probably Nasser who gave the order.[37] Less than a week later, he claimed in a public speech to have been aware of all the implications: "Taking over Sharm al-Sheikh meant confrontation with Israel. It also meant that we were ready to enter a general war with Israel. It was not a separate operation."[38]

Step 3: Closing the Straits of Tiran

In retrospect, though, it was the next decision – to close the Gulf of Aqaba to Israeli access by controlling passage through the Tiran Straits, thus blockading the port of Eilat – that was to prove the most fateful. Egypt's formal decision was made on the morning of 22 May by a meeting

[34] Brian Lapping Associates, *Fifty Years War*: Noufal interview.
[35] Ibid., Fawzi interview.
[36] Rikhye, *The Sinai Blunder*, 49.
[37] Brian Lapping Associates, *Fifty Years War*: Badran interview.
[38] 26 May 1967, *Wathā'iq*, 180; *BBC Summary*, ME2477.

of the Supreme Executive Committee. A vote was taken, but only one representative voted against closure, citing economic concerns.[39] That evening, Nasser made a speech affirming "our rights and our sovereignty over the Gulf of Aqaba, which constitutes Egyptian territorial waters. Under no circumstances will we allow the Israeli flag to pass through the Gulf of Aqaba."[40]

On the following day, Cairo Radio added that the president had also banned "the passage of strategic materials through the Gulf to Israel even on non-Israeli ships." As far as the Israeli economy was concerned, the latter clause was much more important. Nasser may have avoided saying it, so as to leave room for manoeuvre. On the same day, however, Foreign Minister Riad confirmed the decision to newly arrived U.S. Ambassador Richard Nolte.[41] It was also falsely announced that the Tiran Straits had been mined in order to enforce the blockade.[42]

Some controversy exists regarding whether Egyptian decision makers believed this constituted a decision in favour of war. Israeli leaders had long reiterated that they would view the closure of the Gulf of Aqaba as a *casus belli*. Although only five Israeli vessels had passed through during the previous ten years, Cairo Radio's gloss on Nasser's announcement threatened Israeli oil importation, access to Africa and Asia, and most importantly, Israel's deterrent capacity. There was the obvious precedent of 1956, when the Aqaba blockade was a key cause of the Israeli attack. Officers in the Egyptian armed forces learned during training that Israel had laid down certain "red lines," the crossing of which would mean war, and this included the closure of the Tiran Straits.[43] Therefore, it seems certain that Nasser and Riad were being disingenuous when they expressed to U Thant on 24 May the belief that the Gulf of Aqaba was not really important to Israel.[44] According to two of those present at the 22 May meeting, Nasser said then that the blockade would make war 100 percent certain – although in his speech of 23 July, Nasser claimed his actual estimate at that time was 50 percent to 80 percent.[45]

---

[39] Sadat, *In Search of Identity*, 172.
[40] *Wathā'iq*, 175; *BBC Summary*, ME2473.
[41] *FRUS*, 40.
[42] Jeremy Bowen, *Six Days: How the 1967 War Shaped the Middle East* (London: Pocket Books, 2003), 51; Brian Lapping Associates, *Fifty Years War*: Noufal interview.
[43] Brian Lapping Associates, *Fifty Years War*: Fakhr interview. Sami Sharaf uses the same phrase, agreeing that the decision was known to make war inevitable. Author interviews with Sami Sharaf, Cairo, 28 March and 7 December 2004.
[44] Rikhye, *The Sinai Blunder*, 72; Parker, *The Politics of Miscalculation*, 228.
[45] Sadat, *In Search of Identity*, 172; Burdett, *Encounter with the Middle EAst*, 239; *BBC Summary*, ME2525.

The main reason for the Tiran blockade seems to have been the criticism directed at the Egyptian regime by the other Arab states. Amman Radio asked on 19 May: "Will Egypt restore its batteries and guns to close its territorial waters in the Tiran Strait to the enemy?... What would be Cairo's excuse if it fails to do so after the evacuation of the UN force from the area?"[46] Extravagant domestic propaganda had also gathered momentum and raised high expectations.[47] The losses of Suez had long rankled, and there was a deep desire to wipe them out. They endangered the myth that Israel had not been the victor, and they were seen as unfair.

Some observers believed that Nasser never wanted to close the Gulf of Aqaba but was forced into it by the occupation of Sharm al-Sheikh, which was in turn necessitated by the termination of the UNEF.[48] The regime's credibility was involved. As Amer protested at the meeting on 22 May, Egyptian troops could not simply sit in Sharm al-Sheikh and watch the Israeli flag go past.[49] However, even after the UNEF had been asked to leave, the possibility of a blockade was hardly mentioned in the Egyptian press until it became reality. Egyptian and Israeli sources assert that Amer told a group of officers in Sinai on 20 May that the straits would not be closed, which, even if he was lying, must have seemed plausible to his audience.[50] At his trial, Shams Badran also said that Amer had told him that dismissing the UNEF need not mean closing the Gulf. Moreover, to the extent that it was a significant factor, the link between occupying Sharm al-Sheikh and closing the Tiran Straits seems to have been acknowledged earlier in the policy process – implying that the decision was taken then, rather than arrived at by accident.[51] Nasser did not appear to feel trapped by the course of events. Badran has even claimed that "closing the Gulf was the main aim."[52]

It therefore appears that Nasser made a deliberate decision to blockade the Tiran Straits and run a high risk of war, and that decision must be explained. An important factor was the weak and apparently irresolute

---

[46] *BBC Summary*, ME2471.

[47] Walter Laqueur, *The Arab-Israel Reader: A Documentary History of the Middle East Conflict* (London: Weidenfeld and Nicolson, 1969), 90–1.

[48] Rikhye, *The Sinai Blunder*, 52; Brian Lapping Associates, *Fifty Years War*: Noufal interview.

[49] Parker, *The Politics of Miscalculation*, 75; author interview with Mohamed Fayek, Cairo, 25 March 2004; author interview with Ambassador Gamal Naguib, Cairo, 19 April 2004.

[50] Safran, *From War to War*, 288; Mahmoud Fawzi, *Thiwār yūlīyū yita haddithūn* [The July Revolutionaries Speak] (Cairo: Al-Zahra lil-I'lam al-Arabiyy, 1987), 177–8.

[51] Fawzi, *Harb al thalāth sanawāt*, 79–80.

[52] Brian Lapping Associates, *Fifty Years War*: Badran interview.

Israeli response to his previous provocations. In private, Eshkol had sent Nasser secret messages urging deescalation.[53] In public, he continued to assert Israel's peaceful intentions, call for international mediation, and avoid criticism of Egypt. This reinforced the existing image of Egyptian military superiority – if Israel wanted to avoid war, it was presumably because Israel thought it would lose, and if Israel relied on the international community, it must be too weak to stand alone. Nasser was therefore encouraged to believe Israel might not fight, especially if the United States urged a peaceful solution.[54] At the same time, other Arab states were seeking Nasser's leadership. Amer assured him that his armed forces were more than ready to confront Israel – or at least hold Israel off, pending great power intervention.[55]

Step 4: Escalation with No First Strike

Over the following fortnight, from 23 May until the outbreak of war on 5 June, the Egyptian leadership had three options. They could launch a first strike on Israel, continue to escalate the situation (forcing Israel either to attack first or to back down), or attempt to deescalate by making concessions to Israel. In the end, they seem to have chosen the second alternative. However, there are indications that the first was under consideration and was rejected. In the Sinai, there was deep confusion; as late as 5 June officers were still not sure whether their goal was offensive or defensive.[56] Nasser is said by some officers to have added to the chaos by his constant interference in military plans, while Amer was apparently surprised to learn from the commander of his field army "that his forces were not trained for offensive action."[57]

A number of senior Egyptian military figures have denied that there were ever any offensive plans beyond normal contingency scenarios.[58] It has been argued that the captured military documents put forward by the Israeli army as evidence of hostile intentions "are nothing more than the

[53] Ben D. Mor, "Nasser's Decision-Making in the 1967 Middle East Crisis: A Rational-Choice Explanation," *Journal of Peace Research* 28, no. 4 (1991), 371.

[54] Author interview with Yehia Gamal, Cairo, 18 April 2004.

[55] Sadat, *In Search of Identity*, 172.

[56] Gamasy, *The October War*, 23.

[57] Author interview with General Salah al-Din Hadidi, Cairo, 12 December 2004; Gamasy, *The October War*, 41.

[58] Author interview with General Salah al-Din Hadidi, Cairo, 12 December 2004; Brian Lapping Associates, *Fifty Years War*: Gamasy interview; Fawzi, *Thiwār yūlīyū*, 177.

kind of operational orders that any military staff prepares for possible operations."[59] This was also the impression of many outside observers at the time.[60] The contemporary U.S. documents uniformly confirm what Robert McNamara told Abba Eban on 26 May: "that three separate intelligence groups had looked into the matter in the last twenty-four hours and that our judgment was that Egyptian deployments made were defensive."[61]

Nasser openly informed U Thant, however, that the military command had been urging a first strike. Badran admitted as much at his trial.[62] The military command appears to have gone even further. The unfortunate Egyptian commanders were inflicted with "four plans in 20 days" during the 1967 crisis.[63] Replacing the established, defensive Conqueror plan as the troops moved into Sinai, Amer apparently introduced the offensive Operation Lion, which involved an attack on the Israeli port of Eilat and part of the Negev.[64] After the closure of the Tiran Straits, he seems to have broadened his objectives to include the entire Negev, with Operation Dawn and Operation Dusk, the orders for which were to be issued directly from Amer's own house.[65] On approximately 20 May, Saad al-Din Shazly, commander of a Special Forces unit in the Sinai, was given an offensive mission plan involving an advance through Israel.[66] The Voice of the Arabs radio station had also been preparing for a war since 20 May, when it had been ordered to "heat it up." Five days later, Amer told the presenter Ahmed Said that an Egyptian first strike was imminent, and the radio station needed to be prepared to relocate if its transmitters were targeted.[67] As late as 25 May, therefore, everything was set for an attack at daybreak on 27 May.[68]

At a meeting at military headquarters on 25 May, Amer failed to convince Nasser of the case for the offensive operation, necessitating

---

[59] C. Ernest Dawn, "The Egyptian Remilitarisation of Sinai," *Journal of Contemporary History* 3, no. 3 (1968), 201.

[60] Bowen, *Six Days*, 57; *FRUS*, 28.

[61] *FRUS*, 77. See also William Quandt, *Decade of Decisions: American Policy Towards the Arab-Israeli Conflict, 1967–1977* (Berkeley: University of California Press, 1977), 49.

[62] Burdett, *Encounter with the Middle East*, 241.

[63] Fawzi, *Harb al thalāth sanawāt*, 111.

[64] Ibid., 99–104.

[65] Ibid., 109; Oren, *Six Days of War*, 92.

[66] Author interview with Marshal Saad El-Din Shazly, Cairo, 13 December 2004.

[67] Author interview with Ahmed Said, Cairo, 20 December 2004; 2 August 2003, *Al-Bayan* (UAE), 20.

[68] Fawzi, *Harb al thalāth sanawāt*, 113.

a change of plan.[69] Even then, Amer may not have complied with the president's order immediately – on 26 May Nasser and Amer were not on speaking terms.[70] It was only one hour before the planned strike on 27 May that Said's army liaison officer told him the attack had been aborted after a U.S. request to the Soviets. Shazly was not informed of the shift to a defensive posture until about 1 June.[71] Although Nasser reiterated that Egypt would not strike first, tanks and planes in the Sinai were fully fuelled and not concealed, as if they were going to attack, implying that "the political decision did not match with the military one.[72] But eventually, according to Badran, "the situation was turned from attacking to defence," which was fundamentally the cause of all the confusion.[73]

Fawzi implies that Amer and his faction made their plans independently, and that these were not revealed to Nasser until the major showdown during the 25 May meeting, which was followed by a private session between the two leaders.[74] This seems plausible given the evidence that Nasser and Amer were on poor terms on 26 May, and it supports the testimony of Bassiouny, who recalls that when the Washington Embassy reported that Secretary of State Dean Rusk had information that Egypt was going to start the war, Amer wrote on the cable, "Shams, it seems there is a leak." According to an assistant in the secretariat of the presidency, Nasser commented on the behaviour of Amer in these words: "Why is 'Amr upset? Does he think that we shall start the war?"[75]

Abdel Magid Farid, however, suggests that Nasser did actually consider the first strike option until early on 27 May, when he was hauled out of bed at 3 A.M. by the ambassador from the Soviet Union (his only source of arms and spare parts) and warned not to precipitate a confrontation.[76] Some historians go further, suggesting that Nasser was

[69] Gamasy, *The October War*, 42. Confirmed by author interviews with Sami Sharaf, Cairo, 28 March and 7 December 2004, and Mohamed Fayek, Cairo, 25 March 2004.

[70] Oren, *Six Days of War*, 120; Brian Lapping Associates, *Fifty Years War*: Bassiouny interview.

[71] Author interviews with Ahmed Said, Cairo, 20 December 2004, and Saad El-Din Shazly, Cairo, 13 December 2004.

[72] Brian Lapping Associates, *Fifty Years War*: Fawzi, Shazly, and Fakhr interviews.

[73] Ibid., Badran interview.

[74] Ibid., Fawzi interview; Fawzi, *Harb al thalāth sanawāt*, 113–14. See also Bowen, *Six Days*, 57.

[75] L. Carl Brown, "Origins of the Crisis," in *The Six-Day War: A Retrospective*, ed. Richard B. Parker (Gainesville: University of Florida, 1996), 44–5; Brian Lapping Associates, *Fifty Years War*: Bassiouny interview.

[76] Author interview with Abdel Magid Farid, London, 14 June 2004; Robert Stephens, *Nasser: A Political Biography* (London: Penguin, 1971), 484.

fully aware of Operation Dawn from the outset but preferred to overlook it, cancelling it at the very last moment only because he took the Soviet warning to prove that Israel had accessed Egyptian military secrets.[77] Although Nasser gave Amer much latitude, it seems unlikely that he was prepared to allow him to start a war without taking at least a passing interest, and other evidence suggests that he never had any intention of striking first.

All of Nasser's plans depended on the assumption that the Israelis would strike the first blow. The president rejected the first strike option as politically impossible because he thought it would give the United States and Israel the very pretext for which they were looking.[78] International opinion would be alienated, the Soviets might withdraw their support, and the United States could enter the war on Israel's side. When Nasser met his military commanders on 2 June, he told Air Force Chief Sidqi Mahmoud that Egypt had to wait for Israel to attack:

Sidqi just said "Sir," he said it in English, "it will be crippling to me." . . . Abdel Hakim Amer looked at Sidqi and said, "Sidqi, do you accept the first attack or do you want to fight the United States?"[79]

By this time, therefore, Amer had accepted the political parameters within which Nasser was working, especially his expectations of the United States.[80] Badran also says that he tried to persuade Amer to allow a small first strike in order to provoke a war, but Amer unwillingly refused because of the president's policy imperatives, replying, "I wish [I could] but I can't do that, I am obliged with a policy and it's the policy that the President does and I can't do anything about it."[81]

If the Egyptian regime had no intention of attacking first, neither did it make any great effort to defuse tensions with Israel. Though there were some minor concessions, Mohamed Fayek's claim that Nasser "tried by all means to solve this problem politically" is certainly exaggerated.[82] In addition to the reiterated promise not to fire the first shot, Nasser agreed with U Thant to accept a two-week moratorium on action in

---

[77] Oren, *Six Days of War*, 120.
[78] Author interview with Mohamed Fayek, Cairo, 25 March 2004.
[79] Brian Lapping Associates, *Fifty Years War*: Badran interview. But there are conflicting accounts. Salah Nasr claims Nasser promised the air force the chance of a first strike, then later ordered Sami Sharaf to destroy the tape of the meeting. Tariq Habib, *Milaffat thawrat yūlīyū* [The July Revolution Files] (Cairo: Al-Ahram, 1997), 338–9; Salah Nasr, *Mudhakkirāt*, vol. 3 [Memoirs] (Cairo: Dar al-Khiyal, 1999), 227.
[80] Author interview with Abdel Magid Farid, London, 14 June 2004.
[81] Brian Lapping Associates, *Fifty Years War*: Badran interview.
[82] Author interview with Mohamed Fayek, Cairo, 25 March 2004.

the Straits if Israel did the same and to refer the issue of passage to
the International Court of Justice – neither of which was acceptable to
Israel. On 24 May, he seems to have sent an extremely indirect message
to Johnson, emphasizing "that this matter would soon be terminated
without any fighting" and begging him to take no action.[83] More significantly, on 3 June, the U.S. envoy Charles Yost and Foreign Minister Riad
set a date for the U.S. government to receive a visit from Vice President
Zakaria Mohieddin. This seems to have revived the hope in Egypt that
the superpowers might compel Israel to accept the situation and lead to
a military relaxation. Gamal Naguib began preparing the passports on 3
June and still had them on his desk two days later, when he was startled
out of his optimism by news of the Israeli offensive.[84] General Noufal
reports that it was also on 3 June that "we were ordered to de-escalate
and to get back to our offices."[85]

Nasser's small concessions do not suggest that he was making a concerted effort to avoid war. The appearance of reasonableness kept the
international community from turning against him, while every delay
was to his advantage because it gave Egypt time to complete its military
preparations and coordinate with the other Arabs. Israel, by contrast,
could not afford to sustain total mobilization for long. Nasser made use
of belligerent rhetoric to escalate the situation still further, by making the
issue in his public speeches about the rights of Palestine – and thus, implicitly, the existence of Israel. On 22 May, he suggested that peace could
not mean ignoring "the rights of the Palestinian people" and announced
to the Jews: "you are welcome, we are ready for war."[86] Although all of
these threats were explicitly conditional on Israeli aggression, this could
have been small comfort when Nasser was also stating that "the existence
of Israel is in itself an aggression."[87] Moreover, Nasser crossed another
of Israel's "red lines" on 30 May, when he signed a Joint Defence Agreement with Jordan, which Shimon Peres said was the key factor in Israel's
decision to fight because it raised the prospect of encirclement: "we were
now surrounded by a sort of banana filled with Russian weapons."[88]

---

[83] *FRUS*, 78.

[84] Author interview with Gamal Naguib, Cairo, 19 April 2004.

[85] Brian Lapping Associates, *Fifty Years War*: Noufal interview.

[86] *Wathā'iq*, 1, 175; *BBC Summary*, ME2473. See also *Wathā'iq*, 192, 224; U Thant, *International Documents on Palestine*, 553, 579.

[87] Raymond Cohen, *Culture and Conflict in Egyptian-Israeli Relations: A Dialogue of the Deaf* (Bloomington: Indiana University Press, 1990), 105; *Wathā'iq*, 203; U Thant, *International Documents on Palestine*, 562.

[88] Quoted in Randolph and Winston Churchill, *The Six Day War* (London: Heinemann, 1967), 60.

But did Nasser actually expect war? He seems, throughout, to have been of two minds on this issue, making contradictory statements. Rikhye, meeting him on 24 May, thought Nasser believed Israel would not fight without U.S. help, which would not be forthcoming.[89] Fayek claims that the president already expected war at this stage, and Nasser's confidant Heikal proclaimed the inevitability of an armed clash with Israel in *Al-Ahram* on 26 May, recommending that Egypt should wait to receive the first blow.[90] However, he later stated that this was not then Nasser's own opinion, arguing that the president planned to "make intense political efforts to prevent the outbreak of military operations" the probability of which he believed "would reduce with time," as it had with Suez in 1956.[91] At his 28 May press conference, Nasser said that he expected an Israeli attack "daily."[92] But two days later, King Hussein received the impression that Nasser did not want war and did not believe it would happen.[93]

General agreement exists that on 2 June, following the Israeli Cabinet reshuffle, Nasser concluded that war was certain, telling a meeting of the Supreme Command that he expected an attack on the air force on Monday, 5 June.[94] He made the same prediction to other regime members that day. Ali Sabri passed the warning on to the provincial governors whose territories bordered Israel on 3 June, although he does not appear to have informed them of the exact date.[95] This warning has been the subject of some controversy because it seems, on the face of it, incompatible with the demonstrable fact that Egyptian forces were taken entirely by surprise when it proved accurate. For instance, Amer and his senior officers were actually in a plane on the way to the front at the time of the invasion. The explanation appears to have been that the military command did not take Nasser's prediction seriously or did not pass it on to the lower ranks.[96] Amer scoffed to General Murtagi that Nasser, who had been so badly caught out in 1956, "had no transparent soul that

[89] Rikhye, *The Sinai Blunder*, 77.
[90] Author interview with Mohamed Fayek, Cairo, 25 March 2004; 2 June 1967, *BBC Summary*, ME2482.
[91] Heikal, *Li-misr*, 118; Stephens, *Nasser*, 481.
[92] *Wathā'iq*, 203; U Thant, *International Documents on Palestine*, 562.
[93] Hussein of Jordan, *My "War" with Israel* (London: Peter Owen, 1969), 49; Brian Lapping Associates, *Fifty Years War*: Hussein interview.
[94] 23 July 1967, *BBC Summary*, ME2525; Sadat, *In Search of Identity*, 174; Brian Lapping Associates, *Fifty Years War*: Fawzi interview.
[95] Author interview with Governor Hamed Mahmoud, 24 March 2004.
[96] Brian Lapping Associates, *Fifty Years War*: Noufal, Badran, and Fawzi interviews.

would enable him to foresee the future."[97] Amer's own information from Military Intelligence, which had long been engineered to serve the interests of particular groups within the armed forces and hence bought into the myth of Egyptian military superiority, did not lead him to expect war so soon.[98]

Nasser seems not to have been consistently sure whether a war would occur. He changed his mind frequently but not his policies, because, in one sense, the question was unimportant. If war did break out, he believed that "the Egyptian armed forces would be capable of entering a prolonged defensive battle," which "would create a crisis of global confrontation." There would be pressure for an early cease-fire, along the lines of 1956.[99] But if there were no war, Nasser would have achieved a great symbolic triumph for Arabism and regained sovereignty over the Tiran Straits. He expected a political victory in either case.

Nasser's confidence was founded not only on the belief, inspired by Amer, that the Arabs were militarily capable of holding their own against Israel, but also on his perceptions of the international situation. In particular, his expectation of the stance that the Soviet Union would take is crucial to explaining his image of the degree of threat from the United States. Minister of War Shams Badran is alleged to have given Nasser the false impression, returning from a mission to Moscow, that the Soviet Union would provide Egypt with military support if Israel attacked first.[100] Nasser's speech of 26 May certainly might be interpreted as expressing this opinion, which seems to have been prevalent in Cairo. However, it is unlikely that Nasser believed it for long. As he implied at his 28 May press conference, he knew that in such a case the United States would also intervene, perhaps resulting in a direct superpower confrontation. Therefore he suggested that "if war breaks out between Israel alone and

---

[97] Fawzi, *Thiwār yūlīyū*, 174; Mohammed Elwi-Saif, "Nasser's Perception of 1967 Crisis," paper presented at a conference on the United States, the Middle East and the 1967 Arab-Israeli War, U.S. State Department, 12–13 January, 2004, Washington, DC, 22.

[98] Military Intelligence reports are said to have predicted no war on 21 May and only a limited attack on Sharm al-Sheikh aimed at opening the Gulf of Aqaba on 27–28 May. Until 4 June, they continued to rule out the possibility of a full-scale Israeli attack. Elwi-Saif, "Nasser's Perception of 1967 Crisis," 22–3; Author interviews with Sami Sharaf, Cairo, 28 March and 7 December 2004.

[99] Heikal, *Li-misr*, 118; Author interviews with Mohamed Fayek, 25 March 2004; General Ahmed Abdel Halim, 1 April 2004; and Dr. Hoda Abdel Nasser, 1 March 2004 (all in Cairo); Said Aburish, *Nasser: The Last Arab* (Duckworth, UK: London, 2004), 259.

[100] Brian Lapping Associates, *Fifty Years War*: Badran and Fawzi interviews; author interview with Ambassador Mourad Ghalib, Cairo, 19 December 2004.

us alone, I think that it will be restricted to this area."[101] The truth appears to be that although Badran may have embellished a polite Soviet assurance of solidarity and passed it on to Nasser in time to influence his 26 May speech, Deputy Foreign Minister Ahmed Hassan Feki gave the president the true picture that very evening.[102]

Nasser was not, thereafter, relying on the Soviet Union to do more than deter American intervention. King Hussein told a U.S. representative on 31 May that the Egyptian president seemed confident that if the United States took "aggressive action" against Egypt, the Soviet Union would provide "the required support."[103] The Soviet Union did make some moves in this direction, for example, by moving additional naval units to the eastern Mediterranean. Because Nasser knew that the two superpowers had been in touch at the highest levels since 22 May in order to avoid misunderstanding, this action may also have affected his calculations insofar as it seemed indicative of a lowered Soviet estimation of the probability of U.S. intervention.[104]

Nasser's judgement that the Soviet Union would deter U.S. intervention also made it seem less likely that Israel, viewed primarily as a proxy of the United States, would act independently. This was partly because it was not perceived to be strong enough, and partly because Nasser assumed it would follow U.S. orders.[105] From this perspective, the fact that the United States was emphasizing a diplomatic approach, if it could be taken at face value, must also suggest that Israel would not strike first. However, Nasser had an established view of the United States as deeply hostile towards him personally. Therefore, he did not take its signals at face value and did not rule out the possibility of an Israeli strike. His suspicion was reinforced by indications from the American side, such as Richard Nolte's estimate that the chances of Israeli attack were about fifty-fifty and the report that President Johnson had told his aides: "Israel

[101] *Wathā'iq*, 195; U Thant, *International Documents on Palestine*, 555.

[102] Nasr, *Mudhakkirāt*, vol. 3, 219–20; A. Imam, *'Abd al-nā sir: kayf hakama misr?* [Nasser: How Did he Govern Egypt?] (Cairo: Madbouli al-Saghir, 1996), 362; author interview with Ambassador Mohammed Abdel Wahab, Cairo, 30 March 2004; Brian Lapping Associates, *Fifty Years War*: Bassiouny interview; Brown, "Origins of the Crisis," 44. See also Mohammed Hassanein Heikal, *Nasser: The Cairo Documents* (London: New English Library, 1972), 219; author interview with Ambassador Mourad Ghalib, Cairo, 19 December 2004.

[103] *FRUS*, 107n2.

[104] Safran, *From War to War*, 296–7.

[105] *FRUS*, 107n2.

will hit them."[106] However, so deeply ingrained were his assumptions of American hostility and Israeli dependency that these were seen as indications of U.S. hypocrisy rather than a genuine inability to dictate to the Jewish state.[107]

Other factors were also interpreted within the Egyptian regime as further indications of Israeli weakness. The generals seemed to believe that indications of a possible strike by Israel were "only display."[108] Nasser seems to have been encouraged by the fact that Israeli rhetoric condemning the Tiran blockade and subsequent developments was relatively mild.[109] Even the fact that the United States counselled restraint was interpreted as an attempt to protect Israel from Arab wrath – and therefore as further evidence of her need for protection. This Egyptian attitude was fundamentally based on a belief in Israeli military inferiority. Nolte sent a U.S. embassy telegram on 27 May, explaining that Nasser "appears sincerely to believe Egyptians can beat Israelis if we do not intervene and his estimate is shared by every official Egyptian we have talked to."[110] Other foreign observers also noted the confidence of the ruling elite.[111]

The War

When Israel at last launched its attack on Egypt on the morning of Monday, 5 June, the effect was devastating. Most of the Egyptian air force was destroyed within a few hours. Amer, contrary to existing plans, ordered an immediate retreat from the Sinai Peninsula, which rapidly became a rout. By 8 June, the entire Sinai had been occupied. The Egyptian government

---

[106] Riad, *The Struggle for Peace*, 21.

[107] Although Nasser certainly overestimated U.S. control over Israeli foreign policy, there also may have been a few mixed signals and an American tendency not to enquire too closely into Israeli plans. See Avi Shlaim, *The Iron Wall: Israel and the Arab World* (London: Penguin, 2000), 241; Quandt, *Decade of Decisions*, 3; David A. Korn, *Stalemate: The War of Attrition and Great Power Diplomacy in the Middle East, 1967–1970* (Boulder, CO: Westview, 1992), 17–18; Robert McNamara, "Britain, Nasser and the Outbreak of the Six-Day War," *Journal of Contemporary History* 35, no. 4 (2000), 634–8; Robert McNamara, *Britain, Nasser and the Balance of Power in the Middle East* (London: Frank Cass, 2003), 257.

[108] Author interview with Mohammed Abdel Wahab, Cairo, 30 March 2004.

[109] Michael Brecher and Benjamin Geist, *Decisions in Crisis* (Berkeley: University of California Press, 1980), 149, 346.

[110] Parker, *The Politics of Miscalculation*, 242.

[111] Ibid., 224, 235–8; National Archive, Kew: FCO39/250; *FRUS*, 100, 129.

agreed to a cease-fire late that evening. No one in Egypt had expected such a disaster. Nasser, who later described the immediate aftermath of the war as "one continuous nightmare," was overcome by the shock.[112] "We were in a state of confusion, uncertainty and doubt," he recalled. "We did not know, but we feared what the Israelis were going to do."[113] One Egyptian diplomat remembers seeing the president walking in his garden just before the cease-fire, stooped over like a broken man.[114] On 9 June, Nasser publicly resigned his office. "His face was pale," remembers Amin Howeidy, who saw him shortly afterwards. "His eyes were wide open and staring straight ahead."[115] Even then, he failed to comprehend the full scale of the defeat and talked of settling various issues "after the withdrawal," assuming it would follow the Suez pattern.[116]

During the war, Cairo Radio announced that American and British planes were participating in the Israeli attack. Nasser broke off diplomatic relations following this allegation, although it is unclear whether he actually believed it. Abdul Latif Baghdadi, who was in Marshal Amer's office on the morning of 5 June, suggests that the president may have been misinformed by Amer, who was in turn given inaccurate data by Mahmoud, the air force chief.[117] More missions were flown, in a shorter time, than Egypt had thought the Israelis could manage. Nasser's initial response was incredulous. "I will only believe the United States took part if I am shown the wreckage of an American plane," he said angrily, leaving the room. "Unless you can do that I will not accept it." By mid-June, however, Egyptian embassies worldwide were busily issuing "proofs" of Western intervention. Most Egyptian sources suggest Nasser's change of mind was genuine, and it is true that his image of the United States was such that he might well have believed the worst. However, Sadat implies that Nasser only rethought Amer's charge when he realized the magnitude of the disaster, accusing the United States as a political cover-up for domestic consumption.[118] This was also the interpretation of contemporary observers in the United States and the Soviet Union. The case

---

[112] Anthony Nutting, *Nasser* (London: Constable, 1972), 430.
[113] *FRUS*, 500.
[114] Author interview with Mohammed Abdel Wahab, Cairo, 30 March 2004.
[115] Quoted in Bowen, *Six Days*, 290.
[116] Heikal, *Sphinx and Commissar*, 190.
[117] Abdel Latif Baghdadi, *Mudhakkirāt*, vol. 2 [Memoirs] (Cairo: Al-Maktab al-Hadith, 1977), 284–9.
[118] Sadat, *In Search of Identity*, 175.

for deliberate conspiracy is partially supported by Nasser's conversation with King Hussein during the fighting, monitored by Israel:

By God, I say that I will make an announcement and you will make an announcement and we will see to it that the Syrians make an announcement that American and British airplanes are taking part against us from aircraft carriers.[119]

It seems on balance that Nasser believed in the active participation of Western planes only briefly, if at all. However, he saw this as unimportant when set against his deep belief in "imperialist collusion" with Israel.[120] He told Sadat on 9 June that the scenario prepared by the United States and Israel had been carried out "meticulously."[121]

The Consequences

In the longer term, the disaster had a devastating effect on Egyptian morale. Some suggest Nasser was never the same – that he became "a different man" with "a deep scar on his soul."[122] "His hair quickly turned white," wrote Agriculture Minister Sayyid Mar'i, "the spark disappeared from his eyes and he was full of bitterness."[123] There was an immediate regime crisis, in the course of which Badran and Mohieddin were named as possible successors to the presidency.[124] "They'll put me on trial," Nasser told Minister of Information Mohamed Fayek shortly before his resignation broadcast "and hang me in the middle of Cairo."[125]

In the event, Nasser's speech taking full responsibility for the "setback" provoked a massive popular response. The Egyptian people begged him to stay and save them. The remnants of a dangerously discontented army were confined to barracks. Although Amer, who was blamed for the defeat, refused to retire gracefully and his effective patronage structure meant that he retained substantial support among the military,

---

[119] Randolph Churchill and Winston Churchill, *The Six Day War*, 90.

[120] See Abdel Magid Farid, *Nasser: The Final Years* (Reading, UK: Ithaca, 1994), 19; National Archive: FCO17/598.

[121] Sadat, *In Search of Identity*, 175.

[122] Brian Lapping Associates, *Fifty Years War*: Hussein interview; Heikal, *Nasser*, 39; Farid, *Nasser*, 1.

[123] Sayyid Mar'i, *Awrāq siyāsiyya* [Political Papers] (Cairo: 1978), 520.

[124] See Brian Lapping Associates, *Fifty Years War*: Badran and Fawzi interviews; Robert Springborg, *Family, Power and Politics in Egypt* (Philadelphia: University of Pennsylvania Press, 1982) 175; author interview with Dia al-Din Dawud, Cairo, 24 March 2004.

[125] Quoted in Bowen, *Six Days*, 291.

Nasser's backers moved effectively to undermine him. He was placed under house arrest in August and apparently committed suicide soon afterwards. Nasser's much-vaunted grief did not prevent him from taking the opportunity to consolidate control over the army. Amer's supporters were dismissed or imprisoned. Defence Minister Badran, Head of General Intelligence Salah Nasr, and Interior Minister Fathi Radwan were arrested that autumn on suspicion of subversion. The Egyptian military establishment possessed a special status as the founding power of the regime, and Amer's strength had been grounded in its fundamental legitimacy as much as its influence was based on his special access to the president.[126] This legitimacy, however, had been severely damaged by the comprehensive defeat. Popular respect for the army plummeted. Soldiers were mocked in the streets. A joke current in Egypt at that time recounts,

A young lieutenant in a hurry ran after one of Cairo's crowded buses and just managed to get in when he was flung into the lap of an old woman who held him by the shoulder and said tenderly: "Hi sonny, still running?"[127]

In some respects Nasser's position had become less and less secure. Even when he withdrew his resignation in response to popular demand, he felt the need to emphasize that his return to office was conditional and limited.[128] According to Farid, Nasser "became more inclined to consult those around him, even summoning senior army officers and influential government officials who had long since retired."[129]

The structure of the Egyptian regime also changed substantially. There were increased internal divisions between the pro-Western right and the pro-Soviet left. The necessity for increased Soviet assistance to rebuild the armed forces enhanced the power of the left-wing figurehead, Ali Sabri. On the right, even Heikal's *Al-Ahram* became less wholehearted in its endorsement of government policy.[130] There was growing support for the Palestinian *fedayeen*, in defiance of government policy. It was at

---

[126] Shaheen Ayubi, *Nasser and Sadat: Decision-making and Foreign Policy, 1970–1972* (Washington, DC: University Press of America, 1994), 15; author interview with Vice-President Hussein Shafei, Cairo, 11 December 2004; S. Imam, *Husayn al-shāfiʿi wa asrār thawrat yūlīyū wa hukm al-sadāt* [Hussein Shafei and the Sources of the July Revolution and the Rule of Sadat] (Cairo: Maktab Awziris lil-Kutub wa al-Magalat, 1993), 119.

[127] Khalid Kishtainy, *Arab Political Humour* (London: Quartet Books, 1985), 157.

[128] 9 May 67, *BBC Summary*, ME2488.

[129] Farid, *Nasser*, 2.

[130] Sonia Dabous, "Nasser and the Egyptian Press," in *Contemporary Egypt: Through Egyptian Eyes*, ed. Charles Tripp (London: Routledge, 1993), 100.

this juncture that the trend of support for Islamist movements began to become more pronounced in Egypt, in response to the perceived failure of the Arab nationalist experiment.

By early 1968, escalating unrest and student riots forced the government to promise greater representation in the "30 March Programme."[131] Meanwhile, the economic situation continued to deteriorate. Egypt had been saddled with an unserviceable foreign debt estimated at $2 billion even before the war.[132] The new loss of revenue from the Suez Canal, the Sinai oil fields, and tourism was only partially made good by Arab aid. Moreover, receipt of this subsidy from Kuwait, Libya, and Saudi Arabia depended on Egypt's continuation of the fight against Israel.

The international environment was also transformed. In the atmosphere of acute crisis, friendships and enmities became starker. Nasser "tried to promote more harmonious relations" with the Arab monarchies after the war, recalls the diplomat Mohamed Riad. "He felt that as there was an outside threat he should not quarrel with other Arab countries."[133] There were fewer causes of dissension, given that Nasser was no longer able to claim overall Arab leadership. Consequently, he developed a close alliance with King Hussein of Jordan, with both seeking to pursue a relatively moderate policy towards Israel in order to regain their occupied territories. Saudi-Egyptian relations also improved to some extent. In Europe, France was now seen as friendly, and over time, there were even substantial improvements in the Anglo-Egyptian relationship. Whether friendly or hostile, however, these countries all increasingly seemed less significant. As a result of the June 1967 War, Egypt's focus on the principal enemies had narrowed: Israel, the "Zionist" occupier of Arab territory, and the United States, its "imperialist" protector. But, paradoxically, it was this withdrawal from the field of Arab competition that ultimately enabled Nasser's successor, Anwar Sadat, to come to a rapprochement with the United States and Israel – which endures to this day.

---

[131] Mar'i, *Awrāq siyāsiyya*, vol. 3, 570; Mohammed Hassanein Heikal, *Autumn of Fury* (London: Andre Deutsch, 1983), 114.

[132] *FRUS*, 299.

[133] N. Frankel, "Interviews with Ismail Fahmy, Ashraf Ghorbal and Mohamed Riad," *American Arab Affairs* 31 (1990), 97.

3

Syria

Playing With Fire

David W. Lesch

In many ways, the 1967 Arab-Israeli war is still being fought in the Middle East today. This is especially true for Syria, where one cannot engage in any sort of political discussion without soon venturing into the subject of the Golan Heights, the swath of territory Syria lost to Israel in the 1967 conflagration. The essence of Syrian foreign policy today, as it has been for more than four decades, is the return of the Golan Heights to the 4 June 1967 line, the Syrian-Israeli border before the war commenced. It is an emotional issue in Syria; one that has been drummed into the minds of Syrians for two generations. No Syrian leader can enter into a peace agreement with Israel without demanding the return of the Golan.

The role Syria played before the war was critical to its outbreak. Without the Syrian prelude, the war would probably not have occurred or played out in the manner it did. Syria has often been criticized for building up the tension at the inter-Arab and the Arab-Israeli levels, to the point where the two became inextricably intertwined. This brought about the conditions in which Gamal Abdel Nasser felt compelled to follow the fateful path towards the brink of war. For the most part, this criticism is legitimate, although this does not absolve other critical players, primarily Egypt, Israel, and the Soviet Union from their roles in the drama, as they also heightened tensions with opportunism and miscalculation. But it is even more complicated. Why did Syria play the role of agent provocateur in the Arab-Israeli arena? What were the aims of the leadership in Damascus? Did Syria want a confrontation with Israel? This was a time fraught with divisiveness within the politico-military regime. The regional foreign policy that Damascus employed prior to the war contributed to

Syria's loss of the Golan Heights during the war, and it has shaped the nature of Syrian foreign, if not domestic, policy ever since.

The Ba'th Directive

There had been an Arab cold war since the mid-1950s. However, its nature in Syria changed in March 1963, when the Ba'th Party, long an instrumental player in Syrian politics and foreign-policy orientation, captured power in a coup. The very existence of Israel was anathema to the Ba'th. The Ba'th Party's Syrian founders, namely, Michel Aflaq and Salah al-Din Bitar, had cultural roots in the Marxist milieu of the 1930s Sorbonne. They were imbued with antiimperialism as well as doctrinaire socialism. The Ba'th Party slogan of "freedom, unity, and socialism" betrayed the domestic as well as foreign-policy applications of Ba'thist ideology. *Unity* in this sense meant Arab unity, a necessity to fight off the pernicious advances of European imperialism and, during the post–World War II period, the Cold War interference of the superpowers.

Israel was viewed as a wedge to Arab unification, the culmination of which would be an Arab nation united under one flag, leadership, and ideological structure; this would remake the Arab world into the global force. Western imperialism had, in the Ba'th perspective, planted Israel in the heartland of the Arab world, perhaps with the primary objective of keeping the Arabs divided. Thus it would be easy to blame Israel for continued Arab divisiveness during the 1950s and early 1960s, a good portion of which had, in reality, little to do with Israel. One of the main prescriptions for curing the Arab world's weakness brought about by its divisiveness was simply the elimination of Israel. Just as the Prophet Muhammad had used Islam to unite the Arabs during the seventh century into a formidable force of change, so would Ba'thism unite the Arab world during the twentieth century. The goal was to transform the artificial Western constructs called nation-states into a force even more powerful than that which a mere religious-based movement could create.

The immediate aftermath of the 1963 coup was the "volcanic" period of the Ba'thist revolution. Especially, and perhaps unexpectedly, coming on the heels of a Ba'th coup in Iraq in February 1963, Ba'thists everywhere saw this series of events as a portent of things to come. It was a revolutionary period that withstood the setbacks of the failed unification talks with Nasser, persistent intraparty divisions, and political immaturity. As with any revolutionary period, at least in the eyes of those leading it, it was time for aggressive implementation of policy on the domestic and regional levels. It was not today's Ba'th Party in Syria, which is but a shell of its former self, a moribund state vessel through which power is articulated and from which power is co-opted.

The division and internal struggles of the Ba'th Party are the key to understanding Syria's role in the outbreak of the 1967 Arab-Israeli war. The political tumult in Syria fuelled a growing Israeli concern that unpredictability in Damascus would generate an erratic, yet aggressive foreign policy aimed at the Jewish state. Israeli journalist Ze'ev Schiff, who had close ties with the Israeli defence establishment, commented in 1966 that Syria was ruled by "unregulated Arab gangs. Even when there is a chance of reaching an arrangement along the border, we do not know if the person talking with us today will be there tomorrow to fulfil his promises. Syria is dragging Israel into war."[1]

The Ba'thists were relatively unknown commodities in Syria, and it seemed they had to either fight off Nasserist coup attempts, as happened in July 1963, or keep a wary eye on their supposed Arab nationalists compatriots who, according to the Ba'thists, had too easily accommodated themselves to the forces of reaction. Others suspicious of the Ba'th and its anticapitalist policies were the Sunni bourgeoisie and traditional landowning families in Syria who had agitated for the breakup of Nasser's United Arab Republic (UAR) in 1961. The early to mid-1960s was a conspiratorial period in Syria. It was not a political climate that bred calm and stability but rather bred paranoia among the would-be and actual leadership groups. Pitted against the Nasserists and the "reactionaries" (such as the pro-West monarchies of Saudi Arabia and Jordan), the Ba'th Party in Syria succeeded in surviving, but in doing so it also succeeded in isolating its own country from much of the rest of the Arab world.

Within the Ba'th Party there were splits between the Military Committee and the civilian leadership, older and younger party members, rural peasant and urban intellectual party members, and minority groups based on tribal and regional ties. Some of these divisions manifested in the different policy priorities of the Ba'th Party Regional Command and the National Command, in theory the overarching ruling Ba'th organ that included Iraq as well as party branches in other Arab countries.[2] The

---

[1] Quoted in Tom Segev, *1967: Israel, the War, and the Year that Transformed the Middle East* (New York: Metropolitan Books, 2005), 191–2.

[2] The shift in power in Syria from the National Command to the Regional Command can be traced back to a Regional Command Ba'th Party congress of September 1963 and a National Command Ba'th Party congress meeting the following month, when the party's founders, Aflaq and Bitar, were marginalized in the Regional Command. They

differences were in some cases ideologically based, but they were also often based on power, ambition, and personal jealousies. It is not the purpose of this chapter to examine the nature of these multidimensional cleavages, but to comment on the effects these divisions had on the Arab-Israeli front.[3] Remarking on the directional shifts within the Ba'th Party, historian Malcolm Kerr wrote in 1971:

[They] were united by impatience with [Syrian President Amin al-] Hafiz's half-hearted continuation of [Syrian Prime Minister Salah al-Din] Bitar's devious approach to inter-Arab affairs; they blamed Hafiz for his willingness to go along with the Egyptian-sponsored [Arab League] summit meetings instead of unequiv-ocally pressing for militancy toward both Israel and the Arab monarchies. They had no interest in courting Cairo's favour, and indeed there was more than a trace among them of Chinese-like contempt for 'Abd al-Nasir's Soviet-style espousal of peaceful coexistence. Although Ba'thists, they had left behind them the misty *Volksgeist* nationalism of Aflaq and Bitar and indeed the whole preoccupation with Arab unity which had dominated Ba'thist ideology from the beginning, and had become Marxist social radicals committed to the class struggle.[4]

The culmination of this intra-Ba'th struggle was the intra-Ba'th coup of 23 February 1966, the ninth time in the past seventeen years that the Syrian government had been overthrown by force. It was the result of a winnowing process of radicalization within Ba'th Party politics that was intimately tied to the military through the Military Committee of the Ba'th Party ruling apparatus. The rivalries were marked by a combina-tion of holier-than-thou political mantras and actions on the domestic and foreign-policy fronts. Syrian leaders built alliances with military fac-tions based on sectarian, tribal, and regional ties in attempts to isolate other factions. There were thus frequent purges within the military estab-lishment, especially in the officer corps, during the period preceding the outbreak of the 1967 war. As sectarianism was believed to be detrimental to the welfare of the state and of the Ba'th Party, it was intensely frowned

---

were replaced by younger officers of rural, peasant origins, many of whom were Alawite or Druze, including the Alawite Major-General Salah Jadid, who would become the strongman in Syria following the February 1966 coup. Along with Jadid, another military Ba'thist, Hafiz al-Asad, entered the power structure as part of the Military Committee of the Ba'th Party and later became minister of defence when Jadid came to power.

[3] E.g., see Nikoloas Van Dam, *The Struggle for Power in Syria: Politics and Society Under Asad and the Ba'th Party* (London: I. B. Tauris, 1996); Raymond A. Hinnebusch, *Author-itarian Power and State Formation in Ba'thist Syria: Army, Party and Peasant* (San Francisco: Westview Press, 1990).

[4] Malcolm H. Kerr, *The Arab Cold War: Gamal 'Abd al-Nasir and His Rivals, 1958–1970* (London: Oxford University Press, 1971), 118–19.

upon and railed against, yet at the same time it was being utilized to outmanoeuvre rival groups.

What began as a mighty battle that pitted Arab progressive forces against reactionary forces, became an internal struggle between Ba'thists and Nasserists within the progressive camp in the Arab world. Upon gaining power, a struggle developed between the younger, rural, and military Ba'thists against the older, urban, and civilian Ba'thists. In the minds of the younger generation, the leaders of the old generation had obviously lost their ways, and their ideas had grown stale since the party's establishment in the 1950s – in many ways it became a battle between the Regional Command and the National Command. The old guard had abdicated its role when it willingly disbanded the Ba'th Party under Nasserist pressure during the time of the UAR. It was time to restore a Syrian face on leading Arab nationalist ranks.

This basic intra-Ba'thist division devolved into an internal struggle between minority (e.g., Alawite and Druze) Ba'thists, who tended to compose the officer ranks in higher proportions than their numbers warranted, and the Sunni Ba'thists. Sunnis accounted for 75 percent of the Syrian population as a whole, yet were proportionately underrepresented in the officer corps. Sunnis resented the dominance of the minority groups in the ruling apparatus, primarily Alawites and Druze. Further, rivalries complicated the picture, such as those that developed between Salah Jadid and Hafiz al-Asad and among the Alawites based on different family and geographical origins. Throughout the early life of the Ba'th Party in Syria, there was a kind of domestic cold war based on religious and economic ideas, policies, and practices between the new radical ideology of the Ba'th and the still-powerful traditional interests in Syria, particularly in cities such as Hama.

This type of multilayered political struggle in an immature polity was not a place in which moderate policies came to the fore; quite the contrary, they tended to get overwhelmed by activism and bravado. The type of regime this political culture produced in February 1966 was what one of the principal historians of the era, Patrick Seale, called "the most extreme Syria had ever known, rash abroad, radical at home, engulfing the country in war, and attempting to refashion society from top to bottom."[5] The February 1966 movement has often been called neo-Ba'th, reflecting perhaps less a difference in domestic and foreign-policy orientation from its

[5] Patrick Seale, *Asad of Syria: The Struggle for the Middle East* (London: I. B. Tauris, 1988), 104.

Ba'thist predecessor than an intensification and more doctrinaire application of those same policies. Some may focus more on *raison d'état*–driven pragmatism rather than on radical Arab nationalism as being the driving force of Arab policy prior to the 1967 war, as it most surely was after the war. However, although this may be true of Egypt, it is less true of Syria, where policy continued to be shaped by a confluence of forces, from personal antagonisms and sectarian politics to Arab nationalist ideology. The latter was the ideal, which, in the minds of the neo-Ba'th ruling elite, had been betrayed by previous regimes, Ba'thist and non-Ba'thist alike. Similar policies continued, but under the neo-Ba'th they would now be applied correctly and appropriately. Yes, it was more practical than what they viewed as the wishful thinking of Aflaq, Bitar, and others of the old guard, but this must not necessarily be mistaken with less radical Arab nationalism. It was a difference in style and form, not content. This approach is what eventually got the neo-Ba'th in trouble at home and abroad.

The February movement regime inherited a multipronged struggle against Israel. It took on several forms. The first was over the ability to farm, if not control, the agricultural lands in the three demilitarized zones (DMZs) astride the border of Israel and Syria established in 1949 after the end of the first Arab-Israeli war. Second was the Israeli diversion of the headwaters of the Jordan River in its National Water Carrier project and the Arab League–sanctioned Syrian response of trying to carry out its own diversion efforts of the tributaries running through the Golan Heights that feed into the Jordan River. Finally, there was the issue of Syrian support of Palestinian *fedayeen* attacks against Israel, usually from the direction of Jordan rather than directly across the Israeli-Syrian border. All these issues in some ways caused and exacerbated tensions at the Arab-Israeli level and, importantly, at the inter-Arab level.

The Palestinian issue, particularly *fedayeen* raids, by default became a sanctioned Arab response that Syria eagerly supported under successive Ba'thist governments. The Ba'th Party, stung by the experience of the UAR as well as the failed unity talks with Nasser following the Ba'thist advent to power in 1963, were only too willing to call out the Egyptian president for doing too little, too late against Israel. The Arab monarchies had been pummelled by Nasserist propaganda, which was returned in kind, so it was not hard to find issues over which Egypt could be criticized in the Arab world. It was a battle between Syria and Egypt over who was actually implementing true Arab nationalist ideology, not unlike that which was occurring at the same time between China and the Soviet Union over which was the more doctrinaire communist power. In the Middle East between 1963 and 1967, Syria played the role of the radical in the manner of China, belittling what it viewed as the accommodating policies of Nasser just as Beijing ripped Moscow for its perceived concessions to the West and for casting a blind eye towards the anticommunist practices of various client states. It was, in a sense, an internal Ba'th struggle against the older generation of Ba'thists that played itself out on the regional level as well as the domestic front.

The DMZs were relatively small territories along the 1949 armistice line in which neither side was permitted to introduce military units; they were supervised by the Mixed Armistice Commission through the UN Truce Supervision Organization. These three territories had been placed on the Jewish state side of the line in the 1947 UN partition plan, but Syria had taken them by force during the 1948 war. The Israeli-Syrian armistice agreement in 1949 arranged for Syrian troops to be withdrawn and the zones demilitarized. Though small, the territories were a source of contention, and neither side was willing to give them up voluntarily. There had been sporadic clashes between Syrian and Israeli armed units as well as civilians (or on occasion, military personnel dressed as civilians) ever since 1949, with punitive raids by Israel in 1955, 1960, and 1962. Although largely condemned for these raids by the international community, Israel portrayed them as self-defence against both Syrian attempts to redraw the cease-fire line and Palestinian attacks.[6]

The Syrians tried to take control of the Palestinian cause; shifting away from Nasser's more cautious approach by helping the Palestinian guerrillas "burst out of the Arab box" in which Nasser hoped to contain them and "develop momentum to the excitement of the Arab public."[7] Syrian support for Palestinian attacks against Israel was important, especially because Jordan and Lebanon were doing their best to prevent such incursions for fear of Israeli reprisals. More Palestinian guerrillas were killed by Jordanian and Lebanese forces before 1967 than by the Israelis.[8]

---

[6] Fatah, the largest faction within the PLO, launched its first formal act of sabotage against the water carrier in January 1965. It failed. But all three areas of discord between Israel and Syria along the border became linked, reinforcing the intensity of the overall dispute that much more.

[7] Seale, *Asad of Syria*, 123.

[8] Fuad Jabber, "The Resistance Movement before the Six Day War," in *The Politics of Palestinian Nationalism*, ed. William B. Quandt et al. (Berkeley: University of California Press, 1973), 174.

The Palestinian movement was a centrepiece of the Ba'thist ideology. Because Syrians consider Arab nationalism to be their birthright, it was almost a sacred duty to support the Palestinian cause, especially at a time when the elimination of Israel and the return of the Palestinian homeland were still considered viable options. Syria was the country that matched words with deeds, not Egypt, and Cairo was consistently criticized for restraining Palestinian activism. The Palestinians, hoping to engulf the Arab world in war against Israel – for that was the only way they would get their land back – were only too eager to embrace Syrian support for the time being. For the Ba'thists, supporting Palestinian guerrilla activity was a no-brainer: it was ideologically predisposed to do so, made Nasser look impotent, earned Damascus plaudits in most Arab circles, gave Syria the Arab nationalist ideological upper hand, and had practical application in terms of potential results along the border with Israel, and because most of these guerrilla attacks directly emanated from Arab territories other than Syria, there was an element of plausible deniability.

The problem with Syria's aggressive policy was the inability to carefully calibrate it – the inability to accurately assess the reaction of the Israelis. It led to the development of what was called in Israel the "Syrian syndrome." Brigadier General Israel Lior, Levi Eshkol's military secretary, described the Syrian syndrome as something that typically affected almost anyone who served on the northern border with Syria: "Serving on that border, opposite the Syrian enemy, inflames extraordinary hatred toward the Syrian army and people. We loved to hate them."[9] Israeli hostility towards Damascus led to frequent calls for a more muscular and punitive military response, if not all out war, against Syria in the weeks, months, and years preceding the 1967 war. These calls were often leaked to the Israeli press, usually increasing the pressure on the Israeli government to act before cooler heads prevailed. But the confrontational Israeli-Syrian die had been cast.

The Coming of War

Syria was severely unprepared for war. Despite the bombastic and jingoistic rhetoric, the Ba'thist regime viewed its actions against Israel as low-level warfare that was not meant to lead to all-out war. The months and years prior to the 1967 Arab-Israeli war were filled with military purges associated with actual and attempted coups that decimated and

---

[9] Quoted in Segev, *1967*, 195.

further fractured the military and party, resulting in an inexperienced officer corps as well as a deep distrust between the rank and file and officers in the army. In addition, there were uprisings by discontented elements of the Syrian population, less than satisfactory encounters with Israeli forces, and lukewarm Soviet support. At the time, the Soviets were growing more concerned about Syrian policy and had tried to get Damascus to dampen its support for Palestinian raids. Behind all of this was a budding rivalry between the two strongmen of the regime, Salah Jadid and Hafiz al-Asad, which was beginning to manifest. One would be hard-pressed to find a military less prepared for war with a clearly superior foe.

The fifteen months in Syria between the 23 February 1966 coup and the June 1967 War were beset by a new regime struggling to establish its legitimacy and authority. Soon after the coup there were, as one might expect in Syria, countercoup attempts by elements loyal to former President Amin al-Hafiz and the National Command. Naturally, what followed were a series of purges and arrests, particularly devastating to the officer corps of the Syrian military. Throughout the next fifteen months, the regime was constantly on the lookout for coup attempts, especially by opponents who took refuge in neighbouring Lebanon, Iraq, and Jordan. A conspiratorial mentality breeds even more conspiracy, and soon there were coup attempts by disaffected elements within the Movement of February 23. Most notable was an abortive attempt in September 1966 by Colonel Salim Hatum, a Druze; although his troops had been instrumental in the February coup, he felt marginalized by the new Alawite-dominated regime. An intra-Ba'th and intramilitary polarization between Alawites and Druze came to the fore during the summer and autumn of 1966. The subsequent purges in the military and the Ba'th Party were extensive. Hatum was able to escape to Jordan from where he continued his diatribes against the regime. In one September 14 interview to the Beirut newspaper, *al-Nahar*, he commented: "The Alawi officers adhere to their tribes and not to their militarism. Their concern is the protection of Salah Jadid and Hafiz al-Asad. The latest arrests comprised hundreds of officers of all groups, with the exception of the Alawis."[10] The lack of "militarism," particularly in carrying the fight against Israel and on behalf of the Palestinians, was a constant barrage aimed at the regime by the opposition even within what had been its own camp. In a way,

---

[10] Quoted in Van Dam, *The Struggle for Power in Syria*, 57. Hatum returned to Syria during the 1967 June War ostensibly to fight for his country. He was summarily arrested, tried by a special military court, and executed on 24 June.

the pressure that the Syrian regime placed on Nasser was a reflection of similar pressure the regime felt from its own opposition. The regime could in no way seem less than what it said it was or do less than what it said it would do, or it would leave itself open to galvanizing political and propaganda attacks.

As a result, the support for Palestinian guerrilla attacks against Israel, mostly through Jordan, intensified, as well as skirmishes along the border between Israeli and Syrian forces. This particularly became the case after 14 July 1966 when Israeli aircraft bombed and destroyed Syrian engineering works trying to divert the Banias River, one of the tributaries to the Jordan River. Two months later, Israeli aircraft shot down one or two Syrian MiGs (depending upon the source).[11] There were those in the Syrian leadership who were Maoist in their orientation towards guerrilla warfare and others who believed that, with Syrian support, the Palestinians could do to the Israelis what the Algerian rebels had done to the French by 1962: wear down an occupying force by attrition until victory is achieved. Damascus had published Fatah's newspaper *Sawt al-Asafa* (Voice of the Storm) since May 1965. Furthermore, the regime helped organize Popular Defence Army brigades, made up primarily of both Syrian and Palestinian union workers, charged with defending the homeland against "subversive military activities and external attacks."[12] In return for Palestinian assistance with reinforcing regime stability domestically, it appears that the regime stepped up its assistance to Palestinian guerrilla operations against Israel. Again, the relative domestic weakness of the regime, as well as regional isolation, forced it along a road of adopting more radical foreign policies.

One of the important antecedents of the 1967 war was a serious clash between Syria and Israel that took place on 7 April, an event that in retrospect began the march towards war. Israelis within the leadership at the time have since admitted to baiting the Syrians on occasion by provocatively sending armed tractors manned by Israeli soldiers dressed as farmers into the DMZs. This was another occasion, this time on the southern tip of the Sea of Galilee. The Syrians predictably fired on the tractor, prompting a heavy Israeli air response in order to teach Damascus a lesson for its continued support of Palestinian guerrilla raids. These raids had ticked upward in recent months, notably one on 31 March

[11] Edgar O'Ballance, *The Third Arab-Israeli War* (Hamden, CT: Archon Books, 1972), 19.
[12] Fred H. Lawson, *Why Syria Goes to War: Thirty Years of Confrontation* (Ithaca, NY: Cornell University Press, 1996), 44.

that blew up an irrigation pump and railroad tracks near the Jordanian border. The exchanges in the morning of 7 April escalated, and Hafiz al-Asad, who was commander of the Syrian air force in addition to being minister of defence, sent Syrian MiGs against Israeli air forces in what turned out to be a large-scale air battle. Six MiGs were shot down, and Israeli jets humiliatingly buzzed Damascus in the process. It was quite the psychological blow to Damascus, an asymmetrical Israeli response aimed at deterring Syrian activities, conditioning the behaviour of the Ba'thist regime, and possibly encouraging more moderate elements to launch a coup by discrediting the regime. Support for Damascus streamed in from all over the Arab world, as Syria was, once again, matching words with deeds. Consequently, Nasser received some criticism for not having responded in accordance with the Egyptian-Syrian defence pact.

Throughout early 1967, American officials became increasingly angry at Syria, losing what little objectivity they had after years of seeing Damascus as a pro-Soviet pawn in the region. The U.S. ambassador in Tel Aviv referred to Syria as a Stalinist regime, warning that "the paranoiac fear of plots and aggressions, with its constant provocations of Israel, could lead . . . to a military adventure which can only end in defeat." He further warned, on 15 May, that the "situation with Syria is obviously precarious and, if additional serious sabotage incidents . . . continue it [is] impossible to predict GOI [Government of Israel] will sit idly by without reacting."[13] Townsend Hoopes, a senior Defense Department official, stated that "the Syrians are sons of bitches." Even U.S. newspapers were picking up on the anti-Syrian mood. The *New York Times* ran the following headline on its front page on 13 May 1967: "Israelis Ponder Blow at Syrians: Some Leaders Decide That Force Is the Only Way to Curtail Terrorism."[14]

As early as January 1967, the U.S. ambassador in Damascus seemed convinced that Israel was readying itself to launch a major attack against Syria, saying that, "We believe Israel is on the brink of an attack and they [Syrians] cannot count on us to hold Israel back."[15] The fear of and concern over a significant Israeli military action had been building for months, enhanced (or confirmed) by the 7 April air battle and subsequent

[13] Telegram from the Embassy in Israel to the Department of State, May 16, 1967, Department of State, *Foreign Relations of the United States, 1964–1968*, vol. XIX (Washington, DC: U.S. Government Printing Office, 2004), doc. no. 2 [hereinafter referred to as *FRUS*].

[14] Richard B. Parker, *The Politics of Miscalculation in the Middle East* (Bloomington: Indiana University Press, 1993), 16.

[15] Rostow to President, January 16, 1967, *FRUS*, vol. XVIII, doc. no. 380.

bombastic remarks made by both sides, but everyone knew that only the bellicose comments made by Israeli officials could actually be acted upon.

It is under these circumstances that the infamous Soviet warning arrived on 13 May, informing Egypt that Israel was massing troops on the Syrian border primed to launch a full-scale invasion of Syria. Despite repeated examination, there is no generally accepted conclusion regarding who initiated the warning or why and whether it was a genuine warning or disinformation.[16] What is clear is that Moscow was trying to protect the Syrian regime and ward off a potentially catastrophic war. It also appears that the warning did not originate in Syria, although the Ba'th regime certainly did not disagree with the way the Soviets informed the Egyptians. Damascus stood to benefit from the warning both in terms of actually deterring an Israeli onslaught and compelling Nasser to take the initiative.[17] What is equally clear in retrospect is that the Soviets, Egyptians, and Syrians were not expecting a full-fledged war to erupt. The Soviets became concerned that war could lead to a confrontation with the United States if they felt compelled to engage and to a loss of prestige if they did not and the possible loss of an ally in Damascus. The Ba'th regime feared the loss of power in the event of military defeat. The Soviet warning was intended to prevent all of this, but it led to something quite the opposite. In a spate of memoirs by key Syrian figures written after the 1967 war, they almost universally blame Moscow for mishandling the situation. Even though Syria must have known that Israel was not massing troops, it played along with the Soviet warning because of a genuine fear of an impending Israeli attack. The problem for Syria was that the regime lost control of the course of events to the Soviets and Egyptians.

As previously noted, Syria was utterly unprepared to fight a war. The mismatch with Israel in terms of military readiness and materiel capability was compounded by the political and military purges since the February 1966 coup. In addition, there was trouble in Syria. Small craftsmen, artisans, and other elements of the labour force had been manifesting their opposition to the economic policies of the Ba'th regime more vociferously, with strikes and protests becoming more frequent into 1967.[18] These were supported and egged on by the Islamist party in Syria, the Muslim Brotherhood, who were diametrically opposed to the avowedly secular

---

[16] Probably the best among these is Parker, *The Politics of Miscalculation*.

[17] The Soviet ambassador in Damascus in 1967 reported that he did not know the origins of the warning, which, as Parker states, "would seem to militate against a Syrian origin." Therefore, it probably originated elsewhere. Parker, *The Politics of Miscalculation*, 24.

[18] Lawson, *Why Syria Goes to War*, 39–41.

Ba'thist regime. The domestic tension burst out into the open following the publication of an *Army Weekly* article in early May that denigrated religion as anachronistic. This was followed on 5 May by an incendiary attack against the "atheist" regime by one of the leaders of the Islamist opposition, prompting mass protests against the regime over the next few days in Damascus, Aleppo, and Hama. As expected, state security services arrested hundreds in reaction.[19] Naturally the regime blamed agents of imperialism for fomenting the unrest, and in this atmosphere, Syrian officials – and maybe even the Soviets – just might have believed it was true, thinking it may be a prelude to invasion. Whatever the cause, it certainly made an actual war less, rather than more, attractive to the regime given all of liabilities, obstacles, and distractions with which it was saddled.

Syria and the War

The focal point of the crisis shifted to Nasser after 14 May.[20] On that day, ostensibly in reaction to the Soviet warning, Egypt demonstratively mobilized troops and moved them into what had been the demilitarized Sinai Peninsula. The rationale for Nasser's escalatory moves from 14 May on is examined in Chapters 2 and 6 of this book. His actions were in part an attempt to control the crisis and take it out of the hands of the unpredictable Syrian regime. As Nasser's confidant, Muhammad Hasanein Heikal, wrote, "The Egyptian view was that if the frightened Syrians made a wrong move, they could get us all into serious trouble."[21] Maybe Nasser could take the initiative vis-à-vis Israel away from Syria for a change, for now it would be Egypt matching words with deeds. The pressure of the Arab cold war and particularly the constant pressure that successive Ba'th regimes since 1963 had placed on Nasser had finally boxed him into a corner from which he would not emerge unscathed. Although the Syrians and Soviets saw Nasser's mobilizing of troops into the Sinai and the subsequent removal of the UN Emergency Force from the

---

[19] Ibid., 42.
[20] It is interesting that in U.S. government correspondence through May 18, the crisis and potential war was seen as an Israeli-Syrian affair, not Egyptian. That would soon change, especially when Nasser announced the closure of the Strait of Tiran on May 22. E.g., see Memorandum from the President's Special Assistant (Rostow) to President Johnson, May 15, 1967, *FRUS*, vol. XIX, doc. no. 4; and Telegram from the Embassy in Jordan to the Department of State, May 18, 1967, *FRUS*, vol. XIX, doc. no. 12.
[21] Quoted in Seale, *Asad of Syria*, 130.

Sinai, as desirable actions that would help deter Israel, both were probably caught off guard by Nasser's announcement on 22 May that Egypt would close the Strait of Tiran to Israeli shipping, because this action constituted a *casus belli* for Israel. It was, in many ways, the point of no return for Nasser. The rest of the story is well-known. After some more political and military moves by Egypt and Israel, in addition to failed diplomatic attempts by the international community to ameliorate the crisis, Israel launched a devastating air attack against Egypt on June 5 that largely destroyed the Egyptian air force. In effect, the so-called Six-Day War was over in a matter of a few hours.

Despite the mutual defence pact, there had been very little coordination or consultation between Cairo and Damascus as the crisis escalated. An inadequate command and control structure to begin with had become abysmal following the Israeli blitzkrieg. Syria and Jordan were in the dark as to the extent of destruction of the Egyptian air force. Egyptian propaganda led Syrian leaders to believe that they needed to join the fight because the Arab side was winning. Such was the destruction of the Arab control and command system that the Israeli air force was able to successfully carry out its mission against Egypt and return in time to take out the much-smaller Jordanian and Syrian air forces before they had a chance to mobilize. Hafiz al-Asad, the air force commander, sent his small contingent of fighters into the air, and they were quickly shot down by the Israelis on 5 June. With the Arab air forces effectively eliminated, the Arab ground forces were at the mercy of the Israelis.

Except for some sporadic Syrian shelling of Israeli settlements along the border, Syria stayed pretty much out of the war for the first four days. This did not go down well in the Arab world, not least because it was Syria's aggressive posture vis-à-vis Israel that had in large measure brought about war. But the Syrians were confused by what they slowly learned was the scale of the destruction on the Egyptian front. They were astounded. They did not understand what was going on, nor did they have the military experience and capability, especially in the officer corps, to react to the new situation. With no air support, how could they move forward against Israel? They reasoned that if they sat tight, they could emerge from this with little damage. With Nasser possibly irredeemably bloodied, the path towards Arab leadership would be open. Despite repeated pleas, they were in no hurry to come to Jordan's aid either. They also figured that they were operating under a Soviet deterrence umbrella, knowing the Israelis were hesitant to move against Syria for fear of eliciting a Soviet military response, especially as Damascus was so close to the border. In any event, it was assumed that the natural defences of the daunting Golan Heights would make the Israelis think twice.

On all counts the Syrians were almost correct. In many ways, it was these very same calculations and conclusions that led elements of the Israeli high command to decide, after some heated arguments, to engage Syrian forces in the Golan Heights during the last days of the conflict. Even though it could come at great cost in military and diplomatic terms, Tel Aviv simply could not let Syria get away scot-free. Some Israeli leaders believed that it was worth the risk of upsetting Moscow in order to gain the Golan.[22] Eshkol stated that, "The Syrians cannot be allowed to parade in victory.... Israel cannot have overturned all the Arab countries and not Syria."[23] There were some ferocious battles on tough terrain, in which the Syrians fought much more tenaciously then anyone could have anticipated, and which were costly to the Israelis. Israeli Defence Minister Moshe Dayan commented that, "The Syrians are battling like lions." After buying time diplomatically in the United Nations on a cease-fire, and having been reinforced by troops and armour from the other fronts of the war that were now quiet, the Israelis were able to take the Golan Heights by June 10. The admirable performance by Syrian foot soldiers in the Golan was erased by miscommunication and ineptitude in the officer corps and the high command, ending ultimately in an uncoordinated and chaotic retreat from the Golan, including the city of Qunaytra.[24] Once the prize of Qunaytra was taken, Israel finally halted its advance; it was under severe pressure from the United States, the United Nations, and the Soviet Union. The Soviets broke off diplomatic relations with Israel on 10 June to register displeasure with Israeli actions in the Golan and to make sure Israel went no further, especially as the road to Damascus, only some forty miles away, lay wide open.

---

[22] Michael B. Oren, *Six Days of War June 1967 and the Making of the Modern Middle East* (New York: Ballantine Books, 2003), 292.

[23] Quoted in Oren, *Six Days of War*, 292.

[24] Falling for an Israeli feint through Lebanon, and faced with the threat of being out-flanked, Damascus ordered three brigades from the Golan to protect the capital, opening the door for Israeli gains. For a good description of the military and diplomatic activity surrounding the capture of the Golan Heights, see Ahron Bregman and Jihan El-Tahiri, *Israel and the Arabs: An Eyewitness Account of War and Peace in the Middle East* (New York: TV Books, 2000), 109–17. The Syrians prematurely announced the fall of Qunaytra, which led to an *en masse* Syrian retreat from the Golan Heights before it was necessary, unintentionally opening the door for Israeli forces to enter Qunaytra. The Syrian regime may have done this in order to galvanize Soviet and UN efforts to enact an immediate cease-fire; it only accelerated the loss of the Golan Heights.

The Aftermath

In terms of personnel, materiel, and even territorial losses, Syria fared much better than Jordan or Egypt in the confrontation with Israel.[25] Yet of the three major Arab state combatants, it is the only one that to the present day has not resigned itself to the results of the war. Egypt recovered the Sinai Peninsula through the 1979 Egyptian-Israeli peace treaty, and it willingly gave up any claim to the Gaza Strip. Jordan as well effectively renounced any return of the West Bank, including East Jerusalem, and the Hashemite monarchy signed its own peace treaty with Israel in 1994. Syria is still officially at war with Israel, even though during the reign of President Hafiz al-Asad during the late 1980s and throughout the 1990s Syria made peace with Israel a strategic choice and has repeatedly engaged in direct and indirect talks with the Israelis since 1992. The return of the Golan Heights, however, is still a national cause in Syria and still defines Syrian foreign policy. Hafiz al-Asad, as minister of defence and commander of the air force at the time of the war, felt a personal responsibility for losing the Golan. Because he would soon become the president of Syria for thirty years in an authoritarian, neopatriarchal dictatorship, his obsession of getting back the Golan Heights naturally became the country's obsession. His son and successor, Bashar al-Asad, inherited this calling.

Perhaps because Syria could live with the postwar status quo, certainly more so than Egypt with the loss of the Sinai, it could afford to be less conciliatory in defeat than the other Arab combatants over the short and long term. It was a strategic loss; after all, Syria had lost the high ground to Israel, and now Israeli forces were a mere forty miles away from Damascus. But it was more of a strategic gain for Israel in terms of taking away the high ground from Syria and controlling the tributaries that feed into the Jordan River than it was a loss for the Syrians. The intelligence capabilities of Israel vis-à-vis Syria were also greatly enhanced, especially after they occupied Mount Hermon on 12 June, two days after the cease-fire. Located at the apex of the Syrian-Lebanese border, it gave

---

[25] Syria had about 75,000–80,000 troops, 300 tanks, and about 120–130 fighter jets going into the war. Estimates vary widely, but in the war Syria lost about 2,500 soldiers, with 5,000 wounded, as well as 40–50% of its air force and half its tanks. Approximately 80,000–90,000 Syrians fled the Golan Heights, with varying claims as to whether they were forced out by the Israelis or left of their own accord to get out of the way of the fighting (the answer probably lies somewhere in between), with about 7,000 Syrians, mostly Druze, remaining in what became the Israeli occupied Golan Heights.

Israel a clear visual and electronic view of Syrian troop movements and communication traffic in the south throughout the plains that surrounded Damascus.

In Syria, as in other Arab countries, there were desperate – and creative – attempts to mask the scale of the overall defeat. In Egypt, the Nasserist regime loudly asserted that the Americans and British actively engaged in the war. In Syria, the Ba'thist regime proclaimed victory and tried to convince a sceptical Syrian public that even though it had lost the Golan Heights, the primary Israeli objective was to enter Damascus and overthrow the regime; because that did not happen, Syria was able to foil Israeli plans. Bemoaning this attempted regime spin, Mustafa Tlas, a member of the Ba'th military committee and Asad confidante at the time of the conflict, wrote with "grief" in his memoirs that he would "never forget the words of [Syrian] Prime Minister Yusuf Zu'ayyin: Praise be to God, Qunaytra has fallen but the regime has not."[26] Needless to say, not many people in Syria accepted this explanation. As such, a regime that had difficulty establishing its legitimacy prior to June 1967 was now fighting a rearguard action just to try to stay in power.

As expected, recriminations flew back and forth within the regime, with the civilian leadership blaming the military leadership and vice versa. There were also a number of regime adversaries that had been let out of prison or exiles clamouring to come back (and some actually entering) into the country during the war to fight. They now saw an opportunity for a coup against a potentially disgraced regime; some were approached by dissatisfied elements during the war to overthrow the regime, but they wisely demurred for the time being. It was as clear an indication as any that, to some notable Syrians, the primary battles to be fought were now inside Syria's borders. In the end, the regime loyalists temporarily rallied around the flag of self-preservation; to do otherwise would mean their own demise.

In the internal power struggle, Hafiz al-Asad eventually triumphed over Salah Jadid in 1970. Asad viewed the domestic, regional, and international arenas much more pragmatically. He had seen firsthand how a reckless foreign policy could lead to unforeseen – and disastrous – results. Soon after the war he began to play the Syrian political game much more seriously, gathering up loyalists for an anticipated intra-Ba'th coup. It would take some time, and the Jadid regime maintained its radical

---

[26] Mustafa Tlas, *Mir'at Hayati* [The Mirror of My Life], pt. 2, 1958–1968 (Damascus: Dar Tlas, 1995), 874.

positions in public forums, for instance, by not accepting UN Security
Council Resolution 242 and by pulling out of the 1967 Arab League
summit meeting in Khartoum. There were moderate voices (Arab and
Israeli) who believed in the immediate aftermath of the war that a peaceful resolution could be found. Syria was, for the most part, an exception.
It is interesting to note that in a conversation with King Hussein, Syrian
President Nur al-Din al-Atasi mentioned the possibility of a "moderate
solution," but that he believed the Syrian government, as relayed by Hussein in a meeting with President Lyndon Johnson at the White House on
28 June 1967, "could already be too much prisoners of their own propaganda to make this possible."[27] The Jadid regime had become captive of
its own rhetoric and policies – it still could not pull back from this.

As Nasser did soon after the 1967 war, Asad moved to repair relations
with former adversaries in the Arab arena, primarily Saudi Arabia (and
Egypt), thus discarding the policies that resulted in Syria's relative isolation throughout much of the 1960s. Strategically, Asad would focus less
on revolution at home and abroad and more on pragmatic ways to confront Israel and recover the Golan Heights. This meant the military being
resupplied quickly by the Soviet Union; following the resounding defeat
of its allies in the Arab world, Moscow redoubled its efforts to support
them. This meant rebuilding their armies and instilling more profession-
alism and loyalty within the Syrian armed forces. It was imperative to get
more control of the Palestinians and not allow them the free hand that
had contributed to such calamitous consequences in 1967.[28]

Ironically, all of this would lead to another war with Israel in 1973.
In this war, however, there would be much more preparation, planning,
and coordination on the Arab side.[29] The Syrian armed forces performed
much more professionally and effectively than in 1967. In this war, the

---

[27] Memorandum of Conversation, 28 June 1967, *FRUS*, vol. XIX, doc. no. 331.

[28] For an example of the type of action and rhetoric Asad was trying to get away from,
see the notes from a meeting between the U.S. ambassador in Damascus and Syrian
Foreign Minister Makhus on 20 May 1967. Telegram from the Embassy in Syria to the
Department of State, *FRUS*, vol. XIX, doc. no. 27. The summary includes the following:
"SARG (Syrian government) refuses for once and for all take any responsibility for
actions [by] Palestinians in their fight for rights and for despoiled homeland, since
Palestinians not under command [of] Syria."

[29] Although not totally, for Asad would become furious with Anwar Sadat after it became
clear soon after the war began that the Egyptian president had more limited objectives
in going to war with Israel than Asad felt he had been led to believe. When Egyptian
forces dug in and established a bridgehead at the western edge of the Sinai along the
Suez Canal, rather than extending the fight all the way into the Sinai, it allowed Israel
some breathing space to regroup as well as concentrate its forces in the north to repel
the Syrians, who believed they entered the war to regain the Golan Heights militarily.

Soviets would be much more prepared to back a Syrian regime that had been acting in a pragmatic fashion compared to the erratic behaviour of the previous regime. Although Israel would adeptly turn the course of the war around to its advantage, it was to be bloodied by the Arabs; this in turn would, in large measure, set in motion the course of events that would lead to the 1979 Egyptian-Israeli peace treaty as well as direct and indirect Israeli-Syrian negotiations from the early 1990s onwards. In 1972, Syria conditionally accepted UN Security Council Resolution 242. By accepting UN Security Council Resolution 338, which ended the 1973 Arab-Israeli war, Syria officially accepted 242 and thus the land-for-peace formula. In essence, it opted for a negotiated settlement.

With conflicts, contemporary commentators more often than not seek to assign blame, particularly against those who are seen as initiating it. More often than not regarding the 1967 Arab-Israeli war, Syria is held out as the primary culprit. Johnson administration officials certainly thought so before, during, and after the war.[30] The harsh political realities of Damascus moulded regimes that increasingly adopted belligerent policies vis-à-vis Israel and dangerously – too dangerously as it turned out – played the Arab cold war game.

To put it bluntly, if you play with fire, you get burned. This is exactly what happened to Syria. For a variety of reasons, many of which had little to do with Israel, Syria played a very dangerous game. The political-cultural landscape of Syria, characterized by intense political competition and at least the appearance of ideological fidelity among the political elite, won out over pragmatism and advanced radical policies at home and regionally. But the Syrians thought they could get away with it. They did not want war with Israel. Judging from what appears to have been Israeli hesitancy, waffling, and extemporaneousness regarding the question of whether to take the war to Syria in the latter stages of the conflict, the Ba'thist regime almost did get away with it. The Syrians assumed the Soviets, or at least the Egyptians, would protect them. As the crisis heated up in May, the Syrians let it be known to anyone listening that they had unlimited political and military support from the Soviets.[31] They probably were trying to deter the Israelis, but they may have actually believed it. In

---

[30] E.g., see Telegram from the Embassy in Israel to the Department of State, 18 May 1967, *FRUS*, vol. XIX, doc. no. 13; and Telegram from the Embassy in Israel to the Department of State, *FRUS*, vol. XIX, doc. no. 14.

[31] Circular Telegram from the Department of State to Certain Posts, 18 May 1967, *FRUS*, vol. XIX, doc. no. 15; Telegram from the Department of State to the Embassy in Israel, 20 May 1967, *FRUS*, vol. XIX, doc. no. 25; and Telegram from the Embassy in the Soviet Union to the Department of State, *FRUS*, vol. XIX, doc. no. 41.

addition, rather than seeing the November 1966 Egyptian-Syrian defence pact for what it really was – Soviet and Egyptian attempts to control the reckless behaviour of Damascus – they tended to see it as a reinforcement of their strategic policy. The client-state, Syria, after playing the cold war game to its apparent advantage, mistakenly presumed that its patron, the Soviet Union, would go much further than it was prepared to go to protect its client. Only five years after the Cuban Missile Crisis, while Moscow perhaps was not prepared to allow Syria to be destroyed, it was quite wary of the neo-Ba'th regime and was certainly not willing to risk a third world war in order to save the Golan Heights. Mistaken assumptions are behind the anger of many Syrian officials at what the Soviets did and did not do in 1967, but it is equally clear that Syrian naïveté regarding regional and international politics led them to make these mistaken assumptions in the first place and to embark upon a reckless foreign policy bereft of military teeth.

The Israelis and the Americans misread the real causes and intent of Syria's actions, losing sight of inter-Arab and Syrian politics. The cold war paradigm was too Manichean to assess the complex matrix of Middle East domestic and regional cold wars. However one chooses to see Israel in all of this, as a country reluctantly acting in self-defence against Arab aggression or as a hawkish, expansionist state taking advantage of, if not helping to create, an opportune moment, the Syrians provided grist for the mill. Syria was, by far, the weaker state when compared to Israel; had it been stronger it might have been at least more prepared to back up its incendiary support for Palestinian raids and cross-border fire. It was not. Syrian actions against Israel made it that much easier for the hawkish voices in Israel to rise to the fore and implement policies that led to military triumph. The Syrians gambled, but the Israelis ultimately went all in and called their bluff. Syria paid for it with the loss of the Golan.

4

Jordan

Walking the Tight Rope

Avi Shlaim

Jordan was a reluctant belligerent in the third Arab-Israeli war. The principal decision maker on the Jordanian side was King Hussein bin Talal who had ascended the Hashemite throne in 1953 at the tender age of eighteen. Hussein was the heir to a Hashemite legacy of moderation and pragmatism towards the Zionist movement that went back to his grandfather, King Abdullah I, the founder of the Hashemite Kingdom of Jordan.[1] Hussein was also the heir to an even older Hashemite legacy of leadership in the struggle for Arab independence and unity. This legacy went back Hussein's great-grandfather, Hussein the Sharif of Mecca, who staged the Arab Revolt against the Ottoman Empire in World War I.[2] King Hussein's foreign policy was essentially a balancing act between the conflicting claims of Arab nationalism and coexistence with Israel. During the Suez Crisis of 1956, Hussein's commitment to Arab nationalism led him to side with Egypt against Israel. He even offered to open a second front against Israel, but President Gamal Abdel Nasser dissuaded him. After Suez, the pragmatic strand in Hussein's foreign policy came to the fore, and in 1963 he initiated a secret dialogue with Israel's leaders.[3] This dialogue across the battle lines enabled Jordan and Israel to reach a *modus vivendi*, a state approaching de facto peace.

[1] Avi Shlaim, *Collusion across the Jordan: King Abdullah, the Zionist Movement, and the Partition of Palestine* (Oxford: Clarendon Press, 1988).
[2] Adeed Dawisha, *Arab Nationalism in the Twentieth Century: From Triumph to Despair* (Princeton, NJ: Princeton University Press, 2003).
[3] Avi Shlaim, *Lion of Jordan: King Hussein's Life in War and Peace* (London: Allen Lane, 2007).

Jordan's entry into the war against Israel in 1967 alongside the radical Arab regimes calls for an explanation. The explanation offered here is that an ill-considered Israeli military attack upset the delicate balance and launched Jordan on the slippery slope that led to its participation and disastrous defeat during the Six-Day War. It is essential to distinguish Israel's intentions from King Hussein's perceptions. Israel had no intention and no plan to attack Jordan. Hussein misperceived Israel's intentions and these misperceptions guided, or rather misguided, his subsequent policy. The attack destroyed Hussein's faith in Israel's peaceful intentions, although Israel harboured no plans of aggression. It left him feeling that his country was isolated and vulnerable and drove him into a rapprochement with Egypt within the framework of the United Arab Command (which had been set up in 1964) in order to counter the perceived Israeli threat. The alliance with Egypt, however, quickly embroiled Hussein in a war that he neither wanted nor anticipated.

The Samu' Raid

On 13 November 1966, the Israel Defence Force (IDF) launched a devastating attack on the village of Samu', south of Hebron on the West Bank, about four miles from the border with Israel. The attack was staged in broad daylight by a large force with infantry, an armoured brigade, heavy artillery, mortars, engineers, and two Mirage squadrons. A Jordanian army unit was rushed to the scene, but it careered into an ambush and suffered heavy casualties. The attack resulted in twenty-one Jordanian soldiers dead, thirty-seven soldiers wounded, and the destruction of 118 houses, including the police station, the local school, a medical clinic, and a mosque.[4] One Jordanian Hunter aircraft was shot down in an air battle, and its pilot was killed. The attack was a reprisal for a landmine that exploded the previous day on the Israeli side of the border, killing three soldiers.

Israel, as was its wont, exacted an eye for an eyelash, but this time it exacted it from the wrong Arab party. Israel's leaders knew full well that King Hussein was doing everything in his power to prevent Fatah, the largest guerrilla faction within the Palestine Liberation Organization (PLO), from staging sabotage operations from Jordan's territory because they heard it directly from him and from his representatives on the Mixed

---

[4] Yezid Sayigh, *Armed Struggle and the Search for State: The Palestinian National Movement, 1949–1993* (Oxford: Oxford University Press, 1997), 138.

Armistice Commission. The Israelis knew equally well that the militant Syrian regime that came to power in February of that year was training Fatah saboteurs and supporting Fatah operations against Israel from Jordan's territory. For some time, Israel's leaders had been pointing an accusing finger at Syria and threatening dire consequences if these attacks did not cease. So the attack on the Jordanian village came as a complete surprise.

Inside Jordan the effects of the raid were highly destabilizing, exposing the country's military weakness and fragility and touching off large-scale unrest and violent protest against the regime. King Hussein felt personally betrayed by the Israelis because their action seemed to contradict their previously expressed commitment to the safety and stability of Jordan. Furthermore, the raid occurred on his thirty-first birthday and the pilot who was killed was one of his friends. Speaking about this incident thirty years later, Hussein chose to stress the unbalanced and unreasonable nature of the Israeli action:

It really created a devastating effect in Jordan itself because the action, if it had been an action from Jordan, was not something that Jordan condoned or sponsored or supported in any way or form. And to my way of thinking at that time, I couldn't figure out if a small irrigation ditch or pipe was blown up – assuming it was which I didn't necessarily know for sure – why the reaction in this way? Was there any balance between the two? Why did the Israelis attack instead of trying to figure out a way of dealing with the threats in a different way, in a joint way? So it was a shock and it was not a very pleasant birthday present.[5]

At the time, Hussein took a much graver view of the raid on Samu‘, seeing it a signal of a change in Israel's attitude towards his regime and possibly even part of a larger design to provoke a war that would enable the IDF to capture the West Bank. This, however, was a misperception with grave consequences. Meir Amit, the head of the Mossad, said at a conference on the Six-Day War: "The truth of the matter is that we never, never wanted King Hussein to be harmed."[6] Yitzhak Rabin, the IDF Chief of Staff at that time, claimed that some of the more serious consequences of the raid were unintended. "We had neither political nor military reasons," said Rabin, "to arrive at a confrontation with Jordan

[5] Interview with King Hussein bin Talal, 3 December 1996, Ascot, UK. For an abridged text of this interview see Avi Shlaim, "His Royal Shyness: King Hussein and Israel," *The New York Review of Books*, 15 July 1999.
[6] Richard B. Parker, ed., *The Six-Day War: A Retrospective* (Gainesville: University of Florida, 1996), 102.

or to humiliate Hussein."[7] Levi Eshkol, Israel's moderate prime minister, was furious with the IDF for the excessive bloodshed and destruction. The main reason for his anger, however, was that the raid ran counter to his policy of supporting King Hussein and helping him in his struggle against the Palestinian guerrilla organizations.[8]

Hussein interpreted the attack on Samuʿ as an indication that the Israelis were no longer committed to the survival of his regime. For him, Samuʿ was not an isolated incident but part of a wider Israeli design to escalate the border clashes into a full-scale, expansionist war. Prime Minister Wasfi al-Tall was equally convinced that Israel was looking for an excuse to capture the West Bank. He believed that Israel wanted to provoke Jordanian retaliation that would provide the opportunity to go to war.[9] In short, Tall and Hussein suspected that Israel was setting a trap for Jordan, and they took care not to fall into the trap. They resisted the pressure to retaliate and referred the matter to the UN Security Council.

The attack on Samuʿ and Hussein's failure to respond with force widened the rift between the regime and its Palestinian subjects. The regime was accused at home and in the Arab world of neglecting the defences of the country and of failing to protect the inhabitants of Samuʿ against the enemy. The PLO, Syria, and Egypt fanned the flames of popular hatred by launching a fierce propaganda offensive, much of it directed against the king personally. All the pent-up frustrations suddenly came up to the surface and fuelled angry and often-violent protest. Mass demonstrations erupted in the refugee camps and the cities of the West Bank. Serious riots convulsed Hebron, Jericho, Jerusalem, Ramallah, Nablus, Jenin, Tulkarem, and Qalqilyah. Demonstrators marched through the streets carrying nationalist placards and shouting pro-Nasser slogans. The army was called in and instructed to use harsh measures to suppress the riots: curfews, mass arrests, tear gas, and firing live ammunition into the crowd. Even with these aggressive methods, it took the army the best part of two weeks to restore order.[10]

The Samuʿ raid also affected King Hussein relations with Israel. In the words of Israeli expert Moshe Shemesh, Samuʿ was "a turning-point

---

[7] Interview with Lieutenant-General Yitzhak Rabin, 22 August 1982, Tel Aviv.
[8] Interview with Miriam Eshkol, 12 December 2002, London.
[9] Interview with Mreiwad al-Tall, 12 September 2001, Amman. See also Asher Susser, *On Both Banks of the Jordan: A Political Biography of Wasfi al-Tall* (London: Frank Cass, 1994), 110–16.
[10] Moshe Shemesh, "'The IDF Raid on Samuʿ: The Turning-Point in Jordan's Relations with Israel and the West Bank Palestinians," *Israel Studies* 7, no. 1 (Spring 2002).

in Jordan's attitude toward Israel, from a state of guarded coexistence to one of disappointment and pessimism.... At the heart of Jordan's military and civilian estimate," writes Shemesh, "stood the unequivocal conclusion that Israel's main design was conquest of the West Bank, and that Israel was striving to drag all of the Arab countries into a general war, in the course of which it would make a grab for the West Bank. According to this appraisal, in light of Jordan's military weakness and the Arab world's dithering, Israel believed it would have little trouble in seizing the West Bank. After Samuʿ, these apprehensions so obsessed the Jordanians that they should be regarded as the deciding factor in King Hussein's decision to participate in the Six-Day War. He was convinced that Israel would occupy the West Bank whether Jordan joined the fray or not."[11]

Inside the Jordanian national security establishment there were two very different responses to the Samuʿ affair. One group argued that Jordan needed the other Arab states as the only possible defence against future Israeli aggression and that meant drawing closer to Nasser. The other group, led by Tall, argued that Samuʿ showed that the United Arab Command was a broken reed and that Jordan should therefore concentrate on building up its own defences. Tall pursued a confrontational policy towards the PLO, Syria, and Nasser. Hussein recognized Tall's ability, dynamism, and devotion, but he wanted a less abrasive prime minister in order to improve relations with the Arab world. In April 1967, Hussein appointed Saʾad Jumʾa as prime minister but kept Tall by his side as Minister of the Royal Court. Jumʾa had served as ambassador to the United States and was generally regarded as pro-Western and anti-Nasser. But he was a malleable character, and once he reached the top, he faithfully carried out his master's policy of patching up the old quarrels with Cairo and Damascus.[12]

Within six weeks of Hussein's change of course, Jordan was involved in a full-scale war with Israel that culminated in the loss of the West Bank. The loyalist version maintains that Jordan had no choice but to fight alongside its Arab brethren against the common foe. But there was nothing inevitable about the chain of events that plunged the region into war. The June 1967 War was largely accidental and unnecessary, but it had disastrous consequences for all the Arab participants, and especially

---

[11] Ibid.
[12] Lawrence Tal, *Politics, the Military, and National Security in Jordan, 1955–1967* (Basingstoke, UK: Palgrave Macmillan, 2002), 109–12.

for Jordan. The notion of "no alternative" was invented by the Jordanian policy makers to cover up their mistakes and their personal responsibility for the catastrophe that they brought upon their country. King Hussein was admittedly faced with an extremely difficult situation, but he also had a range of options to choose from and he made the wrong choice. Tall kept warning him that jumping on the Egyptian bandwagon would lead to war and to the loss of the West Bank, and this is precisely what happened. It was because he jumped on the Egyptian bandwagon that Hussein lost control over the course of events and ended up by losing one-half of his kingdom.

The Arab Cold War

The decisive factor in triggering the crisis that led to the Six-Day War was inter-Arab rivalries. It may sound perverse to suggest that the war owed more to the rivalries between the Arab states than to the dispute between them and Israel, but such a view is supported by the facts.[13] The Arab world was in a state of considerable turmoil arising out of the conflict and suspicions between the so-called progressive and the reactionary regimes. The militant Ba'th regime that captured power in Syria in February 1966 posed as the standard-bearer of Arab unity and continued to agitate for a popular war for the liberation of Palestine. It not only unleashed Fatah units to attack Israel from Jordan's territory, but it engaged in direct clashes with the Israeli army along the common border.

A major landmark in the spiral of violence was an air battle on 7 April 1967 in which six Soviet-made Syrian MiGs were shot down by the Israeli Air Force (IAF). The air battle started the countdown to the Six-Day War. Syria's conflict with Israel did nothing to improve its relations with Jordan. Relations between the two Arab countries reached their nadir when a Syrian truck loaded with dynamite exploded in the Jordanian customs station at Ramtha on 21 May, causing fourteen deaths and a wave of popular indignation throughout the country. King Hussein was convinced that the radicals in Syria saw Jordan as the real enemy, not Israel. He described terrorism as an instrument designed by his Syrian enemies to bring about Israeli retaliation in order to destroy Jordan. An immediate rupture of diplomatic relations with Syria was ordered by Hussein on his return from the scene of the crime.

[13] Malcolm H. Kerr, *The Arab Cold War: Gamal 'Abd al-Nasir and his Rivals, 1958–1970*, 3rd ed. (London: Oxford University Press, 1971).

For President Nasser, Syrian militancy posed a different kind of problem: it threatened to drag the confrontation states prematurely into a war with Israel. Nasser kept repeating that two conditions had to be met before war with Israel could be contemplated: Arab unity and Arab military parity with Israel. Nasser's dilemma was how to restrain the Syrian wild bunch while working to achieve these conditions. As a first step, Egypt and Syria signed a mutual defence treaty on 7 November 1966. But the treaty merely papered over the cracks. Nasser suspected his Syrian allies of wanting to drag him into a war with Israel while they suspected that, if push came to shove, he would leave them to face Israel on their own. Nasser's failure to come to Syria's aid during the air battle of 7 April exposed the hollowness of the treaty and undermined his credibility as an ally. Jordan seized the opportunity to launch a scathing attack on Nasser, contrasting his anti-Israeli rhetoric with the absence of any concrete action. There were two main thrusts to the Jordanian propaganda offensive: the failure to close the Straits of Tiran in the Red Sea to Israeli shipping and hiding behind the apron of the UN Emergency Force (UNEF) that was stationed in Sinai in the aftermath of the Suez War as a buffer between Egypt and Israel. Jordan's propaganda offensive escalated what Malcolm Kerr called "the Arab Cold War" and contributed to the crisis slide that culminated in a hot war between the Arabs and Israel.

While attacking Nasser publicly, Hussein warned him privately that he had reason to believe that a trap was being laid for him by the Syrian leaders. Hussein invited General Abd al-Mun'im Riad, the Egyptian head of the United Arab Command, to Amman and asked him to convey a most confidential message to Nasser. The message said that the rulers in Damascus were planning to ignite a conflagration on their border with Israel in order to compel Egypt to go to their rescue so that Egypt will become a target to be hit.[14] Ever since the signing of the Egyptian-Syrian defence pact, the Jordanian leaders were convinced that the Ba'th hardliners were plotting to drag Nasser into a military showdown with Israel. They believed that the pact increased rather than decreased the likelihood of war in the region because it spelled the end of Nasser's cautious approach to Israel. All the Jordanian leaders that Samir Mutawi interviewed for his book on Jordan and the June War were convinced that the Syrians were actively trying to involve Nasser in a military confrontation with Israel, not in order to help the Palestinians but in a bid to replace

[14] Mohamed Heikal, *1967: Al-Infijar* [1967: The Explosion] [in Arabic] (Cairo: Al-Ahram, 1990), 435–42.

him as the leader of the Arab world. According to the Jordanian analysis, the Syrians thought they were in a win-win position. If the Arabs defeated Israel, they would claim that they had taken the lead. If the Arabs were defeated, Nasser could be held responsible and be forced to resign. Even if he managed to hang on to power, his position would be gravely weakened.[15]

Nasser was now in a really tight spot. He reacted by taking a series of steps designed to shore up his prestige at home and in the Arab world. Although he appeared to be challenging Israel to a duel, most observers agree that he neither planned nor wished for one. What he did do was to embark on an exercise in brinkmanship that went over the brink. On 13 May 1967, Nasser received a Soviet intelligence report that falsely claimed that Israel was massing troops on Syria's border. Nasser responded by taking three successive steps that made war virtually inevitable: he deployed his troops in Sinai near Israel's border on 14 May; expelled the UNEF from the Gaza Strip and Sinai on 19 May; and closed the Straits of Tiran to Israeli shipping on 22 May. Nasser's first move, the deployment of the Egyptian army in Sinai, was not intended as a prelude to an attack on Israel but as a political manoeuvre designed to deter the Israelis from attacking Syria and to rebuild his authority in the Arab camp. But it unleashed a popular current for war that Nasser was not able to contain.

King Hussein became increasingly apprehensive as the situation was getting out of control. For his part, he was determined to keep calm and avoid incidents. But he told the British ambassador that he found Nasser's threat to close the Straits of Tiran incomprehensible and extremely dangerous. He concluded that Nasser was "behaving like a madman."[16] The situation was complicated. On the one hand, Hussein realized that Nasser's actions increased the risk of war when the Arab side was not ready, when there was no Arab cooperation, no coordination, and no joint plan. On the other hand, Nasser's challenge to Israel dramatically increased his popularity inside Jordan and raised expectations that the much-vaunted "battle of destiny" was at hand and that the liberation of Palestine was imminent. Not only Palestinians but also the majority of Jordanians were swept along by the rising tide of Arab nationalism. This tide posed a threat to the regime. The regime reacted by emphasizing its nationalist credentials, making overtures to the radical Arab states, and

[15] Samir Mutawi in Parker, *The Six-Day War*, 175.
[16] Nigel Ashton, *King Hussein of Jordan: A Political Life* (New Haven, CT: Yale University Press, 2008), 113.

moving ostentatiously armoured units from the East Bank to the Jordan Valley. Egypt, Syria, and Iraq did not reciprocate Jordan's gestures of conciliation, leaving it completely isolated. To break out of his isolation Hussein made the fateful decision to go to Cairo for a grand reconciliation with Nasser. With the help of the Egyptian ambassador to Amman, he arranged to pay a visit to Nasser on 30 May.

The Jordanian-Egyptian Pact

On this occasion, Hussein kept Jack O'Connell, the Central Intelligence Agency (CIA) station chief, in the dark despite the high degree of mutual trust and the close professional ties between the two men. O'Connell went to his office in Amman in the morning and found two CIA intercepts relating to the king's prospective visit to Cairo. The message from Damascus to Nasser went roughly as follow: "Why are you meeting with this traitor? We want to ostracize him. We were not talking to the guy, and all of a sudden you are breaking the rules. What is going on?" The second intercept was Nasser's answer. The main thrust of the message, as O'Connell recalled many years later, was: "Leave me alone. Relax. I know what I am doing. I have a plan and you will approve of it. I'll tell you later. I cannot explain now." Nasser did not say explicitly that he was laying a trap for Hussein. But O'Connell thought that this was a trap. He asked himself: What was Hussein doing? Why was he going to Cairo? O'Connell called the palace to warn Hussein not to go to Cairo, but it was too late: the king was already on the tarmac in the airport, ready to take off.[17]

Wearing a khaki combat uniform with a field marshal's insignia, Hussein took his pliant prime minister and a small group of advisers and piloted his Caravelle plane to the Al-Maza military air base, near Cairo. Nasser, who came in person to the air base to receive his visitor, was surprised to find him in uniform. "Since your visit is secret, what would happen if we arrested you?" asked Nasser. "The possibility never crossed my mind," Hussein replied with a weak smile. This was an inauspicious beginning for the talks in the Kubbah Palace during the course of which Hussein made one concession after another. Hussein began by stating that it was absolutely essential for the United Arab Command to rise out of the ashes. Nasser proposed another solution: to draw up a pact between their two countries there and then. At Hussein's suggestion, Nasser sent

[17] Interview with Jack O'Connell, 4 October 2008, London.

someone to fetch the text of the Egyptian-Syrian mutual defence treaty. By his own account, Hussein was so anxious to come to some kind of agreement that he merely skimmed the text and said to Nasser: "Give me another copy. Put in Jordan instead of Syria and the matter is settled."[18] The manner in which Hussein negotiated this important international treaty was strange, but in character. It reflected the impatient, impulsive, and irresponsible side of his character as well as his propensity for taking risks.

The treaty was one of mutual defence with each party undertaking to go to the defence of the other in the event of an armed attack. The detailed provisions gave Nasser everything he requested. First, the Jordanian armed forces were placed under the command of Egyptian General Riad. Second, Hussein agreed to the entry into Jordan of troops from Egypt, Syria, Iraq, and Saudi Arabia. Third, Hussein had to agree to reopen the PLO offices in Amman and to reconciliation with its chairman, Ahmad Shuqairi, who was summoned to Cairo from Gaza for the occasion. Hussein also reluctantly agreed to take Shuqairi back to Amman with him on his plane. Jordan's role in the event of war was to open hostilities on a limited front in order to tie down a substantial portion of Israel's army that would otherwise be deployed on the Egyptian and Syrian fronts. In return, Nasser agreed to augment Jordan's tiny air force with air support from Egypt and Iraq. This promise went some way towards allaying Hussein's anxiety about conducting ground operations with little or no air cover. Hussein warned his hosts of the danger of a surprise Israeli air attack. He pointed out that Israel's first objective would be the Arab air forces, staring with Egypt. Nasser replied that that was obvious and that they were expecting it. He exuded self-confidence and assured Hussein that his army and air force were ready to confront Israel. The signing ceremony of the treaty was broadcast live on Radio Cairo and was followed by a press conference attended by the two heads of state and Shuqairi. On his return home later in the day, Hussein basked in the glory of his friendship with Nasser. Jubilant crowds lined the streets as the royal procession drove to the hilltop palace. The king was left in no doubt that his people approved his latest move. The following day the Chamber of Deputies voted overwhelmingly in favour of the pact

[18] Vick Vance and Pierre Lauer, *Hussein of Jordan: My "War" with Israel* (New York: William Morrow, 1969), 43–53.

and dispatched cables of congratulations to the king and the Egyptian president.[19]

Hussein won no plaudits from O'Connell for his escapade to Cairo. O'Connell was at the airport when the party returned from Cairo, and he was astonished to see Shuqairi in the king's entourage. That evening O'Connell went to see Jum'a at his home to ask for an explanation of the day's events. Jum'a was in a blithely optimistic frame of mind and had nothing but praise for his master's sudden turnabout. He said that they were no longer ostracized, they were no longer alone, and for the first time he could sleep peacefully at night. O'Connell thought to himself: "You have just signed your death warrant!"[20]

Hussein's pact with Nasser was not the brilliant diplomatic coup that it was widely perceived to be at the time. Within a week Jordan was at war with Israel alongside its new and feckless Arab allies. After the defeat that overwhelmed his country in this war, Hussein frequently repeated that he had no real choice in the matter, that events took their own course regardless of his wishes. To the present author he said:

In 1967 I had the impression that various events happened without one having anything to do with them and that this was going to be a problem. We came under pressure to hand over the control of our army and our destiny to a unified Arab command as part of the Arab League. And when Nasser moved his forces across the Suez Canal into Sinai, I knew that war was inevitable. I knew that we were going to lose. I knew that we in Jordan were threatened, threatened by two things: we either followed the course we did or alternately the country would tear itself apart if we stayed out and Israel would march into the West Bank and maybe even beyond. So these were the choices before us. It wasn't a question of our thinking there was any chance of winning. We knew where we were. We knew what the results would be. But it was the only way and we did our best and the results were the disaster we have lived with ever since.[21]

This account by King Hussein of the sequence of events that led to war is excessively deterministic. He was not compelled to throw in his lot with Egypt. Egypt had lost two wars to Israel, in 1948 and 1956, and there was no reason to think that it could win the third round. Even if one concedes that Hussein had no choice but to sign a mutual defence pact with Egypt, he was responsible for the hasty manner in which it was concluded and

[19] Samir A. Mutawi, *Jordan in the 1967 War* (Cambridge: Cambridge University Press, 1987), 111.
[20] Interview with Jack O'Connell, 4 October 2008, London.
[21] Interview with King Hussein bin Talal, 3 December 1996, Ascot, UK.

for the terms it embodied. Two mistakes stand out above all others. The first and most disastrous mistake was to place the Jordanian armed forces under the command of an Egyptian general. This meant that the most crucial decisions affecting Jordanian security, including the decision to go to war, would be taken in Cairo, not in Amman. It also meant that in the event of war, the Egyptian high command would determine how the Jordanian army would be deployed and how it would fight. Syria had a defence pact with Egypt, but it would have never agreed to place its army under the operational command of a non-Syrian officer. Hussein's second mistake was to agree unconditionally to the entry of Iraqi troops into Jordan. In every previous crisis involving the entry of Iraqi troops into Jordan, Israel reserved its freedom of action. The closure of the Straits of Tiran to Israeli shipping constituted one *casus belli*. The opening of Jordan to Iraqi and other Arab troops raised the perception of threat by Israel and made it more likely that it would take preemptive action. Far from providing political and military insurance, the pact with Egypt increased the external perils and dangers facing Jordan.

Having replaced Tall with a mediocre prime minister, the king was left with no persons of stature to advise and support him in the lead up to the war that he now considered inevitable. The Chief of Staff was General Amer Khammash, a professional soldier and planner who led the reorganization of Jordan's armed forces in the mid-1960s. He was the brightest and ablest individual in the king's inner circle. But he was a strong supporter of cooperation with Nasser and the integration of Jordan into the United Arab Command. Khammash was thus not a constraining influence but a contributor to the policy that led Jordan down the road to disaster. Other generals also pressed for coordinating Jordan's defence plans with the other confrontation states. Failure to stand together, they argued, would results in losing more soldiers and more territory. The CIA reported that "the army's mood was determined, their argument was irrefutable and the King faced serious morale and loyalty problems if he did not respond to it."[22]

Arab overconfidence and Arab overbidding were among the main causes of the 1967 war. The war thus provides a striking illustration of the perennial predicament of the Arab states: they cannot act separately and they cannot act collectively; they have separate national agendas and they keep getting in each other's way. On this occasion, the level of

---

[22] Quoted in Jeremy Bowen, *Six Days: How the 1967 War Shaped the Middle East* (London: Simon and Schuster, 2003), 66.

incompetence displayed by the Arab leaders was quite staggering. After ten years of preparation for what was often referred to as the "battle of destiny," and after raising popular passions to a fever pitch with their bombastic rhetoric, the leaders of the confrontation states were caught by complete surprise when Israel took their threats at face value and landed the first blow on Monday, 5 June.

On the Brink

No less staggering is the degree of mistrust on the Arab side of the hill. The Arab rulers who confronted a common enemy in 1967 profoundly disliked and mistrusted one another. From the outset, there was no possibility of proper coordination of war plans or purposeful collective action. Thanks to the CIA, these rulers did have advance warning of the impending Israeli blitzkrieg. But because they did not trust one another, nothing was done to anticipate it. The warning was conveyed unofficially by O'Connell to King Hussein around 7:00 P.M. on Wednesday, 4 June, when the king was at a dinner party at the home of some friends. O'Connell took the king out to the garden to tell him the alarming news: "The Israelis are going to attack Egypt tomorrow morning at 8:00am, and they are going to destroy its air force and its airfields." O'Connell got this hot piece of intelligence not from his headquarters but from the American assistant military attaché in Amman who had received it from his friend, the American assistant military attaché in Tel Aviv. O'Connell explained to the king that he was not passing on this intelligence officially and went on to advise him in a personal capacity not to get involved in the coming war. Hussein asked whether Jordan and Syria were going to be attacked. O'Connell replied that his source only referred to Egypt and said nothing about Jordan or Syria.[23]

O'Connell had not received any instructions from his superiors in the CIA to warn Hussein. Nor had he cleared his proposed course of action with them. But as he had been assigned to Jordan, he felt a sense of personal responsibility to try to keep the king and his vulnerable kingdom out of trouble. O'Connell was particularly troubled by the plots being hatched in Damascus against Jordan, and he said to the king: "I have no authority to tell you this. I found out this intelligence by chance and I have decided to share it with you. I am not passing it on to you officially. My *personal* opinion, Your Majesty, is that you should not get involved

[23] Interview with Jack O'Connell, 4 October 2008, London.

in this war. You don't have to be more of an Arab nationalist than the Syrians. So if you do get involved, you don't need to do so until after the Syrians get in." It was a wise piece of advice, but it went unheeded.

Hussein's first move was to send an urgent message to Nasser, through General Riad. Hussein warned his new allies of the imminent IAF strike and urged them to take precautions. Despite this clear and timely warning, which was repeated a second time, the Egyptian armed forces were taken by complete surprise. At their first meeting after the war, Hussein asked Nasser why he had done nothing to protect himself against the Israeli air strike despite the two warnings. With disarming candour Nasser replied, "I did not believe you."[24] Jordanians do not like to hear this story because it contradicts the loyalist version which holds that the king had no alternative. But the king did have an alternative: to stay out of this war. The king ignored it; he made his choice and paid the price. For the second time in a week, he fell into a trap.[25]

To understand Hussein's conduct during the June 1967 War it is essential to recall that he had handed over command of his army to Egypt under the terms of his pact with Nasser. On 1 June, General Riad arrived in Amman and assumed command of the Jordanian armed forces. From this point on, it was he who made the key decisions on orders from Cairo. Israel opened hostilities at dawn on 5 June with a brilliantly planned and executed lightening attack that annihilated most of Egypt's air force on the ground. Despite the two warnings from King Hussein, the Egyptians were totally unprepared and as a result virtually lost the war on the first day.[26] Elementary decency required the Egyptian high command to inform its allies of the setback and to warn them to take precautionary measures. But there was no decency and no honesty in the relations between the Arab allies. The Arab coalition facing Israel in this war was one of the most ill-prepared and bitterly divided coalitions in the history of modern warfare with the exception of the Arab front in the 1948 war. As in the war for Palestine, the inability of the Arabs to coordinate their military and diplomatic strategies was a major factor in their ultimate defeat.[27]

[24] Ibid.
[25] Andrew and Leslie Cockburn, *Dangerous Liaison: The Inside Story of the Covet U.S.-Israeli Relationship* (New York: Harper Perennial, 1991), 148–9.
[26] Heikal, *1967: Al-Infijar*, 435–45; Mutawi, *Jordan in the 1967 War*, 122.
[27] Eugene L. Rogan and Avi Shlaim, eds., *The War for Palestine: Rewriting the History of 1948* (Cambridge: Cambridge University Press, 2007).

On 5 June at about 9:00 A.M., Hussein rushed to his army headquarters after being informed that the Israeli offensive against Egypt had begun. Shortly before his arrival, General Riad had received a cable from Cairo. The cable was from First Vice-President and Deputy Supreme Commander Field Marshal Abd al-Hakim Amer. Amer was a nincompoop who largely owed his rapid promotion to his friendship with Nasser. A major and a free officer during the revolution of 1952, Amer rose to the rank of field marshal and minister of war two years later. He was inexperienced in military affairs, impulsive, and prone to wishful thinking. He was personally responsible for the lack of preparedness of the Egyptian air force on the eve of battle; relieved of his command on 9 June; and either committed suicide or was "suicided" after the defeat.

Amer's cable to Riad was a pack of lies. It said that the enemy's planes started to bomb Egypt's air bases, the attack failed, and 75 percent of the enemy's aircraft had been destroyed or put out of action. The cable also said that Egypt's forces engaged the enemy in Sinai and taken the offensive on the ground. On the basis of these alleged successes, Amer ordered Riad to open a new front against the enemy and launch offensive operations. By the time Hussein arrived at the headquarters, Riad had already given the orders for the artillery to move to the front lines and bombard Israeli air bases and other targets; an infantry brigade to occupy the Israeli enclave on Mount Scopus in Jerusalem; the two Egyptian commando battalions to infiltrate enemy territory from the West Bank at dusk; and the air force to be put on combat alert and commence air strikes immediately. Although these decisions were made in his absence, Hussein made no attempt to cancel them or to delay the opening of fire until the information from Cairo could be checked. Jordan was thus committed to war by the decision of an Egyptian general who was acting on the orders of a serial blunderer in Cairo.

Shortly after his arrival at army headquarters, Hussein was given the first of three Israeli messages urging him not to get involved in the war that broke out very early that morning. Israel's main enemy was Egypt, and the government most emphatically did not want war with Jordan, hence the message was transmitted through three different channels. The first channel was the Norwegian general with the implausible name of Odd Bull, Chief of Staff of the UN Truce Supervision Organization. Bull was asked to transmit a message to King Hussein expressing the hope of the Israeli government that he would not join in the war. If he stayed out, Israel would not attack him, but if he chose to come in, Israel would use against him all the means at its disposal. At first Bull hesitated, "This was a threat, pure and simple, and it is not the normal practise of the UN to pass on threats from one government to another." But this message seemed so important that he quickly sent it to King Hussein the same morning.[28]

"I did receive the message," Hussein confirmed, "but it was too late in any event. I had already handed over the command of the army to the United Arab Command. There was a unified Arab command with an Egyptian general in army headquarters in charge of the Jordanian armed forces as a part of the defensive effort. The Syrians were not ready, the Iraqis were far away, eventually they moved even before the Syrians and already the first wave had gone in from Jordan into Israel when the UN general called to say that there is a message to keep out of it. I said: 'Tell him it's too late.' I don't know that the message made any difference because at that time I had these options: either joins the Arabs, or Jordan would have torn itself apart. A clash between Palestinians and Jordanians might have led to Jordan's destruction and left the very clear possibility of an Israeli take-over of at least the West Bank and Jerusalem. We did the best we could in the hope that somebody would stop this madness before it developed any further and help us out."[29]

Israel conveyed the same message to Hussein through Colonel Daoud, his representative to the Mixed Armistice Commission and through the State Department. The message from Secretary of State Dean Rusk to the American ambassador in Amman said, "Israeli Representative here asks us to convey earnest desire government not do any harm to Jordan. They hope that hostilities between the two countries can be avoided or kept to a minimum."[30] Rusk wrote in his memoirs that they tried hard to persuade King Hussein not to become embroiled in the fighting, but he said, "I am an Arab and I have to take part." As an Arab, writes Rusk, Hussein felt honour-bound to assist Egypt, especially because Israel had struck first. Rusk thought that they could have gotten the Israelis to stay their hand, but Hussein insisted on getting in: "It was one of the sadder moments of this crisis because it certainly was not in Jordan's

---

[28] Odd Bull, *War and Peace in the Middle East: The Experiences and Views of a UN Observer* (London: Leo Cooper, 1976), 113.

[29] Interview with King Hussein bin Talal, 3 December 1996, Ascot, UK.

[30] Dean Rusk to Embassy in Jordan, 5 June 1967, Department of State, *Foreign Relations of the United States, 1964–1968*, vol. XIX, *Arab-Israeli Crisis and War, 1967* (Washington, DC: U.S. Government Printing House, 2004), 305 [hereinafter referred to as *FRUS*].

interests to attack Israel, then lose the West Bank and the old city of Jerusalem."[31]

The Outbreak of Hostilities

Jordan did not declare war on Israel but opened hostilities at 9:30 A.M. by firing across the armistice lines in Jerusalem. From Jerusalem the shooting spread to other fronts and involved artillery and tanks. The Israelis hoped that this was just a token gesture of Jordanian solidarity with Egypt. But the Jordanian capture of the Government House and the encirclement of Israeli positions on Mount Scopus were seen as serious acts of war. Jordan also launched an air attack on Israel on Monday morning. This attack was utterly pathetic compared to the IAF attack on the Egyptian air bases. The Jordanian air force was so tiny – a fleet of twenty-two Hawker Hunters – that it could not carry out any large-scale operations on its own. General Riad realized this and issued an order at 9:00 A.M. for a joint Jordanian-Syrian-Iraqi attack on Israel's air bases. Persistent Iraqi and Syrian delays, however, meant that the attack could not be launched before 11:50 A.M. Sixteen Jordanian Hawker Hunters took part in the bombing of air bases and other military targets, but the damage they inflicted was minimal. The Syrian air force made one ineffectual sortie, and the Iraqi air force did not fare much better.

By this time, the IAF had completed the destruction of the Egyptian air force and could turn its full might against the three smaller ones. Amman airport was bombed while all the Hawker Hunters were refuelling and rearming and they were destroyed on the ground before they could take off. Fifteen minutes later, much of Syria's air force and the two Iraqi squadrons suffered the same fate. Israel was now effectively the only air power in the region. By knocking out the Arab air forces so swiftly on the first day, Israel achieved complete mastery in the air, and it proceeded to use it to very good effect in the land battles that followed. In all, four hundred enemy planes were destroyed on the first day, and that basically sealed the fate of all the Arab armies. Never in the history of modern warfare did air power play so decisive a role in determining the outcome of a conflict.

---

[31] Dean Rusk, *As I Saw It: A Secretary of State's Memoirs* (London: I. B. Tauris, 1991), 331.

Israeli pilots appear to have targeted Hussein personally, though he refused to discuss this incident in his extensive interviews with the two French journalists who published the book *Hussein of Jordan: My "War" with Israel*. Zaid Rifa'i, Chief of Protocol at the Royal Palace, was an eyewitness. He saw two Israeli Mystères approaching the palace: one was hit by antiaircraft fire and crashed; the other swept down and fired two missiles that penetrated the conference hall. It came full circle and headed back to the palace at full speed: "This time, it machine-gunned the King's office at point-blank range with a precision and knowledge of its target that was stupefying. Then, finally it disappeared." Rifa'i called Hussein at army headquarters to report the incident. Hussein only asked if anyone had been wounded. The answer was "no." "In that case, it's all right," Hussein said calmly and hung up.[32] O'Connell took the incident more seriously. He reported it to his superiors and asked them to tell the Israelis to knock it off. A message was slipped to the Israelis, and there were no further air attacks threatening King Hussein.[33]

Following the destruction of the Jordanian air force, Israel launched a limited counteroffensive with the aim of repelling the Jordanian soldiers from the Government House, defending Mount Scopus, and capturing key strategic positions around Jerusalem. The next forty-eight hours of fighting on the Jordanian front consisted of a catalogue of errors committed by General Riad, each one worse than the last one. The Jordanians had a carefully laid plan for the defence of the West Bank. Operation Tariq called for concentrating Jordan's forces around Jerusalem, encircling the Jewish side of the city, capturing Mount Scopus, holding on to it until the United Nations imposed a cease-fire, and then using it as a bargaining chip. The Jordanian officers knew the topography of the West Bank well, and this plan was tailored to make the most of their limited military capability. But they were compelled to carry the orders of an Egyptian general who was a complete newcomer to this front and who acted on the basis of orders from Cairo.

Jordan's armoured corps was divided into two brigades of M-48 tanks, the 40th and the 60th. General Riad's worst blunder was to order the 60th armoured brigade to move from Jericho to Hebron and the 40th brigade to move from Damia Bridge to Jericho. The intention was that the Jordanian brigades would join up with an Egyptian force that was

---

[32] Vance and Lauer, *Hussein of Jordan*, 68–70.

[33] Richard Helms, *A Look over My Shoulder: A Life in the Central Intelligence Agency* (New York: Random House, 2003), 303–4.

supposed to be advancing towards Beersheba. But this victorious Egyptian march was a fantasy and a delusion. Riad subjected the Jordanian army to muddled and self-defeating manoeuvres and exposed it to unrelenting attacks from the Israeli air force. The Israelis found Riad's juggling of armoured brigades in broad daylight and without air cover to be extremely strange, to say the least.[34]

The Second Day

At dawn on Tuesday, the second day of the war, the full extent of Jordan's reverses became apparent. At a meeting around 5:30 that morning, General Riad offered Hussein the following options: try for a ceasefire through diplomatic channels or order an immediate retreat so as to fall back at dusk to the East Bank of the Jordan. Riad added, "If we don't decide within the next 24 hours, you can kiss your army and all of Jordan good-by! We are on the verge of losing the west bank; all our forces will be isolated and destroyed." Hussein thought for a moment and then asked the Egyptian general to contact Nasser in order to find out what he thought. Half an hour later, around 6:00 A.M., they got through to Nasser over the regular public telephone system. The United Arab Command had at its disposal an ultramodern system, but the equipment sat idle in Cairo. This was the famous conversation that the Israelis intercepted and publicized round the world. The two leaders agreed to accuse America and Britain of giving Israel air support. "The Big Lie" badly backfired on its inventors by alienating the two governments and public opinion. Hussein maintained, however, that when he charged America and Britain of participation on the side of Israel, he actually believed it.[35]

In the same notorious conversation, Hussein and Nasser also discussed the situation on the Jordanian front. At Nasser's suggestion, Riad sent a written report. Riad's coded cable read as follows: "The situation on the west bank is becoming desperate. The Israelis are attacking on all fronts. We are bombed day and night by the Israeli air force and can offer no resistance because the major part of our combined air power has been put out of commission.... We can try to stay on the west bank another 24 hours. But if we do, the total destruction of the Jordanian army is inevitable. King Hussein has asked me to inform you of the above

---

34 Interview with Moshe Sasson, 21 March 2002, Jerusalem.
35 Vance and Lauer, *Hussein of Jordan*, 95–96.

in order to learn your opinion and your decision at the earliest possible time."

At 12:30 P.M. Hussein sent a personal telegram to Nasser in which he reported: "The situation is deteriorating rapidly. In Jerusalem it is critical. In addition to our very heavy losses in men and equipment, for lack of air protection, our tanks are being disabled at the rate of one every ten minutes. And the bulk of the enemy forces are concentrated against the Jordanian army." Hussein requested Nasser's views as soon as possible. At almost the same moment, Riad received an answer from Amer that said, "We agree to the retreat from the west bank, and the arming of the civilian population." Hussein answered Amer with another message, "We are still holding on. We are trying to put off the retreat as long as possible. The civilian population has been armed for a long time."

Hussein did not hear from Nasser in response to his cable until eleven hours later. From a telephone conversation and a cable Hussein learnt for the first time that Nasser's air force was out of commission, his army was in retreat in Sinai, and the situation on the ground was desperate. "We have been purely and simply crushed by the enemy," Nasser summed up. His advice to Hussein was to evacuate the West Bank and hope that the Security Council would order a cease-fire but not to break off diplomatic relations with London and Washington.[36] The United Nations had called for a cease-fire two hours after the outbreak of hostilities, and Israel responded positively but the fighting continued. On the second day, it became clear that unless Israel could be stopped by political means, the Jordanian front would collapse. Jordan desperately needed a cease-fire, but it could not say so openly nor could it act on its own without consulting its Arab allies. King Hussein got round this problem by asking the Americans to arrange a cease-fire directly with Israel without going through the United Nations. On the morning of the second day, the Americans informed the Israelis of Jordan's readiness to cease-fire immediately but emphasized the need for secrecy so as not to compromise King Hussein's position. This American request had unintended consequences. The Israelis realized that the sand in the political hourglass was running out, and the minister of defence promptly ordered the army to capture the Old City of Jerusalem as quickly as possible.[37]

[36] Ibid., 88–93.
[37] Moshe Zak, *Hussein oseh shalom* [Hussein Makes Peace] [in Hebrew] (Ramat-Gan: Bar-Ilan University, 1996), 117–18.

At 11:00 P.M. on 6 June, an immediate and unconditional cease-fire was ordered by the Security Council. An hour earlier, with Hussein's agreement, General Riad had issued an order for all the Jordanian forces to retreat from the West Bank to the East Bank. The Security Council resolution gave hope of holding on to the West Bank until the cease-fire came into effect. With this prospect in mind, Riad issued a new order countermanding his earlier order and directing the troops to stay in their positions. A few units had already moved back and had to fight to regain the positions they had just relinquished. The counterorder also led to general confusion because of problems of communication between army headquarters and the units in the field. The IDF did not respect the cease-fire. On the contrary, it intensified its offensive in order to gain as much territory as possible. The Israeli offensive destroyed any lingering Jordanian hope of holding on to the West Bank. At 2:30 A.M. on the night of 6–7 June, Riad, once again with Hussein's approval, ordered a complete withdrawal from the West Bank. Both men feared that failure to do so would result in the annihilation of the remnants of the Jordanian army.[38] The retreat of units from the West Bank continued all night.

Wednesday, 7 June, was the third and, to all intents and purposes, the last day of the war on the Jordanian front. Events unfolded at a bewildering speed on both the military and the diplomatic planes. Developments on the two planes were intimately connected: the rapid deterioration in Jordan's military situation led it to intensify its diplomatic efforts to bring about an end to hostilities. The reverse was also true: the unstoppable momentum of the IDF offensive tipped the balance against a cease-fire until the capture of the West Bank had been completed. At noon, Jerusalem, including the Old City, fell after a desperate battle. Following the fall of Jerusalem, a general order was issued for the withdrawal of all the bruised and battered units from the West Bank to the East Bank. The main cities of the West Bank fell in rapid succession. By nightfall, the entire West Bank was in Israeli hands. Last to leave were the three units that secured the bridges across the Jordan River. The Israelis blew up the bridges in order to sever the link between the two banks and consolidate their control of the territory all the way up to the river.

Dialogue across the Battle Lines

All day long Hussein persisted in his frantic efforts to secure a cease-fire and stayed in close contact with the ambassadors of the Western powers

---

[38] Mutawi, *Jordan in the 1967 War*, 139–40; Vance and Lauer, *Hussein of Jordan*, 95–6.

who were bringing pressure to bear on Israel to agree to a cease-fire. Walworth Barbour, the American ambassador to Tel Aviv, forwarded four telegrams that came directly from Amman to the Foreign Ministry, starting at 5:25 in the morning. If the fighting continued, Hussein stated, his regime would be destroyed. In a second telegram that followed half an hour later, Hussein tried to clarify that he was not asking for a formal cease-fire but urging Israel to halt what he described as its punitive actions against his army. Shortly before seven o'clock, he warned again that he was in danger of losing control over the situation. The four messages gave Israel a chance to stop before hundreds of thousands of Palestinians came under its rule.[39] Rusk instructed Barbour to convey at the highest level their insistent demand that Israel agree to a cease-fire. The ambassador was to stress that the flood of refugees to the East Bank and the disintegration of the Jordanian security forces created a real danger for the regime and for the large foreign community in the country.[40] Barbour conveyed the message to Eshkol but gained the impression that it was too late, that Israel was no longer interested in keeping the king on his throne, not after he had bombarded Jerusalem, Kfar Saba, Netanya, and other civilian settlements.[41]

The British Ambassador, Michael Hadow, made similar representations. For the rest of the day the press agencies reported that King Hussein was ready to start negotiations with Israel for a cease-fire. Moshe Dayan, Israel's minister of defence, rejected this request with some vehemence: "We have been offering the King an opportunity to cut his losses ever since Monday morning. Now we have 500 dead and wounded in Jerusalem. So, tell him that from now on, I'll talk to him only with the gunsights of our tanks!"[42] London put pressure on Israel to stop shooting and start talking to Hussein across the conference table. Prime Minister Harold Wilson told the Israeli ambassador that Israel's refusal to respond to Hussein's offer of a cease-fire cast doubt on its claims that its war aims were defensive and not territorial.

Julian Amery, a prominent Conservative politician who was a supporter of Israel and a close personal friend of King Hussein, tried hard to reconcile the warring sides. Amery met with Prince Hassan, Hussein's younger brother, who was studying Oriental languages at Christ Church,

---

[39] Tom Segev, *1967: Israel, the War and the Year that Transformed the Middle East* (London: Little, Brown, 2007), 356–7.
[40] Zak, *Hussein oseh shalom*, 118.
[41] Segev, *1967*, 356; *FRUS*, 324.
[42] Vance and Lauer, *Hussein of Jordan*, 65.

Oxford, when the war broke out. Hassan told Amery that he spoke to his brother on the telephone and that there was a reasonable prospect for signing a peace agreement with his brother. A cease-fire could be made conditional on the immediate start of negotiations for a peace treaty and a comprehensive settlement between the two countries. Amery relayed this report to his Israeli friends and pressed them to act on it.[43] There was not the remotest chance, however, that the Israelis would want to follow up this dubious diplomatic *démarche*. By undertaking it, Prince Hassan revealed how cut off he was from the rapidly unfolding reality. His older brother was in no position to negotiate a separate peace with the enemy at this stage in the war, and in any case, Israel was hardly likely to hand back to him the Old City of Jerusalem, the most glittering prize in this war.

Another meeting in London involved Amery, Air Vice Marshal Sir Erik Bennett, who had been an air adviser to Hussein in the early 1960s, Israeli Ambassador Aharon Remez, and Mossad representative Nahum Admoni. The Englishmen stated, on the basis of their discussion with Prince Hassan, that there was a reasonable prospect of persuading Hussein to agree to a separate peace treaty with Israel. It was likely that Bennett, who was also a close friend of King Hussein, would go to Amman the following day with the approval of the British government. Bennett planned to recommend to Hussein the option of a separate peace with Israel on a fair basis. He therefore asked the Israelis to indicate to Hussein the kind of terms on which a separate peace between Jordan and Israel could be concluded. Bennett realized that the Israelis would need to hold detailed and direct negotiations before entering into a final commitment, but he suggested that it might be decisive to let the king know as soon as possible the kind of terms he might expect to obtain.[44] Bennett's suggestion was not taken up.

Hussein also used a direct British intelligence channel to try to arrest the Israeli assault on his army. Jock Smith, the MI6 representative in Tel Aviv, met his opposite number, Naftali Kenan, at 5:30 P.M. on 7 June in the latter's house. Smith reported that Hussein saw a very bleak situation: he could either withdraw his army from the West Bank and the result would be his fall from power, or he could throw his army into battle with the IDF, in which case his army would be defeated and

---

[43] Remez to Levavi, 7 June 1967, "Hussein," in "The Private Papers of Yaacov Herzog." I am grateful to Shira Herzog for giving me access to her late father's papers.
[44] Remez and Admoni to Levavi, 7 June 1967, ibid.

the result for himself would be the same – the collapse of his regime. Either course would create a situation that would permit the entry of Syrian troops into Jordan. Hussein estimated that the Syrians had eleven brigades that so far had not been committed to the battlefield. Smith asked his colleague to believe that the best long-term interests of both their countries could be served by "reducing fighting immediately to the level of skirmishes; this would enable the Jordanians to hold their positions until the Egyptians are seen to be defeated and a ceasefire arranged by somebody. The internal situation could then be controlled. If this is not done the King believes his regime will fall and you will be faced with a Syrian-type regime in Jordan."

Kenan wanted to know whether this was a service-to-service or a government-to-government approach. Smith replied that it was a service-to-service approach that had the support of the British government. He added that they took into account Hussein's provocative actions during the crisis and after the outbreak of hostilities and his stupid statement about the participation of British airplanes in the fighting alongside Israel, but they still wanted to help him. Kenan asked whether this appeal was instigated by Hussein or by the British side. Smith replied that Hussein turned to their representative in Amman and that the assessment and the conclusions that he presented came from Hussein. The British government shared Hussein's assessment of the situation and his conclusions, and they supported the course of action that he proposed. The British government considered this to be the only way to save Hussein's regime.[45]

These behind-the-scenes manoeuvres did not have any visible effect on Israel's conduct of the war, but they are very revealing of Hussein's state of mind and of his feeling that he and his dynasty might have reached the end of the road. They also reveal the depth of his disenchantment with his Arab allies, especially with the Syrians. Let down by the Arabs and threatened by the Israelis, he was fighting for political survival. For him, the Six-Day War lasted less than three days. In the early hours of Thursday, 8 June, Jordan accepted unconditionally the Security Council's call for a cease-fire. Exhausted, his voice cracking with emotion, Hussein addressed his people in a radio broadcast. First, he paid tribute to the heroism with which Jordan's soldiers had fought against overwhelming odds. He went on to express his deep grief over the loss of all their fallen soldiers. "My brothers," he intoned, "I seem to belong to a family which, according to the will of Allah, must suffer and make sacrifices for its

---

[45] "A conversation between Jock Smith and Naftali Kenan," 7 June 1967, 5:30 P.M., ibid.

country without end. Our calamity is greater than any one could have imagined. But whatever its size, we must not let it weaken our resolve to regain what we have lost."[46]

The reference to Hussein's family may seem odd in this context, but it was not accidental. The Jordanian monarch was the proud heir to a Hashemite heritage that went back to Hussein the Sharif of Mecca and the Great Arab Revolt. Throughout his own career, King Hussein had to walk a tightrope between Arab nationalism and coexistence with Israel. During the mid-1960s, he began to lean towards accommodation with Israel. The tacit alliance with Israel was grounded in a common interest in keeping a quiet border, common enemy in the shape of radical Arab nationalism, and common allegiance with the West in the global Cold War. Israel's attack on Samuʿ suddenly destroyed the trust on which this evolving alliance was based. Contrary to Hussein's perception, Israel had no wish to harm him or to take over the West Bank. Samuʿ was an isolated military operation; it was not part of any sinister plan. Policy, however, is based on perceptions, not on reality. Hussein's misperception of Israel's intentions pushed him into the arms of the radical Arab nationalists. This process culminated in his dramatic reconciliation with Nasser and in the signature of a mutual defence pact with Egypt. From this point on, Hussein was locked to the inter-Arab dynamic of escalation that ended in a full-scale war with Israel.

Consequences

In a strikingly fair-minded biography of the Jordanian monarch, Nigel Ashton wrote, "Hussein's decision to join Nasser in waging war against Israel in 1967 was the greatest calamity of his reign."[47] It would be difficult to disagree with this verdict. Even Hussein accepted this judgement on one occasion in an abrupt departure from his habitual claim that he had no choice. In a candid speech to his countrymen to mark the thirtieth anniversary of the June 1967 War, the king confessed that he considered his decision to fight alongside the other Arab nations to have been a costly mistake. "In reality," he said, "it was probably our duty to try to prevent this country from being part of the battle."[48]

---

[46] Vance and Lauer, *Hussein of Jordan*, 97.
[47] Ashton, *King Hussein of Jordan*, 120.
[48] Christopher Walker, "Hussein Admits Costly Mistake over Six-Day War," *The Times*, 7 June 1997.

The immediate consequences of the war for Jordan were so catastrophic as to raise questions about the regime's prospects of survival.
The government was bewildered and impotent. The army was defeated
and dispirited. Seven hundred Jordanian soldiers had died in the war
and more than six thousand were wounded or missing. Jordan lost its
entire air force, 80 percent of its armour, and a great deal of other equipment. At the end of the war, only four out of the army's eleven brigades
remained operational. The East Bank was left completely defenceless.[49]
The economic consequences of the war were also crippling. The Old City
of Jerusalem was not just a symbol of Hashemite legitimacy but a major
source of revenue from tourism as were some of the West Bank towns
like Bethlehem. The West Bank comprised roughly half of the kingdom's
inhabited territory, half of its industrial capacity, and a quarter of its
arable land. It contained valuable water resources and contributed nearly
40 percent of its gross domestic product.[50] Israel's occupation of the West
Bank resulted in the creation of a new wave of refugees. As a result, the
total number of refugees in Jordan's care increased from about half a
million to nearly three-quarters of a million. Quite apart from the human
suffering involved and the burning sense of injustice, it was a heavy material burden for the truncated and impoverished kingdom to bear.

Yet the balance sheet of the war for Jordan was not entirely negative.
No one could deny that the Jordanian army had discharged faithfully all
its duties to Arab unity during this tragic war. As a direct result of this
honourable war record, Jordan was accepted as a legitimate member of
the society of Arab states. Its right to exist was no longer challenged as
openly and aggressively as it had been during the previous decade. The
war constituted a comprehensive defeat for pan-Arabism. The dichotomy
between "progressive" and "reactionary" regimes disappeared from the
Arab landscape because both camps were equally implicated in the defeat,
and they were all now in the same boat.[51]

A major realignment of forces occurred in the region. The war transformed Nasser from Hussein's worst enemy to his closest ally in the Arab
world. Mahmoud Riad, Egypt's foreign minister at the time, describes
how impressed Nasser was that Hussein stood shoulder to shoulder with
him during the war. On 22 June, Nasser wrote to Hussein, paying tribute

---

[49] Mutawi, *Jordan in the 1967 War*, 164.
[50] Tal, *Politics, the Military, and National Security in Jordan*, 120–1.
[51] Asher Susser, "Jordan and the Six-Day War," in *Six Days – Thirty Years: New Perspectives on the Six-Day War*, ed. Asher Susser [in Hebrew] (Tel Aviv: Am Oved, 1999),
111–12.

to his heroic struggle and offering "to put all we have in the service of the common destiny of our two peoples." He later received Hussein in Cairo and told him that Egypt was ready to share everything it had with Jordan, even if it meant sharing the last loaf of bread between them. "We have entered this war together, lost it together and we must win it together," said Nasser. Nasser also felt that the United States might be more inclined to accommodate King Hussein because he was an old friend of theirs, and so he urged him to negotiate with the Americans in any way he wanted to and for as long as he wanted to for a peaceful settlement in the West Bank as long as he refrained from signing a separate peace treaty with Israel.[52]

The importance of the new alliance with Nasser for Hussein cannot be overestimated. Together the two leaders built up an axis of moderation in the Arab world that others were encouraged to join. On the morrow of their defeat, the Arabs faced a fork in the road: one road led to another appeal to arms; the other involved a fundamental change in the Arab policy towards Israel, an official end to the state of belligerency, and an attempt to recover the occupied territories by peaceful means. By himself Hussein had no chance of persuading his fellow Arab rulers to follow him down the moderate path; with Nasser's support there was at least a chance. Nasser's support provided Hussein with political cover for working with the Americans, negotiating with the Israelis, standing up to the Syrians, and countering the PLO's call for renewing the armed struggle against Israel. It was also crucial for maintaining the legitimacy of the Hashemite regime inside Jordan following the catastrophic defeat on the battlefield.

[52] Mahmoud Riad, *The Struggle for Peace in the Middle East* (London: Quartet, 1981), 46.

5

The Palestinian National Movement

Wendy Pearlman

This chapter explores the impact of Palestinians on the 1967 War and vice versa, with a focus on the Palestinian national movement. Its main argument is that the descent into war was propelled not only by the conflict between Israel and Arab states but also by a multifaceted struggle among Palestinians and Arabs for control over mobilization for the Palestinian cause.

This struggle was defined by three overlapping realms of contestation: that among Arab states, between Palestinians and Arab states, and among Palestinians. During the years leading up to the war, Palestinian groups, principally Ahmed Shuqairi's Palestine Liberation Organization (PLO) and the Fatah movement, advanced competing claims to be the legitimate representative of the Palestinian people and their aspirations. Yet their competition was also testimony to the ambiguous boundaries between the Palestinian national struggle and the larger Arab world. In developing their own conceptions of Palestinian nationalism, they were forced to address its relationship to the call for Arab unity. In vying for resources and power, they could not depend on Arab governments. These governments, themselves competing for stature and security in regional politics, in turn invoked the Palestinian cause as justification for attempts to dictate, restrict, or interfere in Palestinian mobilization. Aspirant Palestinian leaders thus positioned themselves in a matrix of opportunities and constraints constructed by rival Arab state interests. This positioning influenced the strategies that both Palestinian and Arab leaders pursued in the conflict with Israel. It was, therefore, a crucial piece of the story of the third Arab-Israeli war.

Palestinian Nationalism and Arab Politics

From the inception of the conflict between Zionism and the indigenous community of Palestine, the latter's mobilization was shaped by complex connections between Palestinian nationalism and the larger Arab world. Nayef Hawatmeh, head of the Democratic Front for the Liberation of Palestine, explained in 1973:

> The historical and fateful link between the Palestinian question and the conflicts occurring in the rest of the Arab world ... distinguishes the Palestine question from any other cause of emancipation or national liberation in the countries of Asia, Africa and Latin America ... the Palestine question has been dominated by the process of mutual interaction between what occurs in Palestine and what occurs in the neighbouring areas.[1]

This "mutual interaction" between Palestinians and Arab states has had many causes, most notably the active role of Arab states in the conflict with Israel, the dispersion of Palestinian refugees in Arab countries, and Palestinians' situation of statelessness, which has invited Arab heads of state to act as representatives of the Palestinian cause in international forums. These ties, intertwining Palestinian and Arab politics, would surely be sufficient as a source of complexity in the Palestinian struggle. However, they become even more entangled due to their overlap with the multiplicity of interests among Palestinians.

During the British mandate in Palestine, the Palestinian national movement was divided by rivalries among Jerusalem's elite families and the tension between elites and nonelite aspirants. Occasionally siding with some of these groups over others, Arab governments intervened in Palestinians' dealings with the British authorities. During the Palestinians' Great Arab Rebellion from 1936 to 1939, Arab fighters from outside of mandatory Palestine joined the fight and even claimed leadership of it. By the 1947 Partition Plan, it was Arab states that took the lead in choosing or rebuffing Palestinian representatives, if not in speaking directly for the Palestinian people.

The 1948 war ushered in a new stage in the interplay between Arab regimes, intra-Palestinian competition, and the struggle for Palestine. Frontline Arab states were home to most Palestinians: of the 600,000 to

---

[1] "Nayef Hawatmeh," in *Palestinian Lives: Interviews with Leaders of the Resistance*, ed. Clovis Maksoud (Beirut: Palestine Research Center and Kuwaiti Teachers' Association, 1973), 83.

760,000 Palestinians who fled in the course of the war, 10 percent went to the East Bank of the Jordan, 39 percent to the West Bank, 26 percent to the Gaza Strip, 14 percent to Lebanon, 10 percent to Syria, and 1 percent to Egypt.[2] These governments tended to view Palestinians as destabilizing and prohibited or restricted their independent political activity. Palestinians thus tended to join existing Nasserite, Ba'thist, Marxist, Islamist, and other Arab political parties. Palestinians were among the greatest proponents of Arab nationalism, and supporters of Egyptian President Gamal Abdel Nasser. By the early 1960s, however, Nasser was vocalizing his belief that Arab armies were not ready for a war with Israel and should thus avoid seeking one prematurely. Many Palestinians, meanwhile, were becoming impatient with existing political ideologies and longed for a movement that more clearly prioritized the fight for Palestinian self-determination. Towards this goal, Palestinians formed some forty clandestine groups between 1959 and 1963, some containing just a handful of members and others as many as four hundred.[3]

Two of these groups were to become major players in the revival of the national movement. At the American University of Beirut, George Habash and Wadi Haddad assembled a group that called for Arab unity as the means to fight imperialism and recover Palestine. The Arab Nationalist Movement formalized in 1956 and established a Palestinian branch seven years later. The Arab Nationalists developed a close relationship with Nasser. The group thus upheld Nasser's policy against premature military hostilities with Israel, though some of its members were restless to engage in battle.

During the same era, some young refugees in Gaza were joining the Egyptian Muslim Brotherhood as a way of fighting for Palestine. Yet, they too became frustrated with the brotherhood's opposition to taking up arms. At the University of Cairo, Yasser Arafat advocated a position that ran counter to this norm in regional politics: rather than wait for Arab states to unite and attack Israel, Palestinians should rely primarily on themselves to liberate Palestine. Moving from Cairo to Kuwait, Arafat and others formalized their group as the Palestine Liberation Movement, or Fatah. Their clandestine organization grew into a network and began

---

[2] George Kossaifi, "Demographic Characteristics of the Arab Palestinian People," in *The Sociology of the Palestinians*, ed. Khalil Nakhleh and Elia Zureik (London: Croom Helm, 1980), 18.

[3] Baruch Kimmerling and Joel Migdal, *The Palestinian People: A History* (Cambridge, MA: Harvard University Press, 2003), 238.

issuing a magazine, *Filastinuna* (Our Palestine), which facilitated contacts with Palestinians in other countries. In this and other publications, Fatah articulated a vision that challenged the reigning Arab order in two ways. First, in opposition to most regimes' inclination to subordinate Palestinians' struggle to their own government or party, Fatah stressed its ideological and organizational autonomy. Second, in contrast to governments' hope to avoid a war for which they were not ready, Fatah issued an impassioned call for armed struggle against Israel. Its strategy was to pursue a popular campaign of guerrilla operations against Israel through which it would deliberately entangle Arab states in a full-fledged war for Palestine. In the view of Fatah leaders, Arab states would not achieve the necessary preparedness vis-à-vis Israel unless the masses, rallied by the operations of a vanguard force, pushed Arab statesmen to do so.[4]

While most Arabs and Palestinians thus looked to Nasser to lead the Arab states against Israel, Fatah and the Arab Nationalists spearheaded a different kind of mobilization. Their appeals focused on ideology and strategy, but their formation, as nonstate groups, also advanced a new way of representing and leading the Palestinian cause. Nasser also recognized that the status quo of the Arab representation of Palestinians was insufficient. In 1959 he articulated support for the establishment of a Palestinian national entity. Five years later, he brought the issue before his gathering of the First Arab Summit. The thirteen assembled Arab heads of state took different positions on the matter, ranging from Syria's support for designating the West Bank and Gaza Strip as a Palestinian territorial base to Jordan's opposition to any sort of Palestinian entity. In the end, they agreed to authorize Shuqairi, the Arab League's Palestinian delegate, to carry on consultations "with the aim of arriving at the setting up of sound foundations for organizing the Palestinian people and enabling them to play their role in the liberation of their country and their self-determination."[5]

Arab leaders did not intend for the Palestinian entity to become a full-fledged nascent state. In advancing its establishment, Nasser arguably wanted a mechanism that would symbolize his commitment to liberating Palestine, yet assist him in averting war with Israel. This would relieve Palestinian frustrations, yet contain them within the bounds of Arab state interests. He entrusted this task to Shuqairi, who generally deferred

---

[4] Yehoshafat Harkabi, *Fedayeen Action and Arab Strategy* (London: The Institute for Strategic Studies, 1969), 23.

[5] Yezid Sayigh, *Armed Struggle and the Search for State: The Palestinian National Movement, 1949–1993* (New York: Oxford University Press, 1997), 96.

to the Egyptian president's policies. Nonetheless, the Palestinian career diplomat, typically described as ambitious and bombastic, did not shy from pushing the limits of his mandate and seeking to create an authentic national entity. In 1964 Shuqairi assembled 422 Palestinian leaders and declared their meeting to be the first session of the Palestinian National Council (PNC). The assembly approved a Palestinian National Charter and announced the founding of an overarching structure, the PLO. The PNC, confirmed as the PLO's parliament and highest authority, elected an Executive Committee with Shuqairi as chairman. The second Arab summit bestowed recognition on the PLO and its military branch, the Palestine Liberation Army (PLA).

Dynamics of inter-Arab and inter-Palestinian alliances and rivalries infused this initial phase of the PLO's development. As the majority of Jordan's population was Palestinian, King Hussein distrusted any other person or institution that proposed to represent the Palestinian people or might challenge Jordan's sovereignty over the West Bank. Nevertheless, he allowed the PNC to convene in Jerusalem at least in part because he believed this might improve his relations with Nasser.[6] Shuqairi, for his part, went to lengths to reassure King Hussein that he presented no threat to his interests. He thus deferred to Hussein's nomination of most delegates to the PNC, held the assembly under the supervision of Jordanian intelligence, and declared that the PLO made no claims on the West Bank.[7] Shuqairi's concessions remained insufficient to assuage the King's suspicions. Yet they went too far for those Palestinian groups opposed to the Hashemite regime. The Arab Nationalist Movement criticized Shuqairi's decision "to submit continuously to the demands of Jordan and the other reactionary forces."[8] Haj Amin al-Husseini, former Mufti of Jerusalem and still head of the Arab Higher Committee, nominally existent since the 1930s, disparaged Shuqairi's subservience to Egypt as well as his conciliatory steps towards Jordan. On that basis, he condemned the PLO as "a Zionist-imperialist plot."[9] Apart from these problems, Shuqairi's autocratic leadership style inspired criticism even within PLO councils.

---

[6] Moshe Shemesh, *Arab Politics, Palestinian Nationalism and the Six Day War: The Crystallization of Arab Strategy and Nasir's Descent to War, 1957–1967* (Brighton, UK: Sussex Academic Press, 2008), 74.

[7] Sayigh, *Armed Struggle*, 97–8.

[8] Ibid., 100.

[9] Moshe Shemesh, *The Palestinian Entity 1959–1974: Arab Politics and the PLO* (London: Frank Cass, 1988), 51.

The most forceful challenge to the PLO came from Fatah. Though Fatah also endorsed the call for a Palestinian national entity, it suspected that Arab states were sponsoring Shuqairi's initiative primarily as an "envelope" to contain Palestinian nationalism. Compounding its distrust were the aristocratic and upper-class backgrounds of the delegates gathered at the PNC, which stood at odds with the young, refugee social base of the Fatah "revolutionary vanguard." Despite their scepticism of the PLO, Fatah leaders reasoned that they might be able to influence the institution from within. In the words of Fatah leader Salah Khalaf (Abu Iyad), they would thereby transform it into a "legal front for the armed struggle." To that end, Khalaf and others met with Shuqairi and "proposed a secret coordination between his public activities and our underground activities."[10]

The PLO chairman eventually refused, and this refusal demonstrated the complex interplay between Palestinian and Arab circles of political competition. According to Khalaf, Shuqairi claimed that his obligations to the Arab League prevented him from concluding an alliance with Fatah. Khalaf, by contrast, suspected that Shuqairi invoked Arab state opposition as a cover for his own ambitions. In Khalaf's view, this was not a case of Arab states restricting Palestinians as much as one Palestinian invoking the idea of Arab restrictions as a pretext to marginalize his Palestinian competitors. From Fatah's perspective, Shuqairi went on "to fight us tooth and nail."[11]

If the Arab summit had authorized a Palestinian entity with the intent of thwarting guerrilla action, it paradoxically played a role in hastening it. Fatah had slowly been building and training its membership base but, as of 1963, had not planned on commencing military operations. Arab recognition of the PLO and its army, however, created a new sense of urgency. Some Fatah members called for a swift start of guerrilla activity at least in part to preserve their political-military initiative. They worried that otherwise Shuqairi's institution might shunt them to the sidelines of the Palestinian struggle.[12] After an internal debate, Fatah carried out its first sabotage attack against Israel on New Year's Day 1965. It issued a statement in the name of Al-Asifa, which became known as Fatah's military wing.

---

[10] Abu Iyad (Salah Khalaf), *My Home, My Land: A Narrative of the Palestinian Struggle*, with Eric Rouleau, trans. Linda Butler Koseoglu (New York: Times Books, 1981), 41.

[11] Ibid.

[12] Sayigh, *Armed Struggle*, 102.

Fatah claimed its debut as the commencement of the Palestinian revolution. In the years that followed, guerrilla fighters, or *fedayeen*, continued to carry out attacks that included bombing pipelines, water pumps, warehouses, and power plants, as well as planting landmines on roads, highways, and railroad tracks. Fatah accompanied its exploits with bold pronouncements that famously exaggerated the menace that they presented. Fatah's armed struggle soon pressured other Palestinian groups to prove their militant credentials. The Arab Nationalist Movement increased recruitment efforts and undertook preparations for guerrilla action, though it continued to abide by Nasser's preference against irregular attacks on Israel.[13] Also engaging in military recruitment and training was the Palestine Liberation Front (PLF), formed by former Syrian army officers of Palestinian origin, foremost among them Ahmed Jibril. While the Arab Nationalists' efforts concentrated in Lebanon and Gaza, the PLF developed a base among Palestinians in Syria.

From Fatah's launch to the start of the 1967 War, *fedayeen* carried out about one hundred attacks, leaving at least eleven Israelis dead and sixty-two injured.[14] Inter-Palestinian and inter-Arab competition added impetus to this military activity, just as the military activity added impetus to these overlapping dynamics of competition. In carrying out guerrilla strikes, Fatah challenged both Israel and the Egypt-dominated strategy endorsed by the Arab summit. It found an ally in Syria, Egypt's chief rival for leadership of the "revolutionary" Arab camp. Before Fatah's 1965 debut operation, sympathetic officers in the Syrian military, among them Hafiz al-Assad, allowed Fatah to use training camps in Syria.[15] Thereafter, the Ba'th regime offered commandos training and some arms. It permitted Fatah to organize on Syrian soil, distribute its newspaper, transport weapons, and receive shipments of Algerian supplies through its borders. In addition, Syrian media publicized Fatah's announcements and lauded its exploits.[16] As Asad reportedly quipped, "it was in Syria that the lungs of the Resistance were filled with oxygen."[17]

Syria's decision to support Fatah stemmed from its commitment to Ba'th ideology, a commitment that intensified when left-wing officers took power in February 1966, establishing an even more radical

[13] Ibid., 130–1.
[14] Kimmerling and Migdal, *The Palestinian People*, 252.
[15] Abu Iyad, *My Home, My Land*, 42.
[16] Shemesh, *Arab Politics*, 103–4.
[17] Cited in Patrick Seale, *Asad of Syria: The Struggle for the Middle East* (Berkeley: University of California Press, 1988), 124.

"neo-Ba'th" regime and explicitly called for a "popular war for liberation." Yet Syria's support was not due to ideology alone. The *fedayeen* also served the regime's political interests. They were a tool by which it could challenge Cairo for the mantle of leadership of the Arab world and its struggle against Israel. Assisting Palestinian fighters allowed the Ba'th to distinguish their strident commitment to revolution from Nasser's regime, which they accused of submission and defeatism.[18] In the words of one Syrian official, support for the guerrilla offered the Ba'th a chance to "rub Nasir's nose in the mud of Palestine."[19] As most Arabs honoured the Egyptian president's leadership, the *fedayeen* helped the Syrian Ba'th compensate for their relative weakness in the pan-Arabist arena. Nevertheless, Syria welcomed the idea of autonomous Palestinian guerrillas no more than Egypt did. It thus sought to subordinate Fatah to its political and tactical control. Fatah, in turn, sought to avert those constraints.

Not to be trapped by Syria or the Palestinians, in 1966 Egypt continued to take action against the *fedayeen*. It imposed various restrictions on Fatah, gathered intelligence on it, detained its members, and hampered its activities.[20] Nasser accused Fatah of trying to drag him into war and discredited it by alternatively suggesting that it was a front for the Muslim Brotherhood, a proxy of Saudi Arabia, or an agent of the Central Intelligence Agency. Under Nasser's leadership, Arab summit meetings denounced guerrilla actions on the grounds that they would lead to retaliation and escalation. PLO policies mirrored those of Egypt.

King Hussein, for his part, had an even stronger aversion to the Palestinian guerrillas. Fatah, like the PLO, represented an implicit challenge to his rule. It also levelled an explicit threat to the degree that it proclaimed itself to be a destabilizing force. As the king's many Palestinian subjects generally cheered the *fedayeen*, it was politically damaging for him to denounce them directly. Instead he issued warnings and criticized Fatah for violating the orders of the Arab summit's Joint Arab Command. He also made declarations that suggested that Israel was involved in the guerrilla groups as a plot to lure the Arabs into war.[21] Gradually the Jordanian army carried out arrests of Fatah members, put them under

[18] Mark Tessler, *A History of the Israeli-Palestinian Conflict* (Bloomington: Indiana University Press, 1994), 377.

[19] Sayigh, *Armed Struggle*, 104.

[20] Shemesh, *Arab Politics*, 96.

[21] Moshe Shemesh, "The *Fida'iyyun* Organization's Contribution to the Descent to the Six-Day War," *Israel Studies* 11, no. 1 (Spring 2006), 21–2.

surveillance, and intercepted some operations. Highly symbolic was the fact that Fatah's first "martyr" fell at the hands of Jordanian, not Israeli, troops.[22] The Lebanese government's position was similar to that of Jordan. It too worked to block raids from its borders.

The Road to War

Fedayeen activity led directly to tension along the borders between Israel and its Arab neighbours. It aggravated Israel's sense of insecurity and provoked its reprisals against Arab states, both of which contributed to the descent into war. Yet Israel did not view the commandos as an independent Palestinian national movement, still less as a movement navigating the complexities of inter-Palestinian and inter-Arab competition. Holding Arab states responsible for guerrilla attacks emanating from their borders, it charged that Fatah was a Syrian puppet organization.[23] Its activity was thus especially noxious for Chief of Staff Yitzhak Rabin and other officers who held a special antipathy for Israel's neighbour to the north, which some called the "Syrian syndrome."[24] The Israeli press echoed the view that Syria was responsible for guerrilla attacks, making that interpretation widespread among the Israeli public at large. *Fedayeen* activity, and belief in the Syrian hand behind it, accentuated the feelings of malaise that reached extreme levels in Israel by the spring of 1967. The harm that guerrillas wrought on Israeli psyches arguably outstripped the physical injury and damage that they caused.[25]

Israel carried out harsh retaliation against Syria and Jordan, where guerrillas from Syria often launched their raids. Still, through 1966, Israel did not treat guerrilla attacks as a cause for war. This persuaded Nasser that he could adopt a more positive policy towards the *fedayeen* without risking a major conflagration with Israel. At the same time, popular support for the *fedayeen* was convincing him that it was politically imperative to adopt such a policy. Arab publics were cheering the guerrilla strikes and commending Syria for its role in sponsoring them. Lest

---

[22] Eugene Rogan, *The Arabs: A History* (New York: Basic Books, 2009), 345.

[23] Menachem Klein, "The 'Tranquil Decade' Re-examined: Arab-Israeli Relations during the Years 1957–67," in *Israel: The First Hundred Years*, vol. II, ed. Efraim Karsh (London: Frank Cass, 2000), 71.

[24] Avi Shlaim, *The Iron Wall: Israel and the Arab World* (New York: W. W. Norton, 2001), 229.

[25] Tom Segev, *1967: Israel, the War, and the Year That Transformed the Middle East*, trans. Jessica Cohen (New York: Metropolitan Books, 2007), 144.

it be upstaged by Syria, Egypt began to increasingly facilitate *fedayeen* operations.[26]

Similarly, lest he be upstaged by Fatah, Shuqairi echoed Egypt's new support for guerrilla activity. In addition, he undertook initiatives to give the PLO the popular base that the *fedayeen* were increasingly coming to enjoy. The PLO established the Palestinian Popular Organization as a framework for grassroots groups to participate actively in the PLO.[27] It also established its own *fedayeen* squadrons in cooperation with the Arab Nationalist Movement and the PLF. Named Abtal al-Awda (Heroes of the Return), the squads began reconnaissance missions to gather intelligence on Israel and by late 1966 began guerrilla raids as well.[28] *Fedayeen* groups associated with Nasser and the PLO entered the guerrilla field that the Syria-backed Fatah had brought underway. Still, Nasser remained suspicious of Fatah. He continued indirectly to impede its operations, especially by arresting members attempting to infiltrate Israel from the Gaza Strip.

Developments from 1964 to 1967 demonstrated overlapping realms of competition between Palestinian aspirants for leadership of the struggle to liberate Palestine, as well as among Arab states that pursued their own competing interests through attempts to steer that struggle. The years preceding the outbreak of war also revealed how those Palestinian and state interactions shaped the course of Arab strategy in the conflict with Israel. In his classic work on the Arab cold war, Malcolm Kerr wrote, "When the Arabs are in a mood to co-operate, this tends to find expression in an agreement to avoid action on Palestine, but . . . when they choose to quarrel, Palestine policy readily becomes a subject of dispute."[29] In endorsing a Palestinian entity, Arab states arguably cooperated due to their shared belief that they could control Palestinian nationalism and avert the more costly actions which many Palestinians were demanding. To the degree that Arab interests were not identical, however, Palestine remained an idiom for their clashing visions and ambitions. More specifically, they vied with each other by pursuing divergent policies towards the *fedayeen*. Thus Syria aided Fatah at least in part as a way of challenging Egypt. Egypt initially curbed the guerrillas, yet eventually warmed to them at least in part as a way to reassert itself against Syria. Jordan was unable

[26] Shemesh, *Arab Politics*, 99–101.

[27] Shemesh, *The Palestinian Entity*, 81–2.

[28] Sayigh, *Armed Struggle*, 136–8.

[29] Malcolm H. Kerr, *The Arab Cold War: Gamal 'Abd al-Nasir and His Rivals, 1958–1970*, 3rd ed. (London: Oxford University Press, 1971), 114.

to stay aloof from this labyrinth of rival state interests because *fedayeen* frequently crossed from Syria to Jordan to carry out their attacks on Israel. Even though Jordan opposed these attacks, Israel retaliated with destabilizing strikes on Jordanian soil. It was not long, therefore, before Syria and Egypt found themselves in agreement about another benefit of Palestinian guerrilla action: it undermined the political stability of the Hashemite throne.[30]

In 1966 Jordan launched a crackdown on Fatah, which included confiscating its weapons and preventing its border raids. It also carried out a campaign against the Arab Nationalist Movement, severely weakening its organizational presence in Jordanian territory. Nevertheless, Palestinian resistance groups continued to grow in numbers and capabilities, and guerrilla strikes against Israel doubled between 1966 and 1967.[31] Responding to these, Israel carried out a massive retaliatory operation on the West Bank village of Samu' in November 1966, during which it dynamited dozens of houses and buildings. Jordanian troops rushed to the scene and the ensuing battle left fifteen soldiers dead and thirty-five injured, in addition to eight civilian casualties.[32] In the wake of the raid, Palestinian residents demonstrated against the government, calling for the overthrow of Hussein and for arms to defend themselves. Jordanian troops suppressed the protests and redoubled their arrest of PLO, Fatah, Arab Nationalist Movement, and other Palestinian activists.[33]

These events were a turning point for Jordan. As it was clearly Syria that was supporting Fatah, while Jordan was struggling to curtail it, King Hussein interpreted Israel's retaliation as a deliberate effort to escalate border tension into full-scale war. More than that, the king was convinced that Israel wanted such a war as an opportunity to seize control of the West Bank. Hussein had long feared that *fedayeen* activity would serve as a pretext for Israeli aggression. By 1967, he not only believed that war was inevitable, but also he was convinced that, regardless of what he did, Israel was poised to attack Jordanian territory.[34] In consequence, Hussein made preparations to join Arab armies. The mutual defence treaty concluded with Egypt on 30 May 1967 should be understood in this context.

---

[30] Shemesh, *Arab Politics*, 101.
[31] Tom Segev, *1967*, 143–4.
[32] Shemesh, "The *Fida'iyyun* Organization's Contribution," 26.
[33] Sayigh, *Armed Struggle*, 138.
[34] Shemesh, "The *Fida'iyyun* Organization's Contribution," 28.

By the spring of 1967, things were coming to a head. Fatah's attacks quadrupled from March to April 1967 alone.[35] Against this backdrop can be seen a Palestinian contribution to escalation arguably of no less significance than that of the guerrillas' "popular war": Shuqairi's belligerent rhetoric against Israel. After 1967, a heated debate ensued in which Western and Israeli sources accused the PLO chairman of calling on Arabs to "throw Jews into the sea." Though Shuqairi would deny that precise statement, his reputation for bravado did little to exonerate him. More than one newspaper source on the eve of the war quoted him as boasting that few Israelis would survive the coming combat.[36] In its aftermath, Arab critics blamed Shuqairi for recklessly fanning the flames that led to defeat. Yet Shuqairi's radical rhetoric was as much a product of escalation as a cause. He faced Fatah's challenge to his leadership of the Palestinian cause, as well as general pressure to keep up with the growing fervour in Arab media. It was thus unsurprising that the head of the PLO used all the resources at his disposal, including his own oratorical skill, to stake his place in the competitive arena of inter-Arab relations.

Competition among Palestinians for leadership of their national struggle was intimately intertwined with Arab state competition for security or predominance in regional politics. Both forms of rivalry contributed to the destabilizing cycle of *fedayeen* attacks and Israeli reprisals that paved the descent to war. For Fatah, a basic goal of guerrilla strikes was to entangle Arab states in a war that they otherwise would not wage. It was soon to see the fruition of that strategy, earlier than it had expected and with results different than it had hoped.

The Impact of the War

The role of Palestinians in the prelude to the June War was significant. Their role in the war, by contrast, was minimal. The only Palestinian force that participated in the fighting was the PLO's military wing, the PLA. The PLA consisted of infantry brigades based in Syria, Egypt, and Iraq, each of which was more answerable to its host state than it was to the PLO chairman. According to Yezid Sayigh, the months prior to June had seen the PLA wracked by internal dissent and a shakeup of its officer corps. Compounding the PLA's institutional problems were

[35] Sayigh, *Armed Struggle*, 139.
[36] See Moshe Shemesh, "Did Shuqayri Call for 'Throwing the Jews into the Sea'?" *Israel Studies* 8, no. 2 (Summer 2003), 70–81.

logistical shortcomings. Egypt obstructed the PLA's receipt of weaponry purchased from various sources and neglected to inform it of its own war plans until late May. These troubles left the PLA, in Sayigh's words, "completely unprepared" for the coming war.[37] When fighting erupted, PLA units in Gaza engaged in combat to defend the territory from Israeli troops. In Syria, other PLA battalions were also sent briefly to the Golan Heights. PLO leaders made entreaties to send additional PLA forces to Jordan and Egypt, but the outcome of the war was determined before they could take effect.[38]

The *fedayeen* played an even smaller role in the fighting. In Khalaf's account, Arafat and other Fatah leaders reacted to the outbreak of war by immediately deploying to a base in Syria. From there they led *fedayeen* to "infiltrate behind enemy lines" in attempt to block Israel's advance.[39] As combat subsided, guerrilla leaders reacted to the enormity of the defeat as did Arabs everywhere, with shock and sorrow. Fatah writings had claimed that war between the Arab states and Israel could trigger a spontaneous mobilization of guerrilla vanguards and Arab masses that would overwhelm the enemy. The war revealed the hollowness of this vision. Yet it also enabled the creation of a new vision. More than any other Arab force, Fatah was in a position to see an opportunity in the rout. The war thus became a turning point in the history of struggle over representation and leadership of the Palestinian cause. It redefined the balance of power between Palestinian nationalist mobilization and Arab state action, and in so doing transformed the Palestinian national movement.

The most direct impact of the 1967 War fell upon the one million Palestinians in the West Bank and Gaza Strip who came under Israeli military occupation – and the 250,000 to 300,000 new refugees who fled their homes during the fighting and were prevented from returning. In this calamity, however, lay the seeds of nationalist revival. Among Palestinians, the defeat brought many to appreciate what the founders of Fatah had claimed for nearly a decade: that Palestinians could not depend upon the Arab states and rather must take the matter of their national salvation into their own hands. Intensified popular support on the part of Palestinians was mirrored in backing among Arab publics at large. On the bleak post-June political landscape, the Palestinian freedom fighters stood out as symbols of pride, hope, and redemption. They appeared to

[37] Sayigh, *Armed Struggle*, 139.
[38] Ibid., 169.
[39] Abu Iyad, *My Home, My Land*, 51.

be the only force continuing to take up arms against Israel. They defended Arab honour.

Parallel to this surge of popular support for the Palestinian revolution was an auspicious shift in what can be called the structure of political opportunities. The prior system of Arab politics had been based on the upholding of state interests. It facilitated restrictions on the *fedayeen* in accord with basic distrust of autonomous nonstate actors. Moreover, the preexisting configuration of inter-Arab relations bore the heavy imprint of Nasser's personal dominance and hence his general opposition to guerrilla action against Israel. The June defeat, however, brought about the collapse of this Arab political status quo. In its aftermath, governments were politically powerless to oppose the commandos as they once had. These governments found that they had no choice but to endorse the *fedayeen* if they were to divert criticism of the defeat, recuperate their credibility, and prove their continued commitment to the fight for Palestine.

As these changed political circumstances crystallized, Fatah considered how to adapt to the changed military context. After an internal debate, the group resolved to dedicate its efforts to raising funds and acquiring weapons that had been abandoned on the battlefield or had become available on the market. With Arafat's encouragement, it also decided to launch a covert effort to organize a popular war from within the territories newly occupied by Israel.[40] Arafat smuggled fighters and weapons into the West Bank, where they set up a network and began recruiting and training new members. Palestinian guerrillas proceeded to launch dozens of sabotage and other attacks against Israeli targets during the last four months of 1967. The network was poorly organized, however, and Israel easily uncovered, arrested, or killed its members. It also imposed tough reprisals on the population at large with the aim of controlling suspicious activity and deterring civilians from supporting armed insurrection. Arafat's effort soon collapsed, therefore, and he retreated across the border. Regardless, most West Bank leaders were unconvinced by Fatah's call for popular war.[41] More in harmony with local opinion was the large and influential Communist Party, which voiced its opposition to the all but unarmed protest.[42]

[40] Ibid., 53.

[41] Rafik Halabi, *The West Bank Story* (New York: Harcourt Brace Jovanovich, 1981), 191–3; *Arab Report and Register*, 1–15 February 1968, 43.

[42] Shaul Mishal, *The PLO under 'Arafat: Between Gun and Olive Branch* (New Haven, CT: Yale University Press, 1986), 8–9, 32–3.

The Gaza Strip, meanwhile, was in the throes of its own popular war against the Israeli occupation. Fighters, most of them affiliated with the PLF, the Popular Front, and the PLA, used available weapons in a guerrilla campaign to drive out Israeli forces by demonstrating their inability to govern the Gaza Strip.[43] For some eighteen months, underground commandos engaged in gun battles, carried out acts of sabotage, killed Palestinians accused as collaborators, and effectively controlled many neighbourhoods. They carried out more than nine hundred guerrilla attacks from 1968 to 1970, nearly five times the number emanating from the West Bank during the same period.[44] Israel brought the rebellion to a halt by 1971 when General Ariel Sharon led a severe crackdown. This involved imposition of a twenty-four-hour-a-day curfew, house searches, mass roundups, and the transfer of more than twenty thousand residents from their homes.[45]

With the collapse of armed resistance in the occupied territories, the core focus of the Palestinian national struggle came again to centre in the Arab states surrounding Israel. There the transformed relationship between the Palestinian mobilization and Arab state politics had a dramatic effect on the revolution. On the one hand, state restrictions on the *fedayeen* withered. The *fedayeen* thus expanded their bases in Syria, Lebanon, and especially Jordan. On the other hand, state assistance to the *fedayeen* increased. Egypt and Syria provided the guerrillas with new military and logistical aid. In at least two speeches, Nasser explicitly endorsed their actions. The Arab press published Fatah's communiqués and Radio Cairo set aside an hour each day to broadcast its declarations and news about its activity.[46]

The shift in Arab-Palestinian relations set the stage for a shift in relations among Palestinian forces. Fatah and the PLF saw its numbers multiply in the wake of the war because they were the only two *fedayeen* groups with the capacity to absorb the scores of young men wanting to join the armed struggle.[47] The Arab Nationalist Movement understood

[43] See Halabi, *West Bank Story*, ch. 5; Joan Mendell, "Gaza: Israel's Soweto," *MERIP Reports* 136/137 (October – December, 1985), 7–19.

[44] Sayigh, *Armed Struggle*, 209.

[45] Tessler, *A History of the Israeli-Palestinian Conflict*, 473.

[46] Yehoshafat Harakabi, *Fedayeen Action and Arab Strategy*, Adelphi Papers, no. 53 (London: Institute for Strategic Studies, December 1968), 29.

[47] Yezid Sayigh, "Turning Defeat into Opportunity: The Guerillas after the June 1967 War," *Middle East Journal* 46, no. 2 (Spring 1992), 254.

that if it did not join the armed struggle, it risked losing existing members and the opportunity to attract new ones. It thus began preparing for armed actions as well. In December 1967, it came together with the PLF and like-minded military officers to establish the Popular Front for the Liberation of Palestine (PFLP). Like Fatah, the PLF and then the PFLP attempted to build a military presence in the West Bank, yet met with little success. By the end of the year, all *fedayeen* groups were concentrating their efforts on establishing guerrilla bases around the cease-fire lines and launching cross-border raids.

The Palestinian revolution continued to gain pace. In its shadow, Shuqairi struggled to sustain his claims that it was the PLO that was the true representative of the Palestinian people and their national aspirations. The PLA formed its own guerrilla wing to compete with the commandos, or at least stem the outflow of its cadres to join their ranks. Yet no such attempt could compensate for the liability represented by Shuqairi and his overblown rhetoric, which resonated less and less among Palestinians and other Arabs. After earning the disfavour of Arab heads of state and officials within his own institution, in addition to that of the guerrilla groups, the PLO chairman finally resigned in December 1967.

The field of Palestinian political competition narrowed around the *fedayeen*. Fatah stood at the helm, a stature which was sealed by the "Battle of Karameh." In March 1968, Israel invaded a Fatah base on the East Bank. Fatah fighters and Jordanian troops launched an ambush that left a reported twenty killed, three missing, and ninety wounded, in addition to the loss of one airplane and eight tanks or other military vehicles.[48] Arab losses were much greater and Israel achieved its tactical aim before withdrawing. Nevertheless, the day-long battle was hailed throughout the Arab world as a near mythic victory for the *fedayeen*. The fact that the word *Karameh* meant honour in Arabic added to its symbolic significance. By sheer will and resilience, it appeared, the young Palestinian commandos were upholding the dignity and courage of the entire Arab world.

Karameh reinforced and accelerated processes underway since the 1967 war. In the region at large, the Palestinian resistance rose from the humiliation of 1967 "like a phoenix out of ashes" and thus "reaped a

[48] Trevor N. Dupuy, *Elusive Victory: The Arab-Israeli Wars: 1947–1974* (New York: Harper and Row, 1978), 355.

harvest of hero-worship from a wide-spectrum of Arab public opinion."[49] For Palestinians specifically, the commando groups brought the word *Palestinian* to be identified with the "young, vigorous, intelligent, self-sacrificing" guerrilla warrior rather than with the "downtrodden displaced person."[50] A survey of Palestinians in Lebanon confirmed their sweeping identification with the commando groups, as illustrated in young people's statements that the resistance movement "changed the Palestinian identity from refugee to revolutionary," "gave me the answer to who I am," and "was the most important event not just in my life, but in all our lives."[51]

Given this popular groundswell, it became even more difficult for Arab heads of state to appear to take anything but an encouraging stance towards the Palestinian revolution. *Fedayeen* popularity became an issue with which regimes had to cope in managing their relations with their own societies, as well as their relations with each other. "Nowadays," Yehoshafat Harakabi wrote in 1969, "Arab leaders vie with each other in expressing support for *Fedayeen* action."[52] Even King Hussein was compelled to go with the flow. The tide of new recruits accelerated and dozens of new groups formed, though many existed in name only and many more did not endure.[53] The rate for guerrilla attacks also increased. By 1969 the *fedayeen* were carrying out hundreds of strikes each month.[54] During the first year after the war, these operations resulted in a total of 204 Israeli soldiers and 29 civilians killed, as well as 655 soldiers and 238 civilians injured.[55] Apart from attacks on Israel, Palestinian groups also commenced international operations such as aeroplane hijackings and ambushes of Israeli offices and embassies. According to Israeli figures, Palestinian groups carried out forty-seven such operations from July

---

[49] Rosemary Sayigh, *Palestinians: From Peasants to Revolutionaries* (London: Zed Books, 1979), 144.

[50] Don Peretz, "Arab Palestine: Phoenix or Phantom?" *Foreign Affairs* 68, no. 2 (January 1970), 327.

[51] Rosemary Sayigh, "Sources of Palestinian Nationalism: A Study of a Palestinian Camp in Lebanon," *Journal of Palestine Studies* 6, no. 4 (Summer 1977), 34.

[52] Harakabi, *Fedayeen Action*, 30.

[53] John W. Amos, II, *Palestinian Resistance: Organization of a National Movement* (New York: Pergamon Press, 1980), 35; Ehud Yaari, *Strike Terror: The Story of Fatah*, trans. Esther Yaari (New York: Sabra Books, 1970), 199.

[54] Sayigh, *Armed Struggle*, 147.

[55] Harakabi, *Fedayeen Action*, 27–8.

1968 through the end of 1970, with the PFLP leading the way.[56] More Israelis would be killed in hostile action during the three-and-a-half years following the 1967 War than during the war, with about half of these casualties resulting from *fedayeen* attacks.[57]

The combined impact of the June war and battle of Karameh solidified certain patterns in political competition – among Palestinians and between Palestinians and Arab states – that would endure for years to come. Primarily, it led to a resolution of the prior competition between the guerrilla movement and the PLO. An interim chairman took the reins of the PLO after Shuqairi's resignation. Recognizing Fatah's prestige, he reached out to it and other commando groups to join the PLO apparatus. Some suggested that Fatah assume complete command over the PLO and invite other *fedayeen* to participate in its forums as independent voices. Apprehensive, Fatah proposed that each guerrilla organization join the PLO with representation commensurate to its size. Other groups concurred. When the PNC convened in February 1969, they formed the largest bloc. Fatah members came to occupy a significant place in PLO executive councils, and Arafat was elected chairman. Two previously antagonistic organizations, the PLO and Fatah, thus came together under a single head.

The *fedayeen* lent the PLO dynamism, authenticity, and a grassroots base that revitalized it as a national entity. Yet this development transformed more than terminated the phenomenon of intense competition over representation and leadership of the Palestinian cause. Competition thereafter would unfold not between the PLO and rival groups as much as inside the PLO. The fact that all *fedayeen* groups filtered into the PLO elevated it to the status of a legitimate, national representative. That groups retained their autonomy within the PLO, however, rendered it an umbrella group more than a unitary organization. The PLO was part decision maker and part forum for decision making. The PLO leadership, according to one of its leading historians, Helena Cobban, "could never thereafter exercise the degree of monopoly over the national struggle

---

[56] Ariel Merari and Shlomo Elad, *The International Dimension of Palestinian Terrorism* (Jerusalem and Tel Aviv: Jaffee Center for Strategic Studies and The Jerusalem Post Press, 1986), 121.

[57] William B. Quandt, *Palestinian Nationalism: Its Political and Military Dimension* (Santa Monica, CA: Rand, 1971), 86.

which the leaders of most other successful modern-day national liberation movements enjoyed."[58] Although all factions supported armed struggle and the goal of liberating Palestine, their independence impeded the centralization of authority. This entrenched factionalism as an enduring pattern in the organization of Palestinian politics.

Developments, spurred by the war, transformed Fatah just as it allowed Fatah to transform the PLO. Before Karameh, Fatah was a relatively small and clandestine group. After Karameh, its leaders moved from anonymity to the limelight. Arafat stepped out as the group's spokesperson and began engaging with politicians and the press alike. He did not shy from making declarations at odds with the Arab states.[59] In addition, scores of recruits sought to become a part of the movement. As Khalaf recalls, "By the tens of thousands, young and old flocked to join Fatah. High school and university students abandoned their studies to swell our ranks."[60]

This tidal wave in the weeks and months following the June war had important ramifications for Fatah's internal structure. Fatah came to absorb an inflow of new cadres before it had the infrastructural capacity to coordinate their participation. Previously, Fatah had been able to provide each new member with personal training. In the groundswell after Karameh, Fatah leader Khalid al-Hassan recalled, "We were forced to make our mobilization and ideological education to the people in the camps by masses."[61] Fearful that factions might form within the movement's rapidly expanding ranks, Fatah leaders isolated its different sectors lest any unite and attempt to seize control of the entire movement.[62] Organizational fragmentation combined with ideological ambiguity gave the movement a loose framework. Competition within Fatah thus mirrored that within the Palestinian national movement at large. Containing often-extreme differences within its ranks, Fatah would occasionally find it a struggle to unify collective action or to specify what the movement stood for. At times a resource and at times a curse, this vulnerability to internal fragmentation would continue as a key attribute of Fatah, and likewise the PLO, for decades to come.

---

[58] Helena Cobban, *The Palestine Liberation Organization: People, Power, and Politics* (Cambridge: Cambridge University Press, 1984), 140.

[59] Harakabi, *Fedayeen Action*, 30.

[60] Abu Iyad, *My Home, My Land*, 61.

[61] Khalid al-Hassan cited in Cobban, *The Palestine Liberation Organization*, 49; also see Abu Iyad, *My Home, My Land*, 60; Amos, *Palestinian Resistance*, 57.

[62] See Cobban, *The Palestine Liberation Organization*, 26.

The Arab States and the Palestinian Revolution

Intense competition within the Palestinian movement was not limited to Palestinians alone. The June defeat stunned and immobilized Arab leaders. Yet it was not long before they again began to compete for influence in the Palestinian arena. Still, the war dramatically altered the terms of the struggle. Before the war, Arab governments competed with each other and with the Palestinians on whether and how to *restrict* the commandos. After the war, Arab states competed in how to *assist* the commandos, typically with offers of funding or territorial bases. Then they found a new way of competing: by intervening *within* the Palestinian movement. Their main tool was to fund existing *fedayeen* organizations or create their own proxy forces. The latter came to serve as instruments of the Arab states inside the Palestinian struggle and as mouthpieces of their policies and interests.

Thus in the spring of 1968, the Syrian Ba'th Party created Sa'iqa, a Palestinian commando group that effectively became Syria's representative within the PLO. Syria's rival, the Iraqi Ba'th Party, also created its own Palestinian proxy, the Arab Liberation Front. Egypt, meanwhile, lent support to smaller organizations and some Gulf states offered substantial funding to Fatah. Apart from competition between Arab states, even domestic struggles within an Arab state could drive the proliferation or opposition of forces within the Palestinian national movement. In the power struggle in the Syrian army, for example, Salah Jadid used his base in Sa'iqa to compete with his rival Hafiz al-Asad, who in turn took advantage of his ties to the PLA.[63] Competition unrelated to Palestinian affairs thus had the effect of pitting two nominally Palestinian organizations against each other.

For al-Hassan, the race to penetrate Palestinian national politics rendered the kind of competition that existed among Palestinians after 1967 fundamentally distinct from that which existed before it. At the outset of the guerrilla movement, he explained, "Palestinians were forbidden to participate in any political activities related to their cause, the natural consequence being the creation of many clandestine organizations." After 1967 there was also a multiplicity of groups, but this multiplicity was "unnatural." A plethora of organizations formed that were "Palestinian in name only, for in reality they were extensions of the Arab parties they

---

[63] Amos, *Palestinian Resistance*, 101, 104.

represented, desiring to exist within the Palestinian revolution and main-taining their governmental and partisan problems and contradictions."[64] Arab interference in the Palestinian struggle fed competition among Pales-tinian groups, which in turn opened opportunities for further interference.

Less able to suppress the Palestinian movement in the transformed post-1967 political landscape, Arab leaders recouped and attempted to influence it from within. Yet this did not eliminate the essential tension between the interests of states and those of the nonstate PLO. States guarded their political sovereignty and sought to avoid unnecessary hos-tilities with Israel. The PLO craved a territorial sanctuary where it could build its institutional base and continue guerrilla warfare. The incom-patibility of these imperatives became most vivid in Jordan, where the resistance movement came to approximate a "state within a state" with its own police, courts, militias, and media. Uniformed and armed guer-rillas not only moved freely but also set up checkpoints that intervened in the movement of others. Many commandos flaunted their power and violated local laws; the PFLP and other left-leaning factions provoked the Hashemite regime by calling for its overthrow. Guerrilla attacks from Jordan to Israeli-occupied territory provoked reprisals for which Jordan paid a heavy price.

For the monarchy, who had always been distrustful of the indepen-dent Palestinian movement, this behaviour constituted a threat to the country's sovereignty and stability. Three major clashes between the Jordanian army and Palestinian guerrillas suggested that a showdown was inevitable, and this finally occurred in September 1970. The PFLP hijacked four jetliners and landed them on a Jordanian land strip, which it declared to be liberated territory. King Hussein demanded the release of the aircraft and passengers. Arafat suspended the PFLP from the guer-rillas' coordinating body. When a defiant PFLP ignited the planes, the Jordanian army launched a twelve-day onslaught on Palestinian bases that claimed more than three thousand casualties and became known as Black September. The army continued its offensive until it liquidated the last of the Palestinian guerrillas from Jordanian territory in July 1971.

The heyday of the Palestinian revolution, spurred by the 1967 War, had come to an end. Although the resistance movement would build a

[64] "Khalid al-Hassan," in *Palestinian Lives: Interviews with Leaders of the Resistance*, ed. Clovis Maksoud (Beirut: Palestine Research Center and Kuwaiti Teachers' Associa-tion, 1973), 27.

new proto-state base in Lebanon, it lost access to the longest Arab border with Israel. It also lost the air of unassailable confidence and power that events since 1967 had helped in its relations with Arab states. Political changes in other frontline states would continue to bode poorly for the Palestinian revolution.[65] Nasser died shortly after Black September. His successor, Anwar Sadat, articulated an inclination towards diplomacy and peaceful settlement. Hafiz al-Asad seized power in Syria that November, after which he increasingly monitored and restricted Palestinian activity. Syrian authorities began requiring PLO groups to acquire permission before holding rallies, issuing publications, or travelling in and out of the country.[66] Sending a sharp message, Syrian leaders also confiscated a major arms shipment sent from Algeria for Fatah. The frontline state that had once been the greatest supporter of the *fedayeen* thus turned away from them.

The political significance of the 1967 War for the Palestinian national movement thus came full circle. In the years preceding the war, the PLO and the guerrillas had sought to dodge Arab state restrictions in order to carve out political autonomy. The June defeat aided this quest, but the distrust of the Arab states of an autonomous Palestinian movement did not subside. Black September exemplified the lengths state leaders might go to if they perceived it necessary to protect their own interests. If 1967 was the Naksah or "setback" for the Arab states, the final expulsion from Jordan some four years later was the first great setback for the Palestinian revolution. The struggle for Palestinian representation and rights would continue, but only to the degree that it sometimes complemented and sometimes contradicted interests that bound it to the Arab state system.

The 1967 War pushed Palestinians towards a more specifically Palestinian nationalism and forced Arab states to recognize a new generation of Palestinian leaders. These Palestinians became the spokesmen of their cause and the organizers of their struggle. Nonetheless, these developments transformed rather than resolved the tense and competitive relationship between Palestinians and the rest of the Arab world. Before the war, Palestinians with varying political loyalties set their sights on the struggle to build a revolutionary Palestinian movement. After the war, their struggle turned on preserving the independence of this movement, its tactical operations, and its strategy against Israel. Only in the years

---

[65] Fuad Jabber, "The Arab Regimes and the Palestinian Revolution, 1967–71," *Journal of Palestine Studies* 2, no. 2 (January 1973), 97.

[66] Sayigh, *Armed Struggle*, 288–9.

that followed would Palestinians' political struggle evolve to centre on the substance of that strategy.

To sum up, the years leading up to the June war were characterized by heightened contestation among Palestinians and Arab states over strategy and leadership in the struggle for regaining Arab Palestine. These interconnected channels of Palestinian and Arab competition helped fuel guerrilla activity, which was the primary Palestinian contribution to the outbreak of the 1967 War. Guerrilla strikes aggravated Israel's security concerns and sparked its reprisals, which resulted in deaths, destruction, and political tension in Arab lands. The role of the Palestinian national movement in the descent to war was thus not a simple clash between Palestinian nationalism and Israel. Rather, it was a political and military phenomenon that was embedded in and operated through a matrix of relations between Arab state politics and the struggle of Palestinians for direction of their struggle.

Israel's victory in the war transformed this Palestinian-Arab political matrix. It discredited the Arab states and left the *fedayeen* as the main force fighting Israel. As the popularity of the resistance surged, Arab governments found themselves competing to demonstrate their support. Scores of new recruits joined the revolution, commando groups filtered into a reconfigured PLO, and Fatah became the definitive leader of the Palestinian national movement. Nevertheless, competition over the national movement continued. Arab leaders recouped the lost initiative and formed commando organizations with which to influence the Palestinian struggle from within. Fatah's rivals, led by the PFLP, challenged it in matters institutional and ideological. The war was thus momentous not only in confirming the Palestinian national movement as a distinct force in the Arab-Israeli conflict but also in shaping that movement's structure and direction.

The June War settled some of the debates and rivalries that had preceded it but did not signify the end of rigorous and multifaceted competition as a defining feature of the Palestinian national movement. The internal Palestinian struggle with the larger system of Arab states would continue to shape the course of the conflict with Israel. The experience of Palestinians in the June War played not only a vital part in a watershed moment in Middle East history but also demonstrated political dynamics that persist to the present day.

6

The Yemen War and Egypt's War Preparedness

Eugene Rogan and Tewfik Aclimandos

When Israel attacked the Sinai airfields on 5 June 1967, it enjoyed more than the advantage of total surprise. Israeli commanders knew that the Egyptian army was already engaged in a full-scale conflict in the Yemen. Any power would be overstretched trying to fight two wars at the same time. Egypt had neither the logistical means nor the surplus wealth to engage a foe like Israel while pinned down in South Arabia. Egypt's five-year war in Yemen had severely sapped its war preparedness in advance of the third Arab-Israeli war. Although we could not claim that Egypt lost the 1967 War in Yemen – there were too many other variables behind Israel's swift victory – there is no doubt that Egypt's campaign in Yemen fatally impaired its performance in the war against Israel.[1]

Egypt entered the Yemeni civil war in September 1962, almost immediately after the officers' coup that overthrew the monarchy of Imam Badr. Despite some second thoughts, Gamal Abdel Nasser gave his full support to the revolutionary movement as part of his new policy of promoting progressive Arab forces over reactionary regimes. The initial Egyptian military deployment was limited, and Nasser's aides, with Anwar Sadat at the forefront, assured him that a short mission by a small force would be more than enough to ensure victory. Instead, the Egyptians found themselves embroiled in an increasingly complex conflict that divided Arab ranks and drew South Arabia into the superpower rivalries of the Cold War. In the aftermath of the dissolution of Egypt's union with Syria,

---

[1] Although formally known as the United Arab Republic until 1971, we use the name "Egypt" in this essay to distinguish the country from its three-year union with Syria (1958–61).

Nasser was in no position to accept another failure in his Arab nationalist policies. There was no clear point when the Egyptians could declare mission accomplished and withdraw from Yemen without loss of prestige. In this sense, Yemen proved an unwinnable war, Nasser's Vietnam.

Nasser's Egypt was isolated in inter-Arab circles in 1962. Relations with Syria had been strained by the coup that led to the breakup of the United Arab Republic (UAR) the previous year, and revolutionary Iraq was more of a rival than an ally to Egypt. Conservative monarchies that had suffered Nasser's barbs through Voice of the Arabs radio broadcasts from Cairo took advantage of Egypt's exposure in Yemen in order to settle old scores. Jordan and Saudi Arabia threw their support behind the Yemeni royalist movement, helping to prolong a counterrevolutionary movement that might otherwise have been defeated far sooner. Divisions in Arab ranks, provoked by the Yemen War, made concerted military action against Israel far more difficult and contributed to the total Arab defeat in 1967.

The Yemen War was not a purely inter-Arab conflict. Egypt's intervention in South Arabia raised new tensions between Cairo and London. In 1962, Britain still ruled over the Aden Protectorate, which it viewed as a strategic gateway to the oil-producing regions of the Arabian Peninsula. Nasser made no effort to conceal his ambition to drive Britain from Aden, and the British were equally determined to check Egyptian ambitions to convert South Yemen into a "Cairo-oriented Arab nationalist regime."[2] Not only did the British offer covert military support to the Yemeni royalists, but also they involved the Israelis in limited operations. Coming only seven years after the ill-fated Anglo-Israeli collusion in Suez, Israel's involvement in British operations gave the Jewish state valuable intelligence about Egypt's vulnerable position in Yemen during the years immediately preceding the June 1967 War.

Given the extent of Egypt's commitment and exposure in the Yemen conflict, it is all the more astonishing that Nasser's government engaged in the elaborate brinkmanship that led to the June 1967 War. Nasser and his top officers – Field Marshal Abdel Hakim Amer in particular – were all too aware of their vulnerability in Yemen. The fact that one-third of Egypt's most experienced forces were pinned down in a distant battlefield during the summer of 1967 should have made Nasser's generals avoid military action at all costs. Yet the Yemen conflict seems to have had the

---

[2] Clive Jones, *Britain and the Yemen Civil War, 1962–1965* (Brighton, UK: Sussex Academic Press, 2004), 8.

opposite effect on Egyptian war planners. For years, the Egyptian press had portrayed Egypt's actions in Yemen as great victories. Some officials, like War Minister Shams Badran, seemed to take the propaganda at face value and believed their armed forces more capable than they were. This grave overestimation was another fatal legacy of the Yemen War that gravely undermined Egypt's war preparedness in 1967.

Egypt and the Yemeni Revolution

The fourteen-year reign of Yemen's absolute ruler, Imam Ahmad, came to a peaceful end when he died in his sleep on 19 September 1962. He left behind one of the poorest and least-developed countries in the world. A group of reform-minded army officers had already begun to plot a revolution against the Yemeni monarchy before his death. Inspired by Egypt's example, they called themselves the Yemeni Free Officers.

The Yemeni Free Officers were undoubtedly influenced by Egypt's criticisms of Imam Ahmad, broadcast from Cairo on the Voice of the Arabs radio station. The old monarch had enjoyed mixed relations with Cairo throughout the years. He had thrown his support behind Egypt's union with Syria in 1958 – largely, he explained to King Saud of Saudi Arabia, to avoid being a target of Nasser's hostile propaganda. Yet Imam Ahmad condemned Nasser's turn to Arab Socialism and rejected Egyptian nationalization measures that transferred private property to state ownership as contrary to Islamic values. His criticisms of Egypt's state-led development, coming after Syria's secession from the UAR in 1961, antagonized Nasser.[3] Henceforth Egypt would provide support to the Imam's opponents.

Though Nasser denied any prior knowledge of the Yemeni Free Officers or their coup plans, it is clear that the Egyptian government supported the Yemeni opposition. The Egyptian intelligence services certainly knew that a coup was in the air. General Salah al-Din al-Hadidi, head of Egyptian intelligence, confirmed he knew about the coup, but claimed Egypt did not interfere.[4] Another Egyptian intelligence officer, Amin Huwaydi,

---

[3] Paul Dresch, *A History of Modern Yemen* (Cambridge: Cambridge University Press, 2000), 80–8.

[4] Salah al-Din al-Hadidi, *Al-dawr al-misri fi'l-Yaman* [The Egyptian Role in the Yemen] (Cairo: Madbuli, 1984), 18–19. In an interview with Laura James, Hadidi later acknowledged that Egypt had provided "a few small arms" to the Yemeni Free Officers. Laura M. James, *Nasser at War: Arab Images of the Enemy* (Houndmills, UK: Palgrave, 2006), 59.

later recounted that Sadat had told him in early 1962 to expect change in Yemen and to provide assistance to the Cairo-based Yemeni opposition figures.[5] They might not have known precisely when the revolution would occur, but the Egyptian government expected and encouraged an early revolution.

Imam Ahmad's death, and the succession of his son and heir al-Badr, provided the opportunity for the coup plotters to act. Ironically, al-Badr had enjoyed close ties to Cairo. He visited Egypt during the mid-1950s and upheld the Nasserist state as a paragon of progress and modernity. Egypt returned the favour and extended full support to al-Badr through the 1950s. Yet with Nasser's shift to Arab Socialism in 1961, al-Badr found himself lumped together with conservative monarchs as a bastion of Arab reaction. As the newest Arab monarch to ascend to power, he was the most vulnerable. His reign lasted only eight days. By his own account, al-Badr came under attack by junior officers after a late-night meeting of the Council of Ministers in the Royal Palace on 26 September. The leader of the putsch, a young lieutenant named 'Ali 'Abd al-Ghani (in some sources he is given as 'Abd al-Mughny), was killed in the early hours of the coup; one would-be assassin shot himself in the chin and survived "with a disfigured face."[6] Leadership of the revolution fell to Colonel Abdullah al-Sallal, a little-known officer described by his opponents as a puppet of Nasser. In the chaos, al-Badr managed to make his escape and fled the capital to rally loyal supporters in the north of the country. Reports of his death, broadcast on Radio Sanaa, proved premature.

A small detachment of Egyptian troops entered Yemen almost immediately after the coup in order to provide support to the newly declared republic. The first contingent was flown into Sanaa and Taiz two days after the revolution, on 28 September. Thousands more were to flood in throughout the ensuing weeks, reaching fifteen thousand by January 1963. The Cairo weekly, *Ruz al-Yusif*, portrayed this fraternal intervention in a cartoon showing Egypt and Yemen as giants striding hand in hand. The "reactionary" monarchs King Saud of Saudi Arabia and the "boy-king" Hussein of Jordan are shown struggling to pull Imam al-Badr from under the boots of the republican march of progress. "We are with the people of Yemen," the caption reads (see Figure 1).

[5] James, *Nasser at War*, 59.
[6] Cited in Saeed M. Badeeb, *The Saudi-Egyptian Conflict over North Yemen, 1962–1970* (Boulder, CO: Westview Press, 1986), 4.

نحن مع شعب اليمن
اللوحة
• بريشة جمال كامل •

FIGURE I. "We are with the people of Yemen," by Jamal Kamil, *Ruz al-Yusuf* no. 1796, 12 November 1962.

From the outset, the Egyptian intervention in Yemen was ideologically driven. "Why are we fighting in Yemen?" journalist and novelist Fathi Ghanim asked rhetorically in an article in the same issue of *Ruz al-Yusif*. "Why do we send men and arms and provisions to revolutionary liberated Yemen, to preserve its independence, and defend its existence from the infiltration of reactionaries and imperialists?" The answer, Ghanim argued, is that the revolutions in Yemen and in Egypt were one and the same fight for the promotion of socialism and the protection of the rights of workers and peasants from the exploitation of the rich.[7]

Whatever the intellectuals were arguing in Cairo, Egyptian soldiers faced a real war in the Yemen. Imam al-Badr succeeded in rallying loyal tribes in the north to mount a counterrevolution with full Saudi support. The royalists extended the area under their control eastwards to Marib and Harib. In the first phase of the war, which ran from October 1962 until the installation of a UN mission in June 1963, the Egyptian army focused on cutting off the royalists' Saudi supply line and retaking the towns in Eastern Yemen. The Egyptian air force bombed Saudi positions along the Yemeni border and sent troops into the Jawf region of Northern Yemen. They then sent forces to the east, taking Marib on 26 February and Harib on 4 March 1963, in their most successful campaign of the war. The Imam's forces suffered a major setback and withdrew to the mountains in order to continue their struggle against the UAR in guerrilla fashion.[8]

With the failure of the UN Observer Mission to implement a disengagement agreement, the Yemen War resumed with full vigour in September 1963. The Egyptians expanded their forces in Yemen from forty-five thousand in the spring of 1963 to seventy thousand men by the end of 1965. Field Marshal El-Gamasy claimed that by December 1966, some two-thirds of Egypt's armed forces were in Yemen.[9] Yet no matter how many troops the Egyptians sent, they remained locked in a stalemate with royalist forces that proved costly in men and materiel.

Egyptian estimates of the costs of the war vary significantly, but all demonstrate the high price paid for the intervention in Yemen. By the end of 1963, Egypt had sent 130,000 rifles, 5,000 machine guns, 130 antitank guns, 16 antiaircraft guns, and 20 million rounds of ammunition.[10] The

---

[7] Fathi Ghanim, "Limadha nuharib fi'l-Yaman," ["Why we are fighting in Yemen"] *Ruz al-Yusif* 1796 (12 November 1962), 8.

[8] Ali Abdel Rahman Rahmy, *The Egyptian Policy in the Arab World: Intervention in Yemen, 1962–1967* (Washington, DC: University Press of America, 1983), 148–9.

[9] Mohamed Abdel Ghani El-Gamasy, *The October War: Memoirs of Field Marshal El-Gamasy of Egypt* (Cairo: American University of Cairo Press, 1989), 38. For accounts of Egypt's military involvement see Hadidi, *Al-Dawr al-Misri fi'l-yaman*; Muhammad Fawzi, *Harb al-thalath sanawat: mudhakkirat al-fariq awwal Muhammad Fawzi* [The three years war: Memoirs of Lt. Gen. Muhammad Fawzi] (Cairo: Dar al-Mustaqbal al-'Arabi, 1984). Tewfik Aclimandos also consulted the private papers of Gen. Ahmad Fathi 'Abd al-Ghani in Cairo.

[10] Fawzi, *Harb al-thalath sanawat*, 23.

expense of the war was crippling for cash-strapped Cairo and its Soviet patron. Egyptian estimates ranged from £E 20 to 40 million per year ($60–120 million), which more or less agree with foreign observers who estimated the campaign cost the Egyptian treasury more than $125 million in its first two and a half years.[11] Yet the highest price the Egyptians paid was in the lives of their soldiers who died in the Yemen War. Between October 1962 and June 1964, more than fifteen thousand Egyptian officers and men were killed, according to Egyptian official records.[12]

The commander of Egyptian forces in Yemen, Lieutenant-General Anwar al-Qadi, recognized the dangers of an open-ended guerrilla war in the ill-charted, mountainous terrain of North Yemen. In his memoirs, al-Qadi claimed to have filed more than twenty reports to Abdel Hakim Amer describing the Yemen "trap" and its dangers.[13] Following initial Egyptian successes in the battlefield, he returned to Cairo in May 1963 to urge President Nasser to declare victory and withdraw the troops. "We have more than accomplished our duty and must withdraw from this trap as soon as possible," Qadi told Nasser. Yet the Egyptian president seemed oblivious to the military realities in Yemen. "Withdrawal is impossible," Nasser responded. "It would mean the disintegration of the revolution in Yemen. This is more a political operation than a military one," he continued. "I consider it to be a counter-response to the separation from Syria. We cannot leave Yemen."[14] Thus, from the outset, the Egyptian military faced an open-ended intervention in Yemen driven by political rather than military objectives. This meant that, when Egypt began to mobilize in the Sinai during the summer of 1967, one-third of its armed forces were still pinned down in Yemen.

Nasser had a number of political objectives in Yemen, but in the end he set two goals – both equally difficult to achieve: consolidation of the republican regime in Yemen as a blow to conservative monarchies in the region and expulsion of the British from Aden. The Saudis and the British, whose relations had been strained by the Buraimi oasis dispute,

---

[11] Egyptian estimates from Fawzi, *Harb al-thalath sanawat*, 26 and Tal'at Amin Khazbak, *al-General al-tha'ir: Sa'd al-Din al-Shazli* [The Revolutionary General: Sa'd al-Din al-Shazli] (Cairo: al-Dawliyya, 2009), 89. Foreign estimates from Dana Adams Schmidt, *Yemen: The Unknown War* (London: Bodley Head, 1968), 235.

[12] Schmidt claimed the casualty figure was from "official Egyptian army figures, obtained by a foreign intelligence service from Yemenis who had access to the records." *Yemen: The Unknown War*, 234.

[13] Al-Qadi, cited in Muhammad al-Jawadi, *al-Tariq 'ila al-naksa* [The Road to the Setback] (Cairo: Dar al-Khayal, 2000), 251.

[14] Gamasy, *The October War*, 18.

each recognized the threat Egypt's intervention posed to their interests in South Arabia and did their utmost to subvert Egypt's exposed position in Yemen. In this way, the Egyptian intervention broadened the Yemen conflict from an isolated civil war into an international crisis.

The Yemen War and Inter-Arab Politics

The revolution in Yemen, combined with the Egyptian intervention, sent shock waves through the Arab world – and nowhere more so than in Saudi Arabia. Relations between Egypt and Saudi Arabia were already strained. King Saud had been implicated in an assassination plot against Nasser in 1958 and was accused of bankrolling the Syrian rebels who plotted the secession from the UAR during 1961. Egypt had responded with venom, calling for the overthrow of the Saudi monarchy and the spread of progressive republican values in Voice of the Arabs broadcasts across the Arabian Peninsula. A Republican coup in Yemen, followed by an Egyptian intervention, posed very genuine risks to Saudi Arabia.

Saudi Arabia was not a natural ally to Yemen. There was little affection wasted between the two countries' ruling families. The Al Saud and the deposed Hamid al-Din dynasty in Yemen were divided by theological differences and territorial disputes that spanned centuries. It took the threat of republicanism and the Egyptian presence in South Arabia to overcome a long history of antagonism and for the Saudi government to throw its support behind the royalist movement in Yemen.

The political establishment in Saudi Arabia was clearly divided on how best to respond to the coup in Yemen. Shortly after the coup, six members of the Saudi Cabinet (none of them members of the royal family) drafted a memorandum recommending that their government recognize the republican regime in Yemen. As one Western journalist remarked at the time, "Having little faith in the future of the Saudi monarchy and its ability to reform and defend itself, they were inclined to anticipate that President Nasser would succeed in his evident strategy, which was to use the Yemen revolution combined with a threat of armed force to bring down the structure of the Saudi monarchy."[15]

Divisions within the Saudi monarchy and armed forces were quick to appear. Prince Talal bin Abd al-Aziz led a group of young "Free Princes" who declared their support for Nasser's pan-Arabism and called for constitutional reform in Saudi Arabia. Shortly after the coup in Yemen, Talal

---

[15] Schmidt, *Yemen: The Forgotten War*, 51.

and three Saudi princes fled the country for Beirut, where they offered their services to Nasser. They were not the only defectors. On 2 October 1962, a Saudi transport plane carrying supplies for the Yemeni royalists in Najran flew instead to Egypt where its three pilots declared their loyalty to Nasser's government. Over the next six days, three more Saudi aircraft defected to Egypt, prompting the government to ground the entire Saudi air force until pilots could be screened for loyalty to the kingdom.

In order to combat the threat of Nasserism in Arabia, the Saudis committed their support to the Yemeni royalist cause. King Saud gave the royalists a safe haven in Saudi territory along the border between the two countries and began to supply funds and weapons to assist al-Badr in his bid to recover Yemen from the republicans. Along with the Jordanians, the Saudis provided officers to give military training to the Yemeni tribesmen supporting the royalist cause. Saudi support of the Yemeni royalists was a deliberate provocation to the Egyptians who were swift to retaliate.

The Egyptians began to attack towns inside Saudi Arabia as retaliation and deterrence for Saudi assistance to the Yemeni royalists. On 4 November 1962, the Egyptian air force bombed five small villages near the border town of Najran. On 10 November, the Egyptian navy attacked coastal villages around Qizan. Further attacks were carried out in December and January, prompting the Saudis to order a general mobilization and cancellation of all home leave for their military. Three squadrons of Saudi air force jets were sent to a base near the frontier, with anti-aircraft guns, to intercept Egyptian jets. The conflict between Yemeni royalists and republicans risked passing from a proxy war to an open conflict between the Saudis and the Egyptians. Though the Saudis never actually sent their troops to fight in Yemen, their continued support for the royalists provoked further Egyptian attacks through 1963.

Jordan sided with Saudi Arabia in its confrontation with Nasser's Egypt. King Hussein promised his country's support to "the sister Kingdom of Saudi Arabia with all its strength" and asserted "that it regards the aggression against Saudi Arabia as direct aggression against Jordan."[16] A small country with few resources, Jordan was more threatened by than a threat to Nasser. In 1962, the commander of the Jordanian air force and two of his pilots followed the Saudi example and defected to the Egyptian side. They claimed their squadron, based near the Saudi town of Taif, had been given orders to attack republican positions in Yemen.

---

[16] Cited in Rahmy, *The Egyptian Policy in the Arab World*, 136.

It was all Nasser needed to justify a new propaganda campaign against King Hussein.

The Yemen conflict provoked dangerous cleavages in Arab ranks, which gravely undermined any scope for common action against Israel in the years leading up to the 1967 War. West-leaning Arab states hostile to Nasser, like Kuwait and Lebanon, sided with Saudi Arabia and Jordan, while pan-Arab regimes like Iraq and Syria upheld Egypt's position in support of the Yemen Arab Republic. However, as the conflict ran into its second year, the Egyptians grew increasingly concerned about the drain an open-ended war posed to its resources. Nasser took advantage of the Arab summit in Cairo in 1964 to mend fences with King Hussein and prized Jordan away from its support of Saudi Arabia. In July, 1964, the Jordanians extended recognition to the Yemen Arab Republic and cut off their aid to the royalist side.

The thaw in Saudi-Egyptian relations followed in 1964. Field Marshal Amer headed a delegation to Saudi Arabia in March of that year. By the end of his visit, both sides pledged an immediate restoration of diplomatic relations. In September, 1964, Crown Prince Faisal (although he was already the effective ruler, Faisal was only named monarch in November 1964) met with Nasser in Alexandria, and the two leaders agreed to "fully cooperate in mediation with . . . royalist and republican Yemenis, in order to reach a peaceful solution of all problems in Yemen, and to continue these efforts until conditions stabilized there."[17]

Egyptian and Saudi efforts to extricate themselves from the Yemen conflict were complicated by the entrenched differences between the Yemeni factions, and a number of cease-fire agreements collapsed against the wishes of Nasser and Faisal. In August, 1965, Nasser flew to Saudi Arabia to conclude the Jidda Agreement, which called for an end of Saudi aid to the royalists, the complete withdrawal of Egyptian troops from Yemen over a ten-month period, and the holding of a plebiscite to allow the Yemeni people to decide the future of their government. Yet, far from providing the exit strategy for the Egyptians and the Saudis, the Jidda Agreement and subsequent negotiations collapsed. Nasser was unwilling to abandon the republican movement in Arabia, and the royalists were unwilling to concede to republican demands. Rather than withdraw, Nasser expanded Egypt's military presence in Yemen, reaching sixty thousand troops in 1966. Just when he most needed to regroup

[17] Cited in Badeeb, *The Saudi-Egyptian Conflict*, 81.

and concentrate his efforts to face the Israeli threat, Nasser redoubled his commitment to the unwinnable war in Yemen.

Britain and the Yemen War

Egypt's intervention in Yemen created serious tensions between Cairo and Whitehall. Although Britain had abandoned its imperial objectives in the Eastern Mediterranean, it was still firmly entrenched in South Arabia – from Aden to Oman and the Trucial States of the Persian Gulf.

The British first occupied the southern Yemeni port of Aden in 1839, and its strategic importance had only grown throughout the intervening decades. It had served as a coaling station for British steamships in an earlier age and was the crossroads of the shipping lanes between the Persian Gulf oilfields and Western Europe. Britain was keen to retain Aden, which was a formal colony, and the semiautonomous tribal states under British protection – the Protectorate – that stretched northwards to the frontiers of Yemen and east to the border with Oman.

During the 1950s, the challenge to Britain's position in Aden came from the ruler of Yemen, rather than Nasser's Egypt. The Imam Ahmad wanted to absorb the Protectorate into his own state. Yet Aden's strategic importance to the British was only growing in what was otherwise an age of decolonization. The port of Aden had witnessed a massive expansion in population and economic activity. In 1952 the British built a substantial oil refinery, and by 1958 "Aden was said to be the second busiest port in the world after New York."[18] In 1958 the British established the headquarters of their Middle East Command in the Aden colony. It was from Aden that the British coordinated military interventions in Kuwait (1961) and Zanzibar (1964). Driven by the colony's growing economic and military importance, the Colonial Office encouraged a formal federation binding Aden and the Protectorate in order to ward off the Imam's advances. On the eve of the revolution in Yemen, Aden struck an agreement to join the twelve states of the Protectorate in a union known as the Federation of South Arabia. The federation was formally established in January 1963. Immediately it became a target of Nasser's criticism as a bastion of British imperialism in Arab lands.

Harold Macmillan's Conservative government was no more reconciled to Nasser's brand of pan-Arabism than had been Anthony Eden's government at the time of the 1956 Suez Crisis. Faced with the revolution in

[18] Dresch, *A History of Modern Yemen*, 71.

Yemen, the government was divided on how best to respond. Pragmatists in the Foreign Office argued that de facto recognition of the new republican regime was in Britain's best interest. Officials in the Colonial Office, however, held that any form of recognition would provoke a crisis in confidence among the pro-British rulers of Aden and the associated states of the Federation of South Arabia. Indecisive, the British withheld all recognition from the new republic in Yemen, prompting Sana'a to sever ties with London. With encouragement from their Egyptian patrons, the Yemenis began to promote anti-British insurgency within the Federation of South Arabia.

In March 1964 Yemeni forces crossed the border to attack villages in the neighbouring federation state of Bayhan. The British felt compelled to respond in order to demonstrate credible protection of federation territory. On 28 March, Royal Air Force (RAF) warplanes bombed the fortress village of Harib, just across the Yemeni border from Bayhan, killing ten men and wounding seven. The retaliatory attack brought the Conservative government, now under Alec Douglas-Home, international condemnation and domestic criticism. The Yemen Arab Republic submitted a complaint to the UN Security Council, which on 9 April passed Resolution 188 condemning reprisals in general as incompatible with the principles of the UN Charter and "deploring" Britain's military action against Harib. The Arab League was yet more outspoken in its condemnation of British imperialism. Even the British press found the reprisal smacked of discredited Suez-era military interventions.

The humiliation over Harib seemed only to stiffen the resolve of the British government to contain the threat posed by the Yemeni republicans and their Egyptian allies to British interests in Aden. It was clear that direct military action was not an option. Instead, the Conservative government gave tacit support to a covert operation designed to provide weapons, supplies, and training to the Yemeni royalists. By propping up the royalists, the British could deny the republicans sovereignty over all of North Yemen and could pin the Egyptians down in a protracted conflict that would wear down Nasser's armed forces.

The architects of Britain's covert support for the Yemeni royalists were a group of conservative politicians and military men known as the Aden Group. Committed imperialists, the Aden Group had first come together in their support for government action against Nasser in 1956 – when they were known as the Suez Group. They included Macmillan's son-in-law, Julian Amery, who served in a number of junior ministerial posts;

Lieutenant Colonel Neil "Billy" McLean, who had served with Amery in the Special Operations Executive in Albania during the World War II; and Colonel David Smiley, a military adviser to the government of Saudi Arabia who enjoyed direct connections to Prime Minister Douglas-Home. Many dismissed the Aden Group as marginal malcontents, but as a group they exercised disproportionate influence on the one issue that mattered most to them – retaining Aden for Britain's vanishing empire.

The Aden Group had been advocating covert operations in Yemen for at least one year before the Harib incident. In a strategy reminiscent of Suez, they turned to the French to assemble an Anglo-French team of mercenaries in order to assist the royalists and provide intelligence on Egyptian forces. The French had their own scores to settle with Nasser – for his support of the Algerian liberation movement, as well as their own humiliation in Suez – and were happy to exploit Egypt's exposure in Yemen. Numbers were small – by October 1963 there were no more than twenty-five mercenaries at work. Yet between July and October, they oversaw at least four planeloads of French arms and supplies from Djibouti to Aden for reshipment to Bayhan to assist the royalist cause.[19]

Between October 1963 and September 1965, the British took the initiative in the covert war in Yemen. They were still in no position to use RAF aircraft in their operations but, completing the parallel with the tripartite collusion in Suez, turned to the Israelis for assistance in making air drops of arms and supplies to royalists' areas. Of all parties, the Israelis had most interest in exploiting Egypt's exposure in Yemen and seized the opportunity to gain firsthand information regarding the Egyptian order of battle in Yemen. Colonel Smiley went to Israel in the autumn of 1963, where he met with Director General of the Defence Ministry Shimon Peres and Major-General Ezer Weizman, Commander of the Israeli air force, as well as ranking members of Military Intelligence, to broach the subject of Israeli support for covert operations in Yemen. "The Israelis never received payment," Smiley later recalled; "it was in their interests to keep the Egyptians tied down in the Yemen."[20] The Israelis provided aircraft to make drops and surplus arms for the royalists. In return, Smiley provided them with intelligence about Egyptian positions, ordnance

---

[19] Duff Hart-Davis, *The War that Never Was* (London: Century, 2011); Jones, *Britain and the Yemen Civil War*, 130–2.

[20] Smiley, cited by Jones, *Britain and the Yemen Civil War*, 149.

recovered with traces of suspected chemical agents used in Yemen, and knowledge of Egyptian air operations.

The first Israeli airdrop took place in February 1964 and was described by one of the British mercenaries, Major John "Johnny" Cooper. "On the night of the first drop, the Stratocruiser flew down the Red Sea with Egypt on the right and Saudi Arabia on the left. They had to come in almost at sea level to avoid detection by Egyptian radar, and when they reached the port of Hodeidah, they swung inland towards the mountains, climbing to 10,000 feet." Flying at 250 feet above the ground, the plane dropped sixty parachutes of arms and ammunition to the royalist forces below. The royalist commander "was delighted," Cooper claimed. "He had the mortars and bombs he needed together with a plentiful supply of small arms including German Schmeisser submachine guns." The Israelis had taken every effort to conceal the source of the weapons. "Every serial number had been scored out, the parachutes were of Italian origin, and even the wood shavings used in the packing had been imported from Cyprus. Even the most expert intelligence analyst would have had a job to unravel that one," he concluded.[21]

Through mercenary operations, officially denied but given tacit support by the British government, the Aden Group was able to transfer millions of pounds in funds, supplies, and arms in order to keep the flagging royalist cause from collapsing. Yet their efforts were ultimately in vain. In February 1966, Harold Wilson's Labour government announced that Britain would withdraw from Aden in 1968, largely based on economic grounds.

The one enduring result of the mercenary operation in Yemen was to undermine the Egyptian military. Through their support to royalist forces, they drove the Egyptians to devote more arms and materiel to the Yemen War, at the expense of war preparedness on the Sinai Front. The Israelis were in many ways the prime beneficiaries of the operations. They were able to contribute to a conflict that tied one-third of the Egyptian military to faraway Yemen; divided Arab ranks between Saudis, Jordanians, and Egyptians; and secured privileged access to intelligence on Egyptian weapons and tactics – all of which would contribute directly to Israel's victory in June 1967.

---

[21] Johnny Cooper with Peter Kemp, *One of the Originals* (London: Pan Macmillan, 1991), 177–8. Though Cooper never mentions the Israelis by name, Hart-Davis provides full details of Israel's involvements in the airdrops based on the papers of Tony Boyle who organized the flights; *The War That Never Was*, 135–58. See also Jones, *Britain and the Yemen Civil War*, 148.

Conclusion

In his assessment of the 1967 catastrophe, Field Marshal El-Gamasy claimed that the Yemen War played a major role in Egypt's defeat. By 1967, he argued, "nearly a third of our land forces, supported by our air force and navy, were engaged in an operation approximately two thousand kilometres away from Egypt, with no prospects for either a political or a military settlement." El-Gamasy continued:

> We incurred heavy losses in manpower, our military budget was drained, discipline and training suffered, weapons and equipment deteriorated, and fighting capability was seriously affected. Soldiers returning from Yemen were given furloughs during which weapons were overhauled, but levels of training consequently declined. Planes and technical equipment belonging to the air force were subjected to heavy wear and tear as a result of airborne operations and troop movements.[22]

Significantly, he added that the air force had not built a single hangar in five years – leaving all Egyptian aircraft exposed on airstrips, vulnerable to Israeli attack in the opening moments of the war.

As a military man, Nasser of all people should have realized how the Yemen War had left him vulnerable to Egypt's greatest adversary – Israel. With one-third of his military still pinned down in Yemen, he should have reacted with caution, rather than brinkmanship, during the summer of 1967. There could have been no worse time to take on the Israelis. So why did he allow Egypt to go down the path of miscalculation to its third and most disastrous defeat to Israel?

One argument was that Nasser was too weakened by the Yemen conflict not to intervene in the Syria crisis that preceded and led to the 1967 War. After all, Egypt and Syria were bound by a mutual defence pact. Had Israel actually gone to war and defeated an isolated Syria while Egypt was distracted by the Yemen War, Nasser's position would have been even worse than it was in the aftermath of total defeat.

Another of Nasser's miscalculations can be traced back to the Yemen War. On the eve of the 1967 War, Nasser overrode his top commanders' plans and insisted that Israel be left to make the first strike. Egypt would not initiate the war. Although Nasser's decision might have been politically reasonable, it was militarily disastrous. As Egypt's top brass rightly predicted, their defences were not strong enough to absorb Israel's first blow. His army lacked the men and weapons to repel a major Israeli strike. The forces they lacked were all tied down in Yemen.

[22] El-Gamasy, *The October War*, 36–7.

Although there is no doubt that the Yemen War played a major role in undermining Egypt's ability to wage war in 1967, it seems unlikely that Egypt, Syria, and Jordan could have defeated Israel without a much-higher degree of war planning and inter-Arab coordination than was possible in the divided Arab ranks of the late 1960s. In this sense, the Yemen War was a symptom of greater ills dividing the Arab world in 1967.

Despite the crushing defeat at the hands of Israel, Nasser could claim that Egypt ultimately prevailed in Yemen. Although the war between royalists and republicans continued for three years after the last Egyptian soldiers withdrew from Sanaa in October 1967, the Yemen Arab Republic did survive. Moreover, the British withdrew from Aden just six weeks after the Egyptians pulled out of Yemen. The Nasserists could claim victory over both the forces of reaction and imperialism.

There was also a silver lining in the Egyptian troop presence in Yemen. The thirty thousand soldiers, along with their tanks, artillery, and air and naval support, were all spared the defeat and destruction of the June 1967 War.[23] These experienced troops served as the core around which the Egyptians rebuilt their armed forces in the aftermath of the defeat. In this way, the Egyptian war in Yemen contributed not just to defeat in 1967 but also to a much more successful war against Israel in 1973.

[23] Huwaydi, *Harb 1967*, 51; Huwaydi, *50 'aman*, 283.

7

The United States and the 1967 War

Charles D. Smith

America's Middle East policy today exists in the shadow of decisions made during the 1967 Arab-Israeli War. Those decisions were based on positions suggested by Israel, backed by persons close to President Lyndon B. Johnson, and never discussed at any level of the Johnson administration prior to their adoption. The key shift in U.S. policy was to permit Israel to retain territories conquered in the conflict until it could reach peace accords with individual Arab states, a radical change from Washington's previous stance of seeking to maintain the territorial status quo.

The basic question, addressed in 1992 at a conference on the war by retired Ambassador Alfred Atherton, was how that change in policy occurred, especially since the State Department was omitted from the discussion.[1] Input from William Quandt, retired Ambassador to Egypt, Lucius Battle, and White House National Security staffer during the crisis, Harold Saunders, suggested that no policy discussion occurred in the Johnson White House, and that it was impossible to track the developments that led to the positions outlined in President Johnson's 19 June 1967 speech where he left peace up to the respective states; this stance became the foundation of UN Security Council Resolution 242 passed in November 1967. These comments led retired Ambassador to Israel, Samuel Lewis, to declare that "no political scientist or historian would dare write in his book that policy changes could be made in the fashion described by Messrs. Atherton, Quandt, and Battle."

---

[1] Published as Richard B. Parker, ed., *The Six-Day War: A Retrospective* (Gainesville: University Press of Florida, 1994). All remarks noted come from the conclusion, 292, 317–19.

These policy changes were made in this fashion at a time when the Johnson administration was distracted by Vietnam, and Johnson personally was under intense pressure from advisers and representatives of the Jewish community not to replicate America's policy during the 1956 Suez Crisis when President Dwight Eisenhower insisted on Israel's withdrawal from the Sinai Peninsula. Johnson, then Senate Majority Leader, had opposed Eisenhower's threat of sanctions against Israel, a stance he proudly recalled to the end of his career, and one Israel exploited in 1967.

An additional legacy of the Suez Crisis that impacted administration thinking in 1967 dealt with the conditions Israel applied, with Washington's approval, to its withdrawal from the Sinai, and especially from Sharm al-Sheikh, the promontory overlooking the Strait of Tiran. Egypt's Gamal Abdel Nasser had blockaded the Tiran Strait in September 1955, barring Israel's access to the Red Sea from the Gulf of Aqaba. Foreign Minister Golda Meir informed the UN General Assembly in March 1957 that Israel's withdrawal from Sharm al-Sheikh was conditional upon rite of passage through the Tiran Strait, which was considered an international waterway. Any future interference with Israeli ships making such passage would "be regarded by Israel as an attack entitling it to exercise its inherent right of self-defence under Article 51 of the United Nations Charter." At the same time, a UN Emergency Force (UNEF) was established at posts in the Sinai, including Sharm al-Sheikh, to serve as a buffer between Egypt and Israel.[2] Meir's declaration to the UN in March 1957 played a major role in Israeli-American discussions in May and June 1967.

The ultimate result of the 1967 War was Resolution 242, which remains the operative document defining prospective peace talks between Israel and Arab neighbours. Another consequence of the war was the general acceptance in the scholarly literature that the war established a "special relationship" between Israel and the United States that still exists.

American policy makers in various administrations had long known that Israel sought a relationship with the United States that would make Washington Israel's source of weaponry. But Israel had also hoped that this relationship would go beyond military sales to include the coordination of America's Middle East policy with Israel regarding all Arab countries. Members of Congress, encouraged by the Israeli embassy, questioned Washington's assistance to conservative, pro-West Arab regimes, which was justified as strengthening them against opponents who might

---

[2] See T. G. Fraser, *The Middle East, 1914–1979* (London: E. Arnold, 1980), 95–6.

join the Soviet bloc. The Cold War dominated Washington's thinking as it had since the end of World War II. Israel frequently received secret documents or news of White House thinking from sympathizers within various administrations.[3]

Domestic politics was far more salient to Mideast policy during the Johnson administration than it had been under Presidents Eisenhower and John F. Kennedy, influenced by Johnson's personal admiration for Israel and by growing popular opposition to Johnson's Vietnam policies. As a result, Israel's influence in the Johnson administration decision making led to commitments, including the wording of Resolution 242, that suited Israel's goals and contradicted apparent U.S. commitments stated prior to the outbreak of the war, with the State Department excluded from the discussion. It was during the Johnson years that policy making clearly shifted from the State Department to the White House.

The Johnson Administration and Arab-Israeli Tensions: 1964–May 1967

Though he was not blindly supportive of Israel, Johnson's initial sympathies were buttressed by a much greater sensitivity to criticism of his policies than seen in the Eisenhower or Kennedy eras, particularly once he intensified American involvement in Vietnam during 1965. The strongest support for his Great Society programs that legislated equal rights for blacks had come from associates who were Jewish, some of whom had joined him in backing Franklin D. Roosevelt's "New Deal" programs during the late 1930s. Many of these Jewish liberals now openly criticized Johnson's escalation of America's military forces in Southeast Asia. Acutely aware of their views, Johnson approved a military aid package for Israel, far more ambitious than Kennedy's, leading up to the 1964 presidential elections. By this time, State Department personnel included in their reports references to Johnson's political sympathies and how they might influence foreign-policy decisions.[4] Johnson's concern about retaining political backing among American Jews reached the point where he

---

[3] Peter L. Hahn, "Bernarth Lecture: The View from Jerusalem: Revelations about U.S. Diplomacy from the Archives of Israel," *Diplomatic History* 22, no. 4 (Fall 1998), 509–32; Hahn, *Caught in the Middle East: U.S. Policy Toward the Arab-Israeli Conflict, 1945–1961* (Chapel Hill: University of North Carolina Press, 2004).

[4] Arlene Lazarowitz, "Different Approaches to a Regional Search for Balance: The Johnson Administration, the State Department, and the Middle East, 1964–1967," *Diplomatic History* 32, no. 1 (January 2008), 38.

asked Israel's president, Zalman Shazar, when the latter made an official visit to Washington in August 1966, for Israel's "sympathetic understanding" of the American involvement in Vietnam, which he equated with his commitment to Israel.

This shift in emphasis applied also to Johnson's ties to the American Jewish community leadership. President Kennedy had consulted Democratic Party loyalists such as Abraham (Abe) Feinberg and Arthur Krim regarding campaign questions and funding. Both had direct access to high administration officials and were close to Israel's political elite. Feinberg, a New York banker and ardent fundraiser for Israel's nuclear reactor at Dimona as well as for the Democratic Party, advised Israeli Prime Minister David Ben-Gurion on tactics to stall Kennedy's efforts to inspect the plant. Johnson likewise consulted Feinberg and Krim on party issues, but he also used them (Krim was head of the Democratic Party campaign committee) as contacts to explain policy to leading Jewish groups in order to forestall criticism either of Vietnam or of policies that appeared sympathetic to Arab moderates such as Jordan's King Hussein. Finally he employed Feinberg, a frequent visitor to Israel, as a private emissary to the Israeli leadership, including the new prime minister, Levi Eshkol. Feinberg would call the president before his trips to discuss points Johnson might wish to communicate that were distinct from State Department directives also approved by the president.

As for Krim and his wife Mathilde, the latter formerly married to an Israeli and a convert to Judaism, Johnson developed a relationship that went well beyond campaign issues. The Krims were frequent guests at the LBJ ranch in Texas and at the White House, including the days just prior to and during the 1967 War.[5] Like Feinberg, they knew Israeli leaders such as Prime Minister Eshkol, Foreign Minister Abba Eban, and the leading Israeli diplomats in Washington, Ambassador Avraham Harman and Counsellor Ephraim (Eppie) Evron.

Ambassador Harman also had ties to Johnson's closest confidant, Abe Fortas, a successful Washington lawyer whom Johnson had appointed to the Supreme Court. They had met in 1937 when both had backed President Roosevelt's New Deal policies. White House records note

---

[5] Arthur Krim, Interview II with Michael Gillette, 17 May 1982, Oral History, Lyndon Baines Johnson Library [hereinafter referred to as OH and LBJL]. The Krims' daughter served in the Israeli army and Mathilde Krim had fought with the extremist Zionist paramilitary group, the Irgun, in the period leading to Israel's independence. Ibid. and Interview VI, 13 October 1983, OH, LBJL.

"145 LBJ-Fortas meetings between 23 November 1963 and 2 July 1968," not including telephone calls.[6]

These relationships proved crucial as the 1967 War crisis developed, in stark contrast to the U.S. relationship with Egypt that had steadily deteriorated since 1964. Nasser bitterly resented Congress's restrictions on PL 480 food assistance because of Egyptian involvement in Yemen, begun in 1962; PL 480 aid had been critical to Egyptian government policies and economic stability since 1961.[7] An ardent nationalist, Nasser did not respond well to threats that arose in the form of a "short leash" approach to food assistance, renewable if Nasser behaved satisfactorily. This approach was encouraged by Ambassador Lucius (Luke) Battle, who assumed his post in September 1964.[8]

By March 1967, when Battle finished his tour in Cairo, Nasser had halted aid requests; Washington had refused to renew agreements that had expired as of June 1966. The Egyptian leader was convinced that the United States was trying to overthrow his regime; fears that some embassy officials believed justified. The United States was the only Western country not to reschedule Egypt's debts at a time its economy was in shambles, and U.S. activities included suspected Central Intelligence Agency (CIA) operations against Egyptian forces in Yemen and open funnelling of money to Egyptian informants in Cairo and Alexandria.[9]

---

[6] For Fortas-Johnson meetings, Robert Dallek, *Flawed Giant: Lyndon Johnson and His Times, 1961–1973* (New York: Oxford University Press, 1998), 559; Tom Segev, *1967: Israel, the War, and the Year That Transformed the Middle East*, trans. Jessica Cohen (New York: Metropolitan Books, 2007), 119–20, 302, 332, discusses Fortas's ties to Ambassador Harman.

[7] William J. Burns, *Economic Aid and American Policy toward Egypt, 1955–1981* (Albany: State University of New York, 1985), 126, 150.

[8] Battle has given two oral history accounts that treat his ambassadorship in Cairo. They can be accessed online at www.millercenter.org/scripps/archive/oralhistories/detail/2277 and at www.adst.org/Oral_History.htm. For an overview see Burns, *Economic Aid*, 155–70.

[9] The pattern of exchanges between the U.S. embassy in Cairo and Washington can be followed in Department of State, *Foreign Relations of the United States*, vol. XVIII *Arab-Israeli Dispute, 1964–1967* (Washington, DC: U.S. Government Printing Office, 2000) [hereinafter referred to as *FRUS*], from May 1966 onwards, accessed at www.state.gov/www/about_state/history/vol_xviii/a.html. All references to vol. XVIII will be to this site. For the Cairo embassy's belief that Washington sought to undercut Nasser and for complaints of CIA bungling, see David Nes, OH interview with Ted Gittinger, 25 March 1983, LBJL, 5–6, and Richard B. Parker, OH, 21 April 1989 (The Association for Diplomatic Studies and Training), www.adst.org/Oral_History.htm., and Memorandum from the Country Director for the UAR (Donald Bergus) to Lucius D. Battle, 16 March 1967, *FRUS*, vol. XVIII, no. 396. Parker was an embassy political officer.

Battle left Cairo on 5 March. The new Ambassador, Richard Nolte, did not arrive until 21 May. When asked at the airport about the developing crisis, then a week old, he responded "What crisis?" creating an instant impression of being out of touch with the responsibilities given to him.

Crisis and War

In the months preceding the Six-Day War, Johnson and Secretary of State Dean Rusk replaced the top three American officials in South Vietnam, and the president travelled to Guam in March to introduce the new team to the South Vietnamese leadership who were scheduled to oversee elections in the fall. Johnson had approved peace overtures to Hanoi that spring, but when the chance for talks collapsed, he ordered the bombing of the north to be expanded in April, triggering massive demonstrations in America's cities; Martin Luther King Jr. condemned the war. As tensions mounted, Johnson recalled General William Westmoreland, Commander of U.S. forces in Vietnam, for consultations.

Syrian-Israeli clashes intensified during the spring of 1967. Tank and artillery exchanges on 7 April led to an air battle in which Israeli pilots downed six Syrian jets and mockingly buzzed Damascus. A month later, on the eve of Israel's independence day celebrations (14–15 May), both Chief of Staff Yitzhak Rabin and Prime Minister Eshkol publicly warned Syria of major retaliatory raids that could reach Damascus. Johnson administration officials took note but were not overly disturbed.[10] In addition to Vietnam, they had been distracted by a coup by Greek colonels on 21 April that forestalled scheduled May elections.

Washington remained calm when Nasser ordered Egyptian troops into the Sinai on 14 May, a day after the Soviets had warned him of a pending Israeli attack on Syria. The CIA concluded that the Soviet warnings were false but saw Nasser's actions as an understandable response to Eshkol's and Rabin's declarations. The Egyptian ultimatum on 19 May that all UN forces be removed from the posts they had occupied since 1957 changed matters radically. These UN posts included Sharm al-Sheikh, which the Egyptian military occupied on 21 May, the day Ambassador-designate Richard Nolte arrived in Cairo. On 23 May, under taunts of cowardice by both Damascus and Amman, Nasser announced the closing of the Tiran Strait that linked the Red Sea to the Gulf of Aqaba, recreating the conditions that existed prior to the 1956 Suez Crisis. Israel immediately

---

[10] Segev, 1967, 202–13, discusses Syrian-Israeli tensions and speeches made.

reminded Johnson officials of Golda Meir's UN declaration of March 1957 and argued that the United States was now obliged to back Israeli militarily, an interpretation Johnson and his aides rejected.

Johnson strove to keep lines open to all parties. On 17 May he had written Eshkol that "I cannot accept responsibilities on behalf of the United States for situations which arise as the result of actions on which we are not consulted."[11] In reply, Eshkol insisted on the "urgent need to reaffirm the American commitment to Israel's security with a view to its implementation should the need arise."[12] News of the withdrawal of UN forces from the Sinai on 19 May led to further Israeli demands for an American promise of support, causing Ambassador Walworth Barbour in Tel Aviv to recommend that Washington issue a statement to "calm them down" and prevent an immediate attack, advice Johnson accepted after contacting Nasser to ask for consultation.[13]

Johnson's public address the evening of 23 May stressed the U.S. commitment to a peaceful resolution of the crisis "in and outside the United Nations," while criticizing the "hurried withdrawal" of the UN forces from the Sinai. Johnson condemned the blockade of the Gulf of Aqaba to Israeli shipping as "illegal and potentially disastrous to the cause of peace" and then issued a statement of principle that administration policy makers would contradict once war broke out:

To the leaders of all the nations of the Near East, I wish to say what three American Presidents have said before me – that the United States is firmly committed to the support of the political independence and *territorial integrity* of all the nations of the area. The United States strongly opposes aggression by anyone in the area, in any form, overt or clandestine. . . . The record of the actions of the United States over the past twenty years, within and outside the United Nations, is abundantly clear on this point.[14]

[11] Text in *FRUS*, vol. XIX, *Arab-Israeli Crisis and War, 1967* (Washington, DC: U.S. Government Printing Office, 2004), 8, 10. A full chronology of developments is found in "Middle East Crisis, Chronological Guide, May 12–June 20," in National Security Files [hereinafter referred to as NSF], National Security Council Histories, Middle East Crisis, May 12–June 19, 1967, box 17, LBJL.

[12] "Telegram from the Embassy in Israel to the Department of State," 18 May 1967, *FRUS*, vol. XIX, no. 13, 19–21. Eshkol's request for "implementation" meant American military forces fighting with Israel, an interpretation all officials including Johnson rejected.

[13] 22 May 1967, *FRUS*, vol. XIX, no. 34, 58. Johnson proposed that Vice-President Hubert Humphrey visit the region, an idea that led to Egyptian Vice-President Zakariyya Mohieddin's proposed visit to the United States.

[14] Text in *Papers of Lyndon Baines Johnson, President 1963–1969*, "President's Appointment File (Diary Back-Up)," box 67, LBJL, emphasis added.

The situation did not promise easy resolution. The Cairo embassy had informed Washington the same day that Egypt would stop Israeli ships trying to enter the Gulf of Aqaba. The embassy's impression of Cairo's resolve was reiterated by Charles Yost, an emissary sent to Egypt from Washington at the end of May. Yost warned that "there is no prospect for success our present tactic of mobilizing maritime powers to reopen straits, except by exercise military force . . . out of proportion to real US interests at stake . . . [since] force would have to be maintained there indefinitely" with dire political consequences.[15] The Joint Chiefs of Staff agreed and ruled out any American military effort to open the Tiran Strait.

Yost's reference to "maritime powers" called attention to State Department efforts to organize an international maritime force to force the strait, proposed by the British and sponsored by Eugene Rostow, brother of National Security Council (NSC) adviser Walt. Under Secretary of State for Political Affairs Eugene Rostow occupied a key position in the State Department. His office oversaw the routing of cables from U.S. embassies in the Middle East to higher officials; with the crisis he became head of a control group that funnelled information and proposed strategy. Harold Saunders, who represented the NSC on the White House staff, later depicted Eugene Rostow's operating style and staff behaviour as "a floating crap game" in which operational judgements were made "somewhat by the seat of their pants." Saunders added that Johnson's NSC staff could not "get a handle on what and how things were being done in the Department" as the crisis developed, an opinion shared by McGeorge Bundy who had returned at Johnson's request to staff a Special Committee of the NSC handling the flow of information on the crisis. After the war, Bundy recommended to Johnson that he remove Eugene Rostow as head of the control group transmitting information to Rusk and the White House, because Rostow did not have "the good sense and judgment" to oversee a difficult situation.[16]

U.S. embassy personnel and State Department officials in Washington concurred. In the words of the highest-ranking Foreign Service officer at the Cairo Embassy at the time of the war, "United States officials with a working knowledge of the Middle East have no access to the policy-making levels on the seventh floor of the State Department or at

---

[15] "Telegram from the Embassy in the United Arab Republic to the Department of State," "Secstate for Battle from Yost," 2 June 1967, *FRUS*, vol. XIX, no. 128, 231–2.

[16] "Interview with Harold H. Saunders" by Thomas Stern, 24 November 1993, OH, www.adst.org, 12. Bundy's memo is "Memorandum for the President," 25 July 1967, NSF, Files of Special Committee of the National Security Council [hereinafter referred to as SCNSC], box 1, LBJL.

the White House.... From the point of view of Cairo, American Middle East policy seemed to be created in a vacuum."[17] The Israeli embassy in Washington viewed Eugene Rostow as an ardent supporter of Israel, in contrast to his brother Walt.[18]

Another development on 23 May was Rusk's initiative to use Robert Anderson as a private envoy to Nasser. A fellow Texan and prominent Republican with business interests in the Middle East, Johnson often used him as an emissary there and elsewhere. Anderson's visit would result in Egyptian Vice-President Zakariyya Mohieddin's scheduled visit to the United States to discuss possible resolution of the crisis. He was due to arrive on 7 June and his advance party was due to arrive on 5 June, information that Ambassador Harman received from Rusk the afternoon of 2 June.

American information about Arab views came mainly from U.S. embassies abroad, the United Nations, and emissaries such as Yost and Anderson, whereas Israeli envoys had direct access to U.S. officials in Washington and New York, often seeking information. In one such effort, Israel requested, through Washington, the Jordanian order of battle, a demand embassy officials in Amman saw as an attempt to compromise U.S. credibility in that country.[19] Israeli reports, both personal and through embassy cables, often contradicted each other. During Foreign Minister Eban's visit to the United States to sound out President Johnson in a 26 May meeting, Eban assured Arthur Goldberg on 27 May that the "Israeli military was not spoiling for a fight" while Ambassador Barbour cabled the State Department from Tel Aviv the same day that "clearly Israeli military [was] pressing very hard for authority to take pre-emptive action and probably threatening Eshkol with dire military consequences for Israel if he does not do so."[20] Barbour's assessment, not Eban's, was correct.

---

[17] Tom Fenton, "U.S. Ignored Crisis Signs in the Middle East: Despite Clear Warning, No Move Made to Deter Nasser," *Baltimore Sun*, 13 June 1967, quoting David Nes, the Deputy Chief of Mission, on the ship evacuating them from Alexandria. Nes's colleague and later ambassador, Richard Parker, then embassy political officer, agreed with Nes (OH, www.adst.org). Nes's outburst, when published, ended his State Department career.

[18] For Ambassador Harman's praise of Eugene Rostow see Segev, *1967*, 120.

[19] NSF, Country File [hereinafter referred to as CF]/Middle East, Memos and Misc, "Middle East Crisis Cables," box 105, Amman to State, 25 May 1967.

[20] Compare Goldberg's and Barbour's telegrams to the United States from the UN Mission and Embassy in Israel, respectively, in *FRUS*, vol. XIX, no. 81–2, 154–56, both dated 27 May 1967.

In preparation for Eban's visit, Johnson convened a NSC meeting expanded to include long-time confidants Fortas and Clark Clifford. The U.S. military reported that Egyptian forces were in defensive positions and that, in any case, Israel could win a war with ease, against Egypt or, as in later assessments, against Egypt, Syria, and Jordan, a view strongly backed by the CIA.[21] These views countered alarmist messages from Eshkol of an imminent Egyptian attack.

Rusk reported that he had informed Eban that consultation with the United States was essential and that "Israel would not be alone unless it chose to go alone," a remark Johnson adopted. All disputed Fortas's arguments, echoing Eshkol, that if required, U.S. military force should be used to escort an Israeli ship through the Tiran Straits. Johnson noted that congressional approval would be required to use the American military. Congress backed Israel but did not want American forces involved. [22]

At his meeting with Eban that evening, Johnson declared that the United States would use its "best efforts" to keep the straits open to Israeli shipping, but would not act unilaterally; Washington would "do everything we can through the UN . . . even though we do not have great hopes." The president was more enthusiastic about the international maritime force plan backed by Eugene Rostow. He told Eban bluntly that the United States did not believe Eshkol's warnings of an imminent Arab attack, but he assured Eban that if Israel were attacked, "the Israelis would lick them." He then "with emphasis and solemnity . . . repeated twice Israel will not be alone unless it decides to go it alone," and "he could not imagine that they [Israeli Cabinet] could make such a decision."[23]

Johnson left for his Texas ranch the next day (27 May) for the long Memorial Day weekend, accompanied by the Krims, whom he told of his meeting with Eban. During the weekend, Jordan's King Hussein flew to Cairo and entered into a defence pact with Egypt on 30 May, and Johnson's staff exchanged drafts of a speech Eshkol was to deliver to

---

[21] Ibid., Intelligence Memorandum Prepared in the Central Intelligence Agency, "Military Capabilities of Israel and the Arab States," 26 May 1967, no. 76, 138–39.

[22] Ibid., "Meeting on the Arab-Israeli Crisis," 1:30 P.M., no. 72, 127–38, which includes a "draft Statement" for Johnson's delivery to Eban. It included the "Israel . . . go alone" statement along with that stating "we cannot imagine it will make that decision." It stressed as well the United States' intent to rely on the United Nations and the proposed international maritime force, along with emphasis that any military involvement by the United States would require adherence to "constitutional processes," meaning congressional approval.

[23] Ibid., "Memorandum of Conversation," 26 May 1967, 7:15–8:40 P.M., no. 77, 140–6.

the Knesset on 31 May. But Eshkol and others remained dissatisfied with Eban's report of his 26 May meetings in the United States: Would the United States object if Israel acted alone? Mossad head Meir Amit flew to Washington on 31 May where he met with Secretary of Defence Robert McNamara and CIA head Richard Helms, a long-time friend, on 1 June, returning to Israel the next day; he did not meet with any State Department representative.

Twenty-five years later, Amit recalled that he had not sought approval from American officials for an Israeli attack. Instead, he had told them that he would recommend an attack; he wanted their reaction, not their approval. McNamara's response, said Amit, was to say that "it was all right, the president knows that you are here, and I have a direct line to the president," and he also asked Amit how long the war would take and how many casualties Israel expected. According to the official American record of the meeting, Amit said much more. He warned McNamara of a "grand design" in which Nasser and the Soviets intended to establish Arab domination of the entire Middle East up to the Soviet borders and stressed throughout that while this was a matter of concern for Israel, it should be a far greater concern for the United States. He also said that his visit was private and he did not officially represent Israel, a doubtful statement. But Amit did learn from McNamara that the contemplated international naval action in the Tiran Strait "was just one of a number of possibilities . . . under consideration," a clear if inadvertent indication that such an action was unlikely. This remark undercut Johnson's justification for Israel to delay that he had given to Eban.[24]

This meeting supposedly signalled to Israel an American nod of approval to attack. According to Tom Segev, McNamara assured Amit that he found Amit's arguments "persuasive" and would relay his views to the president who supposedly agreed with McNamara. Michael Oren agrees to the extent that Amit concluded that "the president, like his defence secretary, was not telling Israel explicitly *not* to go to war"; this in itself constituted approval for Israeli unilateralism. Admiral Rufus Taylor's detailed summary of the meeting does not bear out these interpretations, which are based on two phone calls Johnson supposedly made to McNamara during his meeting with Amit, calls not noted in Taylor's

[24] Amit's version of his conference with McNamara is in Parker, *Six-Day War*, 136–41. For the American version, see Admiral Rufus Taylor, "Conversation between Major General Meir Amit and Secretary McNamara – late afternoon, 1 June 1967," 1 June 1967, *FRUS*, vol. XIX, no. 124, 223–5. It confirms McNamara's question about Israeli casualties but has nothing about McNamara's assurances of closeness to Johnson.

record. Moreover, in 1992 Amit denied that he had received any sort of light indicating approval for or no objection to an Israeli preemptive strike.[25]

The more important meeting was one that Amit held with Helms on 1 June. Amit, Helms assured Johnson in a report on 2 June, wanted nothing from the United States "except to supply weapons already arranged for, to give diplomatic support, and to keep the USSR out of the ring. He indicated that they have everything they need."[26] In his memoirs, Helms paraphrased his 2 June memo to Johnson but noted that "in passing this information to the President, I added my own conviction that this visit was a clear portent that war might come at any time with no advance warning. Three days later Israel launched its pre-emptive attack. All told we had presented the boss [Johnson] with a tidy package."[27]

American documents indicate that rather than Israel being given a clear go-ahead, administration officials were told of Israeli intentions to attack and did not raise specific objections – that in itself could be read positively by Israel. But did Johnson or other aides suggest to any Israeli official that the United States approved an Israeli assault to launch the war? William Quandt decided the colour was yellow and that Fortas in particular told Israeli officials that Johnson would not disapprove an attack. Johnson had agreed that Fortas could serve as "an informal intermediary" between him and Ambassador Harman.[28]

There were several flashing lights from persons close to Johnson, none of them red. The Israeli embassy had code names for their sources and

[25] Segev, 1967, 330–1; Michael Oren, Six Days of War: June 1967 and the Making of the Modern Middle East (New York: Oxford University Press, 2002), 146–7. Emphasis in original. For Amit's denial of any signals of encouragement see Parker, Six-Day War, 136. An incisive critique of Oren's book is Roland Popp, "Stumbling Decidedly into the Six-Day War," Middle East Journal 60, no. 2 (Spring 2006), 281–309.

[26] Memorandum for the President, CIA, Office of the Director, 2 June 1967. From the George Washington University National Security Archive, www.gwu.edu/~nsarchiv/NSAEBB/NSAEBB265/19670602.pdf. Helms attached to his memo a two-page summary of Amit's views.

[27] Richard Helms with William Hood, A Look Over My Shoulder: A Life in the Central Intelligence Agency (New York: Random House, 2003), 299–300. In a private interview a week after the war ended, Helms said that the CIA had been "certain that at a convenient moment Israel would strike first.... Israel clearly picked its own moment to push off." C. L. Sulzberger, An Age of Mediocrity: Memoirs and Diaries, 1963–1972 (New York: Macmillian, 1973), 346, entry for 17 June 1967.

[28] William B. Quandt, "Lyndon Johnson and the June 1967 War: What Color Was the Light?" Middle East Journal 46, no. 2 (Spring 1992), 198–228, and 215; for Fortas as intermediary, see material updated in his Peace Process: American Diplomacy and the Arab-Israeli Conflict since 1967, 3rd ed. (Berkeley: University of California Press, 2005), 23–52.

had little trouble gaining information. In retirement, Helms scoffed at charges of a CIA-Mossad collusion, arguing that "the Israelis know what goes on in the U.S. government from top to bottom" without requiring a special source. Evron, at the same forum, acknowledged that he and Harman had met with Fortas often, but he issued a dubious denial that Fortas had been a major source in the days leading up to 5 June: "we didn't look at Justice Fortas as a channel to the White House for the simple reason that we didn't need another channel. Too many channels will sometimes get you confused."[29]

Still, Evron had a point – there were many channels. According to Israel's UN Ambassador, Gideon Rafael, he had been told on 27 May by "a most responsible representative of the United States" (possibly Arthur Goldberg, the U.S. Ambassador to the United Nations) that Johnson's reference to Israel acting alone in the meeting the day before did not constitute opposition to Israeli unilateralism; instead, it meant that "if you stand alone you will know how to act," an interpretation urging Israel to go it alone. Ambassador Rafael imparted that news to Amit before he left Israel for his meetings with McNamara and Helms.[30]

However, NSC staffers had also been considering the advantages of not opposing an Israeli assault. On the eve of Eban's visit, Saunders wrote to Walt Rostow that "we are trying to keep the peace because war would lead in unknown directions. However if Eban feels only a strike can solve Israel's problem, we ought to think long and hard before we reject it out of hand. The cost of holding them back may be a tremendous and lasting commitment to meet their long-term security needs which they feel could be met by a strike now – before the Egyptians fully consolidate their position. That cost could be far greater to us than an air-clearing now." Saunders reiterated his argument to Rostow on 31 May, with Rostow then suggesting to Johnson the same day that the United States should reconsider its position on letting Israel go it alone.[31]

---

[29] See Parker, *Six-Day War*, 259, 226 for the Helms and Evron quotations.

[30] Ibid., 149–50. According to Abe Feinberg (Oren, *Six Days of War*, 150), Goldberg had convinced Johnson to unleash Israel. In his own oral history at the Johnson library, Goldberg bragged that Johnson asked him to "take charge" of the 1967 War, and that he had advised Eban, not Rafael, that Johnson's reference to the need to get congressional approval for sending troops meant that Israel should act as it wished, terms identical to advice Rafael said he'd received on 25 May from an "authorized source." Arthur J. Goldberg, OH Interview I with Ted Gittinger, 23 March 1983, LBJL.

[31] "Memo for WWR from Saunders," NSF, CF/Middle East, Memos and Misc, 25 May 2967, LBJL; Memorandum by Harold Saunders to WWR, 31 May 1967, *FRUS*, vol. XIX, no. 114, 208–11; "Middle East Crisis, Chronological Guide," May 31,

The idea of not objecting to an Israeli strike, therefore, had been broached within the NSC staff and shared with Johnson before Amit's visit; it was not simply a question of pressure by pro-Israeli aides and friends. What is clear is that on the evening of 2 June, Johnson informed his overnight guest, British Prime Minister Harold Wilson, that war could not be avoided. His remark echoed two reports that he had received that day stating that war was inevitable, from Helms and from General Earle Wheeler, Chair of the Joint Chiefs of Staff.[32]

Still, when aides drafted Johnson's 5 June response to Wilson's letter of that date, knowledge of Israel's intentions was deleted. The original version read "We had feared that the Israelis might feel compelled to strike but we had no advance indication from them that they had actually taken a decision to do so." Johnson accepted Walt Rostow's advice that this be edited to say: "We had feared that someone might feel compelled to strike. We had no advance indication that a decision had been taken. We believed in fact we had at least a clean week for diplomacy."[33]

Israel's attack was no surprise to Johnson and his advisers, except possibly to Rusk and the State Department who remained invested in the Mohieddin visit, cancelled by the assault, and appear not to have anticipated Israeli unilateralism. At 5:09 A.M. on 5 June, Rusk called Johnson with a draft position statement stating the views of the government, which Johnson approved. Its second sentence read: "We are expecting a very high-level Egyptian delegation on Wednesday (7 June), and we had assurances from the Israelis that they would not initiate hostilities pending further diplomatic efforts."[34]

Wednesday, 13, NSF, National Security Council Histories/Middle East Crisis, May 12–June 19, 1967, box 17, LBJL.

[32] For Wilson's handwritten note to President Johnson, thanking him for his hospitality, NSF, CF/Middle East, box 107, 5 June 1967, LBJL. For Wheeler, Michael Brecher, *Decisions in Crisis: Israel 1967 and 1973* (Berkeley: University of California Press, 1980), 165.

[33] Telegram from the Department of State to the Embassy in London, 5 June 1967, *FRUS*, vol. XIX, no. 168, 317. For editing, see 317n4.

[34] Rusk states that "we were shocked and angry as hell when the Israelis launched their surprise offensive." Dean Rusk, *As I Saw It*, as told to Richard Rusk, ed. Daniel S. Papp (New York: W. W. Norton, 1990), 386. It is doubtful that he knew of the earlier Saunders and Rostow memos to Johnson. For Rusk's phone call to Johnson, Tape WH6706.01, citation no. 11901, LBJ Recordings, CD Track Six, cited in Robert David Johnson, "The Secret Presidential Recordings – Research Paper No. 3" (July 2008), 92, online publication of the S. Daniel Abraham Center for International and Regional Studies, Tel Aviv University, www.tau.ac.il/humanities/abraham/publications/johnson_israel.pdf.

Rostow had made the final case on 4 June for allowing Israel to act alone by breaching the Tiran Strait blockade, an argument couched in terms of there still being a week's leeway to avert a war. He claimed that moderate Arabs and U.S. ambassadors in the Arab world preferred that Israel resolve the crisis without U.S. input, with the goal of "Nasser's being cut down to size." Only then could there be "a new phase in the Middle East of moderation, ... economic development [Rostow's obsession], regional collaboration and acceptance of Israel ... if a solution to the [Palestinian] refugee problem can be found." Further, Israeli action could help "to unify the political base in the U.S. around our Middle East policy, so that we do not weaken the political foundations for our further conduct of the war in Vietnam." American Jews might rally around Johnson's Vietnam policy if the United States gave Israel the go-ahead.[35]

Had Johnson been informed of the date and time of Israel's attack at a campaign dinner in New York? Sources claim that Feinberg told Johnson during the dinner the evening of 3 June that Israel would attack in twenty-four hours, information strongly denied by Israelis in government at the time.[36]

A factor in the Israeli decision was knowledge of the scheduled arrival of the Egyptian vice-president and his advance party in Washington on 7 June and 5 June, respectively. The Cabinet discussed the visit the morning of 4 June in which Eshkol remarked that Johnson had "softened his stand and given Israel political support." He then said, "There is a movement toward a search for compromise, at Israel's expense," referring to the Egyptian delegation whose advance party was scheduled to leave for Washington the next day.[37] Israel's assault preempted a pending negotiating process once the Egyptians arrived in Washington, not a supposed Egyptian attack.

War and the Idea of a Full Peace Agreement

When informed by Walt Rostow of the outbreak of war at 4:35 A.M. on 5 June, Johnson merely acknowledged the news; to one observer

---

[35] Rostow to President Johnson, 4 June 1967, *FRUS*, vol. XIX, no. 144, 272–7.

[36] Quandt, *Peace Process*, 41; Segev, *1967*, 347; Oren, *Six Days of War*, 166. The original source was Merle Miller, *Lyndon: An Oral Biography* (New York: G. P. Putnam's Sons, 1980), 480, who had the wrong date, 4 June, for the banquet; it was 3 June.

[37] Oren, *Six Days of War*, 147, 150; Brecher, *Decisions*, 167, has the Eshkol quotes. Rusk, *As I Saw It*, 386, states that Israel "attacked on a Monday knowing that on Wednesday the Egyptian vice-president would arrive in Washington."

"the President gave no indication of it being anything but a normal day." Nonetheless, Johnson suggested the formation of the special committee under former NSC adviser Bundy, which was formally established on 7 June. Although intended to free Rostow so that he could focus on Vietnam and other issues, he remained deeply involved in policy issues related to Israel and the Arab world.[38]

News of Israel's military successes against Egypt was received "with enthusiasm" by congressional leaders briefed by Johnson. Israel's victories removed concern that U.S. forces might be requested by Israel and lessened chances of a great power confrontation with the Soviets; the "hot line" with Moscow had been activated immediately. Another problem arose when Egypt and other Arab states accused the United States and Britain of collaborating with Israel in the initial air attacks that destroyed 90 percent of the Egyptian aircraft on the ground.[39]

Jordan was another matter, especially when Israel captured East Jerusalem on 7 June with calls for its annexation to Israel, but American attention was diverted on 8 June by an Israeli attack on an American intelligence-gathering ship stationed off the Sinai coast, the USS *Liberty*, by jet aircraft and then by torpedo boats. They failed to sink it but thirty-four U.S. servicemen and intelligence technicians were killed and 172 were wounded. After learning of Israeli responsibility for the attack, the United States immediately alerted the Soviets, including a personal message from Johnson to Soviet Prime Minister Alexei Kosygin, that American naval movements in the Eastern Mediterranean dealt with the *Liberty* and its crew and did not signal U.S. military involvement in the war.[40]

Washington ultimately accepted Israel's apology for the attack, but most in the administration were convinced it had been intentional, including long-time defender of Israel, Clifford, and CIA Director Helms. Helms always believed that Israel attacked to prevent the United States from learning of its planned assault on Syria when Washington sought a ceasefire. The administration rejected the initial Israeli reply to U.S. queries and

[38] For Johnson, "Chronological Guide," NSF, NSC Histories, Middle East Crisis, 12 May–19 June 1967, Monday, 5 June 7:30 A.M., LBJL. For Bundy's role and his special committee, see Walt Rostow, "Memorandum for the Record," 17 November 1968, *FRUS*, vol. XIX, no. 149, 291n12, and Bundy's own account in his OH III, Interview with Paige Mulhollan, 19 March 1969, LBJL.

[39] For congressional enthusiasm, see entries for 6 June 1967 in Papers of Lyndon B. Johnson/President's Daily Diary, 16 April 1967–30 June 1967, box 11, LBJL.

[40] *FRUS*, vol. XIX, no. 210–12, 366–8, all 8 June 1967. The volume has extensive coverage of the *Liberty* question.

Tel Aviv was told to rewrite it.[41] American military bitterness remains to this day. Senior naval officers, once retired, charged that the Johnson administration orchestrated a cover-up to gloss over the incident, relieved that it had not been a Soviet attack. Contrary to some claims, Israeli pilots made no serious efforts to identify the nationality of the *Liberty*.[42] Instead, Israeli ground control instructed the pilots to attack the ship if it was not Israeli; the torpedo boats attacked after positive identification of the ship as American had been made.

A State Department spokesman declared on 5 June that U.S. policy was "even-handed . . . and neutral in thought word and deed." This created a firestorm within the American Jewish community that Johnson and Rusk had to defuse for the rest of the week, with the sympathetic assistance of the Krims and Feinberg; Mathilde was still a White House guest. Arthur Krim called the White House the same day to complain that the neutrality statement meant that no arms could be shipped to Israel and asked the president to intervene personally.[43]

At the United Nations, Ambassador Goldberg sought agreement on a cease-fire resolution with the Soviets. The first draft called for an "immediate cease-fire" and "prompt withdrawal" of forces, something the Israelis opposed. The Soviets objected to a clause in the American draft that would have forced Egypt's withdrawal from Sharm al-Sheikh along with Israel's withdrawal from the land it had taken. As Goldberg hoped, Soviet delays aided Israel's goals given their swift territorial gains. When a cease-fire occurred, all forces were left in place.

News of Israel's early successes prompted the ubiquitous Walt Rostow to propose a plan for Middle East peace on 5 June. At 5:45 P.M. he told Johnson that the United States should try for a full settlement of the conflict. On the afternoon of 6 June, with no UN cease-fire agreement in

---

[41] "Notes of a Meeting of the Special Committee of the National Security Council," 12 June 1967, *FRUS*, vol. XIX, no. 269, 444–7.

[42] Jay Cristol and Michael Oren have argued that Israel made every effort to identify the ship before attacking it, but their data contradicts their assertions: Jay Cristol, *The Liberty Incident: The 1967 Israeli Attack on the U.S. Navy Spy Ship* (Washington, DC: Brassey's Inc., 2002), 75–6; Oren, *Six Days of War*, 265; Oren and Arieh O'Sullivan, "The Attack on the Liberty," *The International Jerusalem Post*, 18 June, 2004; Ahron Bregman, *Israel's Wars: A History since 1947*, 3rd ed. (London: Routledge, 2010), 88–9. For American naval views, see David Walsh, "Friendless Fire?" *Naval Institute Proceedings* (June 2003).

[43] "Editorial Note," *FRUS*, vol. XIX, no. 164, 311–12, notes the comment by Robert J. McCloskey and the call presidential aide Joseph Califano made to Dean Rusk to tell him the remark was "killing us with the Jews in this country." For Krim's call see Dallek, *Flawed Giant*, 428n114.

sight, Rostow advised the president that "a simple cease-fire might be the best answer. This would mean that we could use the *de facto* situation on the ground to try to negotiate not a return to armistice lines but a definitive peace in the Middle East."[44]

The next day Rostow sent Johnson another memo arguing that a definitive peace would require some Israeli concessions, but it would be designed "to split the Arab world" now that Nasser had been humiliated. Twenty minutes later, Fortas called the White House to advise that the United States should not get involved in any peace process but should "let the Israelis and Arabs negotiate this out and save ourselves for the last half of the ninth inning"; Fortas stressed the delicate nature of U.S. involvement with respect to domestic as well as international politics. On 8 June, Goldberg proposed a UN resolution calling for a full peace settlement, indicating that the United States had adopted the idea as its own.[45]

The argument for using the crisis to push for a final settlement had originated with Evron of the Israeli embassy in extensive discussions with Walt Rostow, Saunders, and Johnson prior to 5 June: "this thinking had become embedded in the thinking of top U.S. policymakers" without anyone in the American government thinking through the consequences. Only later did analysts call attention to the implications of a policy to which the United States had already become committed in public statements.[46]

Johnson was receptive to the idea, recalling his opposition to Israeli withdrawal from the Sinai in March 1957, but he now faced a dilemma. How could he adhere to his 23 May declaration that the United States supported the territorial integrity of all states in the regions if the search for full peace allowed Israel to remain in the territories it now occupied and possibly to retain some of them in any peace accord? On 7 June, White House staffers Larry Levinson and Ben Wattenberg noted American Jewish satisfaction that "no [Israeli] withdrawal was stipulated" in the UN cease-fire resolution but warned "*that Israel, apparently having won the war, may be forced to lose the peace again* [as in 1956]. *Only the U.S. could prevent*" the United Nations from selling "Israel

[44] Ibid., June 6, 1967, 5:45 P.M.
[45] Memorandum from Rostow to Johnson, and Memorandum from Califano to Johnson, both 7 June 1967, *FRUS*, vol. XIX, no. 189–90, 339–42.
[46] Parker, *Six-Day War*, 318, n. 1. See also Saunders, OH, interviewed by Thomas Stern, 24 November 1993, www.adst.org, 12–13, in which he states that "Evron had been assigned by the Israeli ambassador to maintain the Rostow connection."

down the river" as had happened under Dulles and Eisenhower. They advised Johnson to send a message to a mass meeting of American Jews to be held in Washington the next day; it "ought not to mention 'territorial integrity'," referring to Johnson's 23 May address. Following this advice might permit the crisis to "turn around a lot of anti-Vietnam and anti-Johnson feeling, particularly if you use it as an opportunity to your advantage."[47]

The same day, Walt Rostow relayed to Johnson Eban's views on withdrawal through Feinberg. Israel would object to any idea of drawback without "definitive peace." Feinberg advised Johnson that this was the route for him to follow if he wished to restore his position with American Jews after the neutrality references of 5 June.[48]

Obsessed with public opinion generally and Jewish opinion specifically, Johnson kept track of the views of the tens of thousands who had been organized by American Jewish groups and had written the White House to express concern about the crisis. He ordered his staff to answer each of the approximately 160,000 letters, tracking how many were pro-Israeli; they wound up in the office of NSC Middle East specialist Saunders, creating "a horrendous work load." As for American Jews and Vietnam, Helms, at Johnson's request, sent him a memo reporting the CIA tracking of domestic Jewish opinion. But Johnson deeply resented this pressure. Following the Levinson-Wattenberg memo of 7 June, he saw Levinson in a hallway at the White House. He revealed his anger at his situation, screaming at him that he and Wattenberg were nothing but "Zionist dupes. Why can't you see I'm doing all I can for Israel."[49]

However attractive avoidance of the phrase "territorial integrity" might have been domestically, it created real problems of policy. At a Special Committee NSC meeting chaired by Bundy, Johnson asked "how do we get out of this predicament?" with McNamara chiming in that "We're in a heck of a jam on territorial integrity." Arab allies interpreted the term as expressed in the 23 May speech and called for Israel's withdrawal, but the United States no longer held that position.[50] Responding

[47] Memorandum from Larry Levinson and Ben Wattenberg to President Johnson, 7 June 1967, *FRUS*, vol. XIX, no. 198, 354–5, emphasis in original.
[48] Ibid., Harold Saunders, "National Security Council Meeting," Wednesday, 7 June, no. 194, 346n1, for the Feinberg message reporting Eban's position.
[49] Dallek, *Flawed Giant*, 429.
[50] NSF, NSC Special Committee Files, [handwritten] Minutes, 12 June 1967, LBJL, reproduced in Notes of a Meeting of the SCNSC, *FRUS*, vol. XIX, no. 269, 444–7, 12 June 1967.

to reporters' questions on 13 June, Johnson expanded on the concept to
say that its implementation would depend on the actions of the Middle
East countries involved, with the goal of achieving peace in the region;
Johnson refused comment when asked if he meant that the United States
would not object to changes in prewar boundaries if the nations involved
agreed to them.[51]

Final resolution of the problem came in a speech that Johnson delivered at the State Department on 19 June, which later became "the bible
of American policy" and the foundation of UN Security Council Resolution 242 passed on 22 November 1967. Here Johnson enunciated five
principles he saw as essential for Middle East peace; the fifth provided the
escape clause from the "territorial integrity" dilemma: "1. Every nation
in the area has a fundamental right to live and to have this right respected
by its neighbours; 2. No nation . . . should permit military success to blind
it to the fact that its neighbours have rights and . . . interests of their own.
Each nation . . . must accept the right of others to live (to which Johnson
added the need to resolve the question of Palestinian refugees); 3. The
right of innocent maritime passage must be preserved for all nations;
4. Limits on the wasteful and destructive arms race in the region;
5. Respect for the political independence and territorial integrity of all the
states of the area. We reaffirmed this principle at the height of the crisis.
This principle can be effective . . . only on the basis of peace between the
parties. The nations of the region have had only fragile and violated truce
lines for 20 years. What they need now are recognized boundaries and
other arrangements that will give them security against terror, destruction
and war . . . [along with] adequate recognition of the special interests of
three great religions in the holy places of Jerusalem."[52]

Having linked territorial integrity to full peace accords in principle
number 5, Johnson rejected the call for "an immediate return to the
situation as it was on June 4." That would trigger renewed conflict.
Instead "there is no escape from this fact: the main responsibility for the
peace of the region depends on its own peoples and its own leaders of
that region. What will be truly decisive will be what is said and what is

[51] Memorandum from Rostow to Johnson, "King Faisal's Reply to Your Letter," ibid.,
no. 283, 486, 13 June 1967. For the press conference, "Lyndon B. Johnson's Press
Conference," no. 102, 13 June 1967, NSF, NSC Histories/Middle East Crisis, box 19,
LBJL.
[52] "Remarks of the President at the National Foreign Policy Conference for Educators,
State Department," 19 June 1967, NSF, NSC Histories/Middle East Crisis, box 18,
LBJL.

done by those who live in the Middle East," essentially what Fortas had argued on 7 June.[53]

The idea of territorial integrity, an absolute on 23 May, was now a relative concept, subject to negotiation. Israel successfully held Johnson to these principles that became enshrined with the same contradictions in Resolution 242. Bundy's special NSC committee had recognized as early as 7 June that Israel would cede territory only in exchange for formal peace treaties with the respective Arab states, while admitting it was "difficult to foresee the political upheavals in the Arab world which would make acceptance of a peace treaty by the Arab states politically feasible."[54] Whereas Johnson and aides assumed Israel would return most of the lands it had taken in return for peace, they had no assurances from Israel that this would be the case.

United Nations Resolution 242: Its Background and Context

Passed by the UN Security Council on 22 November 1967, Resolution 242 has rightly been labelled a masterpiece of British ambiguity and obfuscation attributed to the resolution's author, British UN Ambassador Lord Caradon. It declared the "inadmissibility of the acquisition of territory by war and the need to work for a just and lasting peace in which every state in the area can live in security." Among the "principles" on which this peace should be based were "withdrawal of Israeli armed forces from territories occupied in the recent conflict" and "termination of all claims and states of belligerency and respect for and acknowledgment of the sovereignty, territorial integrity and political independence of every State in the area and their right to live in peace within secure and recognized boundaries free from threats and acts of force."

The resolution considered territorial integrity within the context of final peace agreements. Its reference to Israel's withdrawal from occupied territories, supposedly "inadmissible" in the resolution's preamble, omitted the article *the* before the word *territories* because Israel refused to accept a resolution that specified withdrawal from all the territories as stipulated in earlier drafts.[55]

---

[53] Ibid.
[54] "Middle East Settlement: Introduction," NSF, NSC Histories/Middle East Crisis, 7 June 1967, box 19, LBJL.
[55] The authoritative analysis of the resolution, co-authored by Lord Caradon, stressed the resolution's ambiguity: *U.N. Security Council Resolution 242: A Case Study in Diplomatic Ambiguity* (Washington, DC: Institute for the Study of Diplomacy, Georgetown University, 1981).

Concerned about the question of Israel's retention of territories, Jordan's King Hussein had agreed to Resolution 242 only after being assured by Goldberg and Rusk that "The United States is prepared to support a return of the West Bank to Jordan with minor boundary rectifications. . . . [T]he U.S. would use its influence to obtain compensation to Jordan for any territory it is required to give up . . . [along with being] prepared to use our influence to obtain for Jordan a role in East Jerusalem." But the Israeli Knesset had approved East Jerusalem's unification with West Jerusalem on 27 June. Once out of office, Goldberg denied that the resolution insisted on "minor boundary rectifications," not the interpretation he had given Hussein.[56]

As for Caradon, he cheerfully acknowledged the resolution's lack of clarity. When asked by the Indian delegate whether his draft committed the Security Council to the withdrawal of Israeli troops from all the territories, he declared that "all delegations might have their own views and interpretations and understandings, but only the resolution would be binding."[57] Left unanswered was the question of how the resolution could be binding if it permitted so many interpretations.

Israel's position had evolved during the summer. Eban assured Ambassador Barbour on 5 June and UN Ambassador Goldberg on 8 June that Israel sought no "territorial aggrandizement and had no 'colonial aspirations.'" In Israel on 13 June, Eban acknowledged to Barbour that the rapid changes "had raised opportunities which were inconceivable before" and "the point of reference [could] not really be the pre-June 4th situation." Later that summer, Eban responded to Rusk's query about retaining land by saying, as has been noted in other chapters, "We had changed our minds."[58]

By late August, Israel had become alarmed about an American-Soviet draft proposal to resolve issues created by the war. On 29 August, Saunders alerted Walt Rostow to the latter's forthcoming meeting with Evron, who reflected "his government's almost pathological fear" that the United States would abandon Israel's interests: "They are sticking hard to the

---

[56] "Territorial Assurances to Jordan," Rusk to Embassy in Israel, *FRUS*, vol. XIX, no. 506, 998–9. Ibid., "Present Status of King Hussein's Visit," Rusk to Johnson, undated, no. 513, 1012–13.

[57] Editorial Note, undated, *FRUS*, vol. XIX, no. 541, 1061–2.

[58] Dean Rusk, Telegram from Department of State to Embassy, Israel, *FRUS*, vol. XIX, 5 June 1967, no. 161, 305–6; "Goldberg Talk with Eban," ibid., 9 July 1967, no. 227, 386–7; ibid., Telegram from the Embassy, Israel, to Department of State, 13 June 1967, no. 277, 457–9; Rusk, *As I Saw It*, 388.

President's five principles and feel the draft resolution represents an erosion. The ugliness of this confrontation came out when a senior Foreign Ministry official told Ambassador Barbour that if we backed away from the President's principles, Israel would 'pull out all the stops' on us among its friends in the U.S."[59]

In his session with Rostow, Evron stressed the need for the United States to continue supplying Israel with arms, and then declared:

The heart of the Israeli objection to the joint U.S.-Soviet resolution is its implication that Israel must return to boundaries occupied on June 4. *Even in exchange for a peace treaty Israel is not prepared for a simple return to the June 4 boundaries.* What Israel will seek by agreement with the Arabs are "secure" boundaries, in addition to maintaining the unity of the city of Jerusalem.

Evron insisted that the United States adhere to Johnson's term "secure and agreed borders," meaning that Israel could retain lands it deemed necessary for security, to be accounted for in Resolution 242.[60] Washington had few options. As Saunders wrote to Bundy, "As we all know, what part we play in an Arab-Israeli settlement (if any) may depend precisely on how hard LBJ is willing to lean on Israel."[61]

As the various parties to the conflict sought to define their stances, even before UN discussions on a resolution began, two efforts to start behind-the-scenes peace talks arose involving Jordan and Israel. Israeli Defence Minister Moshe Dayan supposedly instituted one, fearful of calls by General Ariel Sharon and others to annex the West Bank. It involved the CIA and was possibly scuttled by State Department interference. The second saw Jordan's King Hussein approach Ambassador Burns in Amman on 13 July to inform him that he "was prepared to conclude some sort of arrangement with Israel." Possibly reacting to Israel's annexation of East Jerusalem on 27 June, Hussein, with Nasser's tacit approval, proposed secret talks with Israeli representatives, a venture that the United States encouraged.

This endeavour, named "Sandstorm" by U.S. officials, consisted of informal talks between Hussein and Israelis, including Eban at times, who were part of the Cabinet but did not act as their government's

[59] Saunders to Walt Whitman Rostow, "Your Talk with Evron this Afternoon – following issues on his mind," NSF, CF/Middle East, 29 August 1967, box 111, vol. IX, Memos and Misc, LBJL.

[60] WR, Memorandum of Conversation, 29 August 1967, *FRUS*, vol. XIX, no. 431, 811–13. Emphasis added.

[61] Memorandum for Mr. Bundy, NSF, SCNSC, box 13, 21 September 1967, LBJL.

official representatives. The talks lasted from the summer of 1967 to late 1968 with no agreement. Hussein wanted nearly all the West Bank returned and Jordanian access to East Jerusalem, while the Israeli Cabinet remained divided over future policy regarding the West Bank – reports of two Israeli settlements there appeared in September 1967.[62]

1967 and the Special Relationship

With a cease-fire in place, American diplomats and politicians differed over the war's likely significance. Rusk declared in mid-June that if Israel kept territory, "it would create a revanchism for the rest of the 20th c," an opinion shared by most State Department analysts. The same month Bundy foresaw the Suez Canal being "closed only three or four weeks."[63] It remained closed for eight years, until 1975, opening only after Egyptian-Israeli negotiations following the 1973 Israeli-Arab war. U.S. lack of concern for the canal's opening was linked to Vietnam. The canal's closure forced shipments of Soviet supplies to North Vietnam to take the long route around Africa. It also slowed Soviet efforts to establish their influence in South Arabia and the Indian Ocean generally following the British withdrawal from Aden in November 1967. Bundy viewed the war's results in light of Israel's victory and American public opinion agreeing as to "who were the good guys and who were the bad guys." As for policy, "there was no enormous policy question" that arose from the crisis: America's Cold War ally won, the other side lost.[64]

The Arab-Israeli conflict's linkage to the American-Soviet rivalry increased when Richard Nixon took office in January 1969 and further escalated the American involvement in Vietnam. Israel and Iran became strategic allies of the United States, hampering efforts to start Arab-Israeli peace talks. Secretary of State William Rogers and the State Department encouraged UN representative Gunnar Jarring to pursue indirect talks to gain agreement on basic issues. Nixon and National Security Adviser

---

[62] The fullest discussions of Sandstorm are found in Avi Shlaim, *Lion of Jordan: The Life of King Hussein in War and Peace* (New York: Alfred A. Knopf, 2008), 281–311; and Nigel Ashton, *King Hussein of Jordan: A Political Life* (New Haven, CT: Yale University Press, 2008), 121–35. U.S. records for Sandstorm remain heavily sanitized: see NSF, CF, box 113, LBJL.

[63] Rusk's statement is in *FRUS*, vol. XIX, Notes of a Meeting of the NSC Special Committee, no. 287, 478–9. Bundy made his remark to C. L. Sulzberger, *An Age of Mediocrity*, 347.

[64] Bundy, OH III, Paige Mulhollan, 19 March 1969, 22, LBJL.

Henry Kissinger accepted Israel's demands for direct talks and assured Prime Minister Meir in September 1969, through a back channel, that Israel could ignore State Department initiatives.[65] Tensions reached the point where Kissinger and Rogers instructed their staff members not to talk to their counterparts. State Department separation from input into policy discussions, apparent in the run-up to the 1967 War, remained an unresolved issue until Kissinger became Secretary of State while retaining his post as National Security Adviser.[66]

The 1967 War has been seen as establishing the "special relationship" between the United States and Israel "based on a commonality of political and strategic interests" particularly related to Cold War issues.[67] The cementing of this relationship was defined at the time most specifically in military terms. Whereas Israel had relied primarily on France for weaponry up to the war, it would now turn to the United States as its principal arms supplier. But Israel had pursued this goal of arms agreements with the United States throughout the 1960s, well before the war. Although the Kennedy administration first approved weapons sales to Israel, the process greatly expanded during Johnson's presidency to include tanks and jet planes.

Johnson and his aides had seen such agreements as necessary to justify shipments of inferior weaponry to Jordan and to lessen complaints from the Jewish community. They accepted the inevitability of agreeing to selling Israel more arms – the question was when. As early as January 1966, NSC White House staffer Robert Komer asked Johnson that "In the last analysis, can we avoid selling planes to Israel sooner or later?" The only issue, he wrote the president a month later, was *"whether to play hard to get a bit longer as a lesson or begin caving now?"*[68]

The administration agreed to sell Israel Skyhawk jets in February 1966, leading Eban to cable Eshkol noting the progression from defensive Hawk missiles under Kennedy to heavy tanks and now jet bombers under Johnson. This was, he said, "a development of tremendous political value"

[65] Steven L. Spiegel, *The Other Arab-Israeli Conflict: Making America's Middle East Policy from Truman to Reagan* (Chicago: University of Chicago Press, 1985), 185.

[66] Saunders, OH, www.adst.org, 20.

[67] Yaacov Bar-Siman-Tov, "The United States and Israel since 1948: A 'Special Relationship'?" *Diplomatic History* 22, no. 2 (Spring 1998), 231–62.

[68] Komer to Johnson, *FRUS*, vol. XVIII, accessed at www.state.gov/www/about_state/history/vol_xvii/a.html, 12 January 1966 and 8 February 1966, respectively. Emphasis is in the original in the 8 February memo.

that "enabled Israel to strive for a continued intensification of the existing U.S. commitments and the creation of sui generis strategic relations," precisely what Washington hoped to avoid.[69] At least from Israel's perspective, the special relationship had been nearly accomplished more than a year before the 1967 War.

The relationship has survived serious differences over policies that emerged on several occasions, including the 1978 Camp David Accord between Egypt and Israel that led to a peace treaty in March 1979, the first between Israel and an Arab state. President Jimmy Carter and his aides envisioned the accord as the precursor to future agreements with other Arab states. Prime Minister Menachem Begin viewed it as removing Israel's chief military adversary, thereby enabling Israel to further consolidate its hold on the West Bank and the Golan Heights. Whereas the United States assumed that clauses referring to the Palestinians in the territories would be implemented, possibly leading to major changes in their status, Israel rejected this interpretation and intensified its settlement efforts. In short, the relationship has continued despite a lack of commonality of political and strategic interests, not because of it, with the United States eventually raising serious questions about the value of the relationship in light of its perceived strategic concerns, especially in recent years.

Johnson, despite his occasional resentment of Israeli and American Jewish pressure, remained willing to accommodate Israeli requests. He sympathized and identified with Israel, especially when he felt besieged by critics or crises. Reared with a familiarity with the Old Testament, he saw Israelis as a frontier people, "a modern-day version of the Texans fighting the Mexicans."[70] In a phone conversation with Goldberg in March, 1968, both complained about Arab criticism of U.S. policy:

GOLDBERG: The Arabs are impossible down here [United Nations]. . . . They always keep referring to our domestic events. And I have to slap them down. They're . . . a terribly emotional bunch.

JOHNSON: You're the only man I know that's got as mean a type of assignment as I have . . . I sure as hell want to be careful and not run out on little Israel. . . . Because they haven't got many friends in the world.

GOLDBERG: I know they haven't.

JOHNSON: They're in about the same shape I am. And the closer I get – I face adversity, the closer I get to them. . . . Because I got a bunch of Arabs after

[69] Zach Levey, "The United States' Skyhawk Sale to Israel, 1966," *Diplomatic History* 28, no. 2 (April 2004), 274.

[70] In the view of a close Johnson aide. See Spiegel, *Other Arab-Israeli Conflict*, 123.

me – about a hundred million of 'em and there's just two million of us [chuckles; Goldberg joins in]. So I can understand them a little bit . . . my State Department sometimes – I just want to be damn sure that I don't wind up here getting in the shape Eisenhower did, where I want to put sanctions on 'em [after 1956 Suez Crisis].

GOLDBERG: Well we're never going to put sanctions on . . .

JOHNSON: The only people they got in the world they got faith in, I think, [i]s me and you.[71]

At the time of this conversation, Johnson had decided not to run for reelection in 1968, feeling crushed by the North Vietnamese Tet offensive of January that appeared to challenge the administration's handling of the war. Shouted down at public gatherings, he responded to those who listened to him and praised him, sometimes with policy implications. He had decided in early 1968 to sell Phantom jets to Israel, which he justified because of Soviet arms sales to Arab countries, as shown in a revealing conversation with Abe Fortas in June that illustrated Johnson's sometimes graphic discourse.

JOHNSON: I've got to make a decision on those [Phantoms] . . . before I go out of office. . . . But I want the Russians to turn me down on disarmament. I've got a letter on his [Alexsei Kosygin's] lap now. . . . He's not going to pee a drop with me: I know that. But I've got to have that behind me so I can use it as an excuse. . . . I'm not going to give 'em [Phantoms] to 'em [Israel] unless I can protect myself. I'm not going to be a goddamned arms merchant. I'm going to make them [Soviets] be the outlaws if I can.

FORTAS: Sure, that's very good.

JOHNSON: Now that's what I'm trying to do. And this little Eppie [Evron – Israeli embassy] is the only one that's got sense enough in their organization to see it. . . . He's just as bright as that goddamned [*unclear*] dog of mine. He catches everything that comes along without telling him. . . . I haven't had one goddamned bit of trouble with . . . Eppie or Feinberg. They're smart. Arthur Krim.

FORTAS: Isn't this fellow Feinberg wonderful?

JOHNSON: He is just the finest I ever saw. Except Krim. Krim's the best man. . . . Krim's the only one that's like you. . . . I see him damn near every week, . . . *because* [in original] I just like to listen to him. . . . *I let him see every damn document that comes in* [emphasis added]. . . . I have never heard of one little thing he's ever said [passing information].

FORTAS: Yeah. Well he's a saint.[72]

71 Tape WH6803.05, Citation #12843, LBJ Recordings, CD Track 18, cited in Robert David Johnson, "Secret Presidential Recordings," 24 March 1968. Full citation n. 36.

72 LBJ and Abe Fortas, 21 June 1968, posted by Robert David Johnson at www.kc-johnson.com/lbj-and-israel-clips/.

Israel's strategic goals were reinforced in the spring of 1968 when Johnson approved a request that Israel nominate an individual to handle requests for arms shipments or other material, bypassing the State Department; Israel selected Feinberg.[73]

Johnson's empathy for Israel was not always reciprocated. Although delighted that the special relationship appeared to be in place, Israelis who had had contact with Johnson could mock his personal, often crude, behaviour.[74] But that behaviour could be tolerated for the continuation of a special relationship that has lasted to this day, with often apparently successful efforts to isolate the State Department from the decision-making process with respect to ongoing Israeli-Palestinian talks.[75]

[73] W. Marvin Watson, *Chief of Staff: Lyndon Johnson and His Presidency* (New York: Thomas Dunne Books, 2004), 228–9.

[74] For Abba Eban's imitation of Johnson's accent and dialogue, see Amos Elon, "A Very Special Relationship," *The New York Review of Books* 51, no. 1 (January 15, 2004), accessed at www.nybooks.com/articles/16873.

[75] See Glenn Kessler, "A Key Back Channel for U.S., Israeli Ties," *Washington Post*, 6 October 2010, A12, who notes that Israel prefers to bypass the State Department and deal directly with the White House.

8

The Soviet Union

The Roots of War and a Reassessment of Historiography

Rami Ginat

Since the end of the June 1967 War, scholars have offered a variety of explanations as to the origins of that conflict. These interpretations were often based on conspiracy theories, circumstantial evidence, speeches made by Gamal Abdel Nasser and other Arab and Israeli policy makers at the time; including the memoirs of Soviet, Western, and Arab leaders and military high commanders. The recently declassified Eastern European archival material does not provide us with a definitive explanation of the war's origins because some of the most relevant official documents related to the crisis – those of the Soviet Military Intelligence (GRU – Glavnoye Razvedyvatel'noye Upravleniye), the KGB (Komitet gosudarstvennoy bezopasnosti, or Committee for State Security), and the Politburo – remain inaccessible.

The June 1967 War has been the subject of a considerable number of studies. In brief, one may divide the studies into three categories. The first includes works written shortly after the war; that is to say, contemporary works with a narrow historical perspective, which were based on Western, Eastern, Arab, and Israeli sources comprising newspapers, interviews, official declarations, and memoirs of politicians and other figures who were involved in the conflict.[1] The second consists of works written following the declassification of Western and Israeli archival material

---

[1] See, e.g., Avraham Ben-Tzur, *Soviet Factors and the Six Day War* [in Hebrew] (Tel-Aviv: Sifriyat Po'alim, 1975); David Kimche and Dan Bawly, *The Sandstorm* (London: Secker and Warburg, 1968); Bernard Lewis, *The Middle East and the West* [in Hebrew] (Tel-Aviv: Ma'rkhot, 1972); Walter Laqueur, *The Road to War* (London: Weidenfeld and Nicolson, 1969); Lutfi 'Abd al-Qadir, *Ma lam ta'rifuhu'an thawrat Yuliyu*, vol. II (Cairo: Maktabat Madbuli, 1987).

some three decades after the war. These works were more informative and insightful but still could not solve the missing parts of the riddle; particularly, the Soviet conduct in the weeks that preceded the war.[2] The third category consists of works published in the recent years, based on selective declassified official Soviet documents that have attempted to clarify the hitherto obscure aspects of Soviet policy throughout the crisis.[3]

A common view among scholars is that the Soviets concocted the crisis that subsequently led to war. The consensus becomes narrower, however, when the question of their motivation is addressed. The "intentionalist" approach relies on a variety of explanations – some relate to Soviet domestic politics,[4] and some place greater emphasis on external factors connected with the Cold War. The intentionalists may be divided into two further schools: those who argue that the Soviet manoeuvres were

---

[2] Among these studies are Pedro Ramet, *The Soviet-Syrian Relationship since 1955: A Troubled Alliance* (Boulder, CO: Westview Press, 1990); Shlomo Aronson, *Israel's Nuclear Programme, the Six Day War and its Ramifications* (London: King's College, The Mediterranean Studies Programme, 2002); Yosef Govrin, *Israeli-Soviet Relations, 1953–1967* (London and Portland, OR: Frank Cass, 1998); Mohrez Mahmoud El-Hussini, *Soviet-Egyptian Relations, 1945–85* (Basingstoke, UK: Macmillan Press, 1987); Moshe Gat, *Britain and the Conflict in the Middle East, 1964–1967* (London: Praeger, 2003); Ami Gluska, *The Israeli Military and the Origins of the 1967 War: Government, Armed Forces and Defence Policy, 1963–1967* (London: Routledge, 2007).

[3] See, e.g., Uri Bar-Noi, "The Soviet Union and the Six-Day War: Revelations from the Polish Archives," *Cold War International History Project*, e-dossier no. 8, www.wilsoncenter.org/index.cfm?topic_id=1409&fuseaction=topics.publications&doc_id=35467&group_id=13349; Izabella Ginor and Gideon Remez, *Foxbats over Dimona: The Soviet's Nuclear Gamble in the Six-Day War* (New Haven, CT and London: Yale University Press, 2007); see also, Izabella Ginor, "The Long War's Longest Cover-up: How and Why the USSR Instigated the 1967 War," *MERIA* 7, no. 3 (September 2003); Yaacov Ro'i and Boris Morozov, eds., *The Soviet Union and the June 1967 Six Day War* (Washington, DC and Stanford, CA: Stanford University Press and WWCP, 2008); Michael Oren, *Six Day of War: June 1967 and the Making of the Modern Middle East* (Oxford and New York: Oxford University Press, 2002); Guy Laron, "Playing with Fire: The Soviet-Syrian-Israeli Triangle, 1965–1967," *Cold War History* 10, no. 2 (November 2009); R. D. Daurov, *Dolgaya Shestidnevnaya Voyna* (Moscow: Institut Vostokovedeniya RAN, 2009).

[4] Ben-Tzur, *Soviet Factors*, 125. He focuses on the internal power struggle within the Kremlin and its effect on Soviet Middle Eastern politics. The instigation of the Six-Day War was a conspiracy plan aimed at strengthening the positions of Brezhnev and his ally, Minister of Defence Marshal Grechko vis-à-vis Prime Minister Kosygin, Foreign Minister Gromyko, and President of the Supreme Soviet Podgorny. The latter belittled the capabilities of their Arab allies to confront Israel militarily. See also, a recent study by Bar-Noi, "The Soviet Union and the Six-Day War"; Ramet, *The Soviet-Syrian Relationship*, 43–4.

designed to lead to a full-scale Arab-Israeli war, and those who maintain that the Soviets deliberately concocted the crisis believing that they could closely monitor and control it, although a full-scale war was not on their agenda. However, both agree that the Soviets primarily sought to increase their influence in the region and to enhance the prestige of their Arab client regimes domestically and in inter-Arab politics.

The study by Izabella Ginor and Gideon Remez is a prototype of the former group of scholars.[5] According to them, the Soviets deliberately instigated the crisis and war of 1967 in order to block Israel's nuclear program. They posit that the Soviets prepared a plan several months before the outbreak of the conflict. Its alleged purpose was to create a crisis designed to drag Israel into a war, which would lead to a joint Soviet-Egyptian military operation aimed at the destruction of the nuclear reactor in Dimona. If that was the plan, why was it not realized? The authors' explanation and general line of argument failed to convince. Their controversial study met with severe criticism from leading scholars. One writes, "I was convinced neither by the general thrust of their argument nor by the methodology they used."[6] Another remarks that the book has "all the intrigue of a detective story, and all the pace of a novel . . . yet it does not help to resolve one of the great mysteries of the Six-Day War."[7] All critics agree that the interpretation of Ginor and Remez does not fit the pattern of Soviet conduct throughout the Cold War: "always avoid even coming near to a possible clash with the other superpower, certainly not after the fiasco of the Cuban missile crisis . . . the Soviet leadership believed in deterrence, and was cautious and responsible in its relationships with the United States."[8]

Shlomo Aronson also places great emphasis on the Israeli nuclear issue as being a catalyst for the Six-Day War. Although he agrees with Ginor and Remez that the Soviet Union initiated the formative phase of the crisis, he ascribes the escalation that led to the war to regional actors, notably Egypt and Israel. Aronson determines that the Six-Day War erupted as Arab leaders lost control over a crisis, which emanated from their growing concern with Israel's nuclear option. Nasser planned to bomb the Dimona

---

[5] Ginor and Remez, *Foxbats over Dimona*; see also, Ginor, "The Long War's Longest Cover-up."

[6] Ro'i and Morozov, *The Soviet Union*, xxii.

[7] Sir Martin Gilbert is quoted in ibid., xxiii; see also a book review by Amnon Sella in *Journal of Israeli History* 27, no. 1 (March 2008).

[8] A book review by Amnon Sella, *Journal of Israeli History* 27, no. 1 (March 2008).

nuclear reactor if Israel launched an attack on his forces in Sinai. He would thus limit the conflict to conventional weapons, in which case – in Nasser's assessment – Egypt could win.[9]

The full-scale war approach was supported by the U.S. Ambassador to Moscow at the time, Llewellyn Thompson; yet his line of argument is utterly different. A few days before the outbreak of the war, he was of the opinion that the Soviets were interested in an Arab-Israeli war. The ambassador believed that the Soviets could maintain their influence in the region only by giving total support to their Arab allies against Israel, which ultimately meant war. The Soviet Union, he argued, believed that it could avoid direct involvement by restraining the Arabs from actually attacking Israel. Israel, however,

Would be driven by constant provocation into [committing a] concrete act of aggression against one of the Arab states. Then the Soviet Union could rally the whole world opinion plus UN machinery to prevent defeat of the Arabs. The United States could not intervene effectively to prevent considerable damage to Israel or to stop fighting, but would emerge as [a] clear enemy of the Arabs. The result would be final elimination of Western influence from the area.[10]

It is noteworthy that other Western diplomats in Moscow including both the British and Canadian ambassadors did not believe that the Soviets aimed for a full-scale war. Robert Ford, the Canadian Ambassador to Moscow,[11] reasoned that the Soviets appeared to be rather cautious and doubted that they would want to run the risk of a direct confrontation with the United States. Their popularity in the Arab world soared high thanks to their implicit support for their Arab allies against Israel. If the latter "were eliminated or seriously weakened this raison d'être would be removed." Why would they want war "when they appear to be getting all they want quite easily without it?" concluded Ford.

The second "intentionalist" school that constitutes the largest body of literature on the origins of the conflict concluded that the Soviet Union and the United States had no inclination to get involved in a war that neither

[9] Aronson, *Israel's Nuclear Programme.*
[10] Telegram 1529, from Robert Ford, Canadian Ambassador, Moscow, 2 June 1967, British Foreign and Commonwealth Office [hereinafter referred to as FCO] 28/31, Public Record Office, Kew, London.
[11] Ford was described by his Western counterparts as "a first-class Russian speaker and an old Moscow hand" who developed closer relationships with the second-echelon leaders than any other Western ambassador in Moscow. As a former ambassador to Egypt, he also had a particular interest in the Middle East and friends amongst the Arab diplomatic representatives. See remark made by I. J. M. Sutherland, 17 June 1967, FCO 28/32.

of them wanted, yet could not prevent. Pioneer studies representing the first category argue that the Soviet intelligence warnings of 13 May were designed to restrain the Syrian military. The Soviets hoped that moving Egyptian forces into Sinai would deter Israel from taking further actions against Syria. They thus believed that the presence of Egyptian forces in Sinai would also benefit Egypt and the Soviet Union. The former would regain its prestige and leading position of the Arab world, and the latter, as Egypt's patron, would also gain regionally and internationally. The Soviet move was a ruse, which was planned in pursuit of political benefits. An overall Arab-Israeli war, however, was out of question.[12]

Bernard Lewis rules out the possibility that the Soviets intended to lead their Arab allies to war. Focusing instead on Syrian domestic politics, he suggests that the Soviet Union orchestrated the May 1967 crisis in order to prevent the downfall of their most important regional ally – the radical leftist Ba'th regime. The Soviets, he argues, envisaged a great Arab and Soviet diplomatic victory, which would weaken Israel and its Western allies and subsequently increase Soviet influence in other parts of the region.[13] In similar manner, Walter Laqueur centres his arguments on the instability in Syria and on the Soviet interest in strengthening the Ba'th regime domestically and regionally. The Soviets, he maintains, were deeply concerned with the irresponsible actions taken by the Ba'th leaders against Israel and with the support that they extended to Fatah in conducting its guerrilla warfare along the Syrian-Israeli border. All Soviet actions in May 1967 were intended to protect their Ba'th allies. The Soviets, therefore, believed that the concentration of Egyptian forces in Sinai would deter Israel from taking retaliatory actions against Syria.[14]

More recent studies, which may be classified in the second and third categories, elaborate and support the main arguments of the second intentionalist school. Some add that the Soviets used their Arab allies as tools to advance their interests in the Middle East within the context of the Cold War.[15] Yaacov Ro'i argues,

It was the certainty that the UAR [United Arab Republic] under Nasser and Syria under the neo-Ba'th of Salah Jadid could be used to weaken Western, and

---

[12] Kimche and Bawly, *The Sandstorm*, 55, 88–9.
[13] Lewis, *The Middle East and the West*, 159–61.
[14] Laqueur, *The Road to War*, 93–6.
[15] See, e.g., the most recent collection of essays on the Soviet Union and the Six-Day War in Ro'i and Morozov, *The Soviet Union*. See also Govrin, *Israeli-Soviet Relations*, 306–9.

especially, American positions in the Middle East that determined the line the Kremlin took. At the same time, it was the sense that neither Cairo nor Damascus was effectively under Soviet control, and that the logic of Moscow was not necessarily that of its allies that thwarted the Kremlin's initiative and led it to stumble.[16]

In addition, as Michael Oren notes, the Soviets wanted "to maintain a heightened level of tension in the area, a reminder to the Arabs' need for Soviet aid."[17] Shaul Shay also argues that the diffusion of Soviet disinformation was not intended to generate an Arab-Israeli war. The aim was to create a controlled crisis to enhance their regional and global prestige and to consolidate their foothold in the Middle East.[18]

Boris Morozov shows clearly that the Soviet warnings of 13 May were made officially by the Politburo. However, he does not rule out the possibility that similar reports also reached Egypt and Syria through unofficial channels, such as the GRU. Morozov examines several scenarios concerning the motives behind the Soviet decision to diffuse the "false information" to its Arab allies. His conclusion is that the Soviets made mistakes and miscalculations throughout the crisis and found themselves facing an unwanted war, which they tried to prevent as much as they could, but failed to do so.[19]

Military historians place greater emphasis on the Soviet long-term plan for gaining naval and air facilities in Egypt during the 1950s and 1960s – part of an age-old Russian and Soviet dream to find a base in the warm waters of the Mediterranean – as one of the chief considerations in consolidating the Soviet-Egyptian strategic entente.[20] Mikhail Monakov (a professor at the Russian Federation Military Academy) analyzes factors behind the war that go far beyond the narrow perspectives of Soviet interests in the Middle East. He argues that the Soviet endeavours, in the post-Stalin era, to gain naval bases in the Mediterranean met with

---

[16] Ro'i, "Soviet Policy toward the Six Day War through the Prism of Moscow's Relations with Egypt and Syria," in Ro'i and Morozov, *The Soviet Union*, 15–16.
[17] Oren, *Six Days of War*, 55.
[18] Shaul Shay, "The Israeli Evaluation of the Soviet Position on the Eve of the Six Day War," in Ro'i and Morozov, *The Soviet Union*, 122–43. His analysis is largely based on recently declassified Israel Defence Force sources, including intelligence reports.
[19] Boris Morozov, "The Outbreak of the June 1967 War in Light of Soviet Documentation," in ibid., 43–64.
[20] El-Hussini, *Soviet-Egyptian Relations*; Mikhail Monakov, "The Soviet Naval Presence in the Mediterranean at the Time of the Six Day War," in Ro'i and Morozov, *The Soviet Union*, 144–71.

considerable success only after the Six-Day War.[21] Although the military defeat of its Arab allies damaged Soviet prestige, the Soviet navy succeeded in gaining strategic holds in the Mediterranean as a result of the growing dependency of Egypt and Syria on the supply of Soviet weapons and political support.[22]

One may add to the abundant literature another explication drawn from a conspiracy theory such as the one presented by Lutfi 'Abd al-Qadir, the director of Radio Cairo during the late 1960s, who accompanied Nasser to his visits in Moscow. According to him, both the Soviets and the Western powers wanted to topple Nasser or – at least – to reduce his influence. Both blocs did not like Nasser's independent interbloc policies and his desire to create an independent Egyptian identity. The conspiracy plan of both blocs became apparent on the eve of the June 1967 War, when both Soviet and American ambassadors warned Nasser not to be the first to attack Israel – a warning that had grave consequences for Egypt.[23] This groundless conspiracy theory was utterly preposterous because there is no evidence of U.S. – USSR collusion.

The following historical narrative, based on recently declassified Soviet and Western archival material, as well as other primary and secondary literature in various languages, reviews the available evidence in order to reexamine previous accounts of the conflict's origins. In its attempt to answer the question as to whether the Soviet Union is to be held responsible for that war, this chapter sheds new light on the role played by the Soviets in the weeks preceding the war. Its findings challenge the intentionalist approach.

Prelude to the May–June Crisis

Soviet relations with Arab countries – diplomatic, economic, and commercial (including arms deals) – predated the Nasser era. It is clear, however, that Nasser's ascendance to power led to a new era in Soviet involvement in the region. Soviet-Egyptian relations developed more rapidly, culminating in two arms deals in 1955 and the tightening of economic

---

[21] Nevertheless, during the conflict the Soviet navy had a presence of 25 vessels, including 2 nuclear submarines. See Monakov, "The Soviet Naval Presence in the Mediterranean at the Time of the Six Day War."

[22] Ibid.

[23] 'Abd al-Qadir, *Ma lam ta'rifuhu 'an thawrat Yuliyu*, 5–6, 38–9, 54–7, 66–7.

links.[24] Soviet relations with Egypt and Syria had their ups and downs throughout the 1950s and 1960s, yet as far as interbloc politics were concerned, both countries regarded the Soviet Union as their chief ally. The 1960s witnessed a growing dependency of the two countries on the Soviets – the decline of Egypt's position in inter-Arab politics, following the demise of the UAR (1958–61) and Nasser's adventure in Yemen (1962–6), took the edge off his policy of neutralism. After the rise of the Ba'th in Syria in 1963, especially after the removal of the old-guard Ba'th leadership in late 1963, relations with the Soviets improved markedly.[25] Relations became even closer following the officers' coup of 23 February 1966. Syria was now ruled for the first time by military officers of 'Alawi origin, led by Salah Jadid and Hafiz al-Asad – both generals were pro-Soviet, the former in particular.

The Soviet Union had its reasons for supporting the new radical Jadid-Asad regime: First, the Soviets feared that the regime's domestic weakness and its lack of legitimacy might strengthen the Syrian right and induce it to mount a coup. Second, the Soviets were aware that the Arab world was sharply divided into two camps – the conservative and the revolutionary. Saudi Arabia led the conservative camp, which was American-oriented and possessed great influence in the Arab world. The second camp was led by Nasser, whose status and influence in the Arab world decreased during the mid-1960s, among other reasons because of Egypt's involvement in the war in Yemen. The Soviets had important reasons to strengthen Nasser and the revolutionary camp in the Arab world vis-à-vis the pro-Western camp. The inclusion of the radical and pro-Soviet Syrian regime into the anti-Western revolutionary camp could serve Soviet interests in the Middle East, which derived from strategic Cold War goals. The Soviets also hoped that their support for the Damascus regime at this crucial time would pave the way for indigenous communists, who supported the new regime, to penetrate the Syrian establishment. Moreover, there were fears in the Kremlin that if the Soviet Union did not act quickly then China, which had been vying for influence in Syria throughout the previous decade, would seize the opportunity by extending its support for the new regime, thus strengthening its position in the Middle East. It is noteworthy that following the Sino-Soviet split of the 1960s, relations

[24] On Soviet-Egyptian and Soviet-Syrian relations see Rami Ginat, *The Soviet Union and Egypt, 1945–1955* (London: Frank Cass, 1993); Ginat, *Syria and the Doctrine of Arab Neutralism* (Brighton, UK: Sussex Academic Press, 2005).

[25] Rami Ginat, "The Soviet Union and the Syrian Ba'th Regime: From Hesitation to *Rapprochement*," *Middle Eastern Studies* 36, no. 2 (2000), 150–71.

between the two countries became highly tense culminating in a border conflict in 1969.[26]

Throughout late 1966 Soviet-Egyptian relations were increasingly complicated. The Egyptian intervention in the civil war in Yemen in 1962 gave rise to extensive military cooperation with Moscow, which directly and indirectly supported Egypt's military actions at the war's beginning. By late 1966, however, the Soviets exploited the substantial advantages arising from Egypt's growing dependency on Soviet military aid and – not less important – food aid. The war in Yemen had brought U.S.-Egyptian relations to their lowest ebb, and the United States halted its food aid to Egypt. The Soviets manipulated Egypt's vulnerable situation. Egypt was desperate for wheat, and the Soviet Union conditioned its assistance on Egypt's willingness to make strategic concessions, giving the Soviets free access to Egyptian air and sea facilities. Nasser was furious that the Soviets aimed at infringing Egypt's national sovereignty – in his view, this was a new form of imperialism that was no different from the hated British one, which had taken Egypt many years of bitter struggle to get rid of.[27] But the Soviets were not taken aback by Nasser's indignation. By that stage, they had already gained other vital Arab strongholds in Iraq and Syria – a development that allowed them to challenge Nasser's interbloc strategy. The latter's bargaining card was now not strong enough to allow him to pursue his previous policy of positive neutralism – a policy that was based on the following principles:

An independent state that wished to maintain close and balanced ties with both international blocs for the purpose of manipulating the inter-bloc rivalries in order to advance its foreign policy. It wanted to internationally demonstrate its independence and wished to play a major role in international affairs. Positive neutralism was nothing less than the revolt of non-aligned countries against the exercise of monopoly, by either party to the cold war, in the supply of goods, services or capital to underdeveloped lands. It is their protest against unfair practices, discrimination, and the attachment of politico-military conditions to trade, economic aid, or technical assistance.[28]

---

[26] On the Sino-Soviet split of the 1960s see, e.g., Lorenz M. Lüthi, *The Sino-Soviet Split, Cold War in the Communist World* (Princeton, NJ: Princeton University Press, 2008).

[27] Jesse Ferris, *Egypt, the Cold War, and the Civil War in Yemen, 1962–1966* (PhD diss., Princeton University, 2008). See also his "Soviet Support for Egypt's Intervention in Yemen, 1962–1964," *Journal of Cold War Studies* 10, no. 4 (2008), 5–36.

[28] Fayez A. Sayegh, "Anatomy of Neutralism – A Typological Analysis," in *The Dynamics of Neutralism in the Arab World*, ed. Fayez A. Sayegh (San Francisco, CA: Chandler Publishing House, 1964), 70; Ginat, *Syria and the Doctrine of Arab Neutralism*, 235–6.

To strengthen the stability of their shaky ally in Syria, the Soviet Union played a major role behind the scenes in order to facilitate the signing of the Egyptian-Syrian Mutual Defence Pact of November 1966. Some scholars have argued that one of the Soviet objectives was to ease tension along the Syrian-Israeli border because Nasser as the dominant and senior partner would restrain his Syrian allies' inclination towards adventurism.[29]

The next few months were dominated by two central themes in the Cairo-Damascus-Moscow axis: the growing tension along the Israeli-Syrian border increasing the likelihood of an Arab-Israeli war and the situation on the Arab Peninsula in the war in Yemen and the existing tension in Saudi-Egyptian relations. Andrei Gromyko's visit to Egypt (29 March–1 April 1967) left foreign diplomats and political observers puzzled about its content and timing. The purpose of the visit, which was surrounded with particular secrecy, has remained obscure even after the selective declassification of documents in the Soviet archives. Nevertheless, the Ethiopian ambassador, who received information from the Egyptian foreign ministry, has shed new light on Gromyko's visit. Nasser, as is now known, was asked by his guest to restrain his activities in Southern Arabia in order to avoid further regional escalation that might lead "to a major confrontation between East and West...the Soviet Union was not prepared to go to war for South Arabia any more than she was prepared to do so over Israel." The Ethiopian ambassador also disclosed that Nasser expressed concern over the possibility that Israel would manufacture a nuclear weapon. Gromyko was said to have replied that "if Israel did get a bomb, the USSR would give the UAR a [defence] screen."[30]

The Evolution of the Crisis

The content of a conversation between Dmitrii Chuvakhin, the Soviet Ambassador to Tel-Aviv, and his British counterpart, Michael Hadow, demonstrates that by early May the Soviets were deeply concerned that

---

[29] Ro'i, "Soviet Policy," 4; Alexei Vassiliev, *Russian Policy in the Middle East* (Reading, UK: Ithaca Press, 1993), 65–6; El-Hussini, *Soviet-Egyptian*, 176; Ben-Tzur, *Soviet Factors*, 125.

[30] Letter 10312/67 from W. H. G. Fletcher, Canadian Embassy, Cairo, 13 April 1967, FCO 39/263. Recent and earlier studies show convincingly that in their desire to advance a détente policy in East-West relations, the Soviets, at the time, provided countries in the Middle East and in other areas of conflicts mainly with defensive arms. The Soviet efforts to advance détente were reluctantly received by Arab and other Third World allies. See, Laron, "Playing with Fire," 163–75, 180n15.

the prospect for a regional war had increased considerably. On 9 May, Chuvakhin blamed unspecified imperialist forces (such as the Central Intelligence Agency [CIA]) for being responsible for the clashes on the northern Israeli border. The Soviets, Hadow noted, went further to suggest that the British were "now in cahoots with certain 'imperialist reactionary forces' in Israel itself in order to further our policy of raising the temperature between Israel and her Arab neighbours."[31] Similar words were uttered by Chuvakhin during his conversation with Israeli Foreign Minister Abba Eban following the Syrian-Israeli air encounter of 7 April. Chuvakhin, Eban narrates, asked him to give serious consideration to the possibility that "agents of American oil interests and the CIA, disguised as *al-Fatah* infiltrators were laying mines on Israeli roads in order to provoke Israel into retaliation which would, in turn, weaken the regime of Damascus!"[32]

As Hadow reported, Chuvakhin was not "as effusive as usual" during their meeting. That was possibly because he had received intelligence information based on a discussion of the Israeli Knesset's Foreign Affairs and Security Committee, which took place on the 9 May.[33] The Soviets had concluded that the Israeli government was contemplating military operations against Syria – evidenced by the massing of Israeli forces along the Syrian border. The Soviet embassy, moreover, was of the opinion that Eban's recent visit (mid-February 1967) to London was designed to concoct an Israeli attack on Syria with the backing of Western powers.[34] It was not the first Soviet warning to Western contacts of the concentration of Israeli troops along the Israeli-Syrian border. Soviet warnings had been made several times, since the rise of the neo-Ba'th regime in February 1966. For instance, on 25 May 1966, the Israeli embassy in Moscow was given a note stating that "the Soviet government had concrete evidence that Israel was concentrating its forces along its northern border... [we

---

[31] Letter from Michael Hadow, British Embassy Tel-Aviv, 11 May 1967, FCO 17/537.

[32] Abba Eban, *An Autobiography* (London: Weidenfeld and Nicolson, 1977), 317–18.

[33] On the Knesset debate, see Gluska, *The Israeli Military*, 105–6.

[34] On Eban's visit to London see, Gat, *Britain and the Conflict in the Middle East*, 181; Ro'i, "Soviet Policy," 5–6. See the content of the Soviet public statement of 23 May, in Hal Kosut, ed., *Israel and the Arabs: The June 1967 War* (New York: Facts on File, 1968), 51–2. Since mid-1966, Britain did not rule out reprisal actions by Israel, as Gat shows. He quoted Hadow, saying to Eban that, "were Israel to find it necessary to take forceful and aggressive action against the Syrians, Britain though naturally observing the familiar ritual of condemning the reprisal, would in fact understand and indeed sympathize with Israel's dilemma." Gat, *Britain and the Conflict in the Middle East*, 149.

hope] that the Israeli government would not allow external forces to determine the fate of its people and country."[35]

Leonid Brezhnev confirmed that the Soviets were following closely the developments along the Israeli-Syrian border. According to Brezhnev's account,

Many signs led us to the conclusion that a serious international crisis was in the making, and that Israel, relying on the support of Western powers, was preparing aggression. In mid-May – I am drawing attention to this – we received information that Israel was preparing a military attack against Syria and other Arab countries.

Brezhnev stressed that the Politburo took the decision to pass this information on to Egypt and Syria. He made it clear that "the material that I am putting before you was composed on the basis of factual material, and in many places comprises literal citations or accounts from our cipher communications or from cipher communications we received."[36]

It appears the Soviets waited a few days to digest the information they received on 9 May from Tel-Aviv and from other sources (possibly Syria).[37] On 13 May, the day when the Soviets passed on the information to Egypt, Anwar Sadat held talks in Moscow with Soviet Foreign Minister Gromyko during which – astonishingly – the intelligence information was not mentioned. However, several international issues were discussed, most notably the situation on the Arab Peninsula. Sadat told Gromyko that the situation in Yemen had improved, but Egypt and the Soviet Union should closely monitor the situation on the Arab Peninsula and the conspiracy plans of King Faysal and his British allies. As far as the situation in Syria was concerned, Sadat reassured his host that Egypt was committed to the security of Syria in accordance with the joint defence agreement of November 1966: "The struggle against imperialism is all-Arab, not only Ba'thist," Sadat remarked. Gromyko and his deputy, Vladimir Semenov, noted the "strengthening of the extremist factors within the Israeli Military General Staff, who were not satisfied with the Egyptian moderate policy and were looking for a pretext to aggravate the situation."

---

[35] Quoted from Gat, *Britain and the Conflict in the Middle East*, 150. See also Richard B. Parker, *The Politics of Miscalculation in the Middle East* (Bloomington: Indiana University Press, 1993), 11.

[36] See a report by Brezhnev, CPSU Central Committee, 20 June 1967 RGANI/f-2/op-3/d-70, 1.24, in Ro'i and Morozov, *The Soviet Union*, 308 [hereinafter referred to as Brezhnev's report].

[37] Daurov, *Dolgaya Shestidnevnaya Voyna*, 88–90.

Moreover, in line with Chuvakin's words, Sadat was told that the United States was using Israel in order to ignite the region into war.[38]

ʿAbd al-Muhsin Kamil Murtaji, the commander of the Sinai front during the Six-Day War, revealed that intelligence information regarding the concentration of "15 Israeli brigades" along the Israeli-Syrian border and regarding Israel's plan to attack Syria sometime between 15 and 22 May was delivered to the higher military command by the director of Military Intelligence at 9:30 P.M. on the night between 13–14 May, and that the Egyptian army began its moves from that moment on. He stressed, however, that from the information they received it was not overly clear whether Israel would attack Syria or Jordan. The Military Intelligence reports also raised the possibility that Israel might even first attack Egypt as the key Arab state. Another telegram, which arrived from Moscow, reaffirmed the intelligence information and emphasized the need to be prepared and alert, while calling for restraint. Murtaji drew a connection between the intelligence reports and statements made by Israeli statesmen and army generals, particularly "those made by Yitzhak Rabin, the Israeli Chief of Staff, on 12 May, according to which Israel would launch a lightning attack on Syria and occupy Damascus in order to overthrow its government." He also referred to the content of the 9 May debate of the Israeli Knesset's Foreign Affairs and Security Committee.[39]

Sadat recalled that he received the critical information before his departure from Moscow from Semenov and the speaker of the Soviet parliament, who accompanied him to the airport. They talked mainly about the Syrian situation, and he was informed of the concentration of ten Israeli brigades on the Syrian border:

When I arrived back in Cairo, I realized that the Soviet Union had informed Nasser of this. Levi Eshkol, then Israel's premier, subsequently stated that the Israeli forces would, if need be, occupy Damascus. At the time we had a common Defense Pact with Syria. Furthermore, the Russians were trying to . . . provoke Nasser by claiming that the Syrian leadership was more progressive. Nasser therefore ordered Field Marshal [Abd al-Hakim] Amer to concentrate the Egyptian forces

---

[38] Doc. 248, "Zapis' besedy ministra inostrannykh del SSSR A.A. Gromyko s predsedatelem natsional'nogo sobraniia OAR Anvarom Sadatom," 13 May 1967, in V. V. Naumkin et al., eds., *Blizhnevostochnyi konflikt: iz dokumentov arkhiva vneshnei politiki Rossiiskoi Federatsii* (Moscow: Materik, 2003), 551–3.

[39] Abd al-Muhsin Kamil Murtaji, *Al-Fariq Murtaji Yarwi al-Haqaʾiq, Qaʾid Jabhat Sinaʾ fi Harb 1967* (Cairo: Al-Watan al-ʿArabiyyah, n.d.), 49–50.

in Sinai. Although his real aim was to deter Israel, the situation soon got out of hand.[40]

Eban blamed the Soviets for stirring up the crisis. Eban revealed the content of a conversation between Eshkol and Chuvakhin on 11 May, during which the former invited the latter, with his military attaché, on a tour of the northern border to search for the Israeli military brigades. Chuvakhin responded that his "function was to communicate Soviet truths, not to put them to a test."[41] However, one imprecision in Eban's recollection of that conversation exists: its date (11 May).[42]

The question of whether Rabin threatened on 12 May to occupy Damascus and overthrow the Ba'th regime has remained unanswered. According to Carl Brown and Richard Parker, the possible source of the allegation was a report by United Press International that was a distortion of a briefing given by General Aharon Yariv, the chief of Military Intelligence, on that same day.[43] Yariv was quoted as saying, "I could say we must use force in order to have the Egyptians convince the Syrians that it does not pay.... I think that the only sure and safe answer to the problem is a military operation of great size and strength."[44] Whether true or not, this allegation was preceded and followed by a wave of belligerent rhetoric made by Israeli politicians and generals that Eban deemed unnecessary: "If there had been a little more silence, the sum of human wisdom would probably have remained intact," he remarked.[45] These Israeli statements and the intelligence, which was intercepted and leaked to Soviet agents in

[40] Anwar el-Sadat, *In Search of Identity* (London: Collins, 1978), 171–2. Salah Bassiouny, former Egyptian ambassador to the USSR, confirms both Sadat's and Murtaji's versions. See his version to the development of events on 13 May in Carl Brown, "Origins of the Crisis," in *The Six Day War: A Retrospective*, ed. Richard B. Parker (Gainesville: University Press of Florida, 1996), 17–18. See also, Muhammad Hasanayn Haykal, *Harb al-thalathin sanah: al-Infijar, 1967* (Cairo: Markaz al-Ahram lil-tarjama wa-al-nashr, 1990), 442–7.

[41] Eban, *An Autobiography*, 318–19.

[42] Such meeting could not take place before the outbreak of the crisis, which started as soon as the Soviets reported their Arab allies on 13 May of the concentration of Israeli forces along the Syrian borders.

[43] Carl Brown and Richard B. Parker, "Introduction," in Parker, *The Six Day War*, 7.

[44] This briefing was made on 12 May. Although Yariv ruled out the likelihood of a large-scale military invasion of Syria and the conquest of Damascus, his wording was paraphrased liberally by foreign correspondents who reported of Israeli belligerent plans to occupy Damascus and to topple the Ba'thist regime. Brown, "Origins of the Crisis," 32–3.

[45] Eban, *An Autobiography*, 319.

Tel-Aviv, as well as information received from Syria, were poorly digested by the Soviets, who took them literally.[46]

After the June 1967 debacle, Soviet bloc leaders remained faithful to the orthodox version of the origins of the crisis. In his keynote speech at the opening of the VI Polish Trade Union Congress on 19 June, Waldyslaw Gomułka, First Secretary of the Polish United Workers Party, referred again to 12 May as the crucial day. On that day, he stressed, the Israeli government published an announcement threatening to abolish the Syrian government. Moreover, he went on,

Commanders of the Israeli armed forces stated in public that it would take them twelve hours from the beginning of the war to capture the capital of that country, Damascus. In order to deceive the Syrians with regard to the timing of the aggression, Israel announced in the first days of May that a great military parade with the participation of all kinds of troops would be organized on May 14 in Jerusalem.... However, on 14 May a great number of Israeli military formations were sent to the Syrian border instead of Jerusalem.[47]

Gomułka's words indicate that the Soviets took the announcements made by Israeli military men and politicians in the days leading up to the crisis as concrete threats to their Syrian ally and acted accordingly. However, unlike Brezhnev, Gomułka did not refer to "cipher communications" as other modes of intelligence sources, on which the Soviet warnings of 13 May were based.

The Soviet intelligence information was not without foundation, if one relies on what the Egyptian military establishment had reported. The Egyptians doubted, however, the size and extent of the Israeli forces amassing along the Syrian border. On 16 May, the Egyptian Defence Minister Shams Badran discussed the situation on the Syrian-Israeli border in Cairo with Dimitri Pozhidaev, the Soviet Ambassador to Egypt. Badran referred to the alleged concentration of "12 Israeli brigades" along the border as "slightly exaggerated"; yet he agreed that there was an exceptional presence of Israeli forces on the northern border. Badran reassured Pozhidaev that an Israeli attack on Syria would be regarded as an attack on Egypt, which would entail immediate military retaliation. Badran made it clear, however, that Egypt would respond only to an Israeli attempt to occupy Syrian territories – not to border clashes such as those that had occurred in the recent past. Badran seized the opportunity

---

[46] Daurov, *Dolgaya Shestidnevnaya Voyna*, 86–93.
[47] A full text of his speech is attached to letter 10713/23/6, from British Embassy, Warsaw, 23 June 1967, FCO 28/32.

to request modern Soviet arms in order to strengthen the Egyptian army's capabilities.[48] Three days later, Amer reiterated Egypt's request for state of the art arms, including fighter planes and armoured personnel carriers. In his conversation with Pozhidaev, he estimated that Israel would not launch a war by itself, even against Syria alone. Israel's aggressive behaviour, noted Amer, was a result of American support. The Soviet ambassador made no comment.[49]

On 22 May, the day Nasser decided to close the Strait of Tiran, he met with Pozhidaev in Cairo to thank the Soviet government for the important information, which was transmitted to Badran. "Before we received this information, we had no idea of the scope and the placement of the Israeli forces," revealed Nasser. Like the Soviets, Nasser blamed the Western powers for directly encouraging Israeli aggression. When Pozhidaev asked Nasser how the Soviet Union could assist Egypt, he replied that the best help would be the political and diplomatic containment of the United States and its Western allies. During the course of their meeting, Nasser referred to rumours that the Soviet and the U.S. governments were coordinating their actions in the Middle East. Nasser warned that such rumours could hurt the Soviet image in the Arab world. The best way for the Soviets to dispel them, Nasser proposed, was a formal government statement, rather than indirect press reports.[50]

On the same day, the Israeli Ambassador to Moscow, Katriel Katz, who came to the Soviet foreign ministry to remonstrate the imprecise coverage of the Middle East crisis by the Soviet press, found himself instead under attack by A. D. Shchiborin, the head of the Middle East section. The latter reiterated the Soviet accusations that Israel was about to attack Syria.[51]

On 21 May, a day before the closure of the straits, Gromyko, who knew nothing of Nasser's forthcoming move, instructed the Soviet delegation to the United Nations to support the recent steps taken by Egypt

---

[48] Doc. 249, "Zapis' Besedy posla SSSR V OAR D.P. Pozhidaeva S Voennym Ministrom OAR Sh. Badranom," 16 May 1967, *Blizhnevostochnyi Konflikt*, 554–5.

[49] Doc. 251, "Zapis' Besedy posla SSSR V OAR D.P. Pozhidaeva S Pervym vitse-Prezidentom OAR Marshalom A. Amerom," 19 May 1967, *Blizhnevostochnyi Konflikt*, 557–60.

[50] Doc. 253, "Zapis' besedy posla SSSR v OAR D.P. Pozhidaeva s prezidentom OAR G.A. Naserom," 22 May 1967, *Blizhnevostochnyi Konflikt*, 561–3.

[51] Doc. 254, "Zapis' besedy zaveduiushchego otdelom stran blizhnego vastoka mid SSSR A.D. Shchiborina s poslom Israilia v Moskve K. Katsem," 22 May 1967, *Blizhnevostochnyi Konflikt*, 563–4.

and to coordinate the line of arguments with the Egyptian and Syrian representatives. He asked them to stress that the provocative actions against Arab governments taken by Israel with the backing of its Western allies were the reason for the present crisis.[52] Although the Soviet Union supported the Egyptian moves publicly, the Russians were actually not at all pleased with them, regarding them as "ill-advised steps," as Brezhnev disclosed shortly after the war. The UAR leadership, he noted, did not consult with the Soviet Union, "which in the circumstances that had arisen could be interpreted as a step to exacerbate the situation." Brezhnev stressed that Amer viewed these moves as preventative measures intended to deter the Israelis. Israel would have to reconsider its plan to attack Syria with massive force – it would have to take into account the situation on its southern border, with the entrance of Egyptian forces into Sinai.

Nasser felt confident enough on 22 May to inform his Soviet counterparts that the recent Egyptian measures including the blockade of the Gulf of Aqaba for ships and vessels to Israel had proved effective – Israel would now realize that Egypt would not allow an attack on Syria. Although the Soviets saw the short-term gain in Nasser's move, they were also of the opinion that Israel and its allies might use these measures as a *casus belli*. At that time, the Soviets had two options to avoid further escalation: they could either take the required measures to thwart the prospect of an Israeli aggressive adventure, or they could exert pressure on their Arab allies to show restraint and to avoid further provocative steps.[53] As subsequent events demonstrated, the Soviets failed to take the first option and actually came to follow Nasser's lead.

Gromyko expressed Soviet satisfaction on 25 May, following the consolidation of a united front in the Arab world to defend Syria in the face of possible Israeli aggression. In a letter to Nasser, Gromyko leaked the contents of his most recent conversation with Eban and that of a telegram, which he had received from President Lyndon Johnson. Both of them, wrote Gromyko complacently, were deeply concerned about the current situation; this led him to the conclusion that "they would now behave more responsibly and cautiously." For Gromyko, this development was a joint Arab-Soviet achievement.[54]

---

[52] Doc. 252, "Telegramma Ministra Inostrannykh del SSSR Postoiannomu Predstaviteliu SSSR pri OON," *Blizhnevostochnyi Konflikt*, 560–1.

[53] Brezhnev's report, 308–9.

[54] Doc. 255, "Telegramma ministra inostrannykh del SSSR A.A. Gromyko poslu SSSR v OAR," 25 May 1967, *Blizhnevostochnyi Konflikt*, 564–6.

At this stage, the Soviets truly believed that Israel was on the defensive. This would prevent Israel from taking any adventurous step against Syria or any other Arab country. In a conversation with the Lebanese ambassador to Moscow, Semenov praised the Lebanese government for refusing to allow the U.S. Sixth Fleet to use its ports.[55] On 28 May, Gromyko updated the leaders of the socialist countries regarding the current state of affairs in general, and the Soviet position in particular. At this stage, the emphasis was not on Syria but rather was on Egypt: "We received information that Israel was planning provocation against Egypt. Consequently, we warned Israel to avoid committing such a mistake. We correspondingly sent a letter to the U.S. President."[56] The Soviets, however, ignored the Israeli request of 27 May to meet with the Soviet leadership wherever and whenever possible to discuss the crisis in order to prevent further escalation and subsequent regional ignition. At first the Soviets were inclined to reply positively, but after Syria expressed its absolute objection to such a meeting, the Soviets yielded to the pressure from its ally. In retrospect, perhaps Gromyko regretted the Soviet refusal. He made it clear that the Soviets had no intention or any plan to instigate an Israeli-Arab war.[57]

In a conversation with Nasser on 1 June, the Russian ambassador confirmed that his government had refused to meet the Israeli prime minister because of Syrian objections. Nasser opined that such a meeting would be adversely received by Arab public opinion. During this conversation Nasser also complained to the Soviets that the Syrians were against the joint Jordanian-Egyptian agreement despite the current situation: "Jordan was in fact subdued by Egypt, but the Syrians refuse to listen to Egypt's advice." Nasser continued, "Whereas on 15 May Damascus was in panic because of danger of an Israeli invasion, now on 31 May Syrians claim that they don't predict any invasion and don't feel under threat." For Nasser, that was their excuse for not upholding the favourable military arrangements he achieved with King Husain of Jordan.[58]

---

[55] Doc. 256, "Zapis' besedy zamestitelia ministra inostrannykh del SSSR B.C. Semenova s poslom livana v SSSR Naimom Amiuni," 25 May 1967, *Blizhnevostochnyi Konflikt*, 566–8.

[56] Doc. 257, "Telegramma ministra inostrannykh del SSSR A.A. Gromyko poslam SSSR v Pol'she, GDR, Chekhoslovakii, Bolgarii, Pumynii, Vengrii, Mongolii, KNDR, DPV, Kube," 28 May 1967, *Blizhnevostochnyi Konflikt*, 568–9.

[57] Aleksandr E. Bovin, *5 Let sredi Evreev i Midovtsev, ili, Izrailʿ iz okna Rossiiskogo posol'stva: iz dnevnika* (Moscow: I. V. Zakharov, 2000), 104–5.

[58] Doc. 260, "Zapis' besedy posla SSSR v OAR D.P. Pozhidaeva s Prezidentom OAR G.A. Naserom," 1 June 1967, *Blizhnevostochnyi Konflikt*, 572–4.

During the period from 14 May to 4 June 1967, the Soviets were complacent. They did not anticipate an Israeli preemptive attack without direct American involvement. A KGB agent disclosed on 31 May that although the Soviet Union did not encourage Nasser, it did not restrain him either because it saw no reason why it should. As the KGB agent put it, "the Soviet Union could only win [out of this crisis which] . . . was pure power politics. No matter how it went, and whether or not there was an Israeli-Arab war, the United States would suffer a disastrous blow to its prestige and influence."[59] The Soviets thus saw a real prospect for a spectacular diplomatic victory in the Middle East at a time when a mood of frustration was manifest among Soviet leaders.

According to Robert Ford, the Canadian Ambassador to Moscow,[60] there had been a failure

To establish any kind of excitement about the 50th anniversary of the revolution, lack of any dominant personality or theme; and general feeling of apathy in the country and I believe in the CP [Communist Party]. Added to this has been slow but steady deterioration of relations with China, failure to re-establish effective Soviet leadership of the communist movement, lack of progress in Europe, Asia and Africa, stalemate in relations with the United States, and failure to prevent increasingly serious attacks on its communist ally, North Vietnam.[61]

Although the Soviets were not informed of Nasser's plan to close the Straits of Tiran, they tried to use this move to their advantage. Internationally, they manipulated the crisis in order to increase their support in the Arab world by indefatigably supporting the Arab moves. As Leonid Federovich Il'ichev, Gromyko's deputy, put it, could anybody think "of any reason the Americans could give us why we should work with them in the Middle East."[62]

The escalation in the Arab-Israeli dispute had not been given top priority in superpower relations during the period preceding the Six-Day War. The United States pursued a policy of restraining Israel and competing with the Soviet Union for Arab favour. Jeremi Suri, a Cold War historian, has competently shown that Israel's requests for arms met with

[59] Telegram 1631 from Robert Ford, Canadian ambassador to Moscow, FCO 28/32, 6 June 1967. H. F. T. Smith, "Soviet Union and the Middle East," 13 June 1967, FCO 28/32.

[60] See remark made by I. J. M. Sutherland, 17 June 1967, FCO 28/32.

[61] Telegram 1529 from Ford, 2 June 1967, FCO 28/31.

[62] Ibid.

scant success – the United States did not want to be implicated "as a military patron of the Jewish state."[63] Israeli-American relations were quite tense. Israel's security anxieties largely fell on deaf ears and "the United States came to see Israel as a greater threat to Middle East security than the Soviet Union."[64]

With the outbreak of the crisis in May 1967, the United States took pains to coordinate its Middle East policies with the Soviet Union, stressing that the latter "was not behind Nasser's most recent move."[65] Once again, Israel was called to show restraint, while Nasser's move was publicly justified by the Soviet Union. With the outbreak of hostilities, the United States hastily informed Moscow that Israel had not been given a green light to go ahead with its military operation. The Americans feared that the Soviets would retaliate. The United States hoped that they might act together with the Soviet Union in order to bring an immediate end to the hostilities. It would appear that the State Department and the Soviets were unaware that a few days before the outbreak of hostilities, Israel, by means of various clandestine channels, attempted to persuade President Johnson and the Secretary of Defence Robert McNamara to give her a "yellow-green light" to go ahead with a preemptive attack on Egypt.[66] No doubt, Israel's crushing military victory changed its image in Washington – not a needy protégé, but rather a strategic asset – "the most important American ally in the region."[67] Even the KGB agent, mentioned previously, admitted on 5 June that the Soviets miscalculated Israel's capabilities to launch war against "a united Arab world supported by the Soviet Union." He pointed the finger at the Soviet leaders, who "had as seriously over-estimated Egyptian fighting ability as they had under-estimated Israelis." The Soviet leadership, he concluded sarcastically, "mistakably thought of Israelis still in terms of Soviet Jews – downtrodden, intellectuals, artists, etc."[68]

For the Soviets, Nasser's decision to move forces into Sinai and to close the Tiran straits was a show of force. The Soviets, it would appear, employed a twofold tactic. Outwardly, they backed their Arab allies and

---

[63] Jeremi Suri, "American Perceptions of the Soviet Threat before and during the Six Day War," in Ro'i and Morozov, *The Soviet Union*, 107.

[64] Ibid., 110.

[65] Ibid.

[66] See more on this subject in the chapters of Charles Smith and Avi Shlaim (Israel) in this volume.

[67] Suri, "American Perceptions," 119.

[68] Telegram 1631, Ford, 6 June 1967.

provided them with full diplomatic support internationally. As we have seen, however, in the dialogues between the parties, the Soviets called for restraint. Yet things did not evolve exactly the way they wanted or expected them to happen; their belief that they could closely monitor the crisis and master their allies behind the scenes proved to be a grave mistake. On 24 May a high-ranking Egyptian delegation visited Moscow on a four-day mission. Salah Bassiouny, a member of the delegation, claimed that the Soviets called upon Egypt to ease the tensions and to avoid further escalation. Bassiouny suggested, however, that the Soviets were speaking in two voices. During their talks on 26 May, Semenov urged Ahmad Hassan al-Feki, the Egyptian Ambassador to Moscow, to avoid war; whereas, on 28 May, Marshal Andrei Grechko assured Badran (who headed the delegation) before their departure, that the Soviets would provide Egypt with arms as requested, and that they would "enter the war on Egypt's side, if the United States entered the war, and that if something happens and you need us, just send us a signal." The Egyptian diplomats Bassiouni and Feki interpreted Grechko's words as nothing to get excited about, but they realized that Badran and Amer, the supreme military authority, were willing to go further, taking risks that could lead to war.[69]

Evgenii Primakov has confirmed the content of Grechko's remarks to Badran; he regards them as irresponsible statements on Grechko's part. He also argued that they should not have been taken seriously by his Egyptian guests because they were no more than "a stereotype [talk] of an arrogant military man."[70] Primakov noted that Grechko had already made such comments several months earlier. He referred to a conversation with Nasser, during the course of which Grechko declared that "the Egyptian army was prepared to take upon itself all sorts of missions within the regional framework." For Primakov, this statement was made in order to enhance the prestige of the Soviet military aid to the Arabs.[71]

---

[69] Brown, "Origins of the Crisis," 18–19. See also, Tharwat 'Ukashah, *Mudhakkirati fi al-Siyasah wa-al-thaqafah*, vol. 2, 2nd ed. (Cairo: Dar al-Hilal, 1990), 372–3; Evgenii Primakov, *Konfidentsial'no: Blizhnii Vostok na stsene i za kulisami* (Moscow: Rossiiskaia gazeta, 2006), 113–21.

[70] Primakov, *Konfidentsial'no*. Primakov is a well-known Russian orientalist, journalist, diplomat, and politician (foreign minister, 1996–8 and prime minister, 1998–9). He also served as a director of foreign intelligence (1991–6) and held senior posts in the Soviet state apparatus. During the Six Day War he was the *Pravda* correspondent in the Middle East.

[71] Ibid. See similar analysis in Daurov, *Dolgaya Shestidnevnaya Voyna*.

Soviet documents, as well as reports by well-informed Western diplomats in Moscow, rule out the possibility that the Soviets orchestrated the conflict, intentionally hoping for a war that would enhance their influence. A few days before the outbreak of the war, East-West issues captured Soviet attention. For instance, the Soviets blamed the United States on 2 June for bombing a Soviet ship in the port of Cam Pha (the Democratic Republic of Vietnam – North Vietnam). The Soviets described the event as a blatant "violation of the freedom of shipping, an act of piracy, which may have far-reaching consequences."[72] The Soviet press reported of the movements of the U.S. Sixth Fleet in the Mediterranean. Both the United States and Britain were condemned for what *Pravda* described as their plan to attack Arab countries by reviving the old "gunboat diplomacy." Soviet propaganda portrayed the United States as the key source for the problems in Vietnam and the Middle East.[73]

The crisis in the Middle East did not spoil the plan of Brezhnev and the Soviet leadership (including Marshal Grechko and key army figures) to go on a four-day tour (31 May–3 June) to survey the Murmansk and Archangel region.[74] Why would they do so at a crucial time, when the Middle East crisis was reaching its zenith point? The answer may go either way: First, to signal business as usual – the crisis was not severe enough to prevent them from pursuing day-to-day internal business. Second, it was a serious action intended to inspect the preparedness of a central Soviet military arm at a crucial time internationally. One thing is certain – the Soviet leadership was confident enough to leave the Kremlin believing that the likelihood of an immediate outbreak of war in the Middle East was very slim. The two superpowers expressed their objection to war and coordinated their steps shortly before and during the war, despite the anti-American campaign in the Soviet press.[75]

Israel's remarkable military achievements on all fronts during the short six-day confrontation were proof of the extent to which Soviet prestige was harmed. The Soviets and their East European allies reiterated their commitment to the Arab cause, but the pressure they exerted on Israel to withdraw was doomed to fail. The Soviet decision on 10 June to break off diplomatic relations with Israel in order to appease the Arabs was to have adverse long-term implications for Soviet Middle East policies.

---

[72] Telegram 1571, Ford, 5 June 1967, FCO28/31.
[73] See, e.g., *Izvestiia*, 2 June 1967; *Pravda*, 3 and 4 June 1967.
[74] Telegram 1571.
[75] Suri, "American Perceptions," 110–13. See similar analysis in Fawaz A. Gerges, *The Superpowers and the Middle East* (Boulder, CO: Westview Press, 1994), 216–22.

As subsequent events were to demonstrate, the U.S. involvement in the Arab-Israeli conflict increased significantly in light of the new Middle East reality, reaching its pinnacle in the Camp David summit of 1978. The Soviet Union was left behind.

The roots of the Six-Day War are not to found in Moscow, but rather in Cairo, Jerusalem, and Damascus. The Soviet Union's moves in the prewar months were aimed at expanding Soviet political and economic influence over the region. Specifically, the Soviets wanted to acquire naval and air facilities as a counterweight to the presence of the U.S. Sixth Fleet in the Mediterranean. They tried to exploit the May crisis in order to advance that goal. For instance, Brezhnev tried to persuade Nasser in the days preceding the war to allow the Soviets to temporarily transfer "a Soviet air force unit to an UAR airfield" as a measure "toward restraining possible aggression against the independent Arab states."[76] An Arab-Israeli war, however, was not a means by which the Soviets hoped to realize these goals. The intelligence warnings delivered to Egypt and Syria on 13 May were based on a variety of sources, which were allegedly considered reliable by the Soviet security services. After the content of the information had been examined and discussed within the Politburo, it was decided to transmit it at once to Egypt and Syria. As is clear, the Soviets had made similar warnings several times during the months preceding the war, yet the most recent reports were more specific about the date of the planned Israeli attack on Syria. Common wisdom perceives the transmission of Soviet intelligence information as "deliberate disinformation" – an intentional move designed to serve Soviet interests. The question regarding whether the Soviet information was reliable is highly disputable. However, as one study puts it, "the USSR hardly needed an Israeli mole, and Arabs had no need of Soviet intelligence to calculate that Israel might attack Syria. What one [Israeli] government minister called the 'abundance of remarks' by Eshkol, Rabin, and the other Israeli spokespersons before Independent Day left little room for doubt."[77]

---

[76] Brezhnev to Nasser, 24 May 1967, TsVMA, fond 2, op.307ss, d. 139, 34, quoted from Ro'i and Morozov, *The Soviet Union*, 286–7. A letter with a similar notion was sent by Semenov to the Soviet ambassadors in Cairo and Damascus on the same day. See, ibid., 285–6.

[77] Tom Segev, *1967, Israel the War and the Year that Transformed the Middle East* (New York: Metropolitan Books, 2007), 231. On the general feeling in Israel of suffocation in the prewar year, and the unflinching positions as uttered by Israeli high-ranking military

This chapter, nevertheless, categorically confutes allegations concerning the existence of a Soviet plot to concoct a crisis. As post–Cold War studies show, the Soviet Union, generally, was a responsible superpower in the international field and was cautious in its conduct vis-à-vis its main rival, the United States. The USSR was among the first countries to recognize the state of Israel in 1948 and throughout the war of 1948 extended the Jewish state diplomatic and military support, which was of the utmost importance. No evidence exists to indicate that the Soviets ever considered the destruction of Israel. True, the Soviets were not pleased with Israel's alliance with the Western powers, and they had taken the Arab side in the Arab-Israeli conflict since the early 1950s by supporting the Arab states politically, economically, and militarily, but this support was within the context of the Cold War drive for "spheres of influence," and this included Egypt and Syria.

The nature and quality of Soviet-Egyptian relations under Nasser are vital to understand the essence of the May to June 1967 crisis. Nasser's "positive neutralism" aimed to reduce Western influence in the Middle East by skilfully flirting with, but not inviting, Soviet intervention, until his defeat in the June 1967 War. His neutralism was not a policy of opposing both sides in the Cold War, but rather of using each of the two superpowers in an effort to further Egyptian goals. Nasser did his utmost during the 1950s and early 1960s to terminate Western influence in the region, not the least of which were his extended efforts to dissolve the Baghdad Pact. He also successfully combatted Soviet and communist influence in Syria during the late 1950s in an attempt to establish hegemony. His efforts to try this again in Iraq following the demise of the Hashemite monarchy in 1958 were eventually doomed to fail.[78]

Nasser's anticommunist offensive (1958–61) had taken the anti-Western edge off his policy of positive neutralism. The motives behind his anticommunist campaign in the UAR were political and ideological. Politically, he wanted to warn the Soviets that friendly relations with the Arab world could only be based upon respect for Arab neutralism in the interbloc conflict and noninterference in Arab internal affairs. Ideologically, Nasser expressed his dislike of communism because communism and Islam could not coexist because "communism is in its essence atheistic; I have always been a sincere Muslim . . . [and] it is quite impossible to

---

men and senior politicians before the crisis, see, ibid., 14–5, 230–1. See also, Gerges, *The Superpowers*, 211–12.

[78] Quoted from Ginat, *Syria*, 18.

be a good Muslim and a good communist. . . . I [also] realized that communism necessitated certain control from Moscow and the central communist parties, and this, too, I could never accept."[79] Nasser concluded that communism could not provide "an adequate basis for shaping the social and economic future of the Arabs."[80]

The USSR-UAR ideological warfare came to an end soon after the introduction of Nasser's Socialist Laws of July 1961. These laws marked the beginning of Nasser's Arab socialism, a program that constituted his basic principles. The Soviets received this move warmly, though with certain reservations. The introduction of his socialist revolution in July 1961 and the incorporation of key Marxist and communist Egyptian figures into the establishment during the first part of the 1960s signal his growing reliance on the Soviets.[81]

Egypt's dependency is evidenced by Egypt's stance throughout the Cuban Missile Crisis of October 1962. The United States, particularly President John Kennedy, was held responsible by the Soviets because of their belligerent policy towards Cuba. According to Egyptian sources, the Soviets were dragged into this conflict following the irresponsible measures taken by the United States. No accusations directed against the Soviets emanated from Egypt.[82] Soviet-Egyptian relations were quite tense by late 1966, however, because the Soviets conditioned their food aid to Egypt on the latter making strategic concessions by allowing the Soviets free access to Egyptian air and sea facilities.

The gradual decline of Nasser's influence since the early 1960s left him with a very little room for manoeuvre. He was desperate to revive his doctrine of positive neutralism and to free himself of the Soviet clinch. Therefore, he exploited the opportunity created by the delivery of the Soviet intelligence information of 13 May to orchestrate a crisis without consulting his Soviet allies. He believed that the crisis would end in a victory for the Arabs that would enhance Egypt's prestige in the Arab world and beyond.[83] The Soviets were clearly not pleased with his actions,

[79] Ibid., 206–7.

[80] Ibid.

[81] Rami Ginat, *Egypt's Incomplete Revolution* (London: Frank Cass, 1997), 23–45. As we have seen, Nasser was also dependent on Soviet support in his prolonged war in Yemen.

[82] See, e.g., Muhammad Hasanayn Haykal, "Kuba . . . Madha hadith," *Al-Ahram*, 24 October 1962; idem, "hal Hunaka Harb," *Al-Ahram*, 26 October 1962; idem, "al-farq baina ma'rakat al-Suways wa-ma'rakat Kuba," *Al-Ahram*, 2 November 1962.

[83] On Nasser's motives and miscalculations in the weeks preceded the war, see Gerges's analysis, *The Superpowers*, 212–6. Avi Shlaim, *The Iron Wall* (London: Penguin Books, 2001), 236–7.

particularly the closure of the straits on 22 May. Publicly, however, they endorsed Egypt's moves and unquestionably took the Arab side – for them, Israel and its Western allies were to be held accountable for the crisis. The Soviet Union and Egypt failed to predict an Israeli preemptive attack and, moreover, belittled Israel's military might.

Nasser's defeat in the Six-Day War was the swan song of his neutralism. Following Egypt's defeat, Nasser became even more dependent on his Soviet allies. He was now "pro-Soviet neutralist" in domestic and foreign affairs – a situation that prevailed until the mid-1970s – into the reign of Sadat, who succeeded him following his sudden death in September 1970. Thousands of Soviet military personnel were directly and indirectly involved in the war of attrition against Israel. Nasser became fully oriented towards the Soviet bloc, a process that reached its peak in 1968, when he supported the Soviet invasion of Czechoslovakia. His actions created indignation among his close allies of the nonaligned movement – in particular, Josep Broz Tito.[84]

In the short-term, the Six-Day War served Soviet interests. Syria and Egypt now totally relied on Soviet support. The Soviet navy succeeded in gaining strategic bases in the Mediterranean – a most important goal, which the Soviets could achieve only following the Arab debacle. It would take Sadat almost five years to break out of this cycle of dependence and realign Egypt's foreign policy with the West. The transition to the U.S. area of influence was, however, slow and gradual, reaching its peak at the Camp David summit, where the leaders of Egypt and Israel recognized American hegemony and entered a strategic alliance with the United States.

[84] On the Egyptian pangs of conscience on the Czechoslovakia issue, see, idem, "Tshikus-lufakiya," *Al-Ahram*, 28 August 1968; see also, *Al-Ahram*, 25 August 1968.

9

Britain

The Ghost of Suez and Resolution 242

Wm. Roger Louis

In assessing Britain's part in the origins and consequences of the June 1967 War, it is useful to bear in mind a contemporary comment by a shrewd Israeli observer: "Britain's strength is not negligible, but it is greater in causing harm than in being beneficial."[1] Arabs as well as Israelis would have agreed. To the British, the lack of power came as a revelation, though in an unexpected way. In the initial phase of the crisis, the Cabinet assumed an adequacy of military resources and debated the possibility of another Suez expedition – this time without the mistakes of 1956. The motives for possible intervention were to prevent an Israeli preemptive attack that would have profound consequences for the Middle East, above all for Israel. A possible war might even destroy the United Nations by bringing the international organization into a conflict of cataclysmic

---

[1] Haggai Eshed, *Davar* (Israeli Labour Party newspaper, 4 October 1967, cutting in FCO 17/530. All archival references are to records at the Public Record Office, The National Archives. The principal work on Britain and the crisis is Frank Brenchley, *Britain, The Six-Day War, and Its Aftermath* (London: Tauris, 2005), which is succinct, accurate, and perceptive. See also Moshe Gat, *Britain and the Conflict in the Middle East, 1964–1967* (Westport, CT: Praeger, 2003); and Robert McNamara, *Britain, Nasser, and the Balance of Power in the Middle East, 1952–1967* (London: Frank Cass, 2003). Michael Brecher, *Decisions in Israel's Foreign Policy* (New Haven, CT: Yale University Press, 1975), ch. 7, remains indispensable, not least for its carefully constructed chronological and analytical tables. For the UN background, see W. R. Louis, "Public Enemy Number One: Britain and the United Nations in the Aftermath of Suez," in *Ends of British Imperialism* (London: Tauris, 2006), 689–724. It is curious that the British part in the crisis is virtually ignored in Richard B. Parker, ed., *The Six-Day War: A Retrospective* (Gainesville: University Press of Florida, 1996), but nevertheless it is the vital historiographical landmark. For the history of Resolution 242 see especially Sydney Bailey, *The Making of Resolution 242* (Dordrecht, The Netherlands: Nijhoff, 1985).

proportions beyond its capacity to resolve. Faced with what they believed to be an agonizing choice, to intervene or not to intervene, the British were overtaken by events. During the war they were universally blamed by the Arabs for colluding with the Israelis, whereas in fact they had not. The dual theme of saving the Israelis from themselves and preserving the United Nations runs through British thought at the time, but only in the last stage or aftermath did the British significantly influence the course of events.

Six months after the Six-Day War, the British proposed and sustained UN Resolution 242, which was, to the British at least, the epitome of an evenhanded formula. Just as the Balfour Declaration had been incorporated by the League of Nations as part of the mandate, so also did Resolution 242 become a landmark in the history of the United Nations. It corrected the Jewish tilt of the Balfour Declaration, which had included as almost an afterthought the guarantee that the Jewish national home must not damage Arab interests. From the British perspective, the Balfour Declaration loomed large from the beginning to the end of the year, which marked the declaration's fiftieth anniversary. One of the ironies of the crisis is that the events of the war transformed the military and political domination of Palestine at the same time that the British pondered how best to celebrate the anniversary or rather to let it pass by while saying as little as possible.

In the ultimate stage of the 1967 crisis, Resolution 242 seemed to many at the time to be largely the work of one man, Lord Caradon, Minister of State and Permanent Representative at the United Nations. But even with qualification such a statement is no doubt exaggerated. Resolution 242 was the work of many hands. It had American and Russian as well as British origins. Yet it helps in understanding its evolution to focus on Caradon. Previously, as (Sir) Hugh Foot, he had served in the colonial administration in Palestine and Nigeria, and as Governor of the Gold Coast and later Cyprus.[2] To his contemporaries he personified the British colonial mission, and they admired his balanced judgement. Yet there is something puzzling about the end of his life. When the remains of one of the last of the great British proconsuls were lowered into the grave, a flag of the Palestine Liberation Organization (PLO) draped the casket. Edward Heath, shortly after he became Prime Minister, remarked in 1971

---

[2] See his autobiography, Hugh Foot, *A Start in Freedom* (New York: Harper and Row, 1967). There is useful contemporary comment in Hisham Sharabi, "Interview with Lord Caradon," *Journal of Palestine Studies* 5, nos. 3–4 (Spring/Summer 1976), 142–52.

that Caradon was "a traitor to his country."[3] Is there a hidden history here that might reveal more about the part played by the British during the June 1967 War and its aftermath at the United Nations?

Three other British statesmen were conspicuous in the crisis: Harold Wilson, the Prime Minister, George Brown, the Foreign Secretary, and Richard Crossman, Lord President of the Council and Leader of the House of Commons. Crossman was a dedicated and intellectually robust Zionist. Wilson was also a Zionist but throughout proved to be moderate and pragmatic. His decisions usually reflected consensus and common sense. He demonstrated integrity and consistency – along with political agility – during the origins and course of the June 1967 War.[4] In a famous statement about the British Empire, he once said that British frontiers extended to the Himalayas. But to him the empire was not so much a matter of pride as an annoyance, especially in the cases of Aden and Rhodesia. No one at the time would have guessed that Wilson had one passion that put him almost in an unbalanced category of its own. Though he took care to appear judiciously restrained at the time of the June 1967 War, after his retirement he published *Chariot of Israel* (1981). According to Roy Jenkins, who was an historian as well as a member of the Cabinet in 1967, it was "one of the most strongly Zionist tracts ever written by a non-Jew."[5]

At the time of the outbreak of the crisis in May 1967, Brown had the reputation as strongly pro-Arab and had worked to bring about reconciliation with Gamel Abdel Nasser. But he was not an appeaser. A portrait of Palmerston hung in his office. Just as Wilson could be compared with Disraeli, with a wry and quick wit, so also did Brown have mid-Victorian characteristics associated with Palmerston, not least the willingness to use force if necessary.[6] Brown's real hero was Ernest Bevin. He admired the

---

[3] Humphry Berkeley, *Crossing the Floor* (London: Allen and Unwin, 1972), 107.

[4] "Intellectual courage" was the phrase used by Crossman in his diary to describe one of Wilson's attributes. Richard Crossman, *The Diaries of a Cabinet Minister, Volume Two, Lord President of the Council and Leader of the House of Commons, 1966–68* (9 May 1967) (New York: Holt, Rinehart, and Winston, 1976), 348.

[5] Roy Jenkins in the *Oxford Dictionary of National Biography*. The best works on Wilson are by Ben Pimlott, *Harold Wilson* (London: Harper Collins, 1992), and Philip Ziegler, *Wilson* (London: Weidenfeld and Nicolson, 1993).

[6] Jenkins made the point about Wilson and Disraeli in conversation with me, but see also his entry on Wilson in the *Oxford Dictionary of National Biography*. On Brown, see especially Peter Paterson, *Tired and Emotional: The Life of Lord George-Brown* (London: Chatto and Windus, 1993). Brown's own memoir is *In My Way: The Political Memoirs of Lord George-Brown* (New York: St. Martin's, 1970), which is frank and revealing but unreliable in some of the detail.

way in which Bevin had attempted to come to terms with Arab nationalism and, like Bevin, believed the creation of the state of Israel to have been
a mistake. He was also inspired by Bevin's mastery of the Foreign Office
though Brown, unlike Bevin, had an uneasy relationship with permanent
officials.[7] Brown held as his basic tenet the British commitment to the
United Nations. His underlying position throughout the crisis was to preserve the integrity of the international organization whose very existence
might be endangered by war in the Middle East. There was, however, a
problem in Brown's personality, commonly known at the time and hardly
forgotten in retrospect. He was addicted to alcohol. Wilson tolerated his
heavy drinking. By early evening, when Brown held meetings with his
officials at the Foreign Office, he was usually tipsy and erratic in mood
if not in judgement. Yet throughout the crisis of 1967, with a couple
of exceptions, he was relatively sober. He demonstrated brilliance and
dedication to the principle of British support for the United Nations.

Crossman fortunately kept a full diary of the events of May and June
1967. Though he was not able to attend the first meetings of the Cabinet
on the crisis, his account reflects more fully than any other contemporary record the outrage against Nasser, the perplexed reaction to the
Secretary-General of the United Nations, U Thant, and the passionate
discussion about whether to mount another Suez operation. One would
hardly guess from the official minutes the tone of the discussion or for that
matter the details of what actually transpired.[8] Crossman's diary entries
are thus invaluable, all the more because they are perceptive as well as
accurate.[9] He had his own reasons for carefully following the discussions
of May 1967. He had been a member of the Anglo-American Committee
of Inquiry on Palestine in 1946 but had subsequently been kept at a distance, actually snubbed, by Attlee and Bevin because they mistrusted his
ability to make sound decisions. They were not alone. Denis Healey, the

---

[7] The case of Willie Morris is a good example. The head of the Eastern Department,
Morris was one of the most able officials of his generation, unassuming but intellectually
confident. He later became ambassador to Egypt. Brown was unpredictable in his likes
and aversions, but he took a dislike to Morris, permitting him to come to meetings on
the condition that he could listen but not speak. Brenchley, *Six Day War*, xxvi.

[8] Crossman was quite right in complaining that the Cabinet records were distorted and
misleading. Wilson had a habit of making sure that they appeared in as anodyne form as
possible. See Crossman, *Diaries* (19 May 1967), 356. Crossman's books include *Palestine
Mission: A Personal Record* (New York: Harper, 1947); and his most famous work, *The
God That Failed* (New York: Harper, 1949). Crossman believed that academic paradise
can be defined as a vigorous and searching seminar discussion.

[9] On the accuracy of the diaries, see Roy Jenkins, *Portraits and Miniatures* (London:
Macmillan, 1993), 254.

Secretary for Defence in the Wilson government, described Crossman as having "a heavyweight intellect with a lightweight judgment."[10] When Crossman learned that the 1967 crisis had persuaded Wilson to turn to him to speak at the time of the anniversary of the Balfour Declaration, Crossman saw it as an opportunity for revenge against Bevin. Crossman was a radical antiimperialist. He wanted to end the empire as soon as possible, above all the disastrous state of affairs in Aden. Yet on the issue of the expeditionary force, Crossman was torn, his antiimperialist impulses matched by his "fanatical" – his own word – Zionism. He wanted to save Israel but recoiled from the idea of "another Suez," this time by a Labour Government. Others were less ambivalent. James Callaghan, the Chancellor of the Exchequer, turned "pale with anger."[11]

The sequence of early events has two parts. The first part occurred from the time of Nasser's demand for the withdrawal of UN troops and U Thant's quick acceptance of the request in the week following 16 May. The second part in the chain of circumstance was from Nasser's closing of the Gulf of Aqaba on midnight of 22–23 May to the outbreak of war on 5 June. On learning that Nasser had requested the withdrawal of the UN Emergency Force (UNEF); the British were as perplexed as anyone else. The UNEF had effectively served as a buffer between Israel and Egypt for an entire decade. On 18 May, the foreign secretary made a public statement that quite clearly defined his attitude from beginning to end, in private as well as public, drunk or sober:

For a decade now the United Nations emergency force has helped to keep the peace on the border of Israel and the United Arab Republic [UAR]. Its presence there in the Sinai desert has kept tension down on that difficult and potentially explosive border. We don't have to look further for a United Nations success. It is there in U.N.E.F....

It really makes a mockery of the peace-keeping work of the United Nations if, as soon as the tension rises, the U.N. Force is told to leave. Indeed the collapse of the U.N.E.F. might well have repercussions in other United Nations peace-keeping forces.[12]

Defence of the United Nations, not a conversion to Zionism, was Brown's motive. Yet he did not object to the line of reasoning that Britain might

---

[10] Denis Healey, *The Time of My Life* (New York: Norton, 1989), 108.
[11] As recorded by Patrick Gordon Walker in his diary. Gordon Walker was Minister without Portfolio. Robert Pearce, ed., *Patrick Gordon Walker: Political Diaries, 1932–1971* (London: The Historian's Press, 1991), 315. For Callaghan and the crisis, see Kenneth O. Morgan, *Callaghan: A Life* (Oxford: Oxford University Press, 1997), ch. 13.
[12] Brown's speech to the UN Association, 19 May 1967, FCO 17/480.

have to save Israel as well, a point that appealed to the prime minister. "George and Harold passionately advocated intervention to aid Israel," Crossman wrote in his diary.[13] He got it a little wrong about Brown's priorities, but he was right about the emphasis on preventing Israel from launching a preemptive attack. When Nasser closed the Straits of Tiran at the entrance to the Gulf of Aqaba on 23 May, the British believed war to be a near certainty. The Israelis would not tolerate a stranglehold on Aqaba. To mention only one prominent fact that impressed the Chiefs of Staff Committee, 90 percent of Israeli oil passed through the Straits of Tiran.

The foreign secretary and prime minister advocated an expeditionary force to keep open the Straits. Crossman was among the first to remark that British action would carry with it responsibility for the aftermath. But it was Defence Minister Denis Healey who caught the main point: British intervention would be seen by the world at large as a repeat performance of Suez and the attempt to reassert European dominance in the Middle East. But Healey agreed that some sort of action seemed necessary. At this stage of the initial discussion, the foreign secretary and prime minister carried the day. Crossman noted Wilson's "intellectual courage," but it was Brown who dominated the discussion. "We should act now," he stated.[14]

Healey quickly retreated after consulting with the Chiefs of Staff. The immediate military retort, which should have come as no surprise, was that Egyptian naval and air strength dominated the region and that the Royal Navy would be placed in jeopardy (a more sceptical view would have placed more emphasis on Egyptian ineptitude despite Russian assistance). British naval forces were simply not available on such quick notice, and even so would be vulnerable to the Egyptian air force.[15] It remains an academic question whether the British might have taken the straits with bold action and skilful leadership (just as we will never know

---

[13] Crossman, *Diaries* (29 May 1967), 356. Crossman wrote on the same day that a "strange by-product of the crisis" was the invitation "to make the big speech at the Balfour Declaration celebrations next November."

[14] CC (67) 31st Conclusions, 23 May 1967. But compare with Gordon Walker, *Political Diaries*, 314–16; and Barbara Castle, *The Castle Diaries, 1964–70* (23 May 1967) (London: Weidenfeld and Nicolson, 1984), 258: "This is no better than 1956.... It all smelt too much like collusion, 1967 version."

[15] "There would be strong military objection to any plan for concentrating our ships near the Straits of Tiran, in order to counter the UAR threat to the Straits, so long as Egyptian air forces are in a position to dominate that area." Memorandum by Healey, Secret, 24 May 1967, FCO 17/485.

whether Mountbatten's initial plan for a daring strike on Suez might have succeeded immediately after Nasser's nationalization of the Suez Canal Company). What followed was authorization by the Cabinet urgently to consult with the United States about the possibility of a joint task force in the eastern Mediterranean. In Crossman's laconic description of the outcome, it was perhaps as well to "stand aside and let the Americans take the rap." In any event, what emerged from intense Cabinet discussions was a much "dehydrated" plan because it was "too dangerous" to call Nasser's bluff.[16]

Was it a bluff? What were Nasser's motives for what proved to be a suicidal venture?[17] British intelligence had no direct knowledge of the part the Soviet Union may have played in the origins of the crisis, but the British were certain that Russian military assistance and political backing had facilitated Egyptian action. The support of the Soviet Union gave Nasser a confidence that he might otherwise have lacked. In a similar manner, the British did not know whether Nasser had been misled by the commander of the Egyptian army, Field Marshal Abdel Hakim Amer, about the actual strength of Egyptian forces and the probability of victory or for that matter defeat. What the British did know for certain was that Nasser was a political gambler, played for highest stakes, and had been taken aback by U Thant's swift acceptance of the Egyptian demand for the withdrawal of UN troops. In the British view, Nasser had probably hoped for a political victory but was prepared to risk all for military conquest. The mood in Cairo was all or nothing, reflecting "the sense of national humiliation which the defeat of 1948 brought with it."[18]

Wilson and others in the Cabinet did not believe that the Russians wanted a proxy war in which the Arabs would be supported by the Soviet Union and the Israelis by the United States. Thus the historical analogy was not actually Palestine in 1948 but rather Cuba in 1962 and the

---

[16] Crossman, *Diaries* (29 May 1967), 355–56.

[17] The best studies of Nasser and 1967 from a British perspective remain Anthony Nutting, *Nasser* (London: Constable, 1972); and Robert Stephens, *Nasser: A Political Biography* (London: Allen Lane, 1971). See also, esp., Laura James, *Nasser at War: Arab Images of the Enemy* (London: Palgrave Macmillan, 2006).

[18] Memorandum by Willie Morris, 29 May 1967, FO 17/497. See also the minute by D. J. Speares, 30 May 1967, FCO 39/250, in which Nasser is described as "playing for keeps" and "the atmosphere in Cairo... more that of 1948 than that of 1956." From the American perspective, William Quandt later summed up the gist of American thought: "Vietnam and the memory of Suez were powerful background elements in the American thinking in the 1967 crisis." Parker, *The Six-Day War*, 204.

danger of the superpowers losing control.[19] According to a Foreign Office paper drafted by Willie Morris, the head of the Eastern Department who followed the developments of the crisis with insight and grasp of detail, "There is a double confrontation – between the U.S. and the U.S.S.R., and between Israel and the Arabs, and neither the U.S. nor the U.S.S.R. can wholly control their protégés."[20]

Nasser's personality had its own dynamic. There were three times, including the 1967 crisis, when he had demonstrated, to use the word that recurs in the contemporary comment, brinkmanship. In 1955 he had transformed the strategic balance in the eastern Mediterranean by accepting Czech arms, aligning himself militarily with the Soviet Union. In 1956 he had nationalized the Suez Canal Company and, with serendipitous help from President Dwight Eisenhower, had emerged more or less victorious from the Suez encounter. In 1967 he now placed his bet on political and military defeat of Israel. But what had been said about John Foster Dulles now seemed to hold true for Nasser: "three brinks and he's brunk." Whatever the truth of the witticism, brinkmanship was a dangerous game. The Joint Intelligence Committee believed that Israel would emerge victorious over Egypt.[21] But no one would have predicted total defeat, and certainly no one would have guessed that a six-day war would result in the collapse of Nasserism and pan-Arab unity as an ideology. The year 1967 marks a change in the emotional and intellectual climate of the Middle East.

By the end of May the foreign secretary's watered-down plan for another Suez simply amounted to "contingency naval planning" in consultation with the Americans. George Thomson, Minister of State in the Foreign Office and an able and persuasive political figure, went to Washington to discuss the possibility of a multinational concentration of naval power in the eastern Mediterranean.[22] By now the British had second thoughts about taking the lead. They welcomed the proposal of a French initiative put forward by Charles de Gaulle, and they hoped the Canadians and others would join what Walt Rostow, the National Security

---

[19] See, e.g., Harold Wilson's comment about "a second Cuba" in the secret memorandum of 3 June 1967, FCO 17/498.

[20] Memorandum by Morris, 29 May 1967, FO 17/497.

[21] See, e.g., minutes in FCO 17/494.

[22] See Memoranda of Conversations, 24 and 25 May 1967, Department of State, *Foreign Relations of the United States, 1964–1968*, vol. XIX (Washington, DC: U.S. Government Printing Office, 2004), no. 53 and no. 58.

Adviser, called the Red Sea Regatta.[23] Eugene Rostow, the Assistant Secretary in the State Department, embraced the proposal but seemed sceptical whether an international force could be assembled before the Israelis took matters into their own hands. For the British, alas, the anticipation of French support or leadership proved to be a false hope.[24] Nor were the Canadians optimistic that President Lyndon Johnson would welcome the idea. Lester "Mike" Pearson, the Prime Minister – and a key figure in view of his leadership in the United Nations in the aftermath of the Suez fiasco – rightly believed that Johnson would recall the lack of British support he had received in Vietnam. For Pearson, Vietnam was the dominant problem, as related in a jingle, in his own words, to Wilson. Just as Johnson was known as LBJ, so was Mike Pearson known as LBP: "L.B.P. and L.B.J. How many kids have you killed today?"[25] The remark had a direct bearing on the interpretation of Nasser's motives. Nasser probably hoped, in the British view, that Johnson would not be deflected from Vietnam.

President Johnson did remember the skilful and evasive way in which Wilson had avoided British troop commitment in Vietnam – as did Secretary of State Dean Rusk.[26] Yet Johnson had other reasons for doubting whether an effective naval operation could be conducted. By the beginning of June, there was a shift in mood, as if war seemed inevitable. The British did not know of Johnson's message conveyed indirectly – the "amber light" signifying caution but also the implicit signal that the United States would not react negatively in the event of an Israeli attack.[27]

---

[23] Rostow, irrepressible as always, seized the opportunity to explain to Thomson how a reconfiguration of regional power might lead to future economic development – what might be called the takeoff theory underpinning a peace settlement. Thomson's accounts of his conversations with officials in Washington are in FCO 17/485.

[24] Wilson later went to Paris to discuss the Middle East, only to be told by de Gaulle: "There was no reason for the Government of France – or, he suggested that of the United Kingdom – to ruin their relations with the Arabs merely because public opinion felt some superficial sympathy for Israel because she was a small country with an unhappy history" (Record of Discussion, Secret, 19 June 1967, PREM 13/1622). Caradon subsequent summed it up from the British perspective by writing that the French throughout maintained "their usual attitude of superior and negative detachment" (Caradon to Brown, Confidential and Guard, 29 December 1967, FCO 17/516). Willie Morris commented: "The Gaullist instinct will be to do the opposite of what we want" (Minute by Morris, Confidential, 3 August 1967, FCO 17/517).

[25] Memorandum of conversation between Harold Wilson and Lester Pearson, Secret, 1 June 1967, FCO 17/494.

[26] See Louis Heren, *No Hail, No Farewell* (New York: Harper, 1970), 230.

[27] William B. Quandt, "Lyndon Johnson and the June 1967 War: What Color Was the Light?" *Middle East Journal* 46 (Spring 1992).

The British now sensed that it would be up to the Israelis to save themselves, and that Dayan's entry into the Israeli Cabinet as a "national hero" on 1 June symbolized Israeli determination. There occurred at the same time a shift in the British reaction to the crisis. No longer did it seem prudent to take the lead in forcing open the Straits of Tiran. The British in late May had appeared to be, in the words of the head of the planning department of the Foreign Office, "more Israeli than the Israelis."[28] Masterly inactivity now commended itself as the sensible course of action. Any action taken by Britain would be regarded by the Arab world as pro-Israeli. In view of Middle Eastern oil, prudence now prevailed, but prudence characterized by a certain fatalistic attitude – as was also true of Johnson and others on the American side – that everything now would be determined by the outcome of war between the Israelis and Arabs.

On the origins of the war, there is one final and important point to be made about the United Nations. The British archival records help to clarify the mystery of U Thant and the emphatic decision immediately to remove UN troops, thus helping to precipitate the crisis. U Thant's right-hand man was Ralph Bunche, who had firsthand experience of the Arab-Israeli conflict. U Thant, despite the general contemporary view of him as inscrutable, had a sound grasp of principle.[29] He, together with Bunche, devised the formula of O.D.D. – an Orderly, Dignified, and Deliberate withdrawal that would take weeks if not months and would allow Nasser to change his mind. U Thant and Bunche were conscious at all times of Dag Hammarsköld's principle of limiting UN responsibility to tasks that could be kept under control. The precedent that they wanted to avoid was not that of the Suez Crisis but of the Congo. The Middle East crisis of 1967, initiated by Nasser's demand for the withdrawal of the UN contingent, foreshadowed just as vast, dangerous, and unmanageable a problem as that of the Congo.[30]

---

[28] Minute by J. A. Thompson, 29 May 1967, FCO 17/497.

[29] At the British delegation in New York, Lesley Glass, regarded by his colleagues as a man of discerning judgement, wrote of "the courage of the Secretary-General in taking upon himself full responsibility for this decision, which he believed to be the right one and which he believed it to be his duty to take." Glass to FCO, Confidential, 9 August 1967, FCO 58/83.

[30] E.g., "There is little doubt that the Secretary General's 'peacekeeping' advisers were much influenced by their memories of the difficulties UN troops got into in the Congo" (British Mission at the United Nations to FCO, Confidential, 20 May 1967, FCO 17/480). "Previous experience of attacks on United Nations contingents in the Congo were much in the minds of his [U Thant's] advisers, Bunche and [Brian] Urquhart" (Sir Lesley Glass to Brown, Confidential, 9 August 1967, FCO 58/83).

Wilson and Lord Caradon met with U Thant and Bunche on 3 June, two days before the outbreak of war.[31] Bunche was obviously stung by negative comment that the United Nations had been damaged by caving into Nasser's demand.[32] Wilson repeated the criticism. U Thant and Bunche made it clear that UN forces could not remain on Egyptian soil without the permission of Egypt. Nasser possessed the sovereign right to request the UNEF to leave. But there was another compelling reason, one that U Thant could hardly articulate publicly. By taking a stand against Egypt, even by protracting the issue by insisting that it be brought before the General Assembly, the Secretary-General would appear ineluctably and permanently as a creature of western imperialism. It was imperative for the office of the Secretary-General to remain politically nonaligned. Otherwise the United Nations would be divided and perhaps destroyed. It was a shrewd judgement on the part of U Thant and Bunche to act quickly and decisively. Their action stands vindicated by historical perspective on the 1960s, when decolonization had become one of the preeminent purposes of the United Nations.

The June 1967 War and the Postmortems

The British preoccupation with the war itself can be summed up in a single phrase, "The Big Lie." After the Israeli attack on 5 June, Radio Cairo announced the next day that British and American forces had assisted Israel in the attack on the Arab states. The response was understandable enough. The magnitude of the initial defeat included the destruction of the Egyptian air force on the first day of the war. How could it be explained other than by assistance of the Western powers to Israel? The British now reaped the whirlwind of previous commitments. To the Arabs, the logic of collusion seemed as compelling as it had been in 1956. How else could the cataclysm be comprehended? Anti-British demonstrations and rioting erupted throughout the Middle East.

---

[31] Record of a meeting at the United Nations, Secret, 3 June 1967, FCO 17/498. See Brian Urquhart, *A Life in Peace and War* (New York: Harper and Row, 1987), ch. 16; see also the vigorous debate between Urquhart and others in Parker, *The Six-Day War*, ch. 2.

[32] One observer of Bunche at the time believed that he was "slowly getting old, sick, and blind" and infirmity thus may have impaired his judgement (Bailey, *Making of Resolution 242*, 30). Bunche was increasingly ill and suffered from impaired vision, but throughout the crisis his analytical mind remained the same. See Brian Urquhart, *Ralph Bunche: An American Life* (New York: Norton, 1993), ch. 29.

One of the ironies of the attack is that British officials suspected that there might be some truth in the allegation of collusion. The Ambassador in Beirut, for example, was Sir Derek Riches. On the day after the Israeli offensive, he summoned the half-dozen or so senior members of his staff. Everyone had heard the news bulletin saying that British and American aircraft had assisted the Israelis. He asked them, one by one, did they believe the report? He wanted to deny the accusation of collusion immediately to the Lebanese government. But to his annoyance some of his officials were hesitant, saying that, after all, there was the Suez attack only eleven years previously. In exasperation Riches nevertheless picked up the telephone and called directly to the Lebanese Prime Minister, Rashid Karame. Riches said that there was no truth whatsoever in the allegation of conspiracy. He was nevertheless expelled from Lebanon.[33]

The Ambassador in Israel was Michael Hadow, who reported hour-by-hour on the progress of the war, sometimes by telephone. For example on 5 June: "Mr. Hadow rang up at 19.50.... The impression was that the Israelis had scored a notable success in virtually destroying the UAR air-force."[34] Hadow later acknowledged that he, like many others, had underestimated Israeli prowess. In his messages can be traced the transformation in mood from one of anxiety to numbness to exhilaration to euphoria, all in a matter of days.[35] There was no talk of collusion, or of the British as the champions of the Jews. The Israelis had done it on their own.

In Washington, according to reports from the British Embassy, there was a combination of surprise and subdued elation. "The Israelis' action was probably not entirely unwelcome to a number of officials here," according to the ambassador, "and Walt Rostow said at one point that 'If he were trying to stop the war tomorrow he would... [ellipsis in the original].'" Rostow went on "in a Rostowian way" to explain how the aftermath of war might promote regional economic development.

---

[33] I am grateful to Sir James Craig for this information, including the confession that he was among the officials in the embassy in Beirut who suspected that collusion might actually have taken place. There was general unease. The Ministry of Defence felt compelled to place flight logs of the *Victorious* and *Hermes* as well as those of the Royal Air Force stations in Cyprus, Malta, and Bahrain in the House of Commons for confidential inspection. See memorandum by R. A. Sykes, Confidential, 27 June 1967, FCO 17/599.

[34] Minute of 5 June 1967, FCO 17/494.

[35] According to Hadow: At the end of the fighting "there was no general expression of exultation and few outward signs of public jubilation such as marked VE Day in London." The euphoria came later. Hadow to FCO, Confidential, 29 June 1967, FCO 17/526.

"The trend of thought seems to be that the present situation, for all its dangers and difficulties, may provide an opportunity for a fresh start."[36]

In London the main burden of persuading the representatives from Arab countries that collusion was not merely a lie but "a very big and wicked lie" fell mainly to the Permanent Under-Secretary, Sir Paul Gore-Booth. A former High Commissioner (Ambassador) to India, Gore-Booth was familiar with non-European dialogue for which Brown had little patience ("what a confounded cheek & brazen effrontery these chaps have!" Brown had noted a few days earlier about the Arabs).[37] Gore-Booth's method was identical to Caradon's at the United Nations. With patience and an investment in time and energy, he met with each of the Arab ambassadors and deployed a secret weapon, his wife Patricia, or Pat, who with considerable charm usually managed to disarm ideologues.[38] Between the two of them they could almost always, according to Gore-Booth, take off the "chill" while he emphasized, usually successfully, the falsity of the allegation of collusion.

Gore-Booth knew from the time of the outbreak of the war that the British would have little influence on the outcome. In clear and exact language, he put the problem in British perspective on the day of the outbreak of the war:

The levels at which events are now most likely to be influenced are two – on the ground in the fighting between the two sides, and at the super-power level between Washington and Moscow. We must show some activity, but there is much to be said for keeping our heads down at this point rather than seeking to play a major role.[39]

In one of his conversations with the ambassador from Saudi Arabia, an awkward question arose: would it not help simply to admit that Israel was the aggressor? Gore-Booth replied that it was not as simple as all that:

It was clear that UAR leadership had brought about by its methods and objectives a situation of extreme tension which had made an outbreak of hostilities almost

---

[36] British Embassy in Washington to FCO, Secret and Guard, 5 June 1967, FCO 17/491.

[37] Minute by Brown, c. 31 May 1967, FCO 17/491. Gore-Booth had also served as director of Information Services in the United States, which gave him unusual credentials. But perhaps his most striking distinction was that he also held the office of President of the Sherlock Holmes Society. See his memoir, *With Great Truth and Respect* (London: Constable, 1974).

[38] Minute by Gore-Booth, 2 June 1967, FOC 17/491.

[39] Minute by Gore-Booth, 6 June 1967, FCO 17/494.

impossible to avoid – despite the strong efforts by the Americans and ourselves with both sides.[40]

Time and again, with all his interlocutors, especially those from Saudi Arabia and Kuwait, Gore-Booth expressed the hope that the disruption of the flow of oil would be brief and temporary. Clearly the problem of oil was very much on his mind.

For the British, the critical point on the battlefield was Jordan. King Hussein had made the disastrous mistake not only of aligning himself with Nasser but also in handing over operational control of the Jordan army to the Egyptians. By the second day of the war the King's entire regime seemed to be in jeopardy. Hussein "cannot hold it together," according to the estimate of the Joint Intelligence Committee.[41] With the defeat of the Jordan army and the influx of refugees from the West Bank, the King's fate seemed to hang in the balance. According to the Ambassador in Amman, Sir Philip Adams, on the fourth day of the war:

King Hussein... is very depressed, is very uncertain of the future but probably still hopes for help in rebuilding his country....

Two thirds of the army was on the West bank. It has suffered heavy casualties in both men and equipment.... Both armoured brigades are to all intents and purposes non-existent... .The nature of the fighting can be gauged by the fact that a large number of the initial casualties have bayonet wounds.

The defeat in turn gave credibility to reports of British collusion with the Israelis:

A noticeable number of military stragglers coming into Amman... are tired and hungry and full of stories of Israeli air superiority which they believe was achieved with British and United States help and connivance.[42]

In as striking a way as in any other, the case of Jordan thus helps to explain the belief among ordinary soldiers and the Arabs in general that there must be a reason for the defeat other than Israeli ability in combat. How otherwise could three hundred Israeli tanks destroy one thousand Egyptian tanks?[43] For that matter, to ask another fundamental question, how could King Hussein's action in aligning himself with Nasser

---

[40] Record of conversation, 8 June 1967 FCO 17/496.

[41] See records of 6 June 1967, FCO 17/494. For the part played by the local MI6 agent in Amman, see ch. 4.

[42] Adams to FCO, Confidential, 8 June 1967, FCO 17/494.

[43] The round numbers are those used by H. J. Arbuthnott in a minute of 13 June 1967, FCO 17/599.

be explained? According to Michael Hadow in Tel Aviv, "at no time did anyone think of speaking severely to King Hussein about the lunacy of his actions."[44] Jordan ranked low in Israeli priorities. The conquest of the West Bank was an unintended consequence of the war.

By all accounts, Nasser's only success was his propagation of the Big Lie. Everything else lay in ruin. How could his miscalculation be explained? The British had assumed that, as at the time of his nationalization of the Suez Canal Company in 1956, he would sit back and do nothing after his successful demand for the withdrawal of UN troops. In mid-May 1967, he had regained at least some of the mystique lost by disenchantment with lack of economic development in Egypt and the commitment of Egyptian troops to the civil war in Yemen. But he now plunged deeper by closing and mining the Straits of Tiran. In the Foreign Office, the head of the Eastern Department argued that Nasser probably calculated that "great power interest in avoiding a conflict would prevent the Israelis attacking, leaving him in the winning position."[45] In any event, Nasser seemed to believe that "war could be avoided." If so, Morris wrote, "this was brinkmanship at the extreme" that would have repercussions in Egypt and throughout the Middle East, not least for Nasser's successor. At the close of the war, Nasser offered his resignation only to be resoundingly reaffirmed by the Egyptian people. Yet the post-Nasser succession was now widely debated. The British reasoned that he would be succeeded either by "a very violently destructive form of right-wing Arab Nationalism," or – even more unwelcome to the British, by "Egypt putting itself... completely into the pockets of the Communists."[46]

What of the Soviet Union arming Nasser and then leaving him in the lurch? According to the British Embassy in Moscow, the Russian aim had always been predominantly political rather than military.[47] If the Russians could bring Egypt and other Middle Eastern countries into the orbit of Soviet influence, the United States would be increasingly isolated and vulnerable to the worldwide currents against the war in Vietnam. But the Russians never intended to sponsor Nasser's war against Israel – as proven by their inaction during the six-day conflict. One of the more bizarre theories was that the Russians depended on the

---

[44] Hadow to FCO, Confidential, 29 June 1967, FCO 17/526.
[45] Memorandum by Morris, 14 August 1967, FCO 17/498.
[46] R. M. Tesh (Cairo) to D. J. Speares (head of the North and East African Department), FCO 39/250.
[47] See the major assessment, "The Soviet Role in the Middle East Crisis," Confidential, 19 July 1967, FCO 17/498.

United States to restrain the Israelis and then believed themselves to be double-crossed when the Americans failed to do so.[48] In any event, according to Morris, Russian policy could only be explained by a monumental series of "mistakes and miscalculations."[49]

As an episode in British history and the history of the British Empire and Commonwealth, the June 1967 War is significant because of the revelation of the extent of British power in the 1960s. The British did not lack military strength. At the time of the outbreak of the war there were two aircraft carriers and supporting warships that would be able – in a manner reminiscent of the pre-1939 Singapore strategy – to mobilize in a period of seven or eight days. The carrier HMS *Victorious* was stationed at Malta, the HMS *Hermes* near Aden. They were accompanied by frigates and minesweepers. There were also Vulcan aircraft (large bombers) at Malta and fighters in Cyprus. This was not sufficient strength, in Wilson's phrase, "to go it alone" but neither were British military resources negligible. The real problem was political. The British encountered opposition to using their bases by the governments of Malta and Cyprus and by the rulers in the Gulf, especially in Bahrain. The British were in effect paralyzed.[50] Crossman summed it up: "the net effect of this tremendous Israeli victory has been to expose British impotence."[51]

Resolution 242 and the Balfour Declaration

Sometimes in a complicated story it helps to look forward to the end, thereby making clear some of the themes as well as the moral of the tale as contemporaries saw it. To those in the Foreign Office, those in Parliament, and the general public, Resolution 242 of 22 November 1967 was a British triumph, perhaps as significant in its own way as the

---

[48] According to Sir Patrick Dean (Ambassador in Washington), relating a conversation with Dean Rusk: "The Russians probably hoped, and expected, that the U.S., who they believed could control the Israelis completely, would in fact succeed in restraining them. The result might therefore well be that the Russians now thought that they had been double-crossed by the Americans just when they themselves hoped to double cross the Americans." Patrick Dean to FCO, Secret, 6 June 1967, FCO 17/493.

[49] Memorandum by Morris, 14 August 1967, FCO 17/498. True enough about misjudging Nasser, commented the embassy in Moscow, but "it would be ritualistically impossible, in any way other than by palace revolution, for the Soviet leadership to admit that they had been in error, that they had been committed beyond their capacities or that they had failed to meet their obligations." "Soviet Role in the Middle East Crisis," 19 July 1967.

[50] See, e.g., minute by C. E. Diggines, 1 June 1967, FCO 27/179.

[51] Crossman, *Diaries* (13 June 1967), 381.

Balfour Declaration fifty years earlier.[52] The comparison came easily enough because, in the same month that the Security Council passed the resolution, Crossman reflected on the meaning of Britain declaring support for a Jewish national home in Palestine. He spoke to a Zionist gathering in London on the fiftieth anniversary of the Balfour Declaration.

The events at the United Nations leading to Resolution 242 had unfolded from the time of the end of the war. The general view of UN debates, then as now, is that they would usually be pedantic and sterile. But in 1967 there was drama each step of the way. Resolution 242 was, in the Foreign Office post mortem:

A classical case of how a U.N. resolution must be steered through the Security Council, containing all the elements of advance preparation, care in drafting, timing of the initiative, lobbying in New York, lobbying in capitals, and even explanations of vote, as well as subtleties of U.N. procedure such as precedence of resolutions for voting purposes.[53]

The steady and determined course, in the view of the Foreign Office, was "because of Lord Caradon's expert hands."[54] Caradon summed up the aim: to give the Arabs "what they needed, a positive statement on the commitment on Israel to withdraw." And for the Israelis, "a clear declaration in favour of a permanent peace and security within recognised boundaries."[55] In view of the creative ambiguity of the drafting and the nuances of translation from the English into French and other languages, it is not at all surprising that Resolution 242 from the start meant different things to different people. Caradon often referred to it as a "balanced" resolution. It would be more accurate to say that it was as ambiguously balanced as the British could make it in order to get it through the Security Council.

For the British as well as the Israelis, the end of the year turned out to be quite different from a decade earlier in 1956, when Britain stood

---

[52] "Triumph" was the word used by George Brown while reporting to the Cabinet on Caradon's achievement. 23 November 1967, CC (67) 68th Conclusions. For Resolution 242 see, in addition to Bailey, *Making of Resolution 242*, a well-argued article, John McHugo, "Resolution 242," *International and Comparative Law Quarterly* 51 (October 2002); and Bruce D. Jones, "The Security Council and the Arab-Israeli Wars," in *The United Nations Security Council and War*, ed. Vaughan Lowe et al. (Oxford: Oxford University Press, 2008). The best contemporary account, invaluable for detail, is Arthur Lall, *The UN and the Middle East Crisis, 1967* (New York: Columbia University Press, 1968).

[53] Minute by T. F. Brenchley, 19 December 1967, FCO 17/516.

[54] Minute by P. H. Hayman, 17 November 1967, FCO 17/516.

[55] Caradon's summary, Confidential and Guard, 29 December 1967, FCO 17/516.

in the dock at the United Nations, supported only by Australia and New Zealand, while Israel faced universal demands to withdraw from the Sinai. "Greater Israel," as it was already known immediately after the June 1967 War, now extended from the Golan Heights along the River Jordan to the Gaza Strip and the Suez Canal. The Soviet Union demanded withdrawal from all occupied territories. But the Russians could not marshal sufficient votes in the General Assembly or avoid a veto in the Security Council. It proved impossible to forge a resolution calling for Israeli retreat, in part because of the difficulty or impossibility of finding an Arab consensus even on the issue of Israeli aggression.[56] Brown set a precedent in the General Assembly in June 1967 by warning Israel that the world community would never be reconciled to a unified Jerusalem under Israeli control. The British protest had lasting consequences. The new head of the Eastern Department, A. R. Moore (Morris's successor), recalled later: "The Israelis hold a grudge against H.M.G. because we were the first Western government to issue a warning about Israeli actions in Jerusalem after the June war.... We have done so because we believe that if the Israelis maintain their insistence on sovereignty over East Jerusalem, this will be an insuperable obstacle to an Arab-Israel settlement."[57]

The tension between Britain and Israel was reflected in the exchanges between the two governments and within the Wilson Cabinet. There was friction between the pro-Israeli prime minister and the pro-Arab foreign secretary.[58] Brown followed the Middle East crisis in detail, as is clear from his minutes and instructions. Gore-Booth later testified to the foreign secretary's "dynamic persistence in this initiative."[59] Yet the prime minister's hand can also be detected, as if a check on the foreign secretary's anti-Zionist inclination. In the caricature in *Yes, Prime Minister*, a character resembling Wilson bypasses his Arab-centric Foreign Office by following the advice of an Israeli ambassador. Good caricature contains an element of truth: this depiction was penned by Abba Eban's nephew.[60] In a labyrinthine way, the pattern of official behaviour eventually became

---

[56] "The passion and violence of the Arab speeches against Israel suggested that the will to settle on the Arab side did not begin to exist." Lesley Glass to FCO, Confidential, 9 August 1967, FCO 58/83.

[57] Minute by Moore, 9 August 1968, FCO 17/550.

[58] See Brown, *In My Way*, 169–70, 174, 182.

[59] Gore-Booth, *With Great Truth and Respect*, 369. But from the point of view of the UN Secretariat, Brown was "abysmally ignorant." Urquhart, *Ralph Bunche*, 412.

[60] See Jonathan Lynn (the nephew) and Antony Jay, *Yes Prime Minister*, series 1, episode 6, "A Victory for Democracy" (London: BBC, 1986).

lodged in popular culture – perhaps Eban's lasting mark on British public consciousness.

Eban had been Ambassador to the United Nations, then Ambassador to the United States. He was foreign minister during the era of the June 1967 War. He had a Cambridge background, as did Lord Caradon, and spoke in powerful and persuasive Churchillian cadences. He reached the height of his oratorical powers, and they were very considerable, in his speech to the United Nations vindicating Israel's conduct in June 1967. According to a contemporary American newspaper comment, "All of Israel's heritage seemed blended yesterday in the lyrical Churchillian cadences that Eban brought to the finest hour of his life."[61] Beyond the rhetoric, Eban believed, as increasingly did those within the British government, that prolonged occupation of the West Bank might sow the seeds of destruction for the state of Israel. It was also evident to the British that the longer the Israelis remained in place, the more their attitudes would harden. Eban's flexibility narrowed, though he once remarked that two good men from Cambridge could solve any problem. But he never forgot that Caradon reported to the foreign secretary in London.

There were two chronological parts in the run-up to Resolution 242. From the British perspective, they can be called the "George Brown months" from June to November followed by the critical eleven days in November when the Foreign Office unleashed Caradon. At both the Foreign Office and the delegation at the United Nations, the foreign secretary drew on expert advice. In London, Gore-Booth identified the key figures as Frank Brenchley, the supervising Under-Secretary, and Paul Hayman, the head of the UN department. Gore-Booth noted in August 1967 that the two of them had worked something "approaching a 24 hour day for $2\frac{1}{2}$ months."[62] In New York, Caradon's staff included Sir Lesley Glass, a former member of the Indian Civil Service who possessed indispensable contacts with representatives from India and other nonaligned states, and Peter Hope, perhaps the foremost British authority on Latin America.[63] The nonaligned states and the Latin American countries proved to be the key to the outcome on 22 November. Their representatives, according to

---

[61] On 17 June 1967: see Abba Eban, *Personal Witness: Israel through My Eyes* (New York: Putnam 1992), 436, quoting James Wechsler in the *New York Post*.

[62] Minute by Gore-Booth, 3 August 1967, FCO 58/83.

[63] Glass later became High Commissioner in Nigeria. Hope later became ambassador to Mexico and in 1972 was appointed to the Order of the Aztec Eagle, Mexico's highest award to a foreign citizen.

Glass, were in almost "permanent conclave."[64] With the Security Council polarized between the United States and the Soviet Union, the nonaligned and Latin American states refused to follow the lead of either.

Nor did it appear clear that a British initiative stood any chance of success, at least as long as Brown tried to micromanage from London. There were moments of hope, however. In the aftermath of an Arab summit meeting in Khartoum, it appeared that some Arab states, at least, might be willing to make progress towards a political settlement. During a British mission to Washington, it seemed that the Americans and British could work together towards the reopening of the Suez Canal, a British priority. In July, President Johnson met with Premier Kosygin in Glassboro, New Jersey. They came to a sufficient enough understanding for the American and Soviet representatives at the United Nations to try to reach an accord (in what became known as the Gromyko-Goldberg formula). None of these initiatives led to breaking the deadlock, in part because the Americans, at least in the British view, were playing a long hand.[65] The longer the stalemate, the more secure would be the entrenched Israeli position. If anyone were to seize the initiative, in Brown's view, it would be the American Ambassador to the United Nations, Arthur Goldberg, "a *real* politician."[66]

Brown's own inclination was to restore Britain's relations with the Arab states, not least for the powerful reason that the disruption of oil and the continued closure of the Suez Canal contributed to Britain's ongoing financial crisis (which would lead to devaluation in the same month as Resolution 242).[67] Brown wanted above all to repair relations with Egypt. He chose as Ambassador, Sir Harold Beeley, an excellent appointment, but the Israelis recalled immediately that Beeley had been Bevin's adviser

---

[64] Glass to FCO, Confidential, 9 August 1967, FCO 58/83.

[65] According to Caradon, "The Americans . . . seemed to be in no hurry." Caradon to FCO, Confidential and Guard, 29 December 1967, FCO 17/516.

[66] Thus in the judgement of the Foreign Secretary, the locus of American power lay in New York with Goldberg, not in Washington with Dean Rusk (Brown's minute of c. 11 October 1967, FCO 17/529). But this view should be contrasted with that of Lesley Glass in New York, who held that Goldberg's effectiveness was compromised because other representatives identified him with the Israeli cause: "One picture stands out," Glass wrote in reflecting on the debates in the summer of 1967, "the stricken face of Mr. Goldberg, profoundly vulnerable in this dispute, when taunted by the Syrian delegate as being the representative of Israel rather than of the United States" (Glass to FCO, Confidential, 9 August 1967, FCO 58/84).

[67] See the concluding chapter in Steven G. Galpern, "The Devaluation of 1967 and the End of Empire," *Money, Oil, and Empire in the Middle East: Sterling and Postwar Imperialism, 1944–1971* (Cambridge: Cambridge University Press, 2009).

in 1947 and 1948 and thus ranked high in Jewish demonology.[68] By early November 1967, the chances for breaking the deadlock appeared to Caradon to have hit "rock bottom."

By this stage of his career, Caradon was recognized as a UN personality, comparable with one of his predecessors, the inimitable Sir Gladwyn Jebb, who had become a celebrity on American television because of his witty and eloquent denunciation of the Soviet Union. The word *Caradonian* signified total commitment to the cause of the United Nations. Caradon was a man of good will and indestructible optimism. Describing his tactics at the United Nations, he once wrote that he would fight on the resolutions, in the corridors, and in the committees; he would never abstain.[69] But he had complex characteristics. He was vain and egocentric, though in a congenial sort of way. He could be a hard taskmaster while he always took care graciously to acknowledge the work of his staff. He could be engaging and persuasive, even deferential and flattering, while leaving no doubt that he was on top of his case. The full force of the Caradonian cause became apparent to all concerned in November 1967.

Caradon's aims and the sequence of events can be briefly related. He worked towards the solution of five problems: (1) the reopening of the Suez Canal; (2) the question of the refugees, which now numbered more than one hundred thousand in Jordan alone; (3) the future of arms control; (4) the issue of the occupied territories; and (5) the appointment of a UN envoy representing the Secretary-General. The first three points were ongoing business. In final form, the critical passages of Resolution 242 dealt mainly with points four and five. The appointment of an envoy proved to be relatively easy.[70] The problem of the occupied territories and Jerusalem was another matter.

Caradon began by crafting a resolution calling for Israeli withdrawal from the occupied territories in return for Arab recognition of the state of Israel and secure boundaries. The initial Israeli response, in Caradon's

---

[68] By mid-October 1967 the abrasive exchanges between Israel and Britain had broken into a public quarrel. According to the *Sunday Telegraph*, the Israelis suspected Beeley "of over sympathy with the Arab cause... the Israelis are in a fighting mood because they consider the British swung over to an emotive pro-Arab stand at the United Nations." Cutting of 15 October 1967 in FCO 17/529.

[69] See Louis, "Public Enemy Number One," *Ends of British Imperialism*, 705.

[70] For the appointment of Gunnar Jarring of Sweden as UN special representative, see Brenchley, *Britain, the Six-Day War, and Its Aftermath*, ch. 8, "Gunnar Jarring's Mission Impossible."

words, was "immediate and strongly averse." Nor was the preliminary Arab response any more encouraging. Caradon then began to shift to a positive formula that all parties in their own self-interest could embrace. But in the meantime, there were other proposed resolutions that reflected the composition of the Security Council, which in addition to the permanent members included India, Brazil, Argentina, Nigeria, and Mali. India, Nigeria, and Mali represented the nonaligned countries, though each with a voice of its own. Mali, for example, often voted with the Soviet Union. Argentina and Brazil represented the Latin American bloc. Goldberg held out, hoping that a U.S.-USSR formula might still be possible. The Soviet representative, Vasili Vasilyevich Kuznetsov, proposed immediate and total withdrawal and an end to Israeli aggression but failed to gain sufficient support. Yet, as will be seen, Kuznetsov played a critical part in the outcome. In the meantime, Argentina and Brazil put forward a draft resolution that, Caradon believed, would be unacceptable to the Israelis. The Foreign Office exerted pressure in Buenos Aires and Rio as well as in New York, where Caradon had the help of Peter Hope.

The Latin American countries eventually agreed to support Caradon's resolution.[71] Goldberg threw his weight behind it when it became clear that a United States or U.S.-USSR resolution had no chance. The real danger came from the Indian delegation. An Indian draft resolution proved to be "more Arab than the Arabs" and had considerable support because of growing indignation against Israel. Only through the supreme effort of Wilson, writing directly to the Indian prime minister, did the British manage to get the Indian resolution withdrawn. Caradon summed it up in a slightly self-congratulatory way: "We had survived first the opposition of the Israelis, then that of the Russians, then the diversion proposed by the Latin Americans, and lastly the intervention of the Indians." Then he wrote, "We were home."[72] Fifteen unanimous hands went up in favour of Resolution 242. Or, to be more precise, fourteen hands plus one index finger.

---

[71] "Peter Hope's personal good relations with the Latin Americans were most valuable at this time." Glass to Hayman, Secret, 25 November 1967, FCO 17/516.

[72] Caradon to FCO, Confidential and Guard, 29 December 1967, FCO 17/516. The Israeli Ambassador to the United Nations, Gideon Rafael, commented later on Caradon's piecing together different parts of the puzzle with "bits of the defunct Gromyko-Goldberg formula, seasoned with ingredients of a forgotten Latin-American draft and topped with the idea of appointing a special United Nations representative to act as mediator." Gideon Rafael, *Destination Peace: Three Decades of Israeli Foreign Policy* (New York: Stein and Day, 1981), 185.

With the raising of a single finger begins a story within the story, though it can be told in short. Kuznetsov was the Soviet deputy minister of foreign affairs. Though working in concert with his masters in Moscow, he had discretionary authority, which he used to the advantage of the United Nations as well as the self-interest of the Soviet Union. Neither of the superpowers wanted confrontation in the Middle East. Goldberg and Kuznetsov found common ground in the formula arrived at by Johnson and Gromyko in Glassboro (thus allowing Goldberg to claim consistency in American policy and actual authorship of Resolution 242). The vote was scheduled for 20 November.[73] Kuznetsov requested a delay of two days. Caradon was sceptical, believing that he would again try to rally votes for a more radical proposal, but Kuznetsov assured him of something quite different. The delay gave Kuznetsov time to consolidate the pro-Soviet, neutralist, and Latin American factions behind the British draft resolution. Caradon always believed that the Russian support of the resolution was decisive.

The resolution carried because Caradon dropped the definite article "the" before "occupied territories," thereby making the resolution minimally acceptable to the Israelis and by offering something other than total defeat to the Arabs.[74] The critical part of Resolution 242 reads:

(1) Withdrawal of Israeli armed forces from territories occupied in the recent conflict;
(2) Termination of all claims of states of belligerency and respect for and acknowledgment of the sovereignty, territorial integrity and political independence of every State in the area and their right to live in peace within secure and recognized boundaries free from threats or acts or force.

It makes for a remarkable study in ambiguity, not least because the French version of the clause reads: *Retrait des forces armées israéliennes des territoires occupés lors du récent conflit.* French is one of the official languages of the United Nations. Which version should prevail, "territories" or "*des territoires*"? There were further discrepancies in the Russian and Spanish

---

73 For these intricate discussion see especially Arthur Lall, *The UN and the Middle East Crisis, 1967* (New York: Columbia University Press), ch. 14. Lall's work is indispensable for its comprehensive and accurate account of the developments leading up to the passing of Resolution 242.

74 "It was the American decision to support our draft Resolution in New York which brought about the marked change in the Israeli attitude to it." Minute by J. C. Moberly, 29 November 1967, FCO17/526.

versions. Caradon believed there could be no doubt: "Since the resolution was a British resolution it is of course the British text which prevails."[75]

The Arabs later believed they had been betrayed. They assumed that "occupied territories" meant every inch of land taken by the Israelis during the course of the war. Caradon certainly did not misrepresent the draft wording, but neither did he emphasize the significance of dropping the definite article "the." If not in the tradition of perfidious Albion, the draft resolution in its various phases eventually seemed, to the Arabs at least, to be reminiscent of the contradictory promises made during World War I. Or, to use a phrase that comes to mind when describing the assurances given by Caradon to the Arabs, to some extent he may have fudged it – but it should be added that Kuznetsov and Goldberg as well as Caradon assumed at the time that there would be complete withdrawal except for minor border adjustments.[76]

What of Caradon's casket with the flag of the PLO draped over it, and does it have a bearing on his aims in 1967? Did Caradon harbour a secret allegiance to the PLO? The short answer is that it was Caradon's son Paul who was responsible for the flag. Paul Foot had been born in Palestine in 1937. He was a British Trotskyite. He espoused the cause of the PLO as part of his revolutionary philosophy.[77] The flag signified his own extreme position on the British left. He embraced the cause of permanent revolution – with a remnant of upper-class *joie de vivre*. He proposed to offer his friends a glass of champagne before they were shot. I doubt very much if his father would have approved of the flag over the casket. But the longer answer is complicated. Caradon did have pro-Arab sympathy going back to his days in the Palestine administration in Nablus. He was ahead of his time, at least for a figure of his stature in the international community, in becoming a spokesman for the possibility of a Palestinian state in the decade after 1967. He believed it should

[75] Lord Caradon, Arthur J. Goldberg, Mohamed H. El-Zayyat, and Abba Eban, *U. N. Security Council Resolution 242: A Case Study in Diplomatic Ambiguity* (Washington, DC: Georgetown University, Institute for the Study of Diplomacy, 1981), 7.

[76] Caradon later defended himself against criticism of deceiving the Arabs by maintaining that everyone at the time except the Israelis assumed that there would be virtual withdrawal from all of the occupied territories: "We all took it for granted that the occupied territory would be restored to Jordan ... we all assumed that East Jerusalem would revert to Jordan" (Caradon et al., *U.N. Security Council Resolution 242*, 13–14). For a balanced account in the larger context of the Middle East, see Charles D. Smith, *Palestine and the Arab-Israeli Conflict*, 3rd ed. (New York: St. Martins, 1996), esp. 212–13.

[77] See Richard Ingrams, *My Friend Footy* (London: Private Eye, 2005).

consist of a demilitarized region including the West Bank, Gaza, and Arab Jerusalem. "There is no possibility at all of peace if Arab Jerusalem is not under Arab sovereignty."[78] He regarded the PLO as the legitimate voice of the Palestinians. But Caradon's support for the PLO was post-1967. At the time, he was universally acclaimed for his balance and fairness to Israelis and Palestinians. If he had died in November 1967, it would have been a UN flag that adorned his casket.

What of Heath's condemnation of Caradon in 1971 as a traitor to his country? Heath probably had in mind the right-wing Tory view of commitment to the United Nations and African independence. He had a high regard for Caradon. But Heath liked to twit his interlocutors. He enjoyed malicious irony. Sometimes irony is misunderstood. In this case, his comment seemed to reveal more about Heath than about Caradon. Heath not only could be insensitive but also oblivious to the possibility of a lighthearted remark causing great offence. In this case, virtually everyone dismissed it as nonsense.

The ideological tension within the British government did not involve Caradon but rather Crossman and Brown. From June onwards, Crossman no longer believed, as he had earlier, in Brown's integrity. Brown was "in a bad patch again," in other words frequently drunk, and, in Crossman's judgement, unstable and erratic.[79] Brown consistently warned of the danger of prolonged Israeli occupation of the West Bank and the takeover of Arab Jerusalem. He had managed to block the suggestion that Crossman go to Israel to celebrate the anniversary of the Balfour Declaration. Instead Postmaster General Edward Short (Lord Glenamara) represented the British government at the festivity in Jerusalem.[80] In Brown's view, Short was preferable because he was a much more minor political figure

---

[78] Sharabi, "Interview with Lord Caradon," 143. Caradon became increasingly critical of Israel in later years. In 1981 he stated: "These actions of the Israeli Government are in clear defiance of the Resolution 242. They constitute an open rejection of the policy so widely supported in 1967. They are in effect an endeavor to annex all the Arab lands of East Jerusalem, the West Bank and Gaza in an expanded Israel, and to condemn the Palestinian people to permanent subject or exile." Caradon et al., *U.N. Security Council Resolution 242*, 11.

[79] Crossman, *Diaries* (23 June 1967), 395.

[80] The Israelis shifted the location from Tel Aviv to Jerusalem, in part, the British suspected, to emphasize the new status of Arab Jerusalem as part of Israel. Frank Brenchley noted: "As usual, the Israelis have played a fast one on us" (Minute of 4 October 1967, FCO 17/604). Edward Short later served as Lord President of the Council and Leader of the House of Commons in the Labour government of 1974. He was succeeded by Caradon's brother, Michael Foot.

than Crossman yet was acceptable to the Israelis because he was a committed Zionist. But Brown could not prevent Crossman from giving the
keynote address at the Zionist celebration in London on 4 November. He
suggested that Crossman speak in a private capacity rather than as President of the Council and Leader of the House of Commons – a proposal
that made Crossman "wild with anger."[81] The foreign secretary did insist
successfully that Crossman delete two passages. Otherwise Brown threw
up his hands in exasperation, saying that he could not write Crossman's
speech for him.

Crossman prepared the address with great care, believing it to be one
of the most important public statements of his entire career. His argument
was that the Balfour Declaration was "the most unsordid act in history."
He offered an historical analysis, which was not uncritical of the motives
and decisions of the Lloyd George government in 1917. Crossman had
as his guide the recently published volume by Leonard Stein, *The Balfour
Declaration* (1961), which remains today the historiographical point of
departure. Curiously enough, Crossman attached importance to the part
played by Lord Milner in the drafting of the document, thus revealing
the view that the Jews would be British collaborators, keeping out the
French and helping to secure the Suez Canal. Crossman discussed the historical reality as it appeared to those examining the published evidence in
1967. Some of his audience must have been impressed with the historical
sweep of his comment when it ranged from the Russian revolution to the
question of Jews in Germany and to the attitude of the U.S. government.

There was nothing original in Crossman's historical analysis. Nor was
there any surprise at the conclusion, in Crossman's words, that the Balfour
Declaration "remains one of the greatest acts of western statesmanship
in the 20th Century." Nor did anyone in the Foreign Office, not even
Brown, object to this line of interpretation, which was clearly aimed at a
Zionist audience. What is of interest is the passage about the Middle East
that the Foreign Office insisted on deleting:

I myself wholly welcome the end of Britain's suzerainty in the area. It was already
outdated in 1945. If only Attlee and Bevin had decided to wind up our Middle
Eastern empire as completely and unconditionally as we withdrew from India, if
only they had realized the futility of military bases maintained against national
aspirations!

But thank heavens the process of decolonisation is accelerating. The Aden
commitment is now being wound up and we can all be sure that the withdrawal

---

[81] Crossman, *Diaries* (3 November 1967), 553.

from this enormously expensive military base will not only increase the security of our oil supplies but also enable us to make our claim to neutrality in the Jewish/Arab conflict more convincing.[82]

The British had still not withdrawn from the Gulf, which supplied more than 70 percent of British oil. Thus the Foreign Office insisted on the deletion. Crossman lost the chance for a revenge of sorts against Attlee and Bevin, but it is obvious from his diary that he regarded the speech as a success. "A classic oration," he noted.[83]

One thing was certainly clear as a consequence of Crossman's speech. The Balfour Declaration had lost none of its symbolic significance. In the Foreign Office there had been a pertinent comment. Thomson, who tried to check Crossman when his name was proposed earlier in the year, pointed out that the Balfour Declaration remained "at the very heart of Arab distrust" of British motives. "It continues to be a very powerful emotive symbol for the Arabs of Britain's responsibility for the creation of the State of Israel."[84]

Fifty years after the Balfour Declaration, the state of Israel in 1967 controlled more than three times the amount of territory than in the previous year. The British concluded that there had been no master plan on the part of the Israelis. The dynamic of the war had produced the results. Jerusalem was the unsought prize. According to Michael Hadow in Tel Aviv, there was no overarching plan or even deception, but rather a change of heart after the conquest: "There was a complete reversal of policy. Nor do the Israelis attempt to advance any but the most trivial justification for the reversal. A guilty conscience and the dictates of self-interest are masked behind a defiant attitude of self-righteousness." Hadow offered an acute comment on the future of "greater Israel":

The proponents of "greater Israel" oppose negotiations, since they feel these can only lead to Israel making concessions. . . . They accept the danger of fast-breeding Arabs swamping the Jewishness of Israel and seem to contemplate some sort of colonial status for the territories. . . . The Israelis will remain entrenched in their present position for years to come.[85]

---

[82] Crossman's speech and the exchange about the deleted passages are in FCO 17/606 and FCO 17/607.

[83] Crossman, *Diaries* (11 November 1967), 567.

[84] Minute by Thomson, 6 February 1967. George Brown had noted, "I agree." FCO 17/604.

[85] Hadow to FCO, Confidential, 16 January 1968, FCO 17/468.

Hadow's counterpart in Amman, Sir Philip Adams, made an equally interesting comment about the Israelis and Jordan, and about the future: "the Israelis do not care tuppence for King Hussein, and we must assume that his survival is of minimal importance to them. . . . Perhaps we are wrong in thinking Israel is averse to a long period of tension and hostilities on her borders."[86]

The 1967 War brought about a shift in sentiment among British intellectuals and politicians in favour of the Palestine Arabs, or, as they were now more frequently called, the Palestinians. The war occurred during the time that the historic reputation of the British Empire reached its nadir and anticolonial sentiment at the United Nations soared to new heights. Above all the aftermath of the war in Britain led to devaluation and an increasingly acute sense of national decline. Yet there was vitality as well as unease and new preoccupations. The swinging London of the 1960s marked a new era. The changing mood included public amnesia about the British Empire and the Balfour Declaration. Part of Crossman's purpose in speaking on the declaration's fiftieth anniversary was to provide a sharp and positive reminder of Britain's ongoing responsibility for helping to create the state of Israel.

[86] Adams to Sir Denis Allen, Secret, 2 April 1968, FCO 17/550.

10

France and the June 1967 War

Jean-Pierre Filiu

The Israeli-Arab war of June 1967 was a crucial turning point for French diplomacy. The condemnation of the Israeli offensive jeopardized the "best ally" status France had enjoyed in Israel since 1948, even though the much-debated "arms embargo" was not effective until 1969 and Tsahal ultimately won the war with French weaponry. But Charles de Gaulle's opposition to Israel's use of force earned him tremendous prestige in the Arab world, allowing Franco-Arab relations to turn the page on the Suez Crisis and the Algeria war. It was also the launching pad of France's so-called Arab policy, which complemented French opposition to the Vietnam War and the country's withdrawal from North Atlantic Treaty Organization (NATO) military command. This "third way" diplomacy was strongly supported in France by the nationalist right wing and the Communist Party.

De Gaulle took power in May 1958 and founded the Fifth Republic. The main challenge facing him was the war that had been raging in Algeria since 1954, a war that had led the last governments of the Fourth Republic to consider Arab nationalism an archenemy. During the Suez Crisis during the fall of 1956, Guy Mollet's France was much more committed to the Israeli alliance than Anthony Eden's Great Britain. The political failure of that military offensive against Egypt had triggered anti-French riots all over the Middle East and the severing of diplomatic relations with France by the Arab states (with the exception of Lebanon). In the aftermath of such a disaster, Mollet felt a moral duty to safeguard Israel's security, and he ordered a secret cooperation programme in the field of nuclear technology. In addition, France remained the main military supplier of the Jewish state, and together they developed advanced aeronautical and even ballistic projects.

De Gaulle, a great admirer of the Zionist pioneers and an early supporter of the Jewish state, twice welcomed David Ben-Gurion on official visits to Paris.[1] On 14 June 1960, the French president praised the Israeli prime minister as "one of the greatest statesmen of this century."[2] On 6 June 1961, de Gaulle celebrated Israel as "our friend, our ally."[3] The contracts concluded by the Fourth Republic regarding the delivery of sophisticated aircraft were fulfilled, and Israel acquired twenty Super-Mystères after 1959 and seventy-two Mirage IIICs from 1961 to 1967. De Gaulle's government went further and agreed to sell to Israel, in 1965, Super Frelon helicopters and, in 1966, the new generation of Mirage Vs. Regarding nuclear cooperation, France agreed, on 21 February 1961, to supply Israel with 385 tons of uranium over a period of ten years on the condition that the processed uranium be delivered back to France. This is how the Dimona nuclear plant became active in July 1966. The United States, wary of the military dimension of such a programme, monitored this French-Israeli cooperation.[4]

With the Arab world, the main turning point in French relations was the independence of Algeria, on 5 July 1962, which led to the progressive resumption of diplomatic ties between France and the Middle Eastern states. De Gaulle welcomed his Jordanian, Lebanese, and Algerian counterparts to Paris before Egyptian Vice-President Abd al-Hakim Amer visited France on an official trip in October 1966. The French leader never missed an opportunity to stress the historical ties between his country and the Arab world, and he spoke emotionally and positively about Arab culture and civilization.[5] Although de Gaulle considered Mollet's alignment with Israel to have been a strategic mistake, he did not want to replicate the same mistake by switching to the Arab side. Instead, he tried

---

[1] Samy Cohen, "Que voulait de Gaulle?" *Les Nouveaux cahiers* 35 (Winter 1973–4), 30–1.
[2] Michel Bar Zohar, *Ben Gourion, le prophète armé* [Ben Gourion, the armed prophet] (Paris: Fayard, 1966), 355–6.
[3] *Le Monde*, 8 June 1961.
[4] Memorandum from the French Ministry of Foreign Affairs, 20 May 1967, in *Documents diplomatiques français* [hereinafter referred to as *DDF*], 1967, vol. 1 (Paris: Ministère des Affaires Ètrangères, 2008), 525–6.
[5] Samir Kassir and Farouk Mardam-Bey, *Itinéraires de Paris à Jérusalem, la France et le conflit israélo-arabe* [Itineraries from Paris to Jerusalem, France and the Israeli-Arab conflict], 1958–91, vol. 2 (Paris: Les Livres de la Revue d'études palestiniennes, 1993), 38–42.

to restore France's stature in the Middle East by staying conspicuously neutral in the Israeli-Arab dispute.

De Gaulle advocated full implementation of the UN resolutions regarding the conflict in the Middle East and kept pushing for a consensus among the four permanent members of the UN Security Council, the United States, the USSR, the United Kingdom, and France, the so-called Four Powers. This was certainly a way to assert French clout in the international arena, but the proposal stemmed logically from de Gaulle's strategic analysis: the Middle East crisis was a sideshow of the main Cold War conflict, raging in Indo-China, where he believed the American forces could never achieve victory, and France had to avert the serious risk of a third world war by working through the United Nations and ensuring cooperation among the Four Powers.[6] This is how France's attitude towards the Middle East in 1967 fell in line with the rest of its foreign policy, namely de Gaulle's criticism of America regarding the Vietnam War and French withdrawal from NATO military command. This more independent stand was increasingly supported in France by the Communist Party, while it generated heated debates among the ruling right wing, pitting the nationalist faction against the pro–United States one.

May 1967: The Warnings

On 8 and 9 May in Beirut, Secretary-General of the Ministry of Foreign Affairs Hervé Alphand chaired a meeting of the French ambassadors in the Middle East. He then travelled to Syria and Egypt, where he saw at first hand the mounting fears of the Arab regimes. On 10 May, Alphand was received in Damascus by Ibrahim Makhos, the Deputy Prime Minister in charge of foreign affairs. The Syrian official vented his anger at a United States–led "conspiracy" aimed at "strangling" the "progressive Arab states" by encouraging its regional proxies, the "reactionary states" and Israel. Algeria was already the target of such a conspiracy, with Morocco and Tunisia implementing U.S. plots. Damascus was also the victim of "American imperialism," and "Jordan was helping Israel to prepare a new attack" against Syria by concentrating its troops on the Syrian border rather than the Israeli one.[7] Makhos blamed generous U.S.

---

[6] Henry Laurens, "La diplomatie française dans le conflit israélo-arabe, 1967–70," conference at the Collège de France, Paris, 1 October 2008.

[7] Message from the French Ambassador in Damascus, 11 May 1967, in *DDF*, 1967, vol. 1, 488.

military aid to Israel for the fact that Syria had had to acquire expensive Soviet armaments, with two-thirds of the government's budget absorbed by the Ministry of Defence. When Makhos lamented that French-built Mirages had bombed Syrian territory, Alphand answered that "Syrians could also acquire this kind of armament," which was sold on "a commercial basis, not a political one."[8]

The French diplomat heard the same kind of rhetoric in Cairo, where he stayed from 11 to 14 May. Egyptian leaders echoed the Syrian attacks against Jordan, which were alleged as trying to "topple the regime in Damascus."[9] They criticized the U.S. permanent policy of "interference," but they were even harsher on the United Kingdom, especially because of its refusal to deal with the nationalist factions in Aden. They also wanted to know more about French cooperation with Israel in the nuclear field. Alphand reassured them that this cooperation was purely "scientific and industrial" and that "all the steps had been taken to prevent an extension of this cooperation to the military dimensions of atom."[10] Alphand was eventually received by President Gamal Abdel Nasser, who pledged to defend Syria against Israeli "aggression."[11]

Paris monitored very closely the Egyptian initiatives of the following days: the sending of additional troops into the Sinai, the mobilization of the military hierarchy, and, most importantly, the demand on 18 May that UN forces withdraw from the border with Israel. The French Ambassador in Cairo commented that "such war mongering would have been more discreet if a conflict was indeed feared," but he underlined the fact that the situation could now get out of "control."[12] The Quai d'Orsay believed that President Nasser was desperately trying to deter an Israeli offensive against "his new and practically only ally in the Arab world," but this gamble on Syria appeared extremely risky.[13] French envoys were therefore instructed to preach moderation in Damascus as well as in Cairo and Tel Aviv.

Paris repeatedly asked Moscow to rein in the Syrian leaders because any infiltration of Palestinian guerrillas from Syria into Israel could trigger a major conflict. But Soviet officials rejected this logic and placed all responsibility for the escalating crisis on Israel . . . and the United States.

---

[8] Ibid., 489.
[9] Message from the French Ambassador in Cairo, 16 May 1967, in ibid., 496.
[10] Ibid., 497.
[11] Ibid., 503.
[12] Message from the French Ambassador in Cairo, 17 May 1967, in ibid., 507.
[13] Note from the Sous-direction du Levant, 23 May 1967, in ibid., 543.

Paris was even informed that the Soviet Ambassador in Tel Aviv was blaming "CIA agents" for the tension between Israel and Syria.[14] Despite this frustrating response from the USSR, France kept pushing for a quadripartite move in the Middle East in which Washington, London, Moscow, and Paris would join forces to avoid war at all cost. The Quai d'Orsay refused, therefore, to close ranks with the State Department and the Foreign Office, which were pushing for tripartite initiatives at the United Nations and in the region, a move that would fatally antagonize the Soviets.

France also had a hard time trying to deflect the devastating impact of Cairo's feverish propaganda. After an Egyptian newspaper boasted about "non-conventional weapons" being deployed in the Sinai Peninsula, on 22 May Washington asked Paris to substantiate those allegations. The United States argued that the Egyptians had previously used gas warfare in Yemen, and Israel demanded its American ally send an urgent supply of gas masks.[15] In such a volatile context, the Quai d'Orsay interpreted the Egyptian decision to enforce a blockade on the Straits of Tiran on 23 May as a potential *casus belli*.[16] In less than a week, President Nasser had dismantled the security measures established in the aftermath of the Suez Crisis (UN forces on the border and free navigation in the Gulf of Aqaba) in order to ensure Israeli withdrawal from the Sinai and Gaza. In 1957, France was the most vocal ally of Israel in the international arena and supported the Israeli claim that any breach of the Suez settlement would justify "self-defence." The United States had never gone as far in that regard. The Egyptian blockade put France in a very awkward position and strengthened the validity of the Israeli arguments.

On 19 May, de Gaulle had been asked by Prime Minister Levi Eshkol to publicly commit France to defend Israel's territorial integrity, and this message was reiterated with greater intensity on 23 May. Israeli Minister of Foreign Affairs Abba Eban argued passionately for his country's right of "resistance" when de Gaulle welcomed him on 24 May, during a stopover in Paris on his way to Washington.[17] The French president warned him against any "outbreak of hostilities," insisting that such an event would plainly mean "opening fire."[18] Meanwhile, the French Ambassador in Cairo was told that the Egyptian blockade was limited to

[14] Message from the French Ambassador in Washington, 20 May 1967, in ibid., 524.
[15] Message from the French Ambassador in Washington, 22 May 1967, in ibid., 528.
[16] Note from the Sous-direction du Levant, 23 May 1967, in ibid., 545.
[17] Kassir and Mardam-Bey, *Itinéraires de Paris à Jérusalem*, vol. 2, 58.
[18] Ibid.

Israeli ships and strategic supplies, including oil, but that civilian vessels and food supplies would be allowed through the straits. The Egyptian Minister of Foreign Affairs made an interesting distinction between a hypothetical Israeli attempt to lift the blockade on the Gulf of Aqaba, which would be considered an act of "aggression," and an attempt by any other state to ship energy or military supplies to Israel, which would be considered evidence only of an "unfriendly" attitude. De Gaulle summoned the Egyptian Ambassador in Paris on 25 May and warned him that "a war would be disastrous for Egypt."[19] French envoys in Washington, London, and Moscow were instructed to try again to foster a quadripartite initiative and a joint call for peace, but the move was once more frustrated by Soviet obstruction. The Quai d'Orsay feared that the USSR was willing to gamble on a "limited military confrontation between Israel and its neighbours" as a way to "strengthen its hold over its clients."[20]

The Four Powers format was the French formula for bringing the Soviets in, but also for neutralizing Anglo-Saxon military initiatives. British Prime Minister Harold Wilson was secretly urging foreign powers to join a "naval escort" aimed at monitoring freedom of navigation in the Gulf of Aqaba, and according to London, Canada, the Netherlands, Norway, Denmark, and Argentina had agreed to join this force. Washington was pushing for this naval escort as the only way to deter Israel from unilateral action. But U.S. officials were also worried about the sustainability of Israel's defence apparatus. The State Department shared that concern with the French ambassador: "If a war starts, French military supply to Israel will become a pressing and crucial issue, since Israel depends mainly on France for the maintenance of its armaments. The American side is studying what can be done in that regard."[21]

In answer to Eshkol's call for active French solidarity with Israel, de Gaulle tried one more time to ease tensions. On 27 May, he wrote to the Israeli prime minister:

It is to be feared that in the region at the centre of which lies Israel, the suddenly tense and worrying situation could deteriorate into an armed conflict. Nothing could justify [the idea] that this evolution would be in the interest of any of the

[19] Minutes from the meeting between Charles de Gaulle and the Egyptian Ambassador, 25 May 1967, in *DDF*, 1967, vol. 1, 559.
[20] Note from the Sous-direction du Levant, 23 May 1967, in ibid., 547.
[21] Message from the French Ambassador in Washington, 24 May 1967, in ibid., 553.

parties involved. It is not up to me to say that such is the case for Israel: your message is the most authoritative proof of it. And it seems to be that this is also true for Syria and Egypt.[22]

The French president went on pleading in favour of the quadripartite approach and rejected implicitly the presence of any naval escort in the Gulf of Aqaba, saying no outside power should "take sides" in the crisis. The words were chosen extremely carefully in order to be noncommittal.

From Paris, Eban proceeded to Washington to meet with President Lyndon Johnson and Secretary of State Dean Rusk. The French ambassador in Washington was convinced that the Israeli minister had failed to secure all the "commitments expected in Tel Aviv." Johnson was "wavering," caught as he was between "different tendencies": the Jewish community and the state of New York were pushing for unconditional support for Israel, while powerful congressmen from the South instead preferred to provide "moral support" and let France and the United Kingdom take the lead in any "operation." The French envoy added that "if the situation evolves rapidly and if the state of Israel enters directly into military action, it is quite difficult to predict exactly what will be the US position."[23]

Paris was questioning U.S. resolve but was also increasingly anxious about the Soviet attitude. According to the French ambassador in Moscow, "at the beginning of the crisis, the Russians were seeking only to protect the Syrian regime," but the withdrawal of UN forces from the Egyptian-Israeli border, and then the closure of the Straits of Tiran, "had caught the Soviets off-guard." Because "any settlement acceptable to all parties will compel Egypt to back down, more or less openly, on the issue of navigation, serious problems for the Soviets loom ahead." The French envoy doubted whether Moscow even had a plan for getting its Egyptian ally out of this trap. He only believed that the USSR would, in the Middle East as in Vietnam, "try to avoid direct involvement."[24] Paris kept pushing for a quadripartite approach, but Soviet diplomats now argued that "open US and UK support for Israel" left no room for a genuine coordination.[25]

---

[22] Charles de Gaulle to Levi Eshkol, 27 May 1967, in ibid., 570.
[23] Message from the French Ambassador in Washington, 27 May 1967, in ibid., 567.
[24] Message from the French Ambassador in Moscow, 28 May 1967, in ibid., 574–575.
[25] Message from the French Ambassador in Moscow, 28 May 1967, in ibid., 573.

On 28 May, Soviet Prime Minister Alexei Kosygin wrote to de Gaulle about the crisis in the Middle East. He rejected any Four Powers solution, putting all the blame on the U.S. administration:

> It is now up to the US to let the extremist circles in Israel decide whether they will cross the dangerous line. We expressed our concerns to Prime Minister Wilson. We are in permanent contact with the governments of Egypt and Syria. They display moderation, and we know they do not want an armed conflict. Their actions are defensive ones.[26]

De Gaulle carefully noted this position and answered that he could only "regret" this negative answer to his quadripartite proposal.[27] The French envoy at the United Nations was informed of the Soviet position but was also instructed to continue to avoid any tripartite agreement with his American and British colleagues.[28]

Avoiding the Worst in June 1967

Paris feared that the deepening rift between Washington and Moscow would affect the Security Council. The French Ambassador at the United Nations was not empowered to vote in favour of any resolution to ensure freedom of navigation in the Gulf of Aqaba. Abstention was the only option envisioned by French Minister of Foreign Affairs Maurice Couve de Murville, a former Ambassador in Cairo.[29] In the same spirit, France refused to endorse a draft declaration of the "Maritime powers," which was presented by the American and British ambassadors to the Quai d'Orsay on 1 June. Hervé Alphand made clear to the allied envoys, received individually, that any suggestion of military action, even if only implicit in such a text, would prove counterproductive in the tense climate prevailing in the Middle East.[30] France wanted to keep all channels open in order to prevent the outbreak of a conflict.

Although the Anglo-Saxon move was rebuffed at the Ministry of Foreign Affairs, de Gaulle received Ibrahim Makhos. The Syrian deputy

---

[26] Letter from Alexei Kosygin to Charles de Gaulle, dated 27 May, but conveyed on 28 May 1967, in ibid., 578.

[27] Letter from Charles de Gaulle to Alexei Kosygin, 28 May 1967, in ibid., 579.

[28] Message from the French Minister of Foreign Affairs to the French permanent representative at the United Nations, 28 May 1967, in ibid., 580.

[29] Message from the French Minister of Foreign Affairs to the French permanent representative at the United Nations, 29 May 1967, in ibid., 588.

[30] Message from the French Minister of Foreign Affairs to the French Ambassador in Washington, 1 June 1967, in ibid., 596.

prime minister accused Israel of plotting "the destruction" of Damascus and the toppling of the regime. "International Zionism," he said, was waging a "permanent aggression against the Arab countries." The French president listened to this plea before shooting back two questions: "Is your enemy Israel or America?" and "Will you attack or not?" Makhos answered that Israel was the enemy, but that Syria would not attack. De Gaulle then developed his rationale against war, as a "friend" of the Arabs:

You, the Arabs, are many, and you are together. But you lack many things. If you deal with Israel, that will mean fatal casualties and no lasting solution. If you want to destroy Israel, I think your situation will be worse, since many countries believe in the necessity of a settlement. Israel is a people. We, French, have not created it as a state; the Americans, the English and the Russians created it, as you said. But now it exists: it got organized and it worked. We do not approve of all its exaggerations, and we do not approve of its raids against you. If you want to destroy it, you will have many people in the world against you. But if Israel takes the military initiative, if it destroys Damascus, many people will not approve of such an action. You have everything to gain by being patient. In many fields, you are achieving great progress, but if you go to war, you will jeopardize most of it.

I am your friend, and I wish you would not take the military initiative. I wish Nasser would not shoot first. I admit that the issue of the Gulf of Aqaba is now in front of us. But we have to negotiate, find a way, a solution. Not now: you are mobilized because you do not want to be attacked. You have displayed your solidarity; the world is aware of it and does not want you to be destroyed. The Americans are biased against you, and the Soviets are biased in your favour, but do not bet on them going to war on your behalf. Be patient, be strong, be armed, and close ranks. Do not be the first ones to shoot in the Gulf of Aqaba. After two weeks, if there is no war, the issue will be different, since the tension will have diminished and the French will be able to talk in a friendly spirit.[31]

This lengthy quotation illustrates how de Gaulle strove to convince his Arab "friends" to abstain from war against Israel and to work instead for the development of their own countries. The French president followed that line of argument again when he received King Faisal of Saudi Arabia on 2 June: "We are not committed to any side, neither to the Arabs nor to Israel. And we think every state in existence has the right to live. Without shying away from the seriousness of the situation, we believe war would be the worst option. Therefore, any state that shoots first will get neither

---

[31] Minutes from the meeting between Charles de Gaulle and Ibrahim Makhos, 1 June 1967, in ibid., 599–601.

approval nor support from us."[32] This warning was solemnly expressed in the communiqué published after the weekly meeting of the French government, chaired by the president of the republic: "Any state that is the first one to use weapons, no matter where, cannot expect France's approval, and certainly not its support."[33]

When Israel went on the offensive, at dawn on 5 June, it took great pains to avoid being targeted as having initiated the war. France tried to gather intelligence in order to pin down who was responsible for the war, but no final conclusion was reached. Washington claimed that this issue of responsibility would probably stay unresolved, and Paris pleaded at the United Nations in favour of an immediate cease-fire, without blame being assigned to any party.[34] The Soviet ambassador in France informed the French government that there could be no doubt about Israeli "aggression," and he urged Paris to follow up on the warning it had issued three days before.[35] But the issue of Israeli responsibility was not addressed during the exchange of messages between Kosygin and de Gaulle that went through the "green phone" – a direct telex line established between the Soviet and French leaders. They both agreed on empowering the four permanent members of the Security Council to "try and get a cessation of the fighting."[36] The two leaders used the green phone repeatedly during the crisis, and they coordinated their moves at the UN Security Council, whose Resolution 234, voted on 7 June, called for an immediate cease-fire.

De Gaulle had now no longer any doubt about Israel's responsibility for starting the conflict. But he made no public declaration on that crucial point. He even authorized, on 7 June, the delivery of war matériel previously paid for by Israel, including crucial spare parts for Mirage fighters.[37] It was only after this unpublicized shipment that military delivery to Israel came to a halt. During its six-day offensive against Egypt, Jordan, and Syria, Israel never worried about a lack of French military supplies, which

---

[32] Minutes from the meeting between Charles de Gaulle and King Faisal, 2 June 1967, in ibid. 609.

[33] Presidential statement to the Council of Ministers, Paris, Elysée Palace, 2 June 1967.

[34] Message from the French Ambassador in Washington, 5 June 1967, in *DDF*, 1967, vol. 1, 621.

[35] Minutes from the meeting between the Minister of Research and the Soviet Ambassador in Paris, 5 June 1967, in ibid., 628.

[36] Exchange of notes between Alexei Kosygin and Charles de Gaulle, 5 June 1967, in ibid., 634.

[37] This decision was made official in a note dated 8 June 1967, sent by the Presidency of the Republic to the Ministry of Defence (*DDF*, 1967, vol. 2, Paris: Ministère des Affaires étrangères, 2008, 152).

were critical for its air force (the Mirage fighters, but also the Mystères, Super-Mystères, Vautours, and Fougas), and the 7 June delivery was sufficient to replenish its stock until the end of the conflict.

Faced with a military disaster, Egypt tried to convince France that the United States and Great Britain had lent "air support" to the Israeli offensive.[38] Paris gave no credence to these accusations but was impressed by the shock wave they sent all over the Arab world. U.S. embassies and institutions were attacked by angry mobs, just as French representations and symbols had been targeted all over the Middle East after the Suez Crisis. France followed with utmost concern the speed with which popular anger spread to its former colonies in North Africa. Algeria was a longtime supporter of the Syrian and Egyptian regimes, Morocco joined the "United Arab Front" and pledged to send troops to fight Israel, and anti-Jewish riots developed in Tunisia, where President Habib Bourguiba feared "the stubbornness of various Arab leaders, prisoners of their own propaganda."[39]

De Gaulle commented candidly the Middle East crisis on 8 June at a meeting with Richard Nixon, the leader of the Republican Party, who had embarked on a three-month tour around the world:

Israel is not going to take over Damascus, nor Baghdad, not even Beirut. It will stop, and there will be a de facto stabilization that will last for a while. The Arabs will reorganize, recuperate, and recover. Then will come the need for negotiation. I agree with you that the necessary settlement has to be moderate. The Israelis will try to exaggerate, and as you just said, they should not because they cannot resist all the Arabs in the long run. But Israelis always exaggerate – just read the Psalms again. The Arabs also, by the way. So between people prone to exaggeration, the great powers have to let the voice of reason be heard and to compel to reason. The Russians are needed; otherwise, nothing will happen.[40]

The French president was already contemplating the aftermath of a conflict that was still raging: the Egyptian and Jordanian defeat was over, but the Israelis had turned against the Syrians and were moving on the Golan Heights.

When Israel eventually stopped fighting, on 10 June, the French ambassador in Tel Aviv warned that the Israeli press and leaders were widely misrepresenting General de Gaulle's attitude because they believed that "Israel had ceased to be an ally, not even a friend, and has been treated

[38] Message from the French Ambassador in Cairo, 6 June 1967, in *DDF*, 1967, vol. 1, 635.
[39] Message from the French Ambassador in Tunis, 8 June 1967, in ibid., 654.
[40] Minutes from the meeting between Charles de Gaulle and Richard Nixon, 8 June 1967, in ibid., 658.

hour after hour with less equity, only to be sacrificed to the seduction of the Arab mirage."[41] These accusations gained ground not only in Israel but also in the United States. The French envoy in Washington pointed out that the wave of anti-Americanism in the Arab world fuelled "new suspicions regarding France's policy and its relationship with the USA. I cannot say it is the view of the Administration, but it is certainly the most credited interpretation in the country."[42]

While this hostile campaign gained momentum in Israel and in the United States, de Gaulle resisted Soviet pressure to sanction the Jewish state. He stood his ground on 16 June during a face-to-face meeting in Paris with Soviet Prime Minister Kosygin, who had stopped over on his way to a meeting of the UN General Assembly. The French president rejected any concerted approach against the Jewish state, and he even suggested that Israel might keep part of its recent territorial gains.

You tell me the aggressor is to be punished and that Israel was the aggressor. The truth is that it was the first one to use its weapons, but many say it could not have done otherwise. It was threatened, it is a small country lost among the Arabs, and it had to break loose. Everything leads to a situation in which it would be very difficult for the world to band together to punish Israel. Nevertheless, I do not think that Israel should be allowed to exaggerate and keep all its conquests. It could prove possible, after a very long time and very difficult negotiations, to reach a reasonable settlement in the Middle East, if anything like that is even conceivable. I mean a solution accepted by Israel and the Arabs and also acceptable to the powers. Israel would lose part of what it took and keep some of it. Maybe from there, a diplomatic and practical modus vivendi could be achieved on the ground. Failing that, we would still live more or less in a situation of war. If such an agreement cannot be reached, the Arabs will try to get revenge and will accumulate forces to reverse what took place. The United States will support Israel in this armed competition. There would then be very serious international complications, since you and the United States would take sides on this issue and would soon appear on opposite sides. We would then see that the Arabs mean very little, that Israel means nothing, and that the rivalry between the Americans and the Russians is the heart of the matter.[43]

The French president was always linking the Middle East crisis to the Vietnam conflict, and he genuinely feared the escalation of the Cold War into a wider conflict, pitting Washington directly against Moscow. Three days after de Gaulle's meeting with Kosygin, he received Prime

---

[41] Message from the French Ambassador in Tel Aviv, 11 June 1967, in ibid., 682.
[42] Message from the French Ambassador in Washington, 15 June 1967, in ibid., 709.
[43] Minutes of the meeting between Charles de Gaulle and Alexei Kosygin, 16 June 1967, in ibid., 729–30.

Minister Wilson and shared with him his concerns about the new balance of power in the Middle East: "There will be a very serious period, and nobody knows when it will end, before any agreement will be conceivable on anything." De Gaulle therefore warned Wilson against giving in to popular emotion: "In your country as well as mine, people are getting excited about the fate of Israel, unfortunate people for two thousand years who suffered especially during the Second World War massacres. On top of that, there is at home a certain hostility toward the Arabs; it is an old one that developed because of Algeria and is far from being over. But we have to set those feelings aside in order to study the issue in itself."[44]

While the French-British summit meeting was taking place, Johnson and Kosygin failed to meet in New York, and their speeches in front the UN General Assembly were sharply antagonistic. This fuelled de Gaulle's feeling of "impotence" and his pessimism: Israel thought that its victories could pave the way for "talks with some Arab leaders, for instance Hussein [King Hussein of Jordan]. [Israel] will find nobody to negotiate with."[45] On 21 June, the French government publicly renewed the call for a Four Powers–sponsored peace conference in the Middle East, while rejecting any Arab call for the destruction of Israel and blaming the Jewish state for having started the recent conflict. It sounded like a declaration of principles, but one that had no serious possibility of implementation in the short term. De Gaulle was getting ready for the prolonged period of dangerous tensions he foresaw in the Middle East.

The French-Israeli Divorce during the Fall of 1967

Evenhanded diplomacy became increasingly out of touch with French domestic debate, in which vocal support for Israel reached record heights. On 31 May 1967, thirty thousand people, including many popular politicians and intellectuals, demonstrated their solidarity in front of the Israeli embassy in Paris. Protests against the war in Vietnam rarely drew more than a thousand participants during the same period. At the beginning of June, only 2 percent of the French people supported the Arab states against Israel, which was supported by 58 percent.[46] The French press

---

[44] Minutes of the meeting between Charles de Gaulle and Harold Wilson, 19 June 1967, in ibid., 751.

[45] Minutes of the meeting between Charles de Gaulle and Harold Wilson, 20 June 1967, in ibid., 779.

[46] Sondages, 1967, no. 4, 66.

routinely compared Nasser to Hitler and accused the Arab neighbours of
Israel of planning the extermination of the Jewish people.[47] Even among
the ruling right wing, many questioned official French "neutrality," and
on 5 June, three Gaullist Members of Parliament defiantly travelled to
Israel as a public gesture of solidarity with the Jewish state.[48] The Communist Party appeared to be the only organization united in its support
of French policy, while the noncommunist left wing denied the "progressive" nature of the Arab side.[49] This was what de Gaulle had in mind
when he told Wilson that "people are getting excited about the fate of
Israel."[50]

But it became more and more difficult for the French president "to
set those feelings aside,"[51] especially after his flamboyant style led him
to a new anti-U.S. provocation: on 24 July 1967, on the balcony of
Montreal city hall, de Gaulle concluded his official speech by shouting
"Long live Free Quebec" ("*Vive le Québec libre*"). This call for subverting
the Canadian ally caused outrage in France. Valéry Giscard d'Estaing, the
leader of the non-Gaullist right wing, denounced "the loneliness" of the
French president and focused some of his harshest criticisms on his Middle East policy.[52] François Mitterrand, the president of the Fédération de
la Gauche Démocratique et Socialiste (FGDS) and leader of the noncommunist left wing, publicly "condemned the definition of the aggressor the
French government chose" during the Six-Day War.[53] The vibrant debate
went on during the summer and fall of 1967; at the United Nations,
France supported the Israeli withdrawal on the 5 June cease-fire lines.[54]

De Gaulle was shocked by the Israeli decision to "unify" Jerusalem
at the end of June 1967, and France adamantly rejected any change of
the status quo, especially in the holy city. The French president, in a

---

[47] Kassir and Mardam-Bey, *Itinéraires de Paris à Jérusalem*, vol. 2, 132–40.

[48] Pierre Clostermann, Joël Le Tac, and Robert-André Vivien.

[49] On 29 May 1967, Jean-Paul Sartre, Simone de Beauvoir, and forty other leftist intellectuals rejected "the association of Israel with the imperialist and aggressive camp," and
on 2 June 1967, the leadership of the FGDS considered it "hypocritical" to oppose "a
'progressive' camp, based in Egypt, to an 'imperialist' camp, embodied by Israel."

[50] See n. 44.

[51] Ibid.

[52] On 17 August 1967, Giscard d'Estaing attacked publicly "*l'exercice solitaire du pouvoir*"
(the lonely management of power).

[53] Mitterrand's press conference, Paris, 16 August 1967.

[54] When the French Ambassador at the United Nations voted in favour of General Assembly
Resolution 2243 (4 July 1967), calling for a full Israeli withdrawal, he argued that the 5
June cease-fire lines "had in fact become, with the passing of time, real borders" (*DDF*,
1967, vol. 2, 14).

face-to-face meeting with German Chancellor Kurt Kiesinger, accused the Israeli government of planning the "annexation" of Jerusalem and Gaza.[55] Israel's refusal to admit any refugees back into the West Bank after August 1967 and its rejection of the conclusions of the Khartoum Arab summit sharpened French fears. On 22 September 1967, de Gaulle argued to the Egyptian Minister of Foreign Affairs that "the Arabs [had to] recognize the existence of Israel, with borders secured by the military presence of UN troops and with Israeli withdrawal from the occupied territories."[56] He added to the Saudi Minister of the Interior, on 13 October 1967, that "we will support the Arabs in order to get the Israelis to withdraw from the occupied territories."[57]

On 22 November 1967, the UN Security Council unanimously adopted Resolution 242, which demanded the "withdrawal of Israel armed forces from territories occupied in the recent conflict." But the French version called for a "*retrait des forces armées israéliennes des territoires occupés lors du récent conflit,*" implying a comprehensive Israeli withdrawal. Because the English and French languages have the same legal status in UN rules, this opened decades of diplomatic debate about the precise implications of Resolution 242. These considerations went unnoticed by the French public, but the press conference de Gaulle held five days later at the Elysée Palace triggered a political storm. The French president warned that the Israeli occupation of the West Bank and Gaza could generate only "resistance" and that this resistance would be stigmatised as "terrorism."[58] To make matters worse, de Gaulle described the Jewish people as "self-righteous and domineering" ("*sûr de lui-même et dominateur*").

The outcry in France was vociferous, and de Gaulle's Middle East policy became associated with the most ominous designs.[59] Even Raymond Aron went as far as accusing de Gaulle of having "knowingly and voluntarily opened a new era in Jewish and perhaps anti-Semitic history."[60] Ben-Gurion sent a public letter to de Gaulle, who answered that Israel

---

[55] Minutes of the meeting between Charles de Gaulle and Kurt Kiesinger, 12 July 1967, in ibid., 60.

[56] Minutes of the meeting between Charles de Gaulle and Mahmud Riad, 22 September 1967, in ibid., 363.

[57] Minutes of the meeting between Charles de Gaulle and Prince Fahd, 13 October 1967, in ibid., 477.

[58] Charles de Gaulle's press conference, Paris, Elysée Palace, 27 November 1967.

[59] Kassir and Mardam-Bey, *Itinéraires de Paris à Jérusalem*, vol. 2, 148.

[60] Raymond Aron, *De Gaulle, Israël et les Juifs* [De Gaulle, Israel and the Jews] (Paris: Plon, 1968), 20.

was now "a state among the others" and that "its life and longevity will depend on its policy." The French president warned Israel against "the repression and the expulsions that are the fatal consequences of any occupation developing into the annexation" of the conquered territories.[61] The Israeli-Arab polarization about de Gaulle resurfaced during the May 1968 riots: the Israeli media rejoiced at such "serious troubles," while Arab leaders and media often denounced the "dark plot" against friendly France.[62]

Despite all this political turmoil, military cooperation between France and Israel was not interrupted, and Henry Laurens concluded that "the embargo was so selective that, most probably, France delivered more weapons than the United States to Israel from June 1967 to January 1969."[63] But de Gaulle was incensed after an Israeli raid on the Beirut airport on 28 December 1968, which destroyed the civilian Lebanese fleet as a "reprisal" for a Palestinian attack on an Israeli plane in Greece. The special relationship between France and Lebanon had been targeted, while Lebanon was the only Israeli neighbour to have stayed neutral during the Six-Day War. Israel had conspicuously used French helicopters to strike the Beirut airport. Furious, the French president ordered a full-fledged military embargo on Israel, more than eighteen months after the end of the June 1967 conflict.

De Gaulle advocated consistently for the Four Powers formula, even though it proved absolutely ineffective in defusing Middle East tensions. His long-term vision of ending the Indo-China war led him to welcome, in May 1968, the first Vietnam peace conference. But France's proclaimed "neutrality" in the Israeli-Arab conflict did not develop into a mediating role because it clashed with Israel's preferences. Long before the Six-Day War, the Israeli military establishment had planned to switch to the United States as a critical supplier of advanced weaponry, choosing, for instance, the Patton tank over the French AMX-30. As the regional crisis escalated in May 1967, Israeli accusations against France intensified when

---

[61] Charles de Gaulle's letter to David Ben-Gurion, 30 December 1967 (since the Israeli leader had made his initial letter public, so did the French President with his reply), *Articles et documents*, no. 01888, 26 January 1968.

[62] Maurice Vaïsse, ed., *Mai 68 vu de l'étranger* [May 68 seen from abroad] (Paris: CNRS éditions, 2008), 136, 135.

[63] Henry Laurens, "La diplomatie française dans le conflit israélo-arabe, 1967–70," conference at the Collège de France, Paris, 1 October 2008. Only the delivery of the Mirage V was halted, while, for instance, five of the twelve famous "patrol boats of Cherbourg" were shipped to Israel as they were completed, from 1967 to 1968.

de Gaulle refused to lend his support to an Israeli preemptive strike. This is the origin of the myth of the French "betrayal" of Israel, according to which de Gaulle supposedly stabbed in the back a Jewish state fighting for its survival.[64] The French opposition to the Soviet anti-Israeli campaign at the United Nations, as well as the continuation of the military cooperation between France and Israel until January 1969, was brushed aside in order to sharpen the attacks against de Gaulle's "betrayal."

The reversal in France's position in the Middle East, compared with what is was after the 1956 Suez Crisis, was just as striking in the Arab world, where de Gaulle's historical and nationalist rhetoric struck a deep chord, especially after the military disaster. Many Arabs believed Israel had enjoyed direct American and British support that allowed it to achieve such a formidable offensive. French "neutrality" was therefore praised as a brave display of "friendship." This empathy grew when France advocated full Israeli withdrawal from the occupied territories and warned against the dangerous logic of "annexation." But de Gaulle never mentioned a specific "Arab policy," a concept that was coined by his successor, Georges Pompidou, and was developed in the aftermath of the October 1973 war.[65] The founder of the Fifth Republic was careful not to take sides in a dispute that he contemplated with utter pessimism. He nevertheless did not hesitate to go against the current of the pro-Israeli campaign in France in June 1967. He was the first Western leader to qualify as "resistance" the movements confronting the occupation of the West Bank and the Gaza Strip. That was certainly enough for France to lose its "best ally" status in Israel and to pave the way for the "strategic alliance" between the United States and the Jewish state.

---

[64] *Betrayal* is also the title of a vehemently anti-French book in which de Gaulle is portrayed as "increasingly resentful and frustrated" towards Israel: in the Middle East, "his self-importance stranded his country in contradiction, prejudice and grudge." David Pryce-Jones, *Betrayal: France, the Arabs, and the Jews* (New York: Encounter, 2006), 95, 99.

[65] France's "Arab Policy" (*politique arabe*) was then conceptualized by two journalists in a book inspired by the French administration: Paul Balta and Claudine Rulleau, *La politique arabe de la France de De Gaulle à Pompidou* [France's Arab Policy from de Gaulle to Pompidou] (Paris: Sindbad, 1973).

II

The 1967 War and the Demise of Arab Nationalism

Chronicle of a Death Foretold

Rashid Khalidi

It is an established pillar of the seemingly inexhaustible stock of conventional wisdom about the history of the modern Middle East that Arab nationalism was a formidable force before the June 1967 War, and that it visibly waned in its aftermath, largely as a consequence of this crushing defeat of the Arabs and the consequent occupation of vast tracts of their territory. The claim, in essence, is that it was the 1967 debacle that lowered the standing of Egyptian President Gamal Abdel Nasser and of the Arab nationalist ideological current he was seen as representing.[1] Whether this conventional wisdom is correct, there can be little question that for the first two-thirds of the twentieth century, Arab nationalism held a seemingly unassailable position as the hegemonic ideology of the Arab world or that, by the post-1967 era, it had entered into a decline that appears to continue until this day.

The Myth of Demise

However, this chapter argues that while the demoralizing rout of 1967 seriously tarnished the prestige of Egypt and its charismatic president, the war did not sound the death knell of Arab nationalism as a political force. Arabism remained a force among the Arab masses long afterwards and retains its potency with many Arabs until this day. Nor is it only the

---

[1] Thus Adeed Dawisha states in *Arab Nationalism in the Twentieth Century: From Triumph to Despair* (Princeton, NJ: Princeton University Press, 2003), 252–3: "Arabism was merely the remnant of Arab nationalism, what the Arabs were left with after Arab nationalism hit the deck in June 1967. What the Six Day War did was to irretrievably rob Arab nationalism of the crucial element of unification."

case because regimes that proclaimed their Arab nationalist credentials remained in power for many years afterwards in countries like Ba'thist Iraq, Algeria, and Libya. Such a Ba'thist regime still exists in Syria, many decades after 1967. For the most part these regimes were (and the few of them remaining are) "Arab nationalist" only in name, and this was true both before 1967 and afterwards. It is important to specify that this is the case if by Arab nationalist we mean regimes that did not simply pay lip service to the shibboleths of Arabist doctrine but rather had Arab unity as a primary goal and solidly based their external relations on the principle of Arab solidarity. This should be the definition and litmus test of whether a regime was actually "Arab nationalist," not its declaratory policy, or the perhaps sincerely held beliefs of its leaders. More importantly, this chapter contends that the 1967 war and its aftermath simply reinforced and consecrated a preexisting, underlying trend among nominally Arab nationalist regimes. This was one whereby narrow nation-state nationalism – to be sure, covered with a thick cloak of Arabist rhetoric – increasingly became these regimes' primary guiding principle, seconded by powerful considerations of regime security.

Well before the 1967 war, the motive force of the policies of Egypt, Syria, Iraq, and other countries with an ostensibly radical Arab nationalist orientation, as well as of increasingly influential forces like Fatah within the reemerging Palestinian national movement, was essentially *raison d'état*–driven nation-state nationalism. This sometimes took a pragmatic form and sometimes took more radical ones. In cases like that of Egypt under Nasser and the Ba'th regimes in power at various times in Iraq and Syria, this orientation was well disguised under a heavy Arab nationalist veneer. These and other "radical" Arab states, as well as the Palestinian national movement, scrupulously adhered in public to the pieties of Arabism, pieties like unity and Arab solidarity, which the great mass of Arab public opinion believed in and enthusiastically supported. But even during the pre-1967 era, most of these states and the Palestinian national movement operated primarily on the basis of realpolitik rather than nationalist ideology. Achieving relative advantage internationally and in the Arab state system, gaining adherents among Arab public opinion, and staying in power were generally more important than any possible Arabist motivations, although formal adherence to Arabism and ample lip-service to its ideals often advanced these operational aims. The few partial exceptions to this rule during the years before 1967 (the Nasser regime's support for the Yemeni revolution, the Syrian neo-Ba'th regime's adventurist and provocative support for

Palestinian guerrillas, and the dedicated ideologically driven commitment to the policies of Nasser of the Palestinian-dominated Movement of Arab Nationalists [MAN]), important though they were, do not undermine this basic rule, and each will be treated briefly in the following text.

One conventional verity that is incontrovertible is that the 1967 war constituted a gigantic shock to the Arab interstate system. There can be little question that the June 1967 defeat profoundly destabilized Syria, Egypt, Jordan, Lebanon, and, to a lesser extent, several other Arab countries. It thus had a similar effect on the central parts of the Arab world to that of the 1948 war. Its cataclysmic systemic impact notwithstanding, the 1967 war was not the great watershed it may have appeared to be in terms of the decline of Arab nationalism as a driving principle of the policies of the Arab regimes. In practice, respect for the ideals of Arabism, in particular the keystone objective of movement towards Arab unity, was largely a matter of empty genuflection even before 1967. It was even more so thereafter. Arab nationalist regimes, or rather regimes mouthing Arabist slogans, remained in power for many decades afterwards.

Egyptian President Anwar Sadat's acrimonious public break with Arabism, his devil-take-the-hindmost attitude towards the other Arab states, and his overt turn towards Egypt-first nationalism are often cited as post-1967 proof of this shift away from commitment to Arab nationalism. Thus, Sadat told Palestine Liberation Organization (PLO) leaders visiting Egypt just before the 1973 war that he was going to halt the Egyptian offensive after the crossing of the Suez Canal much earlier than he had informed his Syrian allies he would. When his Palestinian interlocutors remonstrated with him about this betrayal, he had told them bluntly: "The Syrians deceived us in 1967. Why should I not deceive them now?" No trace of Arab nationalism, Arab solidarity, or even the minimal respect due to an ally exists, in this attitude, only the vindictive petulance so characteristic of Sadat.[2] Sadat's manifestly un-Arab nationalist policies only consecrated and made more blatant an approach to Egypt's Arab brethren that, in reality, had long animated Egyptian foreign policy under Sadat's predecessor. The fact that that this was true of the Nasser era is obscured for many by the nostalgia with which that era is regarded by some. It is obscured even more by the fact that this approach reached an

---

[2] I was present in Beirut during the spring of 1975 when Yasser Arafat and Salah Khalaf (Abu Iyad) related this story to a visiting delegation. See also Abu Iyad's autobiography, with Eric Rouleau, *My Home, My Land: A Narrative of the Palestinian Struggle* (New York: Times Books, 1981), 121–6, which hints at the same deception of Syria by Sadat.

apogee under Sadat, with his separate peace with Israel and his ostentatious scorn for the concerns of the other Arab countries. It is the further argument of this chapter that for many years before and afterwards, a similar approach was mirrored in the policies of most other Arab countries, including the flamboyantly Arab nationalist Ba'th regimes of Syria and Iraq – their flowery Arabist rhetoric notwithstanding.

In order to demonstrate the validity of this thesis, three cases will be briefly examined both before 1967 and afterwards: those of Egypt, Syria, and the Palestinian national movement. Because this is such a broad theme and this chapter covers a period extending before and after 1967, the treatment of these cases will perforce be cursory. There can be little question of the strong and genuine hold of Arab nationalism on the Arab masses from the Atlantic to the Gulf – *min al-muhit ila al-khalij* as the Arabic phrase went. Nevertheless, by the end of this exposition it will be clear that, although Arab nationalism was a vital legitimating principle for many Arab regimes of this era (and during other earlier and later eras), it was generally not the true well-spring of their policies. Instead, for the most part cold, calculating considerations of *raison d'état* were.

Egypt

The clearest case that demonstrates the validity of the argument of this chapter is that of Egypt. This was true under Nasser, the twentieth century's leading apostle of Arab nationalism and of Arab resistance to domination by the great powers and by Israel. It was even truer of his successor Sadat, who was pilloried by Egyptian and other Arab nationalists for his "apostasy" in diminishing Egypt's Arab role, aligning Egypt with the United States, and making peace with Israel. However much he differed from his much-reviled successor, the idea that Nasser was a radical Arabist who primarily sought to achieve the great ambitions for Arab unity held out by Arab nationalist theorists by unifying the Arab states and overcoming the artificial divisions between them imposed by European imperialism simply does not withstand serious scrutiny.[3] Instead, upon careful examination he appears as a shrewd and perceptive leader who understood perhaps better than any other the power of Arab nationalism

---

[3] Sadat was and is truly a prophet without honor in his own country. His funeral cortège was followed to his grave only by foreigners, who to this day are the only ones who hold him in high regard. Thus visitors to government offices in Egypt for decades could commonly see a portrait of the longtime incumbent, Husni Mubarak, and often one of Nasser, but rarely one of Sadat.

to move the masses. He used this ideology adeptly in order to advance the interest of his regime and his country. The actual unification of the Arab states, however, does not seem to have been a serious or realistic objective of his policy. One only has to look at the Egyptian regime's behaviour in the run-up to the abortive 1958 union with Syria to see the truth of this assessment. For Arab nationalists, this union was a dream come true: bringing together the largest Arab country with the "beating heart of Arabism," as the Syrians saw their country. The best analysis of this topic is that of Patrick Seale, whose book still stands, forty-five years after its publication, as a masterpiece of insight and illumination.[4]

Far from pressing for union with the unstable Syrian regime, or believing in the importance of Arab unity above all other things (as some Syrian Ba'thist leaders and many Arabs, especially in Palestine, Lebanon, and Jordan at the time actually did), Egyptian policy makers were extremely wary of any such outcome. Far from desiring unity with Syria, they feared the consequences of a closer Egyptian alignment with Damascus for the stability and safety of their own regime in Cairo. It was the Syrian Ba'th Party leaders, not Nasser, who were eager for union. It was their insistence on union, domestic political weakness and fear of their political rivals, notably the Communists, and urgent desire for escape from the desperate situation of regional isolation they had gotten Syria into on the eve of union that ultimately overcame the cautious reluctance of the Egyptian president.

Egyptian leaders were increasingly aware of the potential negative impact on Egypt of the collapse of a Syrian regime that was tottering in the face of multiple external threats. In time, they came to fear this outcome more than what they foresaw as the troubled impact of union with Syria. Muhammad Hasanayn Heikal, who was perhaps Nasser's most trusted adviser, recorded later discussions between the Egyptian president and Soviet leader Nikita Khrushchev that make clear Egypt's reluctance to take on the kind of pan-Arab responsibilities that a union with Syria implied.[5] The Egyptian Ambassador in Damascus at the time,

---

[4] Patrick Seale, *The Struggle for Syria: A Study of Post-War Arab Politics, 1945–1958* (London: Oxford University Press, 1965).

[5] The discussion he records was about events a few months earlier, in the lead-up to the 1958 Iraqi coup, and illustrates Nasser's cautious reluctance to extend prior support to its backers, not at all what one might expect of a pan-Arab leader eager to expand further the union just achieved with Syria to encompass Iraq: Mohamed Hassanein Heikal, *The Cairo Documents: The Inside Story of Nasser and His Relationship with World Leaders, Rebels, and Statesmen* (New York: Doubleday, 1973), 126–7. The same incident is also

a close collaborator of the Egyptian president, Mahmud Riad, who would later become Foreign Minister, stated in 1961: "Our policy was in fact to avoid union. We knew that it would arouse all the Powers against us and that we would be accused of annexing Syria – which is in fact what happened."[6] In Seale's words, "Egypt therefore embraced Arabism in a cool and practical spirit."[7] One might have been forgiven for thinking otherwise upon listening to the fiery Arabist rhetoric of the Egyptian radio station broadcasting to the Arab world, Sawt al-'Arab, or the Voice of the Arabs, but overheated propaganda and the actual nature of Egyptian policy must not be confused with one another.

Another demonstration of this unruffled, pragmatic approach of Egypt under Nasser to the burning Arab nationalist issue of unity – by some measures the very core of Arab nationalism – can be seen in the Egyptian government's reaction to the pressure from the Ba'th Party regimes that were (briefly) in power in Damascus and Baghdad during 1963 for a tripartite union among the three countries. The tractions involved are brilliantly analyzed in Malcolm Kerr's pithy monograph *The Arab Cold War: 'Abd al-Nasir and his Rivals, 1958–1970*.[8] Kerr makes it abundantly clear that little or no Arabist ideological fervour animated Nasser's treatment of his Syrian and Iraqi Ba'th Party comrades. Whatever enthusiasm the Egyptian leader and his advisers may have had for Arab unity had been cooled by the unhappy experience of the union with Syria. The Egyptians were especially disillusioned with the abrupt and humiliating end of the union at the instigation of the same Syrian Ba'thists who had rushed Egypt into the 1958 union in the first place, and some of whom now faced Nasser across the conference table demanding a renewed union.

Instead of encouragement for their nationalist fervour, during the negotiations the Syrians generally got a hearty helping of cold realism from the Egyptian leader, together with harsh criticisms of their behaviour during the period of Syrian-Egyptian union, the whole often leavened by a heavy dose of sarcasm. During one session of the unity talks, Nasser mercilessly taxed Syrian Ba'thist leader Salah al-Din al-Bitar: "Don't you read the Lebanese press? . . . Neither the French nor the Lebanese press? . . . But this

---

described in Heikal's *The Sphinx and the Commissar: The Rise and Fall of Soviet Influence in the Middle East* (New York: Harper and Row, 1978), 93.

[6] Riyad said this in an interview with Seale, *The Struggle for Syria*, 314.

[7] Ibid., 313.

[8] The third and fourth chapters of the book are devoted to a detailed analysis of this episode and its aftermath: (3rd ed., [London: Oxford University Press for the Royal Institute of International Affairs, 1971], 59–126).

is incredible! . . . You don't read the Syrian, Lebanese or French press?!
How on earth do you govern your country?"[9] The Egyptians clearly had
absolutely no desire for a repeat of their disastrous experience with the
querulous Syrian Ba'th Party leaders, this time with the latter's dispu-
tatious Iraqi comrades added for good measure. The union talks failed
miserably, which was what Nasser manifestly wanted to happen. This is
made abundantly clear by Kerr's book, which for this episode is mainly
based on a close reading of the transcript of the unity talks, published
in full in Cairo immediately after the failure of the talks.[10] The Egyptian
leadership clearly did not want unity with Syria and Iraq under the rule of
the Ba'th Party. By publishing these transcripts, Nasser was quick to try
to show Egyptian and Arab public opinion, which was animated by Arab
nationalist fervour and desirous of unity, that the fault for the failure of
this effort was not his own.

Egypt under Nasser and his colleagues was not driven by Arab nationalist fervour in its foreign policy: far from it. Rather, what animated the
calculations of Egypt's leaders was a rational, if sometimes erroneous,
reading of what was advantageous for Egypt's position in the Arab world
and for the security of their regime. These errors could best be seen in a
third episode, the Egyptian intervention in Yemen, which is also slightly
exceptional, as ideology does seem to have played some role in Egyptian decision making. Here too, however, it was mainly *raison d'état* that
drove the Egyptian ship of state. Nasser was faced by requests in 1962 for
support from a Yemeni revolutionary regime headed by a group of self-
proclaimed "Free Officers." They asserted that they had been inspired by
the example of the Egyptian group of the same name that had overthrown
the monarchy in 1952. Here Nasser's usually sure instincts failed him.
Back in 1958, when a similar group of Iraqi Free Officers had secretly con-
tacted Egyptian officials for support for their coup against the Hashemite
monarchy, they had been politely told to make their revolution and then
come back to the Egyptians.[11]

For reasons that probably had much to do with the precarious state
of the inter-Arab balance of power and the Egyptian leadership's fears
that archrival Saudi Arabia would gain influence if the Yemeni revolution collapsed under the assaults of Saudi-backed royalist tribesmen, the

---

[9] Ibid., 87.
[10] *Mahadir jalsat mubahathat al-wahda* [Transcripts of the sessions of the unity negotia-
tions] (Cairo: National Printing and Publishing House, 1963).
[11] Heikal, *The Cairo Documents*, 126.

Egyptian leader succumbed to the entreaties of the Yemeni republicans and sent Egyptian troops to back their regime. The consequences of that decision are well-known. Egypt eventually got bogged down in Yemen with sixty thousand of the best troops in its regular army and a large part of its air force, the Egyptian treasury was drained, the royalists went from success to success, and the Egyptian forces came to be hated as heavy-handed occupiers by many Yemenis. To make matters worse, Egypt was still tied down in Yemen in April and May of 1967 when the crisis that led to the June War arose. This massive military commitment in Yemen left Egypt vulnerable at home, and limited drastically its options in the face of Israeli threats to Syria. Ironically, after the June 1967 debacle, when Egyptian troops were withdrawn after a hastily arranged Saudi-Egyptian rapprochement, the Yemeni republican regime managed to survive largely on its own (albeit with significant help in the form of an airlift of arms supplies from the USSR), and it is still shakily in existence to this day.

Unlike the two instances involving union with Syria and the never-consummated 1963 union with Syria and Iraq, in the Yemeni case, solidarity with a revolutionary Arab nationalist regime seems to have played a part in Egyptian decision making. At the same time, it is apparent that other factors were at work: by 1962 the Middle East had become polarized along the lines of what Kerr memorably called "The Arab Cold War," with the radical and revolutionary Arab nationalist regimes led by Nasser pitted against the monarchical and conservative ones led by Saudi Arabia. This Arab cold war eventually began to track with the larger American-Soviet Cold War, in a way that left all the Arab states involved with even less margin for manoeuvre than before.[12] In these circumstances, Egypt responded to an appeal for solidarity that, although it involved elements of *raison d'état*, was also partly ideological in nature, with one radical military-dominated Arab nationalist regime that was the issue of a revolution against a monarchy calling upon another for assistance.

This brings us to the 1967 war, and another illustration of how little Arab nationalism had to do with the actions of Egyptian leaders. It is true that the lead-up to the war witnessed a great deal of fervour in much of the Arab world over the prospect of the Arabs finally being able to stand up to Israel (as most Arabs believed would be the case). Nonetheless, it is evident that the prime motivations of Egyptian leaders were precisely the

---

[12] See Rashid Khalidi, *Sowing Crisis: The Cold War and American Dominance in the Middle East* (Boston: Beacon, 2009) for details.

same kinds of nation-state nationalism-driven concerns for the standing of Egypt in the Arab world, and the regional balance of power, that determined their policies in the Syrian and Syrian-Iraqi cases examined earlier. As in the Yemeni case, the Arab cold war played a role in Egypt's actions during 1967, in particular Jordan and Saudi Arabia's criticism of Egypt for hiding behind UN forces and for failing to act against Israel while fighting and killing Arabs in Yemen.

In 1964 Egypt had been obliged by the outbidding of the weak and unstable Syrian Ba'th regime to hold the first Arab summit meeting in Alexandria.[13] Nasser led the summit in deciding on a joint project for the diversion of the headwaters of the Jordan River in order to prevent Israel from diverting the waters of the Jordan to its National Water Carrier project, which was already well underway. The ongoing need to confront this perceived challenge from Israel, together with the Syrian Ba'th regime's growing support for the rising Palestinian commando groups in this period, marked by the first attack on Israel by Fatah in January 1965, placed Egypt in an exceedingly awkward predicament. Egypt faced a worsening situation in Yemen, where its troop strength had by 1967 risen from forty thousand to sixty thousand, and the war was nevertheless going worse for the republicans. Relations with the United States were also deteriorating after the assassination of President John F. Kennedy and the election in 1964 of Lyndon Johnson, who had even less sympathy than his predecessor for the Egyptian regime, its "Arab socialism," its alignment with the Soviet Union, and its policies in Yemen, and who was even more sympathetic than his predecessor to Israel.[14]

In consequence of these and other factors, when the crisis of April and May 1967 over Syria arrived, all of the fears of Egyptian leaders about being dragged into a confrontation with Israel for which Egypt was manifestly not ready came to the fore. Already in 1963, when the Yemen war had not yet reached its later peak of ferocity, and the inter-Arab situation was slightly less tense than was the case afterwards, Nasser had made this clear. Speaking about the challenge from Israel regarding the diversion of the headwaters of the Jordan, he declared that "we cannot

---

[13] The English word does not do justice to the Arabic term *muzayada*, which has the implication of demonstrative boastfulness.

[14] See Warren Bass, *Support Any Friend: Kennedy's Middle East and the Making of the U.S.-Israel Alliance* (Oxford: Oxford University Press, 2003), 239–53; and Abraham Ben Zvi, *Decade of Transition: Eisenhower, Kennedy, and the Origins of the American-Israeli Alliance* (New York: Columbia University Press, 1998).

use force today because our circumstances do not allow us."[15] In the years leading up to the 1967 war, Egyptian spokesmen bitterly attacked those, like the radical Palestinian commando groups, whom they claimed would "drag" Egypt into a confrontation for which it was not prepared.[16] In reality this was not far from being the actual strategy of Fatah, a strategy that in the event was executed to perfection in the lead-up to the 1967 war, although the Palestinians undoubtedly assumed that Egypt would prevail in a conflict with Israel that they had helped to start.

In the circumstances of a heightened Arab cold war that existed in 1967 and was not going particularly well for Cairo, Egypt could ill afford to alienate one of its few allies, the very radical neo-Ba'th regime that had come to power in Damascus in February 1966. This was the case in spite of the manifest distance between the relatively mature and tame Arabism of Egypt by this stage, and the fiery revolutionary radicalism of the new rulers in Damascus. Some of the civilians among them like Ibrahim Makhos and Yusuf Zu'ayyin had served as doctors and in other capacities during the eight-year war to free Algeria from French colonialism. They had returned to Damascus and won power there convinced that they had seen the future of a "long term people's war of liberation" (to use the then-fashionable Maoist terminology) and that the outcome in Algeria proved that it worked. It was clear to them that the same strategy could be employed in Palestine against what they saw as another settler-colonial regime. Nothing could have been more dissimilar from the deliberate, state centred, conventional military view of Egypt's rulers, nearly all of them military officers. Far from sharing the revolutionary radicalism of the neo-Ba'th, by this stage of its existence the Egyptian regime was mainly focused on economic development and its five-year plans and on the rivalry with the conservative bloc led by Saudi Arabia. In both of these struggles, Arabism had a mobilizing role to play, but it had become essentially instrumental. It was unquestionably secondary to more pragmatic considerations, to the extent that it even constituted a major source of policy inspiration for the post-1952 Egyptian regime.

---

[15] *Nasser's Speeches* (Cairo: Egyptian Book Organization, 1963), 311–12.

[16] See the assessment of Egypt's hostile attitude towards Fatah and other active commando groups preaching "armed struggle" against Israel in Moshe Shemesh, *The Palestinian Entity 1959–1974: Arab Politics and the PLO* (London: Frank Cass, 1988), 58–62, as well as the first-person account of Egyptian hostility to Fatah during this period given by Abu Iyad, *My Home, My Land*, 40–9.

Thus when war came, and with it disaster for Egypt and its army, the turn inwards that followed was far from unprecedented. What followed was merely a continuation of earlier trends. Egypt thereafter had to focus on rebuilding its shattered armed forces and removing the "traces of aggression," which essentially meant ending the Israeli occupation of Sinai. The Egyptian government concentrated single-mindedly on anything that would achieve these aims. Notwithstanding the famous "three no's" of the Khartoum Arab summit of 1968 and the purist Arab nationalist rejection of Israel's very existence that the Egyptians expressed, in practice the overridingly important aim of ending the occupation of Sinai translated into Egypt's willingness to recognize the existence of Israel within its 4 June 1967 borders. This was extended through Egypt's acceptance of UN Security Council Resolution 242 of 22 November 1967. It meant as well accepting the UN mediation of Swedish diplomat Gunnar Jarring, and later that of American Secretary of State William Rogers for a negotiated settlement of the conflict with Israel. All of these policies led inexorably to a break with the PLO, which could not follow Egypt in accepting a UN resolution that reduced the Palestinian national cause to a mere question of refugees. This break was sealed by the awful events of Black September, when Egypt found itself incongruously aligned with Jordan (the only other Arab country that had accepted Resolution 242). In spite of his intensive mediation in the days just before his death, Nasser could do little to prevent the Palestinians from going down to bloody defeat. This was only one of several consequences of the June 1967 defeat. Earlier ones included finally abandoning to their fate Arab allies, like the Yemeni republican regime, and ending the confrontation with Saudi Arabia, whose financial and diplomatic support was now essential to Egypt in its desperate struggle to rebuild its military and liberate the occupied Sinai Peninsula.

However, Egypt's actual policies were no more Arab nationalist before 1967 than they were afterwards. In both eras, they were disguised by the kind of Arabist rhetoric that emerged from the Khartoum summit and from Sawt al-'Arab, but that had little real bearing on the decisions that Nasser and his collaborators took, whether before 1967 or afterwards. These were decisions that were pragmatic and unideological. Ideological or not, some of the decisions taken by Egypt's leaders regarding Yemen, and most especially those taken in the lead-up to the 1967 war, appear not to have been altogether wise ones in the circumstances. This, however, is an entirely different issue.

Syria

The Syrian case does not appear to fit as easily into this argument about Arab nationalism as does the Egyptian one. This is partly because Syria was ruled from February 1966 until November 1970 by a regime that was, in some ways, unique in the Arab world.[17] In an unstable region that at the time was notorious for its radical regimes brought to power by a military *coup d'état*, Syria was undoubtedly exemplary, witnessing a monotonous succession of revolutions and coups starting in 1949, a year in which three changes of regime took place.

The neo-Ba'th faction that took power in the bloody February 1966 army coup, overthrowing the mainstream Ba'thist regime of military strongman Amin Hafiz, may have been the most radical group ever to govern an Arab state (with the possible exception of the period of Marxist rule in South Yemen). This faction was dominated by a group of young Ba'thist military officers and civilians headed from behind the scenes by General Salah Jadid, Army Chief of Staff and Assistant Secretary-General of the Ba'th Party. Many of its leading lights came from deprived Sunni regions and from non-Sunni minorities like the Druze, the Isma'ilis, and especially the 'Alawis. The regime established in 1966 by the neo-Ba'th was extremely "progressive" in its domestic economic and social policies. It pressed forward with the nationalization of industry and with extensive land-reform measures, wielding fiery socialist rhetoric and taking unprecedented and widely unpopular measures to repress public manifestations of Islam.[18] It was also ostentatiously militant and uncompromising in its foreign-policy orientation, even more so than the hard-line government dominated by General Hafiz that preceded it. It may appear at first glance that the post-1966 Syrian regime dominated by Jadid was an intensely Arab nationalist one, and that its replacement by the more cautious and more Syria-centred government of General Hafiz al-Asad in 1970 marked a decline of Arabism after the 1967 war (albeit with a time lag of a few years). If so, that evolution would seem to fit the conventional wisdom and, thus, to run directly counter to the thesis of this chapter.

---

[17] Perhaps the best examination of the politics of this "neo-Ba'th" regime can be found in Nakolaus van Dam, *The Struggle for Power in Syria: Sectarianism, Regionalism and Tribalism in Politics, 1961–1978* (London: Croom Helm, 1979).

[18] For the best study of the social basis of the Syrian Ba'th Party in general and the neo-Ba'th in particular, see Hanna Batatu, *Syria's Peasantry, the Descendants of its Lesser Rural Notables, and their Politics* (Princeton, NJ: Princeton University Press, 1999).

This was not the case. As with so much in the Arab world during this era, appearances could be deceptive. Before 1966, the regime dominated by Hafiz had ratcheted up Syria's confrontation with Israel. This was in response to the near completion of Israel's National Water Carrier, which diverted water from the Jordan River basin towards the centre of the country. This action, and the vocal and militant response of the Syrian Ba'th regime to it, had forced Nasser to convene the 1964 Arab summit and to display his own militancy towards Israel by proposing a pan-Arab water-diversion project, the creation of the PLO, and other anti-Israel measures, all of which were arguably intended primarily for show. Far from being interested in confrontation with Israel, the Egyptian leader had wanted to head off and contain the rising tide of Palestinian militancy and to take the initiative on the Palestine issue away from Syria and its junior Palestinian allies. This was because their radical orientation threatened the Egyptian government's policy goals elsewhere, notably domestically and in Yemen.

Beyond raising the Jordan River water issue, Syria under Hafiz also demonstrated its militancy towards Israel by offering its strong support in the way of bases, arms, and training for a new generation of Palestinian commando groups, notably Fatah. In spite of sporadic tensions with this and later Syrian Ba'thist regimes (which repeatedly imprisoned its leaders), Fatah was in consequence able for the first time to establish itself in a state bordering Israel (it had previously garnered Algerian and Chinese backing). It mounted its first attacks on Israel from bases in Syria during January 1965. This marked what the movement thereafter called the "launching of the Palestinian revolution."[19] These attacks were always carefully carried out from Jordanian or Lebanese soil to avoid the inconvenience to their Syrian hosts of devastating Israeli reprisal raids, which were invariably swift in coming.

After the neo-Ba'th faction – which had already grown more power-ful within the Syrian Ba'th Party during the 1963 to 1966 Amin Hafiz period – seized full control of political power in the sanguinary coup of February1966, it markedly accentuated its support for Palestinian mili-tary operations against Israel. In doing this, it was impelled by the belief of many of its leaders in the Maoist concept of "long term people's war of liberation" as the best way to resolve the conflict with Israel. The

---

[19] The best account of the rise of the commando movement is found in Yezid Sayigh, *Armed Struggle and the Search for State: The Palestinian National Movement, 1949–1993* (Oxford: Oxford University Press, 1997).

central idea of those who supported this strategy was that provoking Israel would ultimately cause it to overextend itself, leading in turn to a lengthy people's war being launched against the Jewish state by the populations of the neighbouring Arab countries. In acting in furtherance of these aims, the neo-Ba'th did what few governments in modern history have been willing to do: imperil its own existence, and the security of the country it governed, by challenging a powerful neighbour in service of a revolutionary ideal. Were the comparison not so far-fetched, one might see in the adventurism of Jadid and his colleagues echoes of Leon Trotsky and his comrades, according to his critics, imperilling Bolshevik power in Russia with revolutionary recklessness in Poland and elsewhere. In this scenario, Joseph Stalin, and his belief in revolution in one country, was personified in the Syrian case by the equally phlegmatic and unflamboyant Defense Minister al-Asad. In any case, it is no wonder that the ultracautious Soviets (whom we have now learned to have been much more fearful of American nuclear power than many at the time believed) would have looked with dismay at the provocative behaviour vis-à-vis Israel of the neo-Ba'th.[20] They were clearly relieved when Jadid and his hot-headed comrades, with their Maoist slogans and advocacy of unconventional warfare, were overthrown in 1970 by the more careful and calculating al-Asad, who represented a more conventional military view of the Arab-Israeli conflict.

The militancy of the neo-Ba'th played a crucial role in precipitating the 1967 war. The new wave of Syrian-supported attacks by Fatah and other Palestinian groups against Israel, although they were not very effective in strictly military terms, precipitated a spiral of events that ultimately led to the June 1967 War.[21] By proclaiming that a long-term people's war was the only way to reverse the humiliations of 1948 and restore Palestinian rights, and by appearing to act in consonance with these slogans, the Syrians and their junior Palestinian allies outflanked from the left Nasser and his regime, increasingly bogged down as it was in Yemen. This in turn

---

[20] See the revelations of a study commissioned by the National Security Archive and released on 11 September 2009: "Previously Classified Interviews with Former Soviet Officials Reveal U.S. Strategic Intelligence Failure over Decades: 1995 Contractor Study Finds that U.S. Analysts Exaggerated Soviet Aggressiveness and Understated Moscow's Fears of a U.S. First Strike," http://www.gwu.edu/~nsarchiv/nukevault/ebb285/index.htm.

[21] A good account of how this occurred can be found in David Hirst, *The Gun and the Olive Branch: The Roots of Violence in the Middle East*, 2nd ed. (London: Faber, 1984), 265–81. Hirst was reporting from the region on these events at the time of the 1967 war.

forced the Egyptians to raise the tone of their propaganda against Israel, and later to act in support of Syria when the exasperated Israelis began to pound Syrian targets, overfly Damascus, shoot down Syrian planes, and finally threaten to march on Damascus in April and May of 1967.[22] For Cairo and for Moscow, the idea of an irregular "popular" war, rather than a war waged by conventional armies, was anathema. So was the spectre of the irresponsible and militant Syrians and Palestinians rather than the more sober Egyptians taking the lead against Israel. However, the prospect of Israel striking Syria and possibly bringing down the Ba'th regime, one of Egypt and the Soviet Union's few close Arab allies, was to be avoided at all costs. Irresponsible though the Soviets and Egyptians felt its actions to be, Damascus therefore had to be supported in a situation in which the Egyptians and the Soviets believed that there were credible Israeli threats to Syria and to its shaky neo-Ba'th regime.[23] The end result of this process was the movement of Egyptian troops into Sinai and the closing of the Straits of Tiran, which ultimately provided the Israeli military with the *casus belli* for their attack on Egypt.

However, the reason why the Syrian case fits the thesis of this chapter does not lie in these important events in the Arab-Israeli arena, or in the fact that the revolutionary radicalism of the neo-Ba'th was replaced by the greater caution and pragmatism of the Asad regime. It can be found rather in earlier developments within the Ba'th Party during the mid-1960s, when its pan-Arab unionist wing led by its founders and traditional leaders like Michel Aflaq and Salah al-Din al-Bitar lost its influence and was gradually moved aside during the Hafiz period. This

---

[22] For a brief account of how this process unfolded, see ibid., 211–17.

[23] Much effort has been devoted to showing that the Soviets falsely warned Cairo against such Israeli threats. The existence of such threats have long been reported (see e.g., ibid., 216). They have been documented more recently and more authoritatively in Tom Segev, *1967: Israel, the War and the Year that Transformed the Middle East* (New York: Metropolitan, 2007), 231, and in Evgenii Primakov, *Russia and the Arabs: Behind the Scenes in the Middle East from the Cold War to the Present* (New York: Basic Books, 2009). Primakov, who was later head of the Russian intelligence service and Russian prime minister, and who was in Cairo in May and June 1967, insists on the basis of "a wealth of information obtained by Soviet intelligence" (107) that Nasser had no intention of launching a preemptive strike and that the Egyptian and Soviet leaderships feared an Israeli strike on Syria. Primakov insists that "the local Soviet foreign intelligence station had got hold of factual materials relating to the Israeli build-up" against Syria, and that "Egypt too had its own intelligence" in this regard (109). He adds that Nasser told the Soviet ambassador in Cairo: "Israel and its backers clearly think that the UAR is tied up in Yemen and can't give Syria any real help. The UAR has to show just how groundless it is to think like that" (110).

once-dominant faction was thereafter removed entirely from power and driven from Syria after the February 1966 neo-Ba'th coup. In assessing the role and importance of Arab nationalist ideology in the making of Syrian policy, these developments were far more significant than the more dramatic ones around the neo-Ba'th regime's support for the Palestinians and its provocations of Israel that helped to bring on the June 1967 War. Important though the latter were, they did not mark any significant shift in Syria's basic posture of confrontation with Israel, which stayed essentially the same through the Hafiz, Jadid, and al-Asad regimes, albeit with important variations of tone and of strategy.

Moreover, in light of this consistency, it must be stressed that important though it was, opposition to Israel was not the main litmus test of the Arab nationalist fervour of Syria's governments. Regarding Israel, all Syrian governments demonstrated a great deal of fervour, in keeping with the strongly pro-Palestinian orientation of Syrian public opinion throughout many decades.[24] The test was rather their position on the touchstone issues of Arab unity, genuine solidarity between the Arab states and commitment to a pan-Arab foreign policy. Here, there was a clear distinction between the conventionally Arabist approach of the Pan-Arab Command of the Ba'th Party, the Qiyada Qawmiyya dominated by Aflaq and Bitar, and that of the party's Syrian Regional Command. Dominated eventually by neo-Ba'thists like Jadid, the latter wing ended up taking over the Ba'th Party in Syria and steered it and the entire country away from the old approach.

Arab nationalists generally were demoralized and pan-Arab movements were in decline in Syria well before the June 1967 War. The classic brand of heroic unitary Arabism represented by the Syrian Ba'th Party's Pan-Arab Command was severely damaged by the failure of the union with Egypt in 1958 and then fatally wounded by the failure of the 1963 union talks with Egypt and Iraq. If the Ba'th Party could not unify the Arab world when it ruled two major Arab countries, and when Nasser ruled a third, what were its ideals worth? The party's fate as a vehicle for Arab nationalism was sealed as the old-guard civilian leadership of the Pan-Arab Command gave way to the hard, young military officers and

---

[24] See Muhannad Salhi, *Palestine in the Evolution of Syrian Nationalism, 1918–1920* (Chicago: Middle East Documentation Center, 2008) for evidence of how longstanding this orientation was. See also Rashid Khalidi, "The Role of the Press in the Early Arab Reaction to Zionism," *Peuples Méditerranéens/Mediterranean Peoples*, 20 July–September 1982, 105–24, for details regarding how much coverage some Syrian papers gave to the issue of Palestine before 1914.

their militant civilian comrades of the Regional Command. The latter group's vehicle for seizing power was aptly named, for it was by their devotion to taking and holding power in one state or *qutr* (a "region" of the larger Arab nation in Ba'thist parlance), that of Syria, that the neo-Ba'th came to be known. For them, in practice what was most important was Syria, "the beating heart of Arabism" (*qalb al-ʿuruba al-nabidh*) according to one Ba'thist formulation, and not the Arab nation that featured so prominently in the central slogan of the Ba'th Party ("one Arab nation with an eternal mission": *umma ʿarabiyya wahida dhat risala khalida*). The slogans remained unchanged and continued to be emblazoned on public buildings (and on antiquities like the Aleppo Citadel). The reality of policy, however, had changed fundamentally.

This "regionalist" orientation was brought to its logical conclusion after 1970 by al-Asad during his nearly three decades in power. As he exalted the power of the Syrian state, he made Syria a major regional player and an Arab power to be reckoned with for the first time in its modern history, and he ruthlessly elevated *raison d'état* (with the *état* needless to say being Syria) over any pan-Arab sentiment or policy. But this post-Arab nationalist "regionalist" orientation had already been well established before the 1967 war by the Jadid faction of the party, and its rise owed little or nothing to that conflict. Its radical appearance notwithstanding, Syria is another case that proves the thesis that 1967 was much less important than is often assumed in the decline of Arab nationalism during the second half of the twentieth century. In Syria, in reality, other factors than the impact of the 1967 war were paramount in this process, notably the failure of the Egyptian-Syrian union from 1958 to 1961 and of the subsequent 1963 unity talks. These resounding failures dashed the hopes of many Syrians in Nasser and the goal of Arab unity, the main purported objective of Arab nationalism.

The Palestinian National Movement

One of the main theses of this chapter has been that nation-state nationalism and *raison d'état* rather than Arab nationalism motivated the policies of most Arab states and nonstate actors even before the 1967 war (a major event that nevertheless made relatively little difference in this respect). But there is a problem when one looks at the Palestinian national movement. This problem is similar to those of explaining the Yemen war in the Egyptian case and the fiery radicalism of Jadid and his colleagues towards Israel in the Syrian case. Both appear to be instances of policy being driven by Arab nationalism, an appearance that was not correct in regard to Egypt and Syria before 1967. The problem with the Palestinian case resides in explaining away the post-1967 decline of the fervently Arabist MAN, a largely Palestinian group of Arab nationalists that dominated the Palestinian scene before the 1967 war while exhibiting intense loyalty to Nasser and Egypt. The MAN appeared to lose ground to the more Palestinian nationalist and less overtly Arabist Fatah in the aftermath of the war. This thus seems to have been a case of a major Arab nationalist movement declining as a direct result of the defeat of 1967.

Here too, it would be unwise to deny everything in the interest of upholding a thesis, but here too appearances are deceiving. MAN was certainly a fervently Arab nationalist grouping, and probably the most prominent force in Palestinian politics from the late 1950s until 1967.[25] MAN consistently offered strong support for Egypt's cautious and deliberate conventional military approach to Israel and stridently opposed "the reckless commando attacks" of Fatah. MAN echoed the arguments of Nasser that it was a mistake for Fatah and other groups to provoke Israel with pinprick attacks that had little serious military impact at a time when the Arab armies were not in a position to defend their countries, let alone take the offensive. Only when these armies had made the necessary preparations for a battle with Israel might such tactics be justified. In any case, it was essential that they be subordinated to a comprehensive military strategy of the Arab regular armies, led by that of Egypt. These positions came to look foolish, and MAN did suffer a precipitate decline in influence that redounded to the benefit of Fatah, after the conventional Egyptian military and those of Syria and Jordan were crushed in a few days in June 1967 by Israeli forces. In the wake of the traumatic events of 1967, Arab public opinion seemed to forget that Fatah and its Syrian backers had been irresponsible, and that by provoking an Israeli military command that was itching for a chance to unleash its powerful air force and army in a "preventive war," they had helped to drag Egypt and the Arabs into a losing conflict that had led to the occupation of more Arab territory.

A couple of points are worth making here that mar this apparently clear picture. The first is that the dominance of MAN in Palestinian politics

---

[25] For a convincing recent statement of this assessment, see Helga Baumgarten, "The Three Faces/Phases of Palestinian Nationalism, 1948–2005," *Journal of Palestine Studies* 43, no. 4 (Summer 2005), 25–48. For more on MAN, see Walid Kazziha, *Revolutionary Transformation in the Arab World: Habash and His Comrades from Nationalism to Marxism* (London: Charles Knight, 1975).

during the years immediately before the June War was more apparent than real. Strongly supported by the Egyptian government, whose interests it served faithfully, and benefiting from the incomparable prestige of Nasser, whose portrait hung on the walls of many Palestinian homes, there is no question that MAN was a major force in Palestinian politics before 1967. Even after MAN's eclipse in the wake of the war of that year, there was strong Palestinian popular support for MAN's offspring, the Popular Front for the Liberation of Palestine (PFLP), which was founded in December 1967. For several years, through the early 1970s, the PFLP posed a credible challenge to Fatah for hegemony over Palestinian politics.

Although all of this is true, the key element to bear in mind is that even before 1967, Fatah was rapidly gaining popularity and prestige among the Palestinian masses with its philosophy of direct armed action (*al-kifah al-musallah*, or armed struggle) against Israel and with its doctrine of Palestinian self-reliance instead of dependence on the Arab regimes. The public profile of Fatah with Arab public opinion rose higher every time Israel publicized the results of the newly founded commando movement's relatively minor military operations against Israeli targets. These operations increased in number after the neo-Ba'th coup of February 1966 led to greater Syrian support for Fatah, with a corresponding rise in Israeli stress on their impermissibility and in the number and ferocity of Israeli retaliatory attacks. This Israeli escalation in turn further raised the profile of Fatah, to the detriment of MAN.

This shift of opinion in favour of Fatah is even more understandable in view of the fact that by the mid-1960s there was great Palestinian impatience, especially among the young, with the apparent passivity of the Arab regimes towards Israel. This translated into criticism of MAN, seen by many as being too closely aligned with Egypt, and increasing support for Fatah, seen as largely independent of the Arab governments. Fatah also caught the mood of young Palestinians in particular, who were disdainful of what they considered to be the inactivity of their parents' generation in response to the *nakba* of 1948 and the intolerable situation it had created for the Palestinian people. By the end of 1966, these popular currents had swept along MAN and the Egyptian-dominated PLO, which both were impelled to swallow their opposition to the tactics of Fatah and were obliged to field guerrilla forces in a vain attempt to compete with its approach.

It is worth considering here the differences between the founding leaders of MAN and Fatah. The former were largely intellectuals and professionals like George Habash and Wadi' Haddad, both medical doctors who had trained at the American University of Beirut (AUB). Having been attracted to the strong Arab nationalist current, which had long existed at AUB, and searching for a way to reverse the disastrous impact of the *nakba*, they saw the Egyptian revolution as providing Arab nationalism with what it had lacked since the demise of King Faisal I of Iraq in 1933: a charismatic leader at the head of a major Arab state.[26] By contrast, the more lower-middle class founding leaders of Fatah, most of whom had come to political maturity in the Gaza Strip, in Egyptian universities, or under other forms of Egyptian tutelage, did not share the starry-eyed view of Egypt and its pan-Arab rhetoric held by many Palestinians farther afield in Jordan, Lebanon, and elsewhere. For the latter, Egypt was a distant potential saviour, and Nasser another Saladin, just waiting for the proper moment to act in the name of Arabism against the alien settler-state that had been planted in the heart of the region. Egypt was seen by them as standing up to the Western powers, and its anti-Israel rhetoric garnered it wide support from Palestinians living at a distance. By contrast, the founders of Fatah, and other Palestinians like those of the Gaza Strip who had had firsthand dealings with Egypt and understood well the practical limits of its stated commitment to the Palestine cause, had a much more jaundiced view of its military regime and its army and security services. This view was born of repression, arrests, and torture at their hands, as is attested by the accounts of the early years of their movement left by such Fatah founding leaders as Yasser Arafat, Khalil al-Wazir (Abu Jihad), and Salah Khalaf (Abu Iyad).[27]

From the announcement of its first attack against Israel in January 1965, Fatah was openly committed to the idea of Palestine first, and that the Palestinians must take charge of their own destiny. Their newsletter, which first announced the existence of the new movement, was entitled *Filastinuna*, "Our Palestine," suggesting its Palestine-centric focus, and the idea that the Palestinians, not all the Arabs, "owned" the Palestine question. This was exemplified in the approach of Fatah's paramount leader. In a political career that stretched from his involvement in the 1947–48 war as a student until his death in 2004, the phrase that best

---

[26] An Arab nationalist grouping at the AUB called *al-'Urwa al-Wuthqa*, "the firm bond," had for years attracted students from all over the Arab word. This Quranic term was also the title of the newspaper edited from Paris during the 1880s by Jamal al-Din al-Afghani and Muhammad 'Abdu.

[27] For personal details see Abu Iyad, *My Home, My Land*, 24–8, and Alan Hart, *Arafat: Terrorist or Peacemaker* (London: Sidgwick and Jackson, 1984), 100–5.

represents Arafat's political credo was his call for *"al-qarar al-filastini al-mustaqil,"* the independent Palestinian decision. This slogan meant that the Palestinian people must be independent of the Arab tutelage under which they had chafed not only since the *nakba* of 1948, but also since the failure of the 1936–39 revolt in Palestine. For Arafat, who was born in 1929 and had long witnessed this humiliating and disastrous dependence, this was an essential element of his political vision. In some respects, it was more fully developed than his attitude towards Israel. This desire for the Palestinians to achieve independence of the Arab states in turn was the driving force of the policy of Fatah, and later of the PLO, which Fatah has dominated since 1968. This was the exact antithesis of the approach of MAN, which preached Palestinian integration into the strategy of Egypt, the Arab nationalist bastion.

This clear distinction between the two movements has often been noted, as have the rise of Fatah and the decline of MAN. However, the degree to which the former was in complete contradiction with not only the key aims of Arab nationalism like Arab unity but also with the orthodoxy of most Arab nationalists, which consisted in subordinating their actions to Egyptian policy, has less frequently been remarked upon. In reality, the rise of Fatah in the years before 1967, its success in winning the initiative from MAN, and its ability, together with its Syrian allies, to drive regional events towards confrontation with Israel against the wishes of the most powerful Arab state, Egypt, not only helped to precipitate the June 1967 War, but they also mark the rise of nation-state nationalism and the demise of Arabism in much of the Arab world even before the 1967 war. This watershed event did no more than bury an Arab nationalism that was already all but deceased in Egypt, Syria, and the Palestinian political arena.

The Transformation of Arab Politics

Disentangling Myth from Reality

Fawaz A. Gerges

This chapter examines the effects of the June 1967 War on the balance of social and political forces in the Arab world and assesses the extent to which Israel's crushing defeat of the Arab armies transformed Arab politics. Did the third Arab-Israeli war mark a paradigm shift from secular pan-Arabism to religious nationalism or pan-Islamism? The question is not whether the 1967 defeat was a turning point in Arab politics. It clearly was. The real question is how, when, and in what ways did the shift from pan-Arab nationalism to pan-Islamism occur? The critical challenge is to contextualize the 1967 War within previous and subsequent developments and to assess its significance and impact on the course of modern Arab history.

To grasp fully the consequences of the June War, it is crucial to examine the internal and external challenges encountered by the Gamal Abdel Nasser pan-Arabist regime on the eve of the war. Domestically, the consequences of the 1967 defeat must be placed within preceding and subsequent developments. By 1965, the Nasser pan-Arabist regime reached a critical deadlock, particularly its much-touted economic program of "populist etatisme," or populist state capitalism, was in crisis. According to John Waterbury, far from increasing productivity, the public sector caused a massive decline: "The crisis that overtook Egypt in 1956–66... was caused by the gross inefficiencies of a public sector called upon

I want to thank my research assistant Andrew Bowen, a doctoral candidate at the London School of Economics, for his help in editing this chapter. My thanks also go to my colleagues, Drs. Tewfik Aclimandos, Katerina Dalacoura, and Yasser Elwy for their comments on the first draft of this chapter.

to do too many things: sell products at cost or at a loss, take on labour unrelated to production needs, earn foreign exchange, and satisfy local demand. It was also caused by the neglect of the traditional agricultural sector which, while taxed, was not reformed so as to become an engine of growth in its own right."[1]

As populist state capitalism was almost brought to a halt during 1965 and 1966, restructuring became inevitable. But the burden of restructuring fell exclusively on the lower-middle and working classes whose income and standards of living declined considerably and threatened the regime's populist coalition.[2]

Expansion of educational opportunities for the young, population growth, and increasing rural migration to urban Cairo overtaxed the ability of the incompetent bureaucracy to provide jobs and essential services and threatened to upset the interests of the rising new middle class. Centralized state planning created swollen bureaucracies but sluggish economic performance, thus producing a systemic overload. Reality did not live up to expectations.[3]

Nasser faced a more hostile and threatening regional environment than before. The flames of the Arab cold war were rekindled. In a textbook case of strategic overreach, Nasser's army was bogged down in a prolonged and costly war in Yemen. The Yemen war literally sapped the strength of the Egyptian state and pit it in a bitter war-by-proxy against one of its regional rivals, Saudi Arabia, and its superpower patron – the United States. To counterbalance Nasser's pan-nationalist appeal, the Saudi monarchy, along with the United States, utilized "Islamic solidarity" and portrayed the power struggle as one between faith and atheism. The result worsened Egypt's already tense relations with the administration of President Lyndon Johnson and forced Nasser into an uncomfortable dependency on the Soviet Union.[4]

---

[1] John Waterbury, *Egypt of Nasser and Sadat: the Political Economy of Two Regimes* (Princeton, NJ: University Press: 1983).

[2] Ghali Shoukri, *Al-Thawra al-modadda fi Misr* [Counter-Revolution in Egypt], 3rd ed. [in Arabic] (Cairo: El Alahi, 1987); Yasser Elwy, *A Political Economy of Egyptian Foreign Policy: State, Ideology and Modernisation since 1970* (PhD diss., Department of International Relations, London School of Economics, 2009).

[3] L. Carl Brown, *Religion and State: The Muslim Approach to Politics* (New York: Columbia University Press, 2000), 130–3.

[4] Mohammed Heikal, *Minutes of a Political Investigation before the "Socialist Prosecutor"* [in Arabic] (Beirut: 1982); Michael Doran, "Egypt," in *Diplomacy in the Middle East: The International Relations of Regional and Outside Powers*, ed. L. Carl Brown (London: I. B. Tauris, 2001), 97–120.

In addition to his rivalry with the so-called reactionary Arab regimes and their imperial masters, Nasser had to contend with a deadlier internal challenge – Arab radicals in Syria, Iraq, Palestine, and elsewhere who questioned his revolutionary credentials and accused him of forfeiting the struggle to liberate Palestine. The intranationalist dispute proved to be Nasser's undoing because, as a self-styled revolutionary, he could not afford another blow to his legitimacy – his leadership of the "Arab cause."[5]

It is within this complex context that the Six-Day War must be placed. Long before the 1967 defeat, the Nasser pan-Arabist regime had overextended itself and got entangled in a web of domestic and international crises.[6] Its very constituency, the new middle class, was restive and anxious about its economic well-being and status. The failure of Nasser's attempts to foster a "transition to socialism" necessitated painful restructuring and put immense stress on the legitimacy of his regime, which partly depended on its populist achievements.[7]

From the mid-1960s onwards, the Nasser regime was pulled and pushed in different directions by competing social groups. The ideological balance that Nasser tried to maintain was fraying under mounting domestic and international pressure. The writing was on the wall.

In addition to the challenges facing pan-Arabism before the Six-Day War, it is essential to take into account the coming to power of Anwar Sadat after Nasser's death of a heart attack in 1970 and the subsequent frontal assault he launched against his predecessor's inheritance and legacy. The long-term consequences of the Six-Day War must consider the pivotal role of the Egyptian state, particularly the transition of power from Nasser to Sadat and the latter's radical change of direction at home and abroad.

Challenging the received wisdom, my central argument is that the 1967 defeat did not lead to the rise of pan-Islamism, but that other causes, such as the role of Sadat and his regime and the oil revolution, were the drivers behind the ideological transformation of Arab politics.

---

[5] Raymond A. Hinnebusch, *Egyptian Politics under Sadat: The Post-populist Development of an Authoritarian-modernizing State* (Cambridge: Cambridge University Press, 1985), 35.

[6] Fouad Matar, *Frankly about Nasser: A 30-hour Interview with Mohammed Hassanein Heikal* [in Arabic] (Beirut: 1975), 166–99.

[7] Yasser Elwy, *A Political Economy of Egyptian Foreign Policy: State, Ideology and Modernisation since 1970* (PhD diss., Department of International Relations, London School of Economics, 2009).

After the 1967 defeat, religiously based activists and movements did not just burst onto the Arab scene, nor did secular Arab nationalism, a deeply entrenched ideological narrative, just fade away.[8] Such a hypothesis neglects the symbiotic relationship between ideas and material interests. Yes, the 1967 defeat undermined the authority and efficacy of Nasser's policies and practices, if not his theoretical and ideological narrative. Nasser was seriously injured and shrewd observers doubted if he could recover. But Sadat's advent to power and his concerted effort to purge Egypt of Nasser's pan-Arabism was the decisive weight that tipped the scale against secular nationalist and socialist ideas in favour of religiosity and, subsequently, politicized religion.

The chapter will chronicle the steps and initiatives taken by the Sadat administration, from 1971 onwards, which empowered religiously based groups and fragmented and weakened secular nationalist and socialist forces. For example, the Sadat regime portrayed the 1973 October War as a divine victory; "God and His angels," proclaimed the state-controlled media, "fought on the side of courageous Egyptian soldiers against the Zionist enemy." Time and again shown on television screens praying at mosques clutching his prayer beads and softly murmuring Allah's name, the "pious president," as opposed to the "apostate" or "atheist," conveyed a sense of piety and symbolic divergence with his predecessor. Nasser's Arab nationalism was criticized as secular or antireligious because it presupposed that the bonds that tie the Arab people are language, history, and a sense of belonging, not only religion.

Religious programmes dominated the airwaves. In Egyptian universities, the state actively supported religiously based students against their

---

[8] It is worth stressing that as a guide to foreign policy (a practiced ideology, not just as a "theory or narrative"), Arab nationalism shifted throughout the 1960s between two competing formulations: the minimalist "unity of ranks," Wihdat al-Saf, implied finding the lowest common denominator amongst Arab regimes with heterogeneous social dispositions and political agenda. The other view, a more radical "unity of goal," Wihdat al-hadaf, implied radicalization of conservative Arab regimes and called for a minimum degree of homogeneity between the Arab countries for any joint Arab action to bear fruition. The 1967 defeat tilted the balance in favour of the "unity of ranks" formula, which manifested in the forced reconciliation of President Nasser and King Faisal in the famous Khartoum summit in 1967. Such transformation rendered the post-1967 subsystem more conservative, and thereby both less attractive to the injured pride of the Arab people (many of whom sought an alternative in the then-glorified "Palestinian Armed Struggle") and more vulnerable to attacks from a host of "conservative" ideologues – pre-1952 "liberal and Westernised" elite and Islamists alike. This shift subsequently facilitated the triumph of ultraconservative religious forces and the transformation of Arab politics.

nationalist and leftist counterparts and dramatically tilted the balance in favour of the former. During the 1970s the "petro-dollar" financed the publications of hundreds, if not thousands, of religious texts every year. An alliance of convenience between the Sadat regime and the Saudi monarchy played a key role in reshaping the sociological and ideological landscape of Arab societies. The Islamic revolution in Iran during the late 1970s, however, turned Sadat's social assets into lethal liabilities.

Although the 1967 defeat inflicted considerable damage on Nasser, nationalist and socialist ideas permeated social space and continued to dominate the Arab/Muslim landscape, with the exception of the Gulf sheikdoms. This point is distinct from the causes of the partial shift from nationalism-socialism to pan-Islamism, a focal point of my analysis. To emphasize this focal point, the chapter is divided into two sections. In the first section, it revisits the flood of writings and the torrent of self-criticism and self-doubt expressed by the Arab intelligentsia in the aftermath of the defeat in order to transport the reader to that painful moment in contemporary Arab history. Readers will get a full portrait of how Arab scholars, theorists, intellectuals, publicists, and activists viewed and interpreted the Six-Day War. The 1967 defeat was seen as a civilizational challenge, not just a military setback, as shattering as the loss of Palestine in 1948.

On the morning after, no one captured the spirit of the moment better than Naguib Mahfouz, a prominent Arab novelist and Noble Prize laureate: "Never before or after in my life had I ever experienced such a shattering of consciousness as I felt at that moment."[9]

The goal of fleshing out the soul searching triggered by Israel's stunning victory over the Arab armies is to show that most critics were part of the Nasser pan-Arabist constituency, not ideological adversaries. The defeat shook the confidence and morale of this constituency to its very foundation but did not shake its belief in the supremacy of secular nationalist and socialist ideas. Critics took Nasser to task for being a centrist who had not broken free of his petty bourgeois class and religious affiliation and identity. They called for a radical shift to the left, not the right, and a clean break with the past. Of all the storm of protests, there was only one religious voice that ascribed the defeat to the Arabs forfeiting their faith in God. Even after the defeat, the secular nationalist and socialist paradigm remained ascendant.

---

[9] Mahfouz's confessions to Ragaa El-Naqqash in *Naguib Mahfouz: Safahat min muzakaratih* [Naguib Mahfouz: Pages from his Memoirs] (Cairo: 1998).

Reconstructing the state of mind of the Arab intelligentsia and the configuration of social forces in the first section allows me to lay out my arguments and evidence about the state's role, or the Sadat regime's role, in helping to engineer an ideological shift or transformation of Arab politics during the 1970s. If after the defeat, leading opinion makers, scholars, and critics called on Arab rulers to abandon the middle ground, turn leftward, and structurally revolutionize backward Arab societies, what then explains the 180 degree turn to the right during the 1970s? What fuelled and caused this historical right-wing shift?

It is worth mentioning that after the Six-Day War, Nasser's domestic and foreign policy moved further and further to the left, with the exception of secularism and class war. "I am an extremist leftist," Nasser sarcastically called himself during his last three years in power. By 1970, when Nasser died, the country's foreign policy was firmly anchored in the Soviet camp.[10]

In the second section, my major task is to show and account for the forces and powers that brought about the reordering and restructuring of the Arab social and political milieu. In particular, it will be shown that the alliance between the Sadat regime and the House of Saud, along with the oil revolution, played a key role in the ideological transformation of Arab politics.

The Morning After: A Torrent of Self-Criticism and Soul Searching

"Defeat goes deeper into the human soul than victory," wrote Albert Hourani, the preeminent historian of the modern Middle East, in his *History of the Arab Peoples*: "To be in someone else's power is a conscious

---

[10] Nasser's overreliance on the Soviet Union to rebuild his broken army after the 1967 defeat went hand in hand with a new economic policy trend at home away from socialist economics toward a more mixed, liberal market. Several measures of economic liberalization were introduced. The March 30th 1968 Manifesto sought to silence the "calls for radicalisation" and the "technocratic discourse" of the regime – arguing that the rightward shift is a result of technical soundness, not ideological backwardness. On this point, see Elwy, *A Political Economy of Egyptian Foreign Policy*; Hinnebusch, *Egyptian Politics under Sadat*; John Waterbury, *The Egypt of Nasser and Sadat: The Political Economy of Two Regimes* (New York: Princeton University Press, 1983); Mourad Wahba, *The Role of the State in the Egyptian Economy 1945–1981* (Berkshire, UK: Garnet Publishing, 1994). Although after the Six-Day War Nasser began the rapprochement with Saudi Arabia, Sadat built a strategic relationship with the Saudis and used it against their common enemies – Nasserists, socialists, and Marxists. That holy alliance was fuelled and cemented by the oil revolution, a development that tipped the balance of social forces in favour of religiously based groups.

experience which induces doubts about the ordering of the universe." Israel's crushing defeat of the Arabs in 1967 was widely regarded as being not only *an-Naksah*, the setback, but also a kind of "moral judgment."[11]

The defeat was painfully personalized and internalized by leading Arab intellectuals, writers, critics, and scholars like Naguib Mahfouz, a prominent novelist, one of the few contemporaries who subtly criticized the Nasser regime at the height of its power.[12] The rupture and psychological trauma that Mahfouz and his generation experienced stemmed from the gravity and totality of defeat and a widely held misperception that the Arabs had finally reached a promising historic moment, one of empowerment and renewal.

Thus, as the cultural critic George Tarabishi notes, the 1967 defeat shocked the Arab imagination because there had existed among Arabs a common tendency to overestimate their strength and power and underestimate that of their enemy.[13] Nourished on illusions of grandeur and an exaggerated sense of self-importance, Arab leaders banished the idea of military defeat from their thinking and planning, promising citizens glorious victories over real and imagined enemies.

In charged, painful reflections, Tawfiq al-Hakim, a leading dramatist and a critic whose earlier writing influenced the formation of a young Nasser's nationalism, notes that "the nightmare of the defeat" was a rude awakening from a sweet dream. When the war broke out on 5 June, al-Hakim describes a festive mood on the streets of Cairo where the ruling party, the Arab Socialist Union, had put up signs with written victory slogans such as "on to Tel Aviv...."

It is worth citing al-Hakim at length – because of his intellectual stature, as well as his harsh criticism of Nasser, which triggered a storm of protests – in order to give the reader a glimpse of the public mood in Egypt and the Arab world on the morning of the outbreak of hostilities:

The whole atmosphere around us almost convinced us that the entry of our armies into Tel Aviv would not be later than nine o'clock in the evening of the same day, 5 June 1967.... The next few days passed and our forces were in a continuous retreat which resembled a rout.

It was impossible, intellectually or logically, easily to believe that our armies could be routed in a few days. Years had passed during which the regime

---

[11] Albert Hourani, *History of the Arab Peoples* (Cambridge, MA: Harvard University Press, 1991), 300, 442.

[12] See Mahfouz's confessions to Ragaa El-Naqqash in *Naguib Mahfouz*.

[13] Tarabishi, *Al-muthaqafoun al-Arab and al-turath* [Arab Intellectuals and the Heritage] [in Arabic] (Beirut, n.d.), 22, 39–40.

emphasized the army's marvels and showed us, whenever there was a revolutionary celebration, military reviews which included the latest models of tanks. During those parades we saw the rockets called al-Qahir and al-Zafir and saw units called al-Sa'iqah, which ran snarling a frightening roar; we saw troops which dropped down from the heights, which hurdled over walls, and which literally tore up and ate snakes. . . .

We had also heard in speeches about the power of our aircraft which had no equal in the Middle East.

We saw ourselves as a major industrial state, a leader of the developing world in agricultural reform, and the strongest striking force in the Middle East. The face of the idolized leader, which filled the television screen and loomed at us from the podia of pavilions and of auditoria, related these tales to us for long hours and explained to us how we had been before and what we had now become. No one argued, checked, verified or commented. We could not help but believe, and burn our hands with applause.

But as the truth of defeat reared its ugly head, "on that day," recollects al-Hakim, I sat in front of the television open mouthed like a moron listening to the collapse of revolutionary Egypt – a process which was complete in a few hours. But the drone continued in the accustomed way all around me: patriotic anthems, the songs of singers and songstresses, and company banners: victory, victory, victory, this Victory Company, that Victory Company, Victory Automobile, Victory Manufacture, Victory Store – everything victory on victory on victory. . . . But Egypt hardly reasoned and was unconscious of the fact that she had become a laughing-stock through these words and descriptions.[14]

In his controversial testimony, *'Awdat al-Wa'i* or *The Return of Consciousness*, al-Hakim paints a grim portrait of political life in Egypt during the 1950s and 1960s where he and other intellectuals lost consciousness and blindly followed the new mahdi Nasser:[15] "Was it a strange case of anaesthetization?" enquires al-Hakim bitterly. "Were we bewitched . . . ? Or was it that we had become used to the kind of life in which the revolution had placed us, a life in which we were stripped of any means of reception – inside a box which was locked on us by lies and delusions . . . ?" Al-Hakim lays the blame squarely at the feet of the Nasser revolution, which "bewitched us with the glitter of hope and intoxicated us with the wine of 'attainment' and 'glory,' and we got so drunk that we lost consciousness."[16]

Regardless if one agrees with al-Hakim's damning indictment of Nasser, whom he calls "the absolute ruler," the substance of his

---

[14] Tawfiq Al-Hakim, *'Awdat al-Wa'i* [The Return of Consciousness], trans. Bayly Winder, (New York and London: New York University Press, 1985), 39–43.

[15] Ibid., 1–73.

[16] Ibid., 44–57.

critique, if not the tone, was echoed by Egyptian and Arab intellectuals and writers from across the ideological spectrum. This was particularly the case amongst ardent supporters of Arab unity and pan-Arabism as well as Marxists. The intelligentsia poured scorn on the military rulers who promised salvation but delivered defeat and called for a new revolution to liberate Arabs from backwardness, patriarchy, and authoritarianism. In their eyes, the war's shocking denouement was a referendum on Nasser's policies and practices.

In the poem "hawamish al daftar al-naksa" ("Footnotes in Setback's Notebook"), memorized by millions of agonizing Arabs and secretly copied and circulated in Egypt after the censorship refused to publish it, Nizar Qabbani, a popular poet and ardent supporter of Nasser, proclaimed the death of the Arab order and cried for revolutionary change:[17]

> 1
> The old word is dead.
> The old books are dead.
> Our speech with holes like worn-out shoes is dead.
> Dead is the mind that led to defeat.
>
> 7
> In short
> We wear the cape of civilization
> But our souls live in the stone age.
>
> 12
> Our enemies did not cross our borders
> They crept through our weaknesses like ants.
>
> 14
> We spend our days practicing witchcraft,
> Playing chess and sleeping.
> Are we the 'the Nation by which God blessed mankind'?
>
> 17
> If I knew I'd come to no harm,
> And could see the Sultan,
> This is what I would say:
> 'Sultan,
> When I came close to your walls
> and talked about my pains,
> Your soldiers beat me with their boots,
> Forced me to eat my shoes,

---

[17] I cite this long poem selectively from Nizar Qabbani, *Complete Political Poems* [al-Amal al-siyasiya al-Kamilah] (Beirut: 1993) III, 71–98, to drive that point home.

Sultan,
You lost two wars,
Sultan,
Half of our people are without tongues,
What's the use of a people without tongues?
Half of our people
Are trapped like ants and rats
Between walls.'
If I knew I'd come to no harm
I'd tell him:
'You lost two wars
You lost touch with children.'

18
If we hadn't buried our unity
If we hadn't ripped its young body with bayonets
If it had stayed in our eyes
The dogs wouldn't have savaged our flesh

20
Arab children,
You will break our chains,
Kill the opium in our heads,
Kill the illusions.
Arab children,
Don't read our suffocated generation,
We are a hopeless case.
We are as worthless as a water-melon rind.
Don't read about us,
Don't ape us,
Don't accept our ideas,
We are a nation of crooks and jugglers.
Arab children
Spring rain,
Corn ears of the future,
You are the generation
That will overcome defeat.[18]

Qabbani questions the very foundation of Arab state and society and even culture. For him, like the 1948 defeat, the 1967 rout exposed the dismal failure of the Arab political system and showed its backwardness and oppressiveness. Labelling Nasser another "sultan" not unlike his predecessors who lost the 1948 Palestine war, Qabbani calls on a new

---

[18] Qabbani, *Complete Political Poems*, 71–98.

generation of Arab children, not tainted or corrupted by power, to smash the existing order and overcome defeat.

The significance of Qabbani's critique is that it came from within the constituency of the Nasser pan-Arab nationalist elite. Although Qabbani was not actively political, he was a vocal advocate of Arab nationalism and unity. Far from an enemy of Nasser, Qabbani publicly supported the Egyptian revolution and celebrated its achievements, particularly its political triumphs in the 1956 Suez Crisis and the 1958 union between Egypt and Syria. He acknowledged he was embittered by the 1967 defeat:

> My grieved country,
> In a flash
> You changed me from a poet who wrote love poems
> To a poet who writes with a knife[19]

Qabbani was the rule, not the exception, among opinion makers and intellectuals who backed Nasser's pan-Arab nationalist vision. The dominant narrative is that the 1967 defeat was "the mother of all defeats," in the words of a nationalist Bahraini writer, Mohammed Jaber al-Ansari, because it has had catastrophic civilizational and psychological repercussions on Arabs: "the defeat was first and foremost existential."[20]

According to al-Ansari, on multiple levels the Arabs still have not recovered from the effects of the defeat – their lands still occupied, their politics and society penetrated by the great powers, and they seem unable to overcome a mind-set of fatalism and impotency. Similar to the loss of the 1948 Palestine War, the 1967 defeat was a turning point that arrested sociological and institutional development of Arab countries and prematurely blocked their quest to achieve genuine self-reliance, independence and empowerment. That trauma, the unrealized promise, the shattered dreams, still haunts the Arab imagination.[21]

Although some zealous Nasserists and pan-Arabists downplayed the significance of the defeat by calling it *al-naksa*, they were a minority, a voice in the wilderness, a counterproductive claim, difficult to sell. In his book, *Mina al-naksa ila al-thawra* (*From Naksa to Revolution*), Nadim Bittar, a zealous nationalist scholar, contended that what happened in the 1967 war was only a setback, and that despite the pain it caused, he

---

[19] Ibid., 73.
[20] Mohammed Jaber al-Ansari, *Al-Nassiriya bimazour naqdi* [Nasserism in a Critical Eye] (Beirut: 2002), 151.
[21] Although written after the Six-Day War, al-Ansari, Mahfouz, and others do capture the temperaments and sensibilities of Arabs.

declared, "We welcome the *naksa*, and its great challenges." Adopted by official circles, that slogan, *naksa*, as opposed to defeat, proved to be a difficult sell for sceptical Arabs. In particular, as time progressed and the consequences of defeat persisted, Nasser's initial pledge to "eradicating the consequences of aggression" no longer resonated.

A consensus has emerged among Arabs that in 1967 their society, not just their military, was defeated and that the catastrophe exposed its civilizational and scientific backwardness. Reputed Egyptian writer, Ahmed Baha' al-Din, argued that the Israeli challenge is more civilizational than military and that the defeat was the failure of modernization.[22] Therefore, it is essential, as the progressive intellectual Yasin al-Hafiz argues, to situate the defeat within a broader context: The deeper meaning of the Six-Day War is much bigger than a military defeat; it is a societal defeat. *The Defeat and the Defeated Ideology (Al-hazima wa al-idioligia al-mahzouma)* is the title of al-Hafiz' book, in which he bluntly contends that in the 1967 war the pan-Arabist ideology of the Nasser regime was dealt a hard blow.

Like al-Hafiz, novelist Tawfiq al-Hakim contends that the political system that emerged out of the 1952 revolution lost its equilibrium and balance after the 1967 defeat and subsequently collapsed. The defeat shook the ideology of the "dictatorial" regime to its very foundation and hammered a deadly nail in its coffin. When Nasser died of a heart attack three years later, centrifugal forces swiftly dismantled the pan-Arabist edifice so painstakingly constructed by Nasser between 1954 and 1967.

Interestingly, immediately after the Six-Day War, Nasser arrived at a similar conclusion. In a stormy session of the Supreme Executive Committee of the Arab Socialist Union (ASU), its highest decision-making body, lasting for two nights in early August 1967, Nasser frankly admitted that the war was disastrous, and it exposed the failure of the country's closed single-party system: "Our system has not been sound," he said. He reminded his colleagues of what citizens were saying in private: "we are devouring one another and that the system is self-destructing." Change or die, Nasser warned his five shaken council members. He lectured them about how "the state broke down into several power centers: Abdel Hakim's power center, Zakaria's [Mohieddin] power center, al-Sadat's power center, Ali Sabri's power center, and so on."[23]

---

[22] Ahmed Baha' al-Din, *Israeliyat wa ma ba'ad Al-udwan* [Israelites and the Aftermath of the Aggression] (Cairo: n.d.).

[23] Abdel Magid Farid, *Min mahadir ijtima'at Abdel Nasser al-Arabiya wa al-dawliya: 1967–1970* [Nasser: The Final Years] (Beirut: 1985), 281–306.

Arab historian, Constantine Zurayk, who during the early 1950s published *ma'na al-nakba* (*The Meaning of the Disaster*), which had vivisected the causes behind the loss of Palestine in 1948, revisited the meaning of disaster, in a book in Arabic, almost two decades later. Zurayk listed two reasons for the 1967 disaster that has befallen the Arabs – scientific underdevelopment and weak spirit of *asabiya* or activism. Israel crushed the Arab armies because it was more advanced scientifically and technologically. The Arabs also lost the struggle because they lacked clarity of purpose, which he attributes to divisiveness and fragmentation into warring "nationalist," socialist," and "reactionary" camps. Zurayk spent a lifetime calling for a transformation of Arab societies along rational and scientific lines, shedding mythology, conspiracy, emotionalism, and illusion: the real challenge facing the Arabs is *Ma'rakat al-hadara'* (*The Battle of Civilization*).[24]

Similarly, Moroccan historian Abdallah Laroui views the Six-Day War as a watershed marking the end of an important epoch in Arab history. According to Laroui, pan-Arabism, a response to the colonial legacy, was an ambitious effort to free the Arab world from the clutches of dependency and achieve real independence. That new historical phase in Arab politics met its waterloo during the Six-Day War, causing a structural crisis that had yet to be resolved.[25]

According to Laroui, what was needed to overcome the crisis in Arab thought was genuine historical understanding and a willingness to transcend the past, to take what was important from it by "radical criticism of culture, language and tradition" and utilize it to create a new future. This process of critical understanding must be guided by the living thought of the age, particularly Marxism if correctly understood, whereby the past is instilled and incorporated into a new system of thought and action.[26]

Other Marxists like the Syrian philosopher Sadiq Jalal al-ʿAzm and Egyptian economist Samir Amin attributed the 1967 defeat to the very religious structure of traditional Arab society and the crisis of the modern nation-state. The postcolonial state, they argued, had not settled vital questions of Arab unity and foreign policy, the class nature of the regime,

[24] Constantine Zurayk, *The Meaning of the Disaster Revisited* (Beirut: 1967), 14, 17. See also his *Battle of Civilization* (Beirut: n.d.).

[25] Abdallah Laroui, *The Crisis of the Arab Intellectual: Traditionalism or Historicism?* (Berkeley: University of California Press, 1976), vii–ix.

[26] See Abdallah Laroui, *L'ideologie Arabe Contemporaine* (Paris: 1977); and Abdallah Laroui, *The Crisis of the Arab Intellectua: Traditionalism or Historicism* (Berkley: 1976); Hourani, *History of the Arab Peoples*, 445.

and the corresponding development strategy. Unlike Laroui, al-A'zm and Amin were neither concerned about reconciliation of past and present nor bridging the divide between *turath* (heritage) and modernity. Al-'Azm stressed that the solution to the Arab predicament lies in authentic scientific Marxism and the total rejection of religious thought. Amin decried the inherent weaknesses of the petty bourgeois nationalist movement of the Nasser variety to carry out an authentic socialist revolution. Both pin the blame indirectly on Nasser's haphazard policies and unwillingness to cut the umbilical cord from the referential framework of the past and his petty bourgeois class.[27]

Although not completely agreeing with the Marxist critique of traditional Arab society, Syrian scholar Burhan Ghalyoun zeroes in on the crisis of the modern nation-state, particularly the tiny power elite that has remained aloof from the Arab masses. In contrast to the journey of its Western counterpart, which emerged as a means of freeing knowledge and reason from the domination of an elitist and obstructionist theocracy, the Arab secular modernizing elite has been given a privileged position by the state and has affirmed and justified the existing undemocratic and unfair system, "either in the name of progress or the logic of history, but always against the freedom of ordinary individual."[28]

The Transformation

It is worth stressing that after the Six-Day War the wave of self-doubt came predominantly from nationalist, Marxist, and liberal quarters, not from those religiously based or with an Islamist orientation. Initially, few critics explained the 1967 defeat in religious terms. For example, in his book, *A'midat al-nakba* (*The Pillars of the Disaster*), Salah al-Din al-Munajjid argued that the Arabs had been defeated because they "forfeited their faith in God, so He gave up on them."[29] But al-Munijjad's was a lone voice in a chorus dominated by pan-Arabists, liberals, and leftists.

---

[27] Sadiq Jalal al-'Azm, *al-naqd al-dhati ba'd al-hazima* [Self-Criticism after the Defeat] (Beirut: 1968); Sadiq Jalal al-'Azm, *naqd al-fikr al-dini* [Critique of Religious Thought] (Beirut: 1969); Samir Amin, *The Arab Nation: Nationalism and Class Struggles* (London: Zed Books, 1978).

[28] See Burhan Ghalyoun, *Ightiyal al-'aql* [The Closing of the [Arab] Mind] (Cairo: 1990), 198, 240–7, 300; and his *Naqd al-siyassa* [Critique of Politics] (Beirut: 1991). For an excellent summary, see Ibrahim M. Abu-Rabi', *Intellectual Origins of Islamic Resurgence in the Modern Arab World* (New York: 1996), 259–61.

[29] Salah al-Din al-Munajjid, *A'midat al-nakba* [The Pillars of the Disaster] (Beirut: 1967), 17.

At the risk of redundancy, what explains the paucity of the religious trend in the critiques of the 1967 war and the dominance of nationalist and secularist writers? How does one then explain the religious awakening that has swept Arab and Muslim lands since the 1970s and the rise of radically politicized religious groups and movements? This is not merely an academic exercise but is essential to deciphering the causes and variables behind the transformation of Arab politics and the surge of political Islam during the last four decades. One of my key arguments is that there is no direct, straightforward line or link between the Arab defeat in the 1967 war and the Islamic revival of the early 1970s. Much more of a link exists to the rise of political Islam than a single cause event, notwithstanding the significance of the 1967 war and its repercussions.

No doubt the 1967 defeat was a transformational development in regional politics, one that undermined the legitimacy and authority of Nasser's pan-Arabist ideology because for more than a decade the Egyptian state claimed ownership of it.

In the eyes of Arabs, the crushing defeat discredited the radical tenets of the thesis of "state and revolution" enunciated by Egyptian leaders at the height of the country's "sacred march" in 1961:

Egypt as a state and as a revolution.... If as a state Egypt recognizes boundaries in its dealings with governments, Egypt as a revolution should never hesitate to halt before these boundaries but should carry its message beyond the borders to the people in order to initiate its revolutionary mission.[30]

Egypt's dual role, as a state and as revolution, was no longer tenable after the 1967 defeat. One of the major consequences of the Six-Day War was that theoretically and operationally Nasser had little choice but to relinquish Egypt's role as a revolutionary vanguard and concentrate on rebuilding his broken army. The logic and survival of the state took priority over Nasser's desire to spread revolution to neighbouring Arab countries and topple rival reactionary regimes.

Nasser's decision to desist from even paying lip service to Egypt's dual role was a product of necessity, not choice. The destruction of the Egyptian armed forces left Nasser with painful, costly options and tied his hands. He became increasing dependent on the economic support of conservative oil-producing states after the Khartoum summit in August 1967. Equally important, the defeat compromised Nasser's revolutionary

---

[30] *Al-Ahram*, Cairo, 29 December 1961. See Adeed Dawisha, *The Arab Radicals* (New York: Council on Foreign Relations Press, 1986), 12–13.

appeal among supporters and battered his reputation as the leader who would bring deliverance and salvation. The Arab mood darkened. A sense of uncertainty, doubt, and questioning of authority set in.

As the late Malcolm Kerr noted, Nasser's popularity and moral standing among Arabs rested on twin pillars: the liberation of Palestine from the Zionist usurpers and the liberation of the Arab world from reactionary rulers and their imperialist masters. Whether Nasser had been actually committed to the liberation of Palestine and the unification of Arab lands, he nourished such an image, one that resonated with Arabs of all walks of life:

Still, ironically enough, it was reputation that mattered in politics; and the fact was that for many Arabs after 1967 Nasir, while still basically respected, was no longer altogether relevant. Whatever miracles he had worked in the past, he had none left for the future. All he could now offer the Arabs was another military defeat, or else a disguised diplomatic surrender. If anyone held the promise of miracles in his hand – and the Arab public lived as always in the hope, if not the expectation, of miracles – it was the Palestinian guerrilla.[31]

Though critically injured with his reserves exhausted, Nasser survived the Six-Day War to fight another day; he attempted to recoup his losses and made a bid to resolve the Arab-Israeli conflict. Although Nasser's "Arab revolution" had run out of steam, the Palestinian *fedayeen*, self-sacrificers, carried the revolutionary torch forward. For a fleeting moment these nonstate actors filled the vacuum left by the discredited ruling elite and captured the Arab imagination. Initially, untainted by official ties and power, the new revolutionaries pledged to undo the defeat and recover lost Arab lands and reputation. A critical segment of the Arab nationalist movement abandoned Nasserism, a "bourgeois" movement destined to fail, and espoused Marxist-Leninist principles instead.[32]

Contrary to received wisdom, in the aftermath of the Six-Day War, Islamists were nowhere to be heard or seen except in their natural pasture, Saudi Arabia and the Gulf. Throughout the 1950s and 1960s, the nationalist, liberal, and socialist trends dominated the Arab social and political space. That was apparent in the soul searching and storm of self-criticism generated by the 1967 defeat, overwhelmingly secular nationalist and leftist. Why were the Islamists out of the picture during the 1960s? It is

---

[31] Malcolm Kerr, *The Arab Cold War: Gamal 'Abd al-Nasir and His Rivals, 1958–1970*, 3rd ed. (Oxford: Oxford University Press, 1971), 135.

[32] Adeed Dawisha, *Arab Nationalism in the Twentieth Century: From Triumph to Despair* (Princeton, NJ: Princeton University Press, 2003), 284.

important to note that from 1954 onwards, the young Egyptian leader, Nasser, brutally suppressed the Muslim Brotherhood, the most powerfully organized religious-based movement in the Arab world, after the Islamist organization challenged his authority and monopoly of power. For almost two decades, the rank and file of the Islamist movement wasted away in Egyptian prisons under hard labour conditions.

However, Nasser's success in marginalizing and weakening the Muslim Brothers stemmed from endowing his regime with an appealing ideology that took the wind out of their sails and stole their thunder. His radical pan-Arabism offered Egyptians and Arabs an alternative paradigm of identity politics to that of the Muslim Brotherhood. Since the mid-1950s, Nasser advanced an ideological narrative that stressed dignity, Arab unity, national independence, economic development, and resistance to foreign domination, which appealed to millions of Arabs and Muslims. As Aweed Dawisha put it, it was the general acceptance of this narrative and ideology that allowed Egypt and its president to carry out the country's radical policies and to do that with popular approval:

Nasser's fiery radicalism fed the anti-colonialist and anti-imperialist orientation of the people. The coincidence of the two phenomena produced perhaps the only true radical mass movement of contemporary Arab history.[33]

Politically and operationally, pan-Arabism climbed on the shoulders of the man on the horseback, Nasser, and thus gained public traction and momentum. If Nasser had not rescued pan-Arabism from oblivion and empowered it through the state, it would have neither turned into a rallying cry for the Arab populations nor eclipsed and cast a shadow over political Islamists of the Muslim Brotherhood variety. If the state was so crucial in the ascendance of Arab nationalism, its voluntary withdrawal from that role under Sadat during the 1970s deprived that ideology of the vital means of public support. But by 1970 Arab nationalism had become a mass movement, a greater social force, beyond Nasser and the Egyptian state.

It is often asked: did Nasser genuinely believe in pan-Arabism or did he simply use it to advance his country's national interests? The question presupposes a clear-cut distinction and a neat divide in Nasser's conduct, which, in reality, did not exist. For most of his tenure he did not have to choose between the two. Some of Nasser's aides told me that he did not see any contradiction between promoting pan-Arabism and serving Egyptian

---

[33] Dawisha, *The Arab Radicals*, 24.

primary interests. Nasser did not even consider pan-Arabism and pan-Islamism as mutually exclusive, only that the latter could not serve as a framework for understanding and advancing national interests. But an appropriate question that has received no analytical attention is the extent to which pan-Arab nationalism was driven and fuelled by Egypt's Nasser?

The role of the Egyptian state, along with its charismatic leader, in promoting and popularizing pan-Arabism is critical to understanding and explaining the configuration of social and political forces in the Arab arena during the 1950s and 1960s. As the cultural capital of the Arab world and its centre of political gravity, Egypt's Nasser operationalized the doctrine of pan-Arab nationalism and turned it into a lethal power with which to be reckoned. Being one of the most powerful weapons in his arsenal, Nasser deployed pan-Arabism to great effects against his domestic and Arab rivals and foreign adversaries.[34]

It is worth noting that pan-Arab intellectuals largely accepted the state's sponsorship of Arab nationalism, assuming that some form of an Arab "Bismarckian Prussia" was required for the achievement of unity. From Sati' al-Husri to Nadim al-Bitar, pan-Arab intellectuals have consistently sang the praise of states that support unity projects.[35]

Although Nasser's architect failed, this did not diminish either the significance of his effort or the intensity of pan-Arab feelings, which he unleashed and which persisted after the 1967 defeat. As Fred Halliday has convincingly argued, "It was easy to say that Arab nationalism had later failed. But nationalism is partly a matter of sentiment and a shared sense of collective grievance; neither in August 1900 nor in the aftermath of March–April 2003 would it be said that these feelings had disappeared."[36]

[34] A background point to this question is the simple distinction, in foreign-policy analysis, between a realist policy that is driven by the pragmatic pursuit of the national interest and uses ideology as subordinate to it and an ideologically based foreign policy that prioritizes the pursuit of ideology and, in a sense, subordinates the national interest to it. For Nasser, there was a happy coincidence, at least until the Six-Day War setback, between the Egyptian national interest and pan-Arab nationalist ideology. But even after 1967, when ideology ceased to serve the Egyptian national interest, Nasser did not fully abandon Arab nationalism, though he injected a heavy dose of realism into Egyptian foreign policy. In contrast, Sadat waged all-out war on supporters of Nasser's pan-Arabism and relied on advocates of pan-Islamism to vanquish his nemeses. Utilizing a religiously based ideology as cover for a statist-realist policy, Sadat, more than anyone else, tipped the scales in favour of political Islam.

[35] Nadim Bitar, *Min al tajzi'ah lal al-wihdah* [From Fragmentation to Unity] (Beirut: 1983).

[36] Fred Halliday, *The Middle East in International Relations: Power, Politics, and Ideology* (Cambridge: Cambridge University Press, 2005), 86.

But the patronage of the state and its sponsorship of pan-Arabism was a double-edged sword. The fortunes and prospects of the pan-Arabism doctrine became organically and inextricably tied to that of the state. When the state and its leader, Nasser, were at the height of their prowess during the 1950s and 1960s, pan-Arab nationalism seemed unstoppable – the wave of the future. In the aftermath of the defeat, pan-Arabism suffered a crippling setback. With Nasser's death in 1970, that ideology was at the mercy of the new ruler of the Egyptian state.

It is true that by 1970, pan-Arab nationalism had become a mass social movement that acquired its own momentum and had taken on a life of its own, beyond Nasser and Egypt. Nevertheless, in the short and medium term, the withdrawal of the support of Sadat and the Egyptian state had a crippling effect on Arab nationalism as a political project, though not as a popular sentiment.

Sadat's Coup against Pan-Arabism

It was not until the 1970s that religiously oriented activists or Islamists openly reappeared on the Arab horizon and began to flex their muscle. Political Islam returned after the death of Nasser, and his successor, Sadat, made a fundamental decision to wrap himself with religious garb and cleanse his regime from the Nasserist legacy. Islamism did not just burst into the Arab scene after the exhaustion and weakening of the pan-Arabist order in 1967. Like its ideological rival, political Islam was fuelled in considerable part by state patronage and sponsorship.

The Six-Day War did not automatically usher in a dramatic shift from one ideological narrative, pan-Arabism, to another, pan-Islamism. That hypothesis is a simplistic sketch of a much more complex social and political reality.

Like Nasser's adoption of pan-Arabism during the 1950s and 1960s, Sadat and his state apparatus played a key role in the rise and expansion of pan-Islamism. In his effort to rid Egypt of his predecessor's inheritance, the "pious president," as Sadat insisted on being called, Islamized social space and systematically dismantled the entrenched main core of the Nasserist ruling group. In less than a year after gaining power, Sadat carried out a putsch and charged Nasser's all-powerful inner circle with conspiracy; this included Vice President Ali Sabri, General Mohamed Fawzi, and senior ministers and heads of security, particularly Shaarawi Gomaa and Chief of Staff Sami Sharaf. In one strike, reminiscent of the old sultans, Sadat wiped out most of the Nasserists and locked them away behind prison walls.

It is now forgotten that the revolt against Nasser's pan-Arabism came from *within* the regime's power structure. From the onset of the Egyptian revolution, Sadat was a loyal associate of Nasser and blindly and fanatically defended the regime's policies. Sadat dutifully earned the nickname, the "yes man," because he hardly ever dissented and served on revolutionary courts that persecuted dissidents, particularly the Muslim Brothers. He showed no mercy or leniency towards political Islamists who challenged the authority of his boss, Nasser, and the pan-Arab nationalist order.

Immediately after Nasser's death in September 1970, however, Sadat radically changed the state's direction and launched a frontal assault on his predecessor's pan-Arabist legacy. He purged Nasser's most trusted aides and lieutenants from various ministries and institutions and replaced them with his own men. Moreover, Sadat laboured hard to cleanse the Egyptian landscape from the very ideology that had powered the revolution from the mid-1950s until 1970. That was not easy because, although Nasser's appeal and aura weakened after the 1967 defeat, his pan-nationalist ideas were deeply entrenched in Egypt and neighbouring Arab countries.

Contrary to the dominant narrative in the West, pan-Arab nationalism did not just disappear into the sunset. There was no "end" to Arab nationalism as some writers have wrongly suggested.[37] The shift was gradual, assisted and expedited by the Sadat regime that, systemically over several years, rehabilitated a rival contrarian narrative, political Islam.

The gradual nature of the transition from pan-Arabism to pan-Islamism was obvious if one traces Sadat's words and actions. In a major speech to the ASU after Nasser's death, Sadat said that Egyptians "belong to the Arab nation both historically and by common destiny" and also pledged that Egypt, under his leadership, would "serve as the vanguard of Arab nationalism," calling Nasser's principles and attitudes

---

[37] See Fouad Ajami, *The Arab Predicament: Arab Political Thought and Practice since 1967* (Cambridge: Cambridge University Press, 1981); Fouad Ajami, "The End of Pan-Arabism," *Foreign Affairs* 57 (1978–79), 355–73; Adeed Dawisha, "Requiem for Arab Nationalism," *Middle East Quarterly* 10, no. 1 (2003); Hilal Khashan, *Arabs at the Crossroads: Political Identity and Nationalism* (Gainesville: University Press of Florida, 2000); James G. Mellon, "Pan-Arabism, Pan-Islamism and Inter-State Relations in the Arab World," *Nationalism and Ethnic Politics* 8, no. 4 (2002): 1–15; Bassam Tibi, *Arab Nationalism: Between Islam and the Nation-State* (Houndmills, UK: Palgrave Macmillan 1980).

"an inexhaustible treasure for us all."[38] Less than two years later, Sadat fully distanced himself from the overbearing shadow of Nasser and carried out a palace coup against his successor's legacy.

After Sadat removed Nasser's right-hand men from their seats of power, he knew he needed to offer an appealing oppositional doctrine to Nasser's pan-Arabism and take ownership of it. Keep in mind that by the early 1970s, no rival competitive ideologies existed that could fill the ideological and leadership vacuum left by the departure of Nasser and his inner circles from power. Since the mid-1950s, the rank and file of the Islamist movement was either underground or in prison. The Nasser state decimated the social infrastructure of the Muslim Brotherhood and appropriated its functions in society.

It is no wonder then that in 1965 the Nasser security apparatus was shocked to discover that, despite years of suppressing the Muslim Brothers and trying to discredit it, the Islamist movement plotted to assassinate Nasser. Said Qutb, while in prison, led a paramilitary group called *al-Tanzim al-Sirri* (a Secret Apparatus), with a membership of a few hundred strongmen, whose goal was to overthrow the political system. Also while incarcerated, Qutb authored a subversive manifesto called *Milestones*, challenging the hegemony of pan-Arab nationalism and offering an alternative revolutionary vision – a Qur'anic state based on the early Prophet's model. The Nasser security machine unleashed its fury against all Muslim Brothers, as well as other sympathizers and religiously oriented activists who had little or nothing to do with the brotherhood. The second wave of repression, which was much more brutal than the one in 1954, culminated with the hanging of Qutb and the silencing of most voices of religious dissent.

In my interviews with top jailed leaders of the Muslim Brotherhood of the Nasser era in 2007 and 2008, they paint a dark portrait of a hellish existence, and hardly anyone says there was a ray of light at the end of the prison tunnels. More than fifteen years of incarceration and suppression left the Islamist organization broken and lifeless, with the exception of some Islamist dissidents in the diaspora. Some of Qutb's ardent disciples, who spent a decade in prison with him, told me that on the morning after the 1967 defeat a fact dawned on them that this could mean the beginning of the end of the Nasser regime. But they said they had no idea how and who and when this "end" might come about. One thing is clear: they

---

[38] British Broadcasting Corporation, Summary of World Broadcasts, Part IV: The Arab World, Israel, Greece, Turkey, Iran, November 16, 1970, 3–4.

did not and could not imagine that the winds of political fortune would blow their way and sweep away their bitter tormentors – the pan-Arab nationalists.[39]

"The shameful 1967 defeat exposed the bankruptcy of Nasserism and decadent secular nationalism," said Sayyid Eid, Qutb's confidant and soul mate inside and outside prison. "It was a divine punishment." When pressed if he and other Muslim Brothers viewed the defeat as a godsend opportunity to rebound and reclaim their vanished mandate, Eid and other incarcerated Islamists said they could not envision such an ambitious scenario because they had been out of circulation for two decades and lost touch with their social base and constituency, not to mention society at large.

"Remember that beginning in 1954 we [the Muslim Brothers] were subjected to several waves of oppression and were kept off balance and on the run till the first half of the 1970s," said Ahmed Abd al-Majid, a senior lieutenant in Qutb's al-Tanzim al-Sirri. Abd al-Majid was sentenced to death with his mentor, but Nasser commuted his sentence to life in prison. "The Nasser regime temporarily silenced the Islamist movement and terrorized its sympathizers into either submission or inaction. But in the deepest depth of our being, we believed that *iman* [faith] will triumph over *kufr* [apostasy in this context]."[40]

Mustafa Mashour, who spent almost a decade in prison and was subsequently elected supreme guide of the Muslim Brotherhood, acknowledged the hegemony of secular Arab nationalism and said he believed that Islam was ultimately bound to return to all Arab lands, including Egypt; it was a matter of time and God's will. Did he perceive the 1967 defeat and Nasser's death as a catalyst for the reawakening of the Islamist movement and the Muslim Brotherhood from their prolonged political slumber? "Not really," recalled Mashour in an interview in the Muslim Brotherhood's Cairo headquarters in 1999. "We were not in a position or a state of mind to envision such a comeback, although our faith in God and our Islamic mission never lessened or wavered despite the suffering and humiliation we endured at hands of Nasser and his thugs."[41]

By 1970 the Egyptian state had almost succeeded in breaking the backbone of the Islamist movement and consolidating the dominance of

[39] See my forthcoming, *Sayyid Qutb and His Disciples: How One Man Radicalized the Middle East.*
[40] Interview with Ahmed Abd al-Majid, Cairo, Egypt, 15 December 2007.
[41] Interview with Mustafa Mashour, Cairo, Egypt, January 1999.

pan-Arabism. That was the context under which Sadat laboured to purge Egypt of Nasser's inheritance and make it in his own image. He released hundreds of Muslim Brothers from prisons and allowed them to move freely, organize themselves, and publish and distribute their publications. During the first half of the 1970s, Sadat provided the broken Islamist movement with a new lease on life.[42]

Visiting notorious Egyptian prisons, the "pious president" spoke solemnly about his opposition to the violation of human dignity of Egyptians and, before the hungry cameras, chipped away with a hammer at their thick walls. He pledged to shut them down and put an end to abuse and torture; this implied a radical departure from his predecessor, Nasser, who persecuted the Muslim Brothers and other dissidents. Sadat forgot to remind his audience that he was a senior official who did Nasser's bidding.

Sadat's officials targeted the universities where Arab nationalists and socialists held the upper hand in student unions. The state authorities actively supported religious students and cracked down hard against Nasserists and leftists in general. The struggle for political dominance in the universities was a microcosm of a greater struggle in society at large where the state took sides and tipped the balance of social forces in favour of religiously based activists. In his autobiography, *Al-din wa al-thawra in Egypt (Religion and Revolution in Egypt)*, philosopher Hassan Hanafi, at that time a junior academic at Cairo University, recollects how the Sadat authorities built up religious-oriented groups and unleashed them against Nasserists and socialists. The so-called al-Jama'at al-Islamiya (Islamic Groups) imposed a reign of terror on universities under the watchful eyes of Sadat's officials.[43]

Throughout the 1970s, the Sadat regime played a key role in empowering Islamic-oriented students on campuses and weakening their secular counterparts. A new generation of politically radicalized young religious activists was born, one that subsequently spread its subversive ideas outside the university walls to urban centres, Upper Egypt, and other Muslim lands.[44]

---

[42] Hassan Hanafi, *Al-din wa al-thawra fi misr: 1952–1981* [Religion and Revolution in Egypt: 1952–1981] (Cairo: 1989), 62–8.

[43] Ibid., 65–71.

[44] Hanafi, *Al-din wa al-thawra in Egypt* [Religion and Revolution in Egypt] (Cairo: 1989), 65–71.

The October 1973 War and the Petro-Dollar Revolution

In his effort to marginalize the Nasserists, Sadat sowed the seeds of religious revivalism and radicalism. The October 1973 War added momentum and impetus to the religious milieu nourished by Sadat. Unlike the Six-Day War, the regime and its clerical allies portrayed the 1973 war as a divine victory fought under a religious banner – Allahu Akbar (God is Great); although, the Sadat regime did not fully deploy the war-cry "Allahu Akbar" until the intensification of its de-Nasserization campaign in 1975.

Time and again Egyptians were told that "God and His angels" fought on the side of advancing Egyptian soldiers and helped them triumph over the enemy. The airways were filled with gripping stories about divine intervention on behalf of Sadat's pious green-clad army. Religious fervour reached new heights. Far from dead, "God and His Prophet" joined the fight and tipped the scales in favour of the virtuous Arabs who returned to Islam. The Sadat regime and Islamists alike insinuated that in 1967 God punished Egypt because it forfeited the faith, while in 1973 God rewarded it for reembracing Islam. The tide had decisively shifted against the pan-Arabist paradigm and secular, liberal trends.

The dominance of Saudi Arabia's "petro-dollar" or "petro-purse" supplied plenty of ammunition to the religiously based narrative and fuelled it further. One of the major effects of the 1967 war was the rise in Saudi influence and assertiveness, which received another major boost with the October 1973 War and the subsequent quadrupling of crude oil prices. After the Six-Days War, Nasser had swallowed his pride and relied on Saudi money to rebuild his army and finance the costly War of Attrition with Israel. At the Khartoum summit in August 1967, Saudi Arabia, Kuwait, and Libya agreed to provide Egypt with EGP135 million annually until the occupied land and lost revenue had been recovered.[45] Chequebook diplomacy allowed the House of Saud to consolidate its authority at home, exercise a greater regional role, and spread its ultraconservative ideas far and wide.

The close alliance between the Sadat regime and the Saudi monarchy had far-reaching consequences on the configuration of social forces in Arab and Muslim societies. Now two pivotal Arab states actively promoted an ideological narrative intrinsically opposed to Nasser's secular

---

[45] Elwy, *A Political Economy of Egyptian Foreign Policy.*

pan-Arabism. The resources and assets of these two powerful regimes were fully deployed in the service of conservative religious narratives and the reinterpretation of contemporary Arab history. Once again the role of the state was critical in spearheading the transition or shift from one ideological paradigm to another.

One of the least examined chapters in this unfolding drama is the convergence of interests between the Sadat regime and the House of Saud in creating a religiously oriented constituency: a community of opinion makers, public intellectuals, and clerics. Ideas do not move in a vacuum but are sustained and nourished by material interests and social networks. Since the 1970s, millions of Arabs, including workers, professionals, educators, and writers, found employment opportunities in Saudi Arabia and the small Gulf sheikdoms and returned home with monetary savings and a new conservative sensibility and way of life.

The Saudi ultraconservative model migrated with the returnee migrants and fertilized the Arab and Muslim soil. Resistance was futile; according to many activists and scholars who lived in the midst of this ideological transformation. "It was impossible to stem the conservative religious tide that struck Egypt and other Muslim countries," said Gamil Mattar, a nationalist public intellectual. "The petro-dollar revolution swept people off their feet and transformed the social landscape. Oil money fuelled the rebirth of political Islam at the expense of Arab nationalism."

Heikal conceded that the rise of the statist, oil-rich countries and the growing respect of the political power of money all made the earlier focus on "revolutionary struggle" a thing of the past.[46] In short, the oil revolution trumped the pan-Arab revolution.

"If it was not for Sadat and the Saudi connection, Islamists would not have had the resources to spread their influence inside and outside Egypt. . . . In the 1970s the merchants of religion had unlimited sums of money at their disposal and the backing of the two most powerful states in the Arab world. We [nationalists and liberals] struggled against great odds and fought a losing war," recollected Sayyed Yassin, a progressive intellectual at the Al-Ahram Centre in Cairo, in his spacious office clogged with hundreds of books and mountains of Arabic newspapers.

Unlike Saudi Arabia, other Gulf sheikdoms abandoned Arab nationalism because they wanted to preserve their authority as separate states, a

---

[46] Dawisha, *Arab Nationalism in the Twentieth Century*, 256.

haven of privileged wealth. "Oil nationalism" clashed with "Arab nationalism" and vanquished it.[47]

Another Egyptian liberal, Wahid Abd al-Majid, stressed to me the pivotal role of oil, money, power, and globalization in bringing about social and political transformation of Muslim countries during the 1970s. "Sadat played on peoples' hopes, fears, and greed to bury Nasserism and portray himself as the leader who would bring salvation," said Abd al-Majid, who does not hide his contempt for Sadat. "The name of his game was religion and the manipulation of religious symbols to restructure social and political space." Abd al-Majid contends that Sadat's shortsightedness and recklessness brought ruin to Egypt, as damaging, if not more so, than the 1967 defeat.[48]

Regardless of the extent of the damage that Sadat and his alliance with the petro-dollar wrought, his policies altered the debate in Egypt and created fertile ground for conservative religious revivalism and political Islam. During the second half of the 1970s, radical religious sensibility reigned supreme, fed by the proliferation of publications financed mainly by Saudi Arabia and Gulf money. A concerted systemic effort led by the Saudi and Egyptian states existed to indoctrinate, educate, and shape public opinion.

The second half of the 1970s witnessed the migration of many prominent nationalist and Marxist intellectuals and scholars to the religiously oriented camp. Leftists and pan-Arab nationalists found solace, refuge, and answer in religion and shed their former beliefs for an "authentic" identity. These included Adel Hussein, Tariq al-Bushri, Munir Shafiq, Mohmmad Ama'ra, Abed al-Wahab al-Masiri, Ra'fat Sayyid Ahmed, Hassan Hanafi, and others.

The late Adel Hussein is a fascinating example of a hard-core Marxist who turned Islamist during the late 1970s. Although he said he was very critical of the conduct of the Six-Day War and the Nasser regime in general, he still supported Nasser's progressive agenda at home and his foreign policy, particularly the quest for Arab unity. More than ever, Hussein said he felt the need to stand by Nasser's side in order to prevent reactionary forces from outflanking the Egyptian revolution and to prepare for the coming fight against Israel.

---

[47] Aparajita Gogoi and Gazi Ibdewi Abdul Ghafour, *Arab Nationalism: Birth, Evolution and the Present Dilemma* (New Delhi: 1994), 220.

[48] Interview with Wahid Abd al-Majid, Cairo, Egypt, December 2007.

What is fascinating is that the generation of militant Islamists who turned their guns on Sadat and killed him has taken a second look at his presidency. Although throughout the years, radical activists whom I interviewed insist that they were not creatures of the Sadat regime but were their own men, many now concede that they felt free to organize, build a social base, and spread their ideas on campuses all over Egypt and beyond.

"Come to think of it, during the Sadat era we were a healthy generation," said Kamal Habib, a founding father of Egyptian Islamic Jihad who, along with a few cohorts, engineered the assassination of the Egyptian president. "We had space and freedom of speech and movement; and unlike our brethren in the Nasser period we were not harassed and persecuted," reflected the middle-aged activist who spent more than a decade behind bars and whom I profiled over a period of several months during the 1990s. "To be honest with you, the Sadat moment was golden age for the Islamist movement, and we squandered it away."

Habib is not the only radical Islamist who looks nostalgically at the Sadat era. Mountasser al-Zayat, known as an attorney for an army of incarcerated militant activists during the 1980s and 1990s and himself an early member of Egyptian Islamic Group (*al-Jama'at al-Islamiya*), confessed that his generation made a strategic error by rising up against Sadat. "In comparison to Nasser, Sadat was a God-send for the sons of the Islamist movement. He released Islamic activists from Nasser's prisons and contributed to the religious revival that swept the *ummah* in the 1970s. If we had patience and forbearance, we could have gradually transformed Egypt into a truly Islamic society."

In an unprecedented gesture, more than two decades after assassinating Sadat, the leadership of al-Jama'at al-Islamiya made a formal apology and called the late president a "martyr" because, in their opinion, he protected and defended the faith. Though politically and ideologically costly, al-Jama'at's decision to call Sadat a martyr shows that even (former) Islamist hard-liners now recognize Sadat's contribution to their movement, an historic testament.

Conclusion

No doubt exists that the Six-Day War was a catalyst that changed the regional balance of power in favour of pro-American Middle Eastern allies like Israel, Saudi Arabia, and Iran. In the eyes of Egyptians and Arabs, the defeat undermined the authority of the Nasser pan-Arabist regime and temporarily empowered a new generation of nonstate Palestinian actors who pledged to be the new standard-bearers and vanguard of the Arab revolution. Rhetorically and literally, Egypt could no longer afford to play a dual role as a state and as a revolution and reached a rapprochement with the "reactionary" Arab regimes; it voluntarily surrendered its revolutionary function to the Palestinian *fedayeen* who, for a fleeting moment after the defeat, captured the Arab imagination.

On the intellectual and ideological level, a soul searching of what went wrong swept the Arab lands. Marx, God, and Kant were called to the rescue – to set things right. A common denominator of the torrent of self-criticism by the intelligentsia focused on the crisis of the modern nation-state, particularly the lack of institutions, and the backwardness of Arab societies.

Ironically, most of the critiques were internal, part of the broader constituency of the Nasser pan-Arabist regime, not external or adversarial. The defeat undercut the confidence of the Nasser constituency in the regime, thus weakening its immunity system and making it vulnerable to external attacks. Abandoning Nasser, Arab nationalists joined Marxist-Leninist organizations signalling disillusionment with Nasserism.

Beyond that, it would be misleading to argue, as some writers do, that the Six-Day War marked the end of pan-Arab nationalism and the onset of a new epoch, a new ideological framework that has dominated Arab politics till today. We must be weary of single-factor explanations that ascribe massive causality to a specific event, regardless of how pivotal. That principle applies to the 1948 defeat and the 1967 defeat alike.

For example, contrary to the received wisdom, on its own the 1948 Palestine War cannot explain the outbreak of armed coups and revolutions that destroyed the old regime in the Arab world. Rather, the 1948 defeat was the final nail in the coffin of the old regime because Egypt had been ripe for a revolution. The loss of Palestine and the defeat of the Egyptian army accelerated the erosion of the legitimacy and authority of the colonial-sponsored ruling elite. In the 1952 coup, it took fewer than a hundred junior officers to destroy the British-supported monarchy.

The consequences of the 1967 war defeat must be similarly contextualized within preceding and subsequent developments, internal and external. The coming to power of Sadat and his radical change of direction was pivotal, particularly the use of the state to purge the country of Nasser's pan-Arab nationalism and substitute Islam as the public face of his regime. I have argued that the role of the Egyptian state was pivotal in dismantling the Nasserist political and security apparatus and marginalizing and weakening pan-Arabism. The state also invested critical resources in empowering religiously based groups that have dominated the Arab landscape since the late 1970s.

One of my central arguments is that after the Six-Day War, writers who penned the obituaries of pan-Arabism and the return of Islam did not fully consider the real sources and forces that brought about this sociological transformation. These included a concerted effort by the Sadat regime, the 1973 October War, the petro-dollar revolution, and an alliance between the Egyptian state and the Saudi monarchy.

A counterfactual question is in order: would not the received wisdom be turned on its head had Nasser lived beyond 1970 to fight another battle or to resolve the Arab-Israeli conflict? Surely, the course of contemporary Arab history would not have been the same. If Nasser had survived and Sadat had not gained power, political Islam would have unlikely swept Arab lands and replaced pan-nationalism as the dominant paradigm.

Before and after the 1967 war, we must look at the role and functions of the Egyptian state first in advancing pan-Arabism as its operational doctrine and then in shifting to promote a contrarian ideological narrative based on religion. Time and again the state tipped the balance of power in favour of competing social forces, a testament to the enduring hegemony of statism in the postcolonial Arab world.

Index

List of Books in the Series